THE COLLECTED WORKS OF JEREMY BENTHAM

General Editor

J. H. Burns

Correspondence

Volume 1

JEREMY BENTHAM
as a boy, from the portrait by Thomas Frye (*c.* 1761)

The
CORRESPONDENCE
of
JEREMY BENTHAM

Volume 1: 1752-76

—————

edited by
TIMOTHY L. S. SPRIGGE

—————

UNIVERSITY OF LONDON
THE ATHLONE PRESS
1968

Published by
THE ATHLONE PRESS
UNIVERSITY OF LONDON
at 2 Gower Street, London wc1
Distributed by Constable & Co Ltd
12 Orange Street, London wc2

Canada
Oxford University Press
Toronto

U.S.A.
Oxford University Press Inc
New York

485 13201 X

Printed in Great Britain by
WILLIAM CLOWES AND SONS, LIMITED
LONDON AND BECCLES

GENERAL PREFACE

Jeremy Bentham (1748–1832), leader of the Utilitarian reformers who became known as the Philosophical Radicals, was a major figure in the history of ideas, of law, and of social policy in the nineteenth century. Even today his influence survives in many fields. Yet there has been no modern critical edition of his works. This situation—in striking contrast with the editorial treatment of writers like Jefferson, Ricardo, and Coleridge—is in part explained by the very nature of Bentham's work. He wrote so voluminously on so many subjects that no single editor, no group of editors from any single field of scholarship, could undertake to present his work as a whole in acceptable critical form. The huge mass of manuscript material left by Bentham at his death reflected his dwindling concern, as his long life advanced, for the eventual published form of what he wrote. The task of reducing to order the uncoordinated statements and restatements of his thought he left to his 'disciples and editors'. And in fact the French redactions by Etienne Dumont which first made Bentham's ideas widely known, and the version of Utilitarianism developed by John Stuart Mill largely took the place of Bentham's own writings for most readers. The consequence has been an impoverished and at times a false picture of Bentham's thought.

For those seeking Bentham's own writings the principal resource has inevitably been the collected edition completed in 1843 under the supervision of his executor, John Bowring. This has long been out of print; and even when accessible its eleven volumes of small type in daunting double columns (two volumes comprising what Leslie Stephen called 'one of the worst biographies in the language' —Bowring's *Memoirs of Bentham*) are defective in content as well as discouraging in form. Bowring excluded Bentham's anti-clerical writings, and for many works the texts in his edition derive at least as much from Dumont's French versions as from Bentham's own manuscripts. For half a century after 1843 these manuscripts lay neglected; and even now, despite the valuable work during the present century of such scholars as Elie Halévy, C. W. Everett, C. K. Ogden, and W. Stark, relatively little has been done to remedy these defects. When Bentham is known at all today at first hand, he is known largely from reprints of his *Fragment on Government*

v

and *Introduction to the Principles of Morals and Legislation*—both dating from the first decade of an active career of over sixty years.

The present edition is an attempt to present definitive versions of Bentham's writings based, wherever possible, on the original manuscripts. The greatest single collection of Bentham papers is of course that which has been in the custody of University College London since the middle of the nineteenth century. Second only to this in importance is the large group of manuscripts—including a large part of Bentham's correspondence—acquired by the British Museum in 1889. A third source of great importance lies in the collection of the papers of Etienne Dumont now in the Bibliothèque Publique et Universitaire at Geneva. Other papers and letters, together with the various editions of Bentham's writings, will also form part of the foundation upon which the edition is built.

The edition is intended to be comprehensive in scope as well as definitive in text. All the works included by Bowring and his associate editors will be included here (though not always in the same form). Works omitted or overlooked by Bowring, but published either during Bentham's lifetime or since his death, will also be included. To these will be added any work, large or small, which exists in reasonably complete and coherent form in the manuscripts, together with any fragments judged by the editors to be of particular interest and importance. The straightforward policy of printing everything Bentham wrote is ruled out by Bentham's own method of working, his constant rehandling of the same themes and reshaping of earlier materials. But much of what he wrote, both in familiar and in unfamiliar or unknown works, will now for the first time be made available in Bentham's authentic words.

An important—indeed a fundamental—part of the edition will comprise the first comprehensive presentation of Bentham's extensive correspondence. If knowledge of Bentham's thought has been limited by the factors indicated above, understanding of his life and personality has at times been distorted by lack of access to the essential biographical data contained in his letters. Reflecting as they do the evolution of a man and his world over a period of three-quarters of a century, the volumes of Bentham's correspondence may well be among the most important, as they can hardly fail to be among the most readable, parts of the edition.

The edition is sponsored by a National Committee set up in 1959 on the initiative of University College London, and since 1961 the detailed planning and supervision of the work has been in the hands of Professor **J. H. Burns** as General Editor. Cooperative scholarship on a large scale over many years will undoubtedly be required before the edition is completed, each volume or group of volumes being entrusted to a scholar in the appropriate field. Editorial problems must vary widely in character from volume to volume; but in every case the introduction will indicate the basis of the texts presented, their historical context, and their mutual relationships.

The whole project will, it is estimated, require some thirty-eight volumes for its completion, though further exploration of the materials may naturally impose some revision of this estimate. The structure of the edition has been based on an attempt to classify Bentham's writings, so far as possible, according to subject matter. The working plan outlined below does not seek to be comprehensive but merely to list some of the main items within each section heading.

I. CORRESPONDENCE

II. PRINCIPLES OF LEGISLATION

Introduction to the Principles of Morals and Legislation; Of Laws in General; Essay on the Influence of Time and Place in Matters of Legislation; Essay on Indirect Legislation; General view of a Complete Code of Laws; Pannomial Fragments; Codification Proposal; Nomography; Comment on the Commentaries; Fragment on Government.

III. PENOLOGY AND CRIMINAL LAW

Principles of Penal Law; Penal Code; Letters to Count Toreno; View of the Hard Labour Bill; Theory of Punishment; Panopticon.

IV. CIVIL LAW

Principles of the Civil Code; Letters on Law Reform.

V. CONSTITUTIONAL LAW

Constitutional Code; Three Tracts relating to Spanish and Portuguese Affairs; On the Liberty of the Press and Public Discussion; Securities against Misrule; Jeremy Bentham to his Fellow Citizens of France; Jeremy Bentham to the Belgic Nation.

VI. POLITICAL WRITINGS

Essay on Political Tactics; Anarchical Fallacies; Book of Fallacies; Parliamentary Reform; Defence of the People against Lord Erskine;

Radicalism not Dangerous; Principles of International Law; Letters of Anti-Machiavel; Junctiana Proposal.

VII. JUDICIAL PROCEDURE

Principles of Judicial Procedure; Draught of a Code for Judicial Establishment in France; Scotch Reform; Equity Dispatch Court Proposal; Jury Analysed; Elements of the Art of Packing; 'Swear not at all'; Lord Brougham Displayed; Rationale of Judicial Evidence.

VIII. ECONOMICS AND SOCIETY

Defence of Usury; Institute of Political Economy; The True Alarm; Defence of a Maximum; Manual of Political Economy; Rationale of Reward; Emancipate your Colonies!; Rid Yourselves of Ultramaria; Pauper Management Improved; Observations on the Poor Bill.

IX. PHILOSOPHY AND EDUCATION

Essays on Language, Logic, Universal Grammar, and Ontology; Deontology; Table of the Springs of Action; Chrestomathia.

X. RELIGION AND THE CHURCH

Analysis of the Influence of Natural Religion; Not Paul but Jesus; Church of Englandism and its Catechism Examined.

The thanks of the Bentham Committee are due to the following bodies for financial assistance towards the cost of the editorial work on Volumes 1 and 2 of the Correspondence:

The Rockefeller Foundation
The Pilgrim Trust
The British Academy

PREFACE

The thanks of the Bentham Committee are due to the following for access to and permission to print Mss. in their possession as well as for assistance afforded to the General Editor and the editor of the two volumes now published: The Trustees of the British Museum; The Librarian, University College London; The Provost and Fellows of King's College, Cambridge; The Free Library of Philadelphia; The Most Hon. the Marquess of Lansdowne; Miss Lloyd Baker, Hardwicke Court, Gloucester.

As editor I also wish to express my gratitude to the following for their assistance in the work of preparing these two volumes: Professor C. W. Everett of Columbia University, from whose projected volume of selections from Bentham's correspondence the present comprehensive enterprise took its origin, and under whose supervision the early work on the volumes was carried out; the late Mr W. D. Hogarth, Secretary of the Athlone Press of the University of London, whose close interest in the edition throughout its formative stages was a great source of encouragement and whose practical advice was invaluable; Professor J. H. Burns, who as General Editor of the edition as a whole since 1961 has become more and more closely associated with the work on these volumes, more especially with the annotation of the letters; Mrs. Hilary P. Evans, now of the Library staff at University College London, who as editorial assistant from 1959 to 1965 played an active and essential part throughout the preparation of the volumes; Mr J. W. Scott, Librarian of University College London, who apart from his indispensable official aid as custodian of the largest single collection of Bentham papers, and his work as Secretary of the Bentham Committee from its inception until 1966, took throughout a most helpful interest in the work and was of particular assistance in the editing of Bentham's letters in Latin and Greek; Mr R. H. Elvery of the Department of Civil and Municipal Engineering, and Mr K. J. Wass of the Department of Geography, University College London, who made the drawings for the reproduction of the at times somewhat baffling technical diagrams in certain of the letters; Mrs Sandra Hole for preparing the indexes.

Among the members of the Bentham Committee, I should like to express my particular thanks to Lord Evans, Provost of University College London from 1951 to 1966, and to Professor R. A. Humphreys, for their encouragement.

These two volumes consisting mainly of Bentham's own words and much of the editorial work having been a co-operative venture, it is not for me to make a formal dedication of them. However, I should like to dedicate my share in their production to the memory of my mother, a great reader of history, who lived to read them through in typescript, but not in print.

It remains to add a note on additional letters discovered since the main work on the volumes was completed. Wherever possible these have been inserted in their proper places in the series. In the case of letters located too late for this to be possible publication will be delayed until they can be collected in an appendix to the final volume of correspondence in the present edition. Information about relevant letters will be welcomed by the General Editor.

University of Sussex T. L. S. S.

CONTENTS

LIST OF LETTERS IN VOLUME 1

INTRODUCTION TO VOLUMES 1 AND 2

1. THE LETTERS

The only attempt hitherto made to publish the extensive correspondence of Jeremy Bentham was incorporated by his executor,
John Bowring, in the two volumes of memoirs which closed the
first collected edition of Bentham's works in 1843. Besides correspondence these volumes contain Bowring's record of a large number of word of mouth accounts which Bentham gave him of his
early life. It should perhaps be emphasised that these provide an
essential complement (though one to be used with caution) to the
picture of Bentham's early years, especially of his childhood, which
can be obtained from the correspondence which follows. Only a
small part of the relevant material is reproduced in the notes to
these volumes. Bowring also quotes from a commonplace book
belonging to Jeremiah Bentham which does not, so far as is known,
survive. But very little of the correspondence before 1780 appears
in Bowring's *Memoirs*. He was avowedly selective in his treatment
of the material at his disposal, and indeed for the period with which
the present volumes are concerned that material was virtually non-
existent. The vast majority of surviving Bentham letters down to
1780 are family letters; and while Bowring seems to have had
access to family papers which cannot now be traced (e.g. the
commonplace book kept by Bentham's father), he seems to have
seen very few of Bentham's early letters. Bentham himself evidently
believed in old age that his stepmother, Mrs Sarah Bentham
(d. 1809), had destroyed these letters. In Bowring's annotated copy
of his *Memoirs of Bentham*, now in the British Museum, the following Ms. note appears at the end of chapter II (vol. x, p. 45):

It is to me a subject of great regret that so little remains of Bentham's
early correspondence with his father and family. He believed that the
letters were destroyed wilfully by his mother-in-law, and his suspicions
added not a little to the severity of judgement with which he visited
that lady.

In fact the letters and a great many other family documents survived. They were consulted by Mary Sophia Bentham (d. 1858),
the widow of Bentham's brother Samuel, when she was writing
the brief life of her husband which was published in 1862. From

her they passed to her son George, Bentham's nephew, the eminent botanist (d. 1884), who bequeathed them to his colleague Sir Joseph Dalton Hooker. It was Hooker who sold to the British Museum the twenty-eight volumes which now form the greater part of the Museum's holding of Bentham manuscripts.

By far the greater number of the letters now published is drawn from this collection. A second principal source is the great corpus of Bentham papers in the library of University College London. Most of this collection was deposited by John Bowring in the College on his departure for China in 1849. These papers are naturally the focus for editorial work and research on Bentham's works in general. For his correspondence their importance is substantial, but limited. What we find for the most part consists of drafts or copies, and it is by no means always clear that corresponding letters were in fact sent. The problem is particularly acute in respect of the substantial body of draft letters to sovereigns and statesmen which Bentham wrote in the late 1770's. It would clearly be misleading to regard these as forming part of his correspondence in any genuine sense; but some specimens of particular interest (and reasonable brevity) are included in the present collection. Where there are good grounds for thinking that letters bearing some relation to the drafts were actually sent, the drafts have been printed in default of more definitive texts.

The original collection in University College has at various times been supplemented, and the additions have often taken the form of autograph letters of Bentham. Of special importance here is the collection originally assembled by C. K. Ogden and subsequently acquired by the College. This includes an important series of letters to Richard Clark which give us virtually our first knowledge of Bentham's correspondence outside his family circle.

Other letters have been found in a number of libraries and private collections, the courtesy of whose owners in the matter is acknowledged elsewhere. Particular mention may properly be made of the important group of Bentham letters in the Lansdowne Mss. at Bowood. The items falling within the period of these first two volumes are few and brief; but they represent the beginning of one of the most influential associations in Bentham's career.

Only a few of the letters now published have appeared in print before, and hardly any have appeared complete. The main sources were virtually unknown until Elie Halévy published his great work on philosophical radicalism in 1902, and no extensive biographical use was made of Bentham's early correspondence until Professor

C. W. Everett published *The Education of Jeremy Bentham* in 1932. More recently, the letters have been used by Mrs M. P. Mack in her *Jeremy Bentham: an Odyssey of Ideas* (New York and London, 1962). In the circumstances, therefore, it has been neither necessary nor possible to draw upon printed sources, and only where the full text or a very substantial extract has appeared in print has it been judged necessary to draw attention to the fact.

2. Method of Editing

Every letter of Bentham's down to the end of 1780 which has been found is printed in full. Bentham's spelling and punctuation have been followed throughout except in a few places where obvious slips have been corrected. Bentham's approach in both respects was highly individual. The same statement applies with even greater force to the French in which a fair number of his letters are wholly or partly written: here too his orthography and his use or non-use of accents have been reproduced. The ampersand which Bentham frequently, but by no means invariably, employs in his letters is in every case replaced by 'and'. Other abbreviations are in general retained, but suprascript letters in abbreviated words have been printed on the line except in a few cases where ambiguity might have resulted.

Special mention must be made of Bentham's habit, even in his letters, of writing alternative words and phrases above the line without deleting the original. In draft letters his intention was presumably to make a final choice at a later stage. But when writing to intimates he often left these alternatives standing; and this is at times a literary device of a distinctive character, the effect of which is that the sense of the passage arises from an amalgam of the two (or more) readings. (Bentham had perhaps the perfectly balanced mind described by Lewis Carroll in the preface to *The Hunting of the Snark*.) To print all these alternative readings would seriously imperil the readability of the text; in most cases therefore Bentham's 'second thoughts', written above the line, have been preferred in the printed texts. But in some instances it has seemed best to leave the alternatives standing, that written above the line being here printed between oblique strokes / /. Other editorial symbols are elucidated in the key which follows this introduction.

The notes to each letter are individually numbered. In every case they open with a general note, giving the location of the Ms. the address, postmark, dockets, etc. Where appropriate this general note also supplies background information to elucidate the context of the letter. Indicator numbers in the letter-headings are not given for these notes, but for reference purposes they are numbered '1' in each case. The annotation as a whole is intended, among other things, to identify, as far as possible, all persons, books, and (where it seems necessary) places mentioned in the text of the letters. So far as the identification of persons is concerned, two exceptions should be noted. First, it would have seemed pedantic to include notes on such persons as King George III and Dr Samuel Johnson. Second, where a person's occupation or profession is mentioned in the text and investigation has yielded no further information about him, no note has been inserted. Otherwise, unidentified persons have been signalized as such in the notes.

In accordance with the general policy governing the edition of which these volumes form part, explanatory editorial comment has for the most part been incorporated in the notes rather than in a discursive introduction. It is hoped that in this way the comments will serve their purpose at the point where they are most likely to be required—during the actual reading of the letters themselves.

A word is required on the inclusion or exclusion of items other than Bentham's own letters. Inclusion of all extant letters received by Bentham during the period would have been impracticable, but an attempt has been made to mention all such letters at appropriate points in the notes. A selection of letters to Bentham has been included, amongst which special mention should be made of the letters written by Bentham's brother Samuel. The inclusion of a fairly substantial number of these, either in full or in extensive extracts, seems justified, not only because many of the letters are of special interest and charm on their own account, but also because the relationship between the brothers is at this period so intimate and so central in Bentham's life that a clear picture is virtually impossible without this representation of Samuel's side of the correspondence.

The letters between Bentham's parents which open the first volume have been included in the hope that they will assist in forming a picture of Bentham's family environment in his early years and, more particularly, to fill out the portrait of Bentham's father, who (with Samuel) largely dominates Bentham's life in the period here covered. (A longer perspective in Bentham family history is indicated in the note by Professor J. H. Burns appended to this introduction).

3. Outline of Bentham's life to 1780

1745 3 October (O.S.): Jeremiah Bentham marries Mrs Alicia Whitehorne (née Grove).

They live in Church Lane, Houndsditch; but spend a good deal of their time in Barking, where Jeremiah's mother, Mrs Rebecca Bentham (née Tabor), lived, and at Browning Hill in Baughurst, which belonged to Alicia's family.

1748 15 February (N.S.): Birth of Jeremy Bentham.

1749 Birth of Thomas Bentham; who died in early childhood.

1751 Birth of Alicia Bentham (d. 1752).

1752 Birth and death of Rebecca Bentham.

1753 Birth of William Bentham.

1755 Bentham, aged seven, goes to Westminster School and lodges with Mrs Morell.

Birth of Anne Bentham.

1757 11 January: Birth of Samuel Bentham.

Family move from Church Lane, Houndsditch to Crutched Friars. Death of William Bentham.

1759 6 January: Death of Bentham's mother Alicia Bentham.

1760 Death of Anne Bentham.

June: His father takes Bentham to Oxford and enters him at Queen's College.

October: Bentham, aged twelve, takes up residence at Queen's.

November: First meeting with John Lind.

1761 Translates Cicero's Tusculan Questions for his father.

Observes transit of Venus in June.

In September sees coronation of George III.

His maternal grandmother, Mrs Grove, probably died late in this year.

1762 Jeremiah Bentham and family move to Queen's Square, Westminster.

1763 January: Admitted to Lincoln's Inn.

June: Becomes Senior Commoner at Queen's (age fifteen).

November: Begins to eat his commons at Lincoln's Inn and to attend the Court of King's Bench as student.

December: Starts attendance at the first Vinerian Lectures given by William Blackstone.

1764 Graduates B.A.

Visits France with his father.

1766 August: Goes on a tour through the North of England with Richard Clark.

14 October: His father marries Mrs Sarah Abbot (née Farr). At about this time Bentham moves into chambers in the Middle Temple.

1767 27 March: Takes his M.A. degree.

During March and April attends scientific lectures given by Thomas Hornsby, Professor of Astronomy at Oxford.

1768 7 August till early September: Tour of the North of England with his uncle and aunt Grove. (It may have been in this year that Bentham began attending a club which met for supper and discussion. He was introduced to it by Dr George Fordyce, the chemist, and the other members included such distinguished men as Sir Joseph Banks, Daniel Solander, Robert Milne the architect, and Alexander Cumming the watchmaker. He was uncomfortable at these meetings where he felt much less distinguished than the others, (see letter 169, n. 7) but he continued to attend until at least after 1775 (see letter 309 at end).)

1769 15 February: Comes of age.

Moves from chambers in Middle Temple to Lincoln's Inn.

Admitted to the Bar. Does not practise but lives on for many years at Lincoln's Inn (until 1792 when he inherits his father's house) hard at work on his plans for a reformed law.

1770 9 September: Leaves England for visit to Paris. Arrives home 4 November.

3 December: Letter to John Glynn Esq., Serjeant-at-Law (signed *Irenius*) published in *The Gazetteer and New Daily Advertiser*.

1771 1 and 18 March: Two further letters signed *Irenius* appear in the same journal. They defend Lord Mansfield against an attack.

For many years hereafter the correspondence shows the education of his brother Samuel, just bound shipwright's apprentice at Woolwich, as a main preoccupation (cf. letter 92).

1772 Spends some of the summer with Richard Clark at Chertsey. He is by now at work on the analysis of offences and punishments which issued partly in the *Introduction to the Principles of Morals and Legislation*.

Early **1773** (or late **1772**).   Beginning of Bentham's (adult) friendship with John Lind (see letter 99).

1774 Drawing up abstract of Priestley *On Airs* (see letter 105).

Publication of Bentham's (anonymous) translation of *Le Taureau Blanc* (by Voltaire).

July: Meets and falls in love with Miss Mary Dunkley, a moneyless young lady of Colchester, while he and Lind are on a visit to Lind's sisters (see letters 114 and 122).

October: Inspired by a work by John Lind, Bentham starts work on the *Comment on the Commentaries* (i.e. on Blackstone's *Commentaries on the Laws of England*), first published in 1928, edited by C. W. Everett (see letter 122).

November: Writes to Joseph Priestley on chemical experiments (see letters 123, 124, 129, and 143).

1775 April: Samuel (still a shipwright's apprentice) starts to lodge at Chatham with Joseph Davies and his wife Elizabeth (née Nairne) and this soon leads to a close involvement of both brothers with the Davies family, especially with Mrs Davies's sister, Sarah, and her husband Robert Wise.

28 April: Bentham informs his father of his attachment to Miss Dunkley. His father opposes it strongly. Bentham ponders the possibility of marrying and supporting himself and his wife by his pen (letters 133 and 134).

On midsummer's day (24 June) Bentham left his chambers at Lincoln's Inn to lodge with Mr and Mrs John Lind. He had been taking his meals with them already for some time. He stayed on in the house alone when they went (perhaps late in August) to spend some time in a house they had taken for the summer at Stanmore. Bentham also spent some of the time with Lind's sister at Colchester. Meanwhile his father had departed early in July to spend the summer in France with his wife, Samuel, and the two stepsons. They stayed there until around the end of October.

Bentham and Lind seem to have been working in close co-operation on various political and legal writings at this time. Bentham was hard at work on the *Comment on the Commentaries*. Decision on the fate of his alliance with Miss Dunkley appears to have been suspended while his father was away in France, but he was certainly seeing something of her, and was probably still considering whether with Lind's help he could support himself and his wife as a professional writer. By early September Bentham was back at Lincoln's Inn, a certain coolness having grown up between himself and Lind (see letters 139 and 148). This had to some extent blown over by February of next year.

1776 17 January: Bentham informs his father that his courtship of Miss Dunkley is finally broken off. Bentham was however at least occasionally in touch with her until the end of the year (see letter 149 n. 6).

About this time Bentham made the acquaintance of George Wilson who was for some years to be his most intimate friend (see letter 149, n. 12).

Having seen the Miss Dunkley affair terminated, Jeremiah Bentham now sought to find a suitably moneyed wife for his son Jeremy. On 19 February he introduced him to a Miss Stratton. Bentham agreed to pay court to the young lady. Her mother, Mrs Brickenden (twice widowed), had an estate at Ripley, and in July Bentham and George Wilson took rooms at Fetcham near by, allegedly as a reading retreat but in fact mainly to pursue this project. There Bentham spent most of the time until early October, his hopes alternatively raised and dashed by Miss Stratton and her mother. By 1 October, however, failure had become certain, and he could write to his father in the more dignified role of one quite absorbed in composing his *Critical Elements of Jurisprudence* (see letter 186).

A Fragment on Government, Bentham's first major publication, had appeared in April. It was a fragment torn from the *Comment on the Commentaries* (see above), and published anonymously. The question of its authorship occasioned a good deal of gossip. William Pulteney, a Member of Parliament, sought, through the publisher, to put a brief into the hands of its author. But Bentham had long given up all thought of a career devoted to law as it is, and needed all his time for his labour on law as it ought to be.

1777 By the beginning of this year the Bentham brothers had become deeply concerned with the fate of Mrs Wise and her four children (with another on the way), as Robert Wise was in serious financial difficulties. Bentham, as well as giving some financial help, worked hard at a project for saving the family from destitution by conveying Wise's property to Mrs Acworth, the mother of Mrs Wise and Mrs Davies and a creditor of Wise, so that she would have a certain priority over his other creditors and thus be able to help her daughter, Mrs Wise. Wise was a most irresponsible fellow and Bentham had a hard task in persuading him to take the necessary steps. In June Bentham and George Wilson went to board with the Wises in Battle, Sussex, with a view to bringing a little money in for Mrs Wise. They stayed, it would seem, until some time in October, Wilson pursuing his studies for the Bar and

Bentham his literary projects as the year before at Fetcham. There were those in the Wise-Davies circle who thought that Bentham's interest in helping Mrs Wise arose from something more than friendly feeling (see letter 217) and there are various indications which point in this direction, but the exact nature of their relationship remains unknown. Since Mrs Wise was expecting a baby in August it is perhaps unlikely that Bentham was there primarily to prosecute an amour. Towards the end of November Wise deserted his wife, and the Sheriff's officers removed some of the effects from his house on behalf of his creditors (the property having been conveyed to Mrs Acworth, she brought a successful action in July 1778 against the Sheriff for trespass). About this time the Wises moved to humbler quarters in Maresfield. Later the family moved to London, where Mrs Wise supported herself by working for Lind and others. She died in 1779 (see letter 313).

Bentham was at work throughout this year on a translation of Volume I of *The Incas* by Marmontel for Elmsly (see letter 193, n. 3). He was also busy writing on the theory or policy of punishment. Part of this work was eventually incorporated in the *Introduction to the Principles of Morals and Legislation*. We catch glimpses of him reading parts of it to George Wilson and to the chemist Dr George Fordyce (for advice on the physiological sections). There are various remarks in the letters of this year showing that Bentham's mind was running a good deal on the idea of presenting his work on Punishments to Catherine the Great with a view to her putting its proposals into effect in Russia (see letter 211).

1778 On 11 January Samuel Bentham came of age, and his apprenticeship finished at the month's end. With the help of friends and family he turned over various plans for his future, while he cultivated influential acquaintances and added to his naval education by becoming a pupil at the Royal Naval Academy in Portsmouth (around June) and serving for a time in Lord Keppel's fleet. The letters Bentham wrote Samuel in August when he thought he was likely to be involved in engagements with the French show the intense devotion he felt for his brother. He also regarded him as an ally in the cause of reform and wanted Samuel to make a career which would allow them to be of mutual assistance.

In March Bentham wrote *A View of the Hard Labour Bill* and it was published shortly after. It was a critique of a Bill, passed the next year, for the erection of two new prisons, of which Bentham had seen a preliminary draft. He forwarded the Ms. preface of *A*

View to William Eden (one of the Bill's authors) and some correspondence ensued. When it was published he sent copies to all the judges, including Blackstone, another author of the Bill. He also sent copies together with the *Fragment on Government* to the French *philosophes*, d'Alembert, Morellet and Chastellux, from the last of whom he received a reply of fulsome praise. The *View* also occasioned a visit to Bentham by John Howard, the prison reformer.

In April Bentham was nearly successful in an effort to travel to America as assistant to George Johnstone, one of the Peace Commissioners dispatched to treat with the American Congress. William Eden was also a commissioner on this abortive venture (see letter 243, n. 2).

That spring Bentham could say (writing to the Rev. John Forster in St Petersburg) that he hoped to publish his *Theory of Punishment* in two or three months as a middle-sized quarto volume. He also described himself as at work on a *Treatise on Offences* which would include a Code of Criminal Law covering matters not peculiar to any one country. The latter became in part the *Introduction to the Principles of Morals and Legislation* (without the Code however), while most of the former had to await the attentions of Dumont in 1811. In a letter to Samuel in September (letter 274) Bentham says that he has just begun his Code of Criminal Law, which he now proposed to enter for a prize competition announced about a year earlier by the Oeconomical Society of Berne (the closing date being 1 July 1779).

In August Bentham spent a week in Colchester with the economist Nathaniel Forster, who offered to work under Bentham as a kind of disciple. Another acquaintance of Bentham's at this time who probably took some interest in his work was Sylvester Douglas, a barrister of Lincoln's Inn, who later entered politics with some success (see letter 254). George Wilson was now Bentham's closest friend though he still saw quite a lot of Lind and met influential people through him.

Late in the year he made the acquaintance (through Nathaniel Forster) of Francis-Xavier Schwediauer, an Austrian medical author with some distinguished acquaintance. Bentham's main interest in him, as in any such person, was as a means of access to sovereigns and national leaders who might put his ideas concerning a penal code into practice, or let Bentham do so himself. Schwediauer knew the chemist Ingenhousz, who was a friend of Benjamin Franklin, and Bentham, though he took an anti-American point of view on the War of Independence, saw a possible path here for the introduction of his ideas to America (see letter 181). Schwediauer also had Russian connections and Bentham looked to him more seriously as opening up an avenue to Catherine the Great. Bentham cherished the hope of entering the Empress's service in some manner allowing him to forward his ideas to Russia. Schwediauer was also one of the several people who embarked on abortive plans to translate Bentham's work on Criminal Law.

1779 By the beginning of the year Samuel was very seriously considering travelling to Russia, as a post in a Royal Dockyard to suit his rather peculiar qualifications was proving hard to come by. To his family, and to those who might assist him with introductions, he talked as though his plan was simply to make a tour of the dockyards of Northern Europe and Russia in order to increase his knowledge of naval architecture, but presumably he already had in mind the possibility of service in Russia. The main alternative he considered was service of some sort in a ship bound for the East Indies. Jeremy Bentham favoured the Russian scheme. For one thing it fitted in with his own hopes of finding a patron in Catherine II. In the earlier part of the year the brothers cultivated all the Russian connections they could, and Samuel took on some young Russians, studying shipbuilding in England, as his pupils. This was arranged with the chaplain at the Russian Embassy, largely through Jeremy Bentham's efforts. Through Bentham's acquaintance, Baron Maseres, Samuel obtained an introduction from Lord Shelburne to the Principal Lord of the Admiralty in Russia, and to the British Ambassador, Sir James Harris.

Samuel eventually left England in August. He travelled overland to Russia through Holland and along the Baltic Coast, reaching St Petersburg in March 1780. His letters to Bentham describing his travels are full of interest. Bentham sent Shelburne a number of extracts from them containing intelligence possibly useful to him.

George Wilson had taken up quarters for the summer at Thorpe near Staines. There Bentham stayed with him from 2 to 25 September, and again from a date in late October till 4 November. On this latter visit his eyes, which had been troubling him for some time, became much worse and he had to keep them covered. The excellent Wilson acted as nurse (applying leeches etc.), as scribe and as reader. By 9 November Bentham could report himself recovered and ready to sit down again to 'Code' and 'Punishments', as he familiarly termed his two main literary projects.

Apart from this interruption Bentham may be supposed to have been writing on Criminal Law throughout the year with his usual vigour. The closing date for the Berne competition was put off for a whole year till July 1780, which was a great relief to Bentham (though it seems clear that in the end he did not compete). His letters to Samuel show what high hopes he now pinned upon presentation of his Penal Code to the Empress. His plan to have it published straight off in translation was largely for her benefit. He was now thinking of his acquaintance Rudolf Eric Raspe (known to posterity as the creator of Baron Munchausen) as its translator into German, rather than Schwediauer.

About this time Bentham seems to have been forming quite a wide acquaintance among continental men of letters and diplomats resident in England. Recent acquaintances included G. S. Poli and Felix Fontana, both Italian men of science whom he probably met through Schwediauer. He probably met Jan Ingenhousz, the Dutch chemist, and his friends among fellows of the Royal Society now included a Hungarian Baron Podmaniecsky, who introduced him (in 1780) to Baron Ragersfeldt of the Imperial Embassy (see letter 370). The latter read some of 'Code' and helped Bentham find a German translator for it. Among old friends, Bentham continued to see Joseph Davies and his family at Chatham, John Lind, and, of course, George Wilson.

1780   The bulk of the correspondence for this year, as for previous years, is between Bentham and Samuel. It is concerned in large part with Samuel's hopes of employment and gainful activity in various places which he visited, including the little dukedom of Courland and, above all, St Petersburg. There continue to be frequent exchanges on the best way of bringing Bentham's Penal Code to the attention of the Russian Empress.

Bentham spent most of February and March staying with Mr and Mrs Davies in Brompton (near Chatham). There he relaxed from his serious labours on 'Code' by dictating to Mrs Davies a translation of a work on *The Usefulness of Chemistry* by the Swedish chemist Bergman, working from a rough translation done by Schwediauer.

At the beginning of April printing of the introduction to 'Code' was actually started and was completed, so far as it ever was completed, by the end of the year. It was Bentham's original intention that it should be published as the introduction to his detailed Code of Criminal Law which would appear shortly after. In fact it was not published until 1789, when it appeared as *An Introduction to the Principles of Morals and Legislation,* and the Code itself was never completed.

By May a translation of the Introduction into German had already been begun. The translator was neither Schwediauer nor Raspe, whose general unreliability had become obvious, but a German called Leonardi. Later in the year Leonardi dropped out and one J. F. Schiller (who had translated *The Wealth of Nations*) took over. It seems that Schiller must have actually translated the bulk of the work, but apparently the translation was never put to any use.

About this time Bentham came to know James Anderson, the Scottish writer on agriculture. He asked Samuel to send communications to a paper Anderson was starting (which paper however proved abortive). Anderson also supplied Samuel with agricultural information required in Russia.

Bentham had continued to send extracts from Sam's letters to Lord Shelburne, and in July Shelburne invited Bentham to visit him at his London house. Bentham found an excuse for avoiding this, as he wanted to meet him for the first time when he had himself acquired more reputation, though it seems probable that Lord Shelburne already appreciated him as author of *A Fragment on Government.*

Bentham again spent much of the summer of this year at Thorpe with George Wilson: there they saw something of Colonel Horace St Paul, the soldier and diplomat, who promised to be an influential friend to Bentham in those schemes for publicizing 'Code' with which our second volume leaves him still engrossed. These schemes, above all that of presenting his book to Catherine II and thereafter seeing a Benthamic code introduced into Russia, petered out in the next decade. The real triumphs of Benthamism were reserved for the next century and his own country.

4. BENTHAM'S FATHER AND BROTHER

Bentham's main correspondents throughout the period covered by the present volumes were his father and brother. A more consecutive account of these two key figures in his early life than can be gathered from the preceding section is given here.

JEREMIAH BENTHAM

Jeremiah Bentham, father of Jeremy and Samuel, was born in 1712 in Aldgate, the second son of Jeremiah Bentham (1684–1741) and his wife Rebecca (née Tabor). He was the great-grandson of

Bryan Bentham, Bowring's 'prosperous pawnbroker in the city of London', not grandson as Bowring has it (Bowring, x, 1). Jeremiah Bentham followed his father's profession as an attorney from the beginning of the 1730's at least, but it seems that his not inconsiderable prosperity arose from his dealings in property rather than from his professional activities. In 1745 he married a young widow, Mrs Alicia Whitehorne, daughter of Thomas Grove, a mercer of Andover. They had six children, of whom only the oldest and the youngest, Jeremy and Samuel, long survived. They lived originally in Jeremiah's house in Church Lane, Houndsditch, moving to a house in Crutched Friars sometime in 1757. Alicia died in 1759, an event which, though not referred to in the correspondence, must have had a profound effect on Jeremy Bentham's childhood, as she appears to have been a most loving wife and mother. The way in which Jeremiah, finding his son a prodigy, devoted himself to pushing him into unwelcome prominence on every possible occasion, and imposed burdensome extra studies and pursuits on him throughout his childhood, emerges clearly enough in this correspondence, and is underlined by the talk of the aged Bentham reported by Bowring in his memoirs. One wonders what comparisons Bentham may have drawn later between his own childhood and that of John Stuart Mill, urged on in something like the same way by a father with very different ambitions. In 1763 Jeremiah moved into the house in Queen's Square, Westminster, which Bentham inherited on his father's death and lived in for the rest of his life. The house was known as Queen's Square Place and this supplied Bentham and his brother with the nickname 'Q.S.P.' by which they generally refer to their father in their correspondence.

In 1766 Jeremiah remarried, his wife being Mrs Sarah Abbot (née Farr), widow of a Colchester clergyman and Fellow of Balliol. At the same time chambers were taken for Bentham in the Middle Temple, so that he never lived in the household of his stepmother, for whom he developed no great devotion. There were, of course, tensions between Bentham and his father. Jeremiah was disappointed in his early hopes that Bentham would pursue the orthodox ambitions of the Bar, and in 1775 he was certainly not going to let this folly be compounded by that of an imprudent marriage. As time wore on he seems, however, to have learnt to appreciate Bentham rather more for what he was, and even to have realized that he might after all have cause for pride in him. He was glad to assist Bentham in the publication of his writings, and by the end of the period covered in these volumes a fair mutual understanding between father and son seems to have been achieved, which lasted until the former's death in 1792. It is perhaps appropriate to quote the following speech of Bentham as reported by Bowring:

While my father lived, from my birth to his death, I never gave him any ground to complain of me. Often and often have I heard from him spontaneous and heartfelt assurances of the contrary. My conduct may indeed have sometimes been a cause of regret and dissatisfaction to him; but on what ground? My 'weakness and imprudence' in keeping wrapt up in a napkin the talents which it had pleased God to confer on me—in rendering useless, as he averred, my powers of raising myself to the pinnacle of prosperity. The seals were mine, would I but muster up confidence and resolution enough to seize them. He was continually telling me that everything was to be done by 'pushing'; but all his arguments failed to prevail on me to assume the requisite energy. 'Pushing', would he repeat—'pushing' was the one thing needful; but 'pushing' was not congenial to my character. . . . How often, down to the last hours of our intercourse when we were sitting on contiguous chairs, has my father taken up my hand and kissed it! (Bowring, x, 4).

SAMUEL BENTHAM

Samuel Bentham, born in 1757, was nine years younger than his brother Jeremy. Like him he went to Westminster School, but he did not go to Oxford. At the age of fourteen he was apprenticed to William Gray, Master Shipwright at Woolwich, with whom he later moved to Chatham. More general instruction was also arranged for him in such subjects as mathematics and French. From an early stage Jeremy Bentham assumed the role of tutor in relation to Samuel. It was doubtless largely as a result of his persuasions that their father agreed to let Samuel pursue his enthusiasm for naval architecture rather than go up to Oxford. As the letters show, Samuel was soon as fertile in ideas for improvement in shipbuilding as Jeremy was in ideas for improvement in the law. Bentham did his best to bring some of Samuel's mechanical devices to the attention of the Navy Board, but without any great success. By 1778 when his apprenticeship was finished Samuel had been somewhat unusually educated, with most of the accomplishments expected of a gentleman added to the more practical expertise of a shipbuilder. He could not find a suitable position in the royal dockyards and, after various projects had been considered, he set out in 1779 for Russia, stopping on the way at many places in northern Europe, with a particular view to seeing dockyards, thereby improving his knowledge and increasing his useful acquaintance. In

St Petersburg he enjoyed the patronage of the British Ambassador Sir James Harris, and became known at court. In 1783 he entered the service of the Empress, with the rank of lieutenant-colonel, and accompanied Prince Potemkin to Krichev in White Russia, to assist him in his grandiose schemes for the development of the southern steppes. Jeremy visited him in 1785, staying for almost two years, and it was at Krichev that Bentham wrote the *Defence of Usury,* publication of which was arranged by his father back in England. He also wrote the original *Panopticon* letters there, which concerned the application to prisons of a method devised by Samuel for keeping workers under constant observation. In 1787 during the Russo-Turkish war, Samuel Bentham was in command of a flotilla based on Kherson. Using a new system devised by himself for fitting guns without recoil, he was able to arm his boats with far heavier armament than the enemy could expect them to be carrying. The result was so devastating for the Turks that Samuel Bentham was awarded the military cross of St George, the rank of brigadier-general, and a sword of honour. Later he obtained the King's permission to use his Russian title in England. He returned home in 1791 in time to see something of his father before he died in 1792. He remained in England assisting his brother with the *Panopticon* scheme and touring the dockyards under the authority of the Admiralty with the object of suggesting improvements in construction and organization. In 1796 he was appointed Inspector-General of Naval Works, an office especially created for him. While holding this appointment he introduced a series of improvements in the construction of dockyards and ships, which did much to strengthen Britain's sea power in those vital years. His proposals for reorganization show some of the ideas at work which loomed large in his brother's thought, for instance, the importance of associating duty with self-interest. He was married in 1796 to Mary Sophia Fordyce, the eldest daughter of Dr George Fordyce, the chemist. In Russia, incidentally, a socially more ambitious marriage project had failed. His wife bore him several children, amongst them George Bentham, the botanist, who assisted his uncle Jeremy in his logical investigations and published a book expounding Benthamic logic, which attracted little notice. Samuel's attacks on abuses and mismanagement in the dockyards did not serve to make him popular, and in 1807 on his return from a mission to St Petersburg, his office of Inspector-General was abolished. He was appointed to the Navy Board where his relations with his colleagues were strained by various divergences of opinion, especially over the best site for a new dockyard. In 1812 he was retired with a pension of £1500 a year, equal to his full pay. He then removed with his family to France, settling eventually in the neighbourhood of Montpellier, where he worked on various papers on naval topics. John Stuart Mill stayed with him there as a boy. In 1827 Samuel returned with his family to London, where he died in 1831, a year before his brother. His widow, who died in 1858, aged ninety-three, wrote a life of her husband, to vindicate his memory from various aspersions, which was published shortly after her death.

APPENDIX

Notes on the History of the Bentham Family[1]

by J. H. Burns

The common ancestor of the branches of the Bentham family mentioned in these volumes of letters was Thomas Bentham (c. 1514–78/79), who was born at Sherburn in Yorkshire, became a Fellow of Magdalen College, Oxford, in 1545, was exiled during the reign of Mary Tudor, and became Bishop of Coventry and Lichfield in 1559. Thomas Bentham married Matilda Fawcon of Hadleigh, Suffolk (d. 1607) and had four sons who survived into manhood. From one of these four—it is not as yet clear which—Jeremy Bentham's family traced its descent through the bishop's grandson Francis Bentham, a draper of Stafford, who migrated to London and died there in 1670. Francis's son Bryan Bentham (the name Bryan had long been established among the Yorkshire Benthams) was Jeremy Bentham's great-great-grandfather: he may have been, as Bowring states (x, p. 3), 'a prosperous pawnbroker in the City of London'; certainly this branch of the family was now well established in the city. Bryan's son, another Bryan Bentham (born c. 1657) became Master of the Clothworkers' Company in 1693, and when he married Ann Gregory in 1680/81 was living in the parish of St Botolph, Aldgate, where his great-grandson Jeremy was born sixty-seven years later.

Bryan Bentham of the Clothworkers had three sons. One was Bryan Bentham of Sheerness (d. 1748), whose son Edward Bentham of the Navy Office (d. 1774) figured in Bentham's early recollections (cf. Bowring, x, p. 4). Edward's son Edward William Bentham (d. 1785) was Jeremy's 'shabby cousin' of letter 104. Another son of Bryan

1. A fully documented account of the material summarized here will, it is hoped, be published elsewhere. Detailed references are therefore not given below; but the principal source other than the Bentham papers themselves has been found in wills and other testamentary documents in the Prerogative Court of Canterbury registers at Somerset House.

Bentham of the Clothworkers, conjectured to have been given his mother's surname of Gregory for his Christian name, was the father of Gregory Bentham of Sheerness, who died sometime between 1774 and 1778 and was himself the father of Gregory Bentham, mentioned towards the end of the period covered by these volumes, who served as purser aboard one of the ships in Captain Cook's last voyage.

From these cousins of Jeremy and Samuel Bentham we return to the brothers' own line of descent. Their grandfather was Bryan Bentham's third son Jeremiah (1684/5–1741), with whom, so far as is known, the legal connections of the family began. Jeremiah Bentham became an attorney, a profession in which he was followed by his son Jeremiah (1712–92), father of Jeremy and Samuel.

At this point it is convenient to consider Jeremy Bentham's family connections through his paternal grandmother (who herself played a part of some importance in his upbringing). Jeremiah Bentham the grandfather married Rebecca Tabor in 1706. She was the daughter of John Tabor (1649–1709) of Ramsden Belhouse in Essex and of Dorothy Croxall, herself the daughter of an Essex clergyman. The Tabors were a well-established family in the county, and some of them had close connections with Cambridge University and with the diocese of Ely. One member of the family, Robert Tabor (c. 1642–81), became physician to Charles II and a Knight of the Bath. Much of the Essex property which formed so important a part of Jeremy Bentham's patrimony must have come from the Tabor side of the family. It was probably also through that branch of the family that Bentham and his father were connected with the Suffolk clergymen Samuel and William Ray to whom and to whose families there are frequent references in the early letters.

Before turning to Bentham's maternal ancestry and relatives, it is necessary to elucidate the connection between him and two other Benthams mentioned in his letters: Edward Bentham (1707–76), Regius Professor of Divinity at Oxford, and his brother Thomas (c. 1714–90), who became vicar of Stockport in 1768, shortly before Bentham visited him there. These brothers formed part of a remarkable dynasty of Anglican clergymen all descended from Bishop Thomas Bentham through his son Joseph (born c. 1560). The Bishop's grandson Joseph Bentham (c. 1594–1671) became rector of Broughton in Northamptonshire. His sons—a third Joseph (d. 1692), who became vicar of Lowick, and Samuel Bentham (c. 1624–1703), who became rector of Knebworth—both continued in their own children the ecclesiastical tradition of the family. Here our concern is with one of Samuel Bentham's thirteen children, another Samuel Bentham (1653/4–1730), canon of St Paul's and Westminster (he is buried in the Abbey). One of his seven children, yet another Samuel Bentham (1681–1732/3), vicar of Witchford and Registrar of Ely Cathedral, was the father of Edward and Thomas Bentham whom Jeremy Bentham met in the 1760's.

APPENDIX

On the mother's side our knowledge of Bentham's ancestry is much less complete. His maternal grandfather, Thomas Grove (d. 1750), was probably a son of James Grove of Andover, where Thomas Grove was in business as a mercer: beyond this nothing is certainly known of the Grove connection. In the case of Bentham's 'grandmother Grove' rather more is known. She was Alice Woodward, daughter of William Woodward (c. 1640–1703), rector of Baughurst in Hampshire. The ancestry of the Woodward family in Hampshire and the Isle of Wight can be traced well back into the seventeenth century. William Woodward's son Thomas, Bentham's great-uncle, was for many years in business as a London bookseller. Thomas's sister Ann married John Mulford (d. 1747/8), clockmaker of London; and their son John (1721–1814) was the 'cousin Mulford' so often mentioned in Bentham's letters.

Bentham's mother had one brother, George Woodward Grove (d. 1784), who played a part of some importance in the early lives of his nephews Jeremy and Samuel Bentham. It seems that he was unmarried during the early part of the period covered by the volumes now published. Sometime in the 1770's, however, he appears to have married his housekeeper Elizabeth Riley or Ragg, by whom he had by then had two daughters, who later adopted the name of Grove. Bentham had two aunts on the mother's side, George Woodward Grove's sisters Deborah and Susan. The former was apparently the elder and is presumably the 'aunt Grove' of Bentham's letters in the 1760's. Neither sister married. Susan Grove evidently predeceased her sister Deborah, who died in 1769.

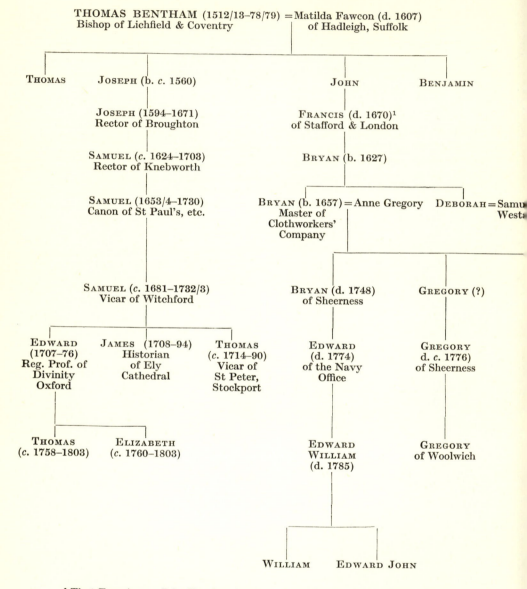

THOMAS BENTHAM (1512/13–78/79) = Matilda Fawcon (d. 1607)
Bishop of Lichfield & Coventry   of Hadleigh, Suffolk

THOMAS   JOSEPH (b. c. 1560)   JOHN   BENJAMIN

JOSEPH (1594–1671)   FRANCIS (d. 1670)[1]
Rector of Broughton   of Stafford & London

SAMUEL (c. 1624–1703)   BRYAN (b. 1627)
Rector of Knebworth

SAMUEL (1653/4–1730)   BRYAN (b. 1657) = Anne Gregory   DEBORAH = Samu
Canon of St Paul's, etc.   Master of   West:
                           Clothworkers'
                           Company

SAMUEL (c. 1681–1732/3)   BRYAN (d. 1748)   GREGORY (?)
Vicar of Witchford   of Sheerness

EDWARD   JAMES (1708–94)   THOMAS   EDWARD   GREGORY
(1707–76)   Historian   (c. 1714–90) (d. 1774)   d. c. 1776)
Reg. Prof. of of Ely   Vicar of   of the Navy   of Sheerness
Divinity   Cathedral   St Peter,   Office
Oxford   Stockport

THOMAS   ELIZABETH   EDWARD   GREGORY
(c. 1758–1803) (c. 1760–1803)   WILLIAM   of Woolwich
                                               (d. 1785)

                                      WILLIAM   EDWARD JOHN

[1] That Francis was John Bentham's son is a hypothesis: what is clear is that he was a
grandson of Bishop Thomas Bentham.

(Names of members of the BENTHAM *family are in capitals)*

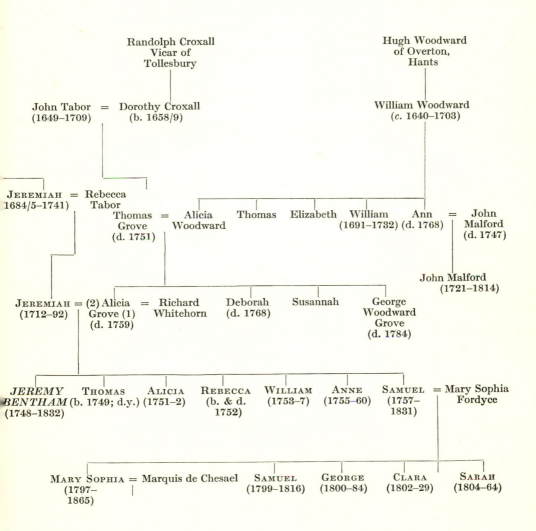

KEY TO SYMBOLS AND ABBREVIATIONS

SYMBOLS

/ In /   Interlineations. Sometimes these are insertions, sometimes alternative versions. Interlineations are not indicated in all cases.

| | Space left in Ms.

~~Oxford~~ Word crossed out in Ms.

[to]   No such word in Ms.; it has been supplied by the editor according to sense.

< so >   Conjectural restoration of mutilated word.

<...>   Word torn away or hidden in binding of Mss.

[?]   Reading doubtful.

[...?]   Word proved illegible.

Editorial comments are printed in italics within square brackets.

ABBREVIATIONS

Apart from standard abbreviations, the following should be noted:—

B.M. I, II, ... etc.: refers to the main series of Bentham papers in the British Museum, Additional Mss. 33537–64, the volumes of which are numbered from I to XXVIII. Thus B.M. I = Add. Ms. 33537 and so on.

U.C.: refers to the Bentham papers in the Library of University College London. Roman numerals refer to the boxes in which the papers are placed, Arabic to the leaves in each box.

Bowring: refers to *The Works of Jeremy Bentham*, published under the superintendence of ... John Bowring (11 vols.), Edinburgh, 1838–43. Volumes x and xi contain Bowring's Memoirs of Bentham.

NOTE

Apart from sources cited in the notes, a number of standard works of reference have, it will be evident, been heavily drawn upon, notably the following:—

Biographie Universelle (1811–33)
Clowes, W.L., *The Royal Navy: A History* (1897–1903)
Court and City Calendar
Dictionary of National Biography

Foster, J. (ed.), *Alumni Oxonienses* (early series, 1891–2; later series 1887–91)

Musgrave's Obituary prior to 1800 (ed. G. J. Armytage, Harleian Society, 1899–1901)

Namier, L. B. & Brooke, J., *The Commons 1754–90* (History of Parliament, 1964)

Royal Kalendar

Venn, J. & J. A. (ed.), *Alumni Cantabrigienses* (Part 1, 1925–7; part 2, 1940–54)

Correspondence

1752-76

JEREMIAH BENTHAM TO ALICIA WHITEHORN

24 August 1745

Aldgate London 24 Augt. 1745

My dearest Life!

Cou'd my Thoughts, as easily as they are conceiv'd, be committed to paper, you my dearest Creature! who have so large a Share of 'em, had need have no other Employment than reading my Letters for they wod. furnish a Packet every hour, and you wod. daily receive Expresses by the Dozen; such possession have you taken of my Mind that nothing can find admittance there but what some way or other relates to your dearself; whether I am riding in

---

1. ¹ B.M. I: 4–5. Autograph.

Bentham's father, Jeremiah Bentham (1712–92), had been intended by his mother to marry a certain young lady with 'a jointure of £10,000'. But he decided that he had found a wife for himself when he met Mrs Alicia Whitehorn 'at a place of entertainment on or near Epping Forest, called Buckholt Acres' (Bowring, x, 5). (This must be meant for Ruckholt House, Leyton, which had been opened in 1742 as a place of public entertainment.) Mrs Whitehorn was a widow, the daughter of Thomas Grove (d. 1750), a mercer of Andover. (Thomas Grove had married Alice Woodward, daughter of William Woodward (1640?–1703), rector of Baughurst, Hampshire.) Jeremiah Bentham's mother strongly disapproved of this match, and used later to tell the infant Jeremy that his father had made a great mistake in marrying his mother. Jeremiah resisted family pressure and chose love rather than fortune, perhaps aided by the fact that his father, also Jeremiah, had died in 1741—an advantage not enjoyed by Bentham himself in 1775 when he had to make a somewhat similar choice. Jeremiah Bentham and Alicia Whitehorn were married at All Hallows', London Wall, on 3 October (O.S.) 1745, and Jeremy was born on 15 February (N.S.) 1748. Alicia Bentham died on 6 January 1759, and therefore figures little in the recorded part of Bentham's life. Talking of the time when his French tutor, La Combe, delighted him, aged about seven, with a book of fairy stories in French, he told Bowring: 'My mother—it was a point of principle with her—refused me access to every book by which amusement in any shape might be administered' (x, 10). This implied gloominess of character is not borne out by the tone of her correspondence with Bentham's father, and Bentham himself remembered her as having a gentle and beautiful character (cf. Bowring, x, 5, 26).

This letter was presumably written at Jeremiah Bentham's house in Church Lane, Houndsditch; Alicia was shortly to return (probably from Andover) to Browning Hill, the house at Baughurst which belonged to her mother's family.

Jeremiah's assurance that his mother approved 'her Son's happy Choice' may have been less than wholly candid. In another love-letter written before the marriage (B.M. I: 6–7, unpublished), dated 3 September 1745, Jeremiah urges Alicia to feel no regret at leaving her relatives at Browning Hill, as they shall often visit her at Barking (where Jeremiah's mother had a house in which Jeremiah and later his family also, spent the weekends).

my Coach or walking in my Garden, where ever I am, or what ever I am
doing, I can never forbear thinking how much happier I shod. be
was I still blessed with your sweet Company, and how forlorn I am
for want of it: while I was present with you Time bore me on his
rapid Wing, so swiftly did the delightful hours pass on, but no
sooner was I gone from you than that Wing became pinion'd and
cou'd no longer fly, or was rather chang'd into leaden Feet, so
slowly do the sluggish Minutes now creep forward—Such is the
Difference caused by mighty Love! which prompts my eager Breast
again to Joyn itself with your's, in the rapturous Embrace of the
most cordial Affection—O how hard it is to part from what One
entirely loves! how surpassingly great must our Enjoyment be,
whose last Moments will be ever sweeter and more valuable than
the former, where mutual Love cemented by the most perfect
Esteem will secure us from ever knowing Satiety that necessarily
palls the *Happiness* of the Animal-unthinking-Part of Mankind
who follow the blind Guidance of Simple Nature, no wonder *It* is
seen to terminate so soon when Desire once Sickens and becomes
Stifled for want of that true and lasting Spirit of Love which
Shou'd ever feed the Torch of Hymen to preserve it's sacred Flame
perpetually burning, without which it can produce nothing but the
foggy Fumes of Smoak, such as we may Imagin have blear'd the
Eyes of our inconsiderate P—r—n and urg'd him to his ruin—
what a Wretched Scene must the nuptial State afford where
Reflection when ever it once takes place, instead of height'ning,
must soon extinguish all Desire, and transform the Inclination to
abhorrence and Distaste—but let us Shift the Scene and view the
happy side of the Contraste in ourselves my dearest Charmer,
what solid and rational transport and Satisfaction may we not feel
in the pleasing Consciousness of a well plac'd affection in the Choice
we have made in Each other, for since I have been so happy to
be yours I have learn'd to think myself of no small worth nor can I
possibly avoid entertaining some favourable Opinion of myself
when I consider the Singular happiness I enjoy in the Esteem of so
good a Judge and so nice an Observer as my dear Girl, but at the
same time the reason I have given forces me to make this acknowledgment I am ready to own with all, that whatever there may be
commendable in me is owing to my Ambition to approve myself
worthy your Affection and Esteem So little else have I to boast
besides what I derive from you—Therefore I can allow myself my
Dearest, as much merit as you please since 'tis all your own, without reproaching myself with the least Degree of Vanity—

2

I made my Mother[2] your obliging Present of your Duty who receiv'd it with all the gratitude and regard due to the charming and deserving Object of her Son's happy Choice of which She has conceiv'd the highest Opinion—you may well imagin what pleasure She took in the Account I gave her of my happiness in you—as nothing can be more engaging than the Tenderness and affectionate regard so remarkable in your carriage and behaviour to your own Parents and Relations, that alone wou'd be sufficient to prepossess her in your favour, and I may both venture to assure you, and Answer for her that no Relation you have can love and value you more than She will do when She comes to know you, so well satisfied am I that you will never be wanting in whatever may render you deserving of it—in Short if I am capable of forming any Judgment at all, no Three Persons cou'd ever come together so perfectly suitable and agreable in our several capacities and Relations as ourselves, among whom there is all the Reason in the World to expect the most lasting and uninterrupted Harmony Love and Friendship—O that the Time wod. come for its Commencement from whence it may date its Continuance which I am satisfied will know no other period than Life itself—Pray make my affectionate Compliments to Miss Suky[3] and tell her I hope your Charioteer will take more care of her Charge in driving you back to Baghurst than my Phaeton did of your humble Servt. in the Post Chaise. I think you told me, my Love, you had visits to make at some Distance out of Town pray let me conjure you to take care of catching Cold, and not stay out late now the Evenings are grown Winterish raw and cold—as you regard my Welfare, be tender of your own health, and let me know how you Do— . . .[4]

. . . Be so good to let me hear from you on Wednesday and tell me where I shall write to you next, and when I may certainly expect to see you up—God bless you, the dear Wife of my Soul and ever have you in his Special favour and Protection, and be asur'd I shall always continue to be no less than I am at present my dearest Dear

Your Grateful and ever faithful Lover and m⟨ost⟩ oblig'd
humble Servt. Jer.ʰ Bentham.

Pray make my Duty Love and best Service acceptable to your Papa Mama Brother and sisters,—and to your Uncle and Aunt

---

[2] Mrs Rebecca Bentham (née Tabor), Bentham's paternal grandmother.

[3] Alicia Whitehorn's sister, Susannah Grove.

[4] About five hundred words omitted at this point, concerned with the interest friends and relatives take in his engagement.

when you remove to Baghurst[5]—I hope you receiv'd the few lines I wrote you by Thursdays Post—

2

ALICIA BENTHAM TO JEREMIAH BENTHAM

Autumn 1745

Mon Cher Ami

I have just had the Closet clean'd that I might set down to write to you, for it's but just you shou'd have the first fruits of the favours you bestow—I mean the use of the Closet. I supose Sr. you expect a Journal of all the remarkable Occurencies which has happened since your departure, you know the grand Affair in hand was the business of returning Visits in which we made a begining yesterday—but first let me tell you how Monday past with us after you was gone—dull enough, till tea time and then we began to pluck up our Spirits, tell old Stories and talk of you till Evening which we spent very agreably in drinking your health (not in small beer) No, no, we knew better what was good for ourselves, and due to you, tuesday morning I wash'd my hands and did a *little* work then it was time to dress and set down to dinner, which we did, to an excellent Pudding not without wishing you a Slice—then after Mr. Bentham's health we finish'd dressing and made our first Visit

5 Presumably Mr and Mrs Mulford, the parents of Bentham's cousin John Mulford (cf. letter 10, n. 12). John Mulford's father, citizen and clock-maker of London (d. 1749), had married Ann Woodward (d. 1768), Alicia Whitehorn's aunt.

2. 1 B.M. I: 8–9. Autograph. Docketed by Mary Bentham (?): 'Mrs Alicia Bentham to her husband Jeremiah Bentham. / The father and mother of Jeremiah and Samuel B.'
  Addressed: 'To / Mr Bentham / near Aldgate / London.'
  This letter seems to have been written at the house in Barking, where Alicia Bentham was living with her mother-in-law ('my mother'), to Jeremiah Bentham at his house in Aldgate. It appears to have been written shortly after their marriage, when introductory 'visits' were still being paid (see letter 10, n. 13).
  This is the only surviving letter from Alicia Bentham of which the whereabouts are known to us. But Bowring possessed some others from which he quoted. In one letter, dated 6 August 1749 (Bowring, x, 5), 'she speaks of her anxiety about "her sweet boy" (Bentham), and of "an uneasy dream" she had had respecting him. In another letter, of the following week, she writes of the "longing expectation" with which she had waited for her husband's letter, of the "joy of hearing from a beloved absent one;" and implores a frequent repetition of such "absent interviews". She says, "I try to divest myself of all uneasy cares, and think of nothing at home but the joys I left behind—my sweet little boy, and his still dearer papa; though there are little anxious fears about death and fever, and too great a hurry and perhaps vexations in business, which may perhaps overpower

to Mrs. Finch,[2] then to Mrs. Barry[2] and so home where I was
agreably surpris'd to find a letter from dear Mr. Bentham but I
must not forget to tell you that your Pupil behaved her self very
well abroad she desires you may be told that my Mother says She
held up her head very well considering she had the tooth Ach—poor
Girl she is sighing and groning with it now, but to return to my
Journal at supper we again sent out our best wishes to you—had
they been good Carriers your table wou'd have been furnish'd with
better cheer than roasted Potatoes, I am glad of the Occasion to
write to my Uncle which I think you shou'd do imedeatly and by all
means accept of the horse for a time, but not as a present, I have
nothing particular to say unless you aprove of saying that the
interest money which my father sent by my Sister is left with my
Uncle Mulford he will then perhaps recollect that it ought to be Pd.
to you, as to the Cake affair I don't think it proper to mention it it
was only a little rust of the old Batchelour[3] which by this time the
tranquillity of the Country with my good Aunts Assistance has
rub'd of, I suppose you will thank him for his Company, but how
will you have the horse up won't it be proper for you to offer to
send for him or at least to mention it to my Uncle Mulford,[4]
excuse my giving you these hints I thought you seem'd to desire it,
they are of no weight but submitted to your better judgment to
improve or reject we are sorry to hear the sad Acct. of Mr. Pugh,[2]—
but are you not ashamed to own that you fell asleep in such a
pretty Ladys Company—shou'd it be known in the beau Monde I
shou'd blush for you and then the excuse you alledge is still worse—
what bestow your Gallantry and good humour on your Wife fie
upon it what an unfashionable thing you are, pray take a View of
Mariage a la Mode[5] before you come down again—

the spirits, and I not present to bear my part, and soothe those cares; which, I
flatter myself, would be in my power, were it only from my desire of doing it. Shall
you see the dear little creature again? I dreamed he had been like to have been
choked with a plum-stone. Surely nurse will not trust him with damsons. God preserve him from all evil accidents!" It would appear from this letter that Mr Bentham
had some aspirations after a knighthood; for she says—"I am vastly angry with the
title of ladyship. I have taken so great a disgust to it that I hope you will *not* get
yourself knighted in haste, for I don't believe I shall ever be reconciled to it. It has
robbed me, I fear, of some sweet epithets, and exchanged what I value above all the
world for an 'humble servant.' However it shall not deprive me of a title I value
above all others that could ever be conferred on me: even that of your faithful and
affectionate wife. A.B.'"

    [2] Unidentified.

    [3] Probably Alicia's uncle, Thomas Woodward, for whom see letter 7, n. 1.

    [4] Cf. letter 1, n. 5.

    [5] Hogarth's drawings were exhibited from May 1745 to June 1751 at the Golden
Head and at Cock's Auction Rooms.

I am glad we Escaped the Serenade sure they will not think of makeing a second Visit a Month hence—and so you was too late for your Appointment my Mother and I thought how it wou'd be—O my Uncle Mulford—

when I see Miss Waldoe[6] I shall tell her that I expect to be treated at her expence for if your stay depends on my writeing you shall not want for impertinence of which I here give you a Specimen and indeed you need not regrett your absence from the country for it's very unpleasant the weather is so bad it breaks all our visiting Schemes, and now I hope you will allow that I have exceeded my Copy in Quantity—in Quality its deficient—I shall never arrive to the perfection of the dear Original but give me leave to Assure you that with equal sincerity I am my Dearest

Your most Affectionate Wife
& Obliged humble Sert.
A Bentham

3

JEREMIAH BENTHAM TO ALICIA BENTHAM

26 April 1750

My dearest

Your sweet obliging Answer gave me a pleasure far beyond any I have or cod. have enjoyed since your Absence—and your little Jerry-Boy I asure you seem'd to take a part in it with his Papa—upon my telling him it was a Letter from his dear Mama—he cryed Kish, Kish—and Kiss'd it several times—and when I ask'd him what it was—he cryed Pape (for Paper) Mama—your pretty agreable Expressions cod. not fail to Kindle in me that Glow of Heart—which is peculiarly your's to give and me to receive—you see I am not for ascribing to you the whole of my happiness, since I am for placing some of it to my own Account—not that it is the l⟨east⟩ detracting from your own merit—for foreign Experience Shews us /in our observation of others/ (thank God! it is not our own) that how great so ever the Cause of Love may be of one side

---

[6] In the unpublished part of letter 1, a Mrs White and her niece Miss Waldoe are mentioned as Barking people. They turn up again later as guests of Dr Leigh, Master of Balliol (see letters 44 and 70).

3. [1] B.M. I: 11. Autograph.
    Addressed: 'Mrs Bentham / Andover / Hants.'
    This letter was evidently written to Alicia while she was staying at her parents' house in Andover. Their son, Jeremy, was just over two years old at this time.

6

in whatever is engaging indearing amiable—unless it meets with another mind suitably sensible—susceptible—of the tender Passion —the Elements of Fire and Water may as soon mix in Simpathy— as minds and Dispositions equally opposite to Each other—as it is not every thing in nature yt. is found to be capable of being Electrifyed, so as to produce what has the appearance of material Fire— Fewer still are the Instances of minds so happily paird, as to be both fitted and capable to Strike the Cordial Fire of Hearts—such an Electricity, how much more valuable wod. be the Discovery of its Art, than the Phylosophers Stone— . . .[2]

but my little Tiny[3]—indeed I am sorry for it's Elopement Jerry says he shod. love his little Sister—a Miss Becky—I fear it may spoil the good Effects of Country Air—and throw you back in Health and good Plight—pray my dearest—let me soon hear how you do after it—make my respectful Compliments and be asured that I am, and hope ever to be

Your affectionate as well
as beloved Husband
J B

London 26th April 1750

P.S. Jerry desires me to add his
[. . .?] [. . .?]mas—To—Grana—To—Tom etc.[4]

4

JEREMY BENTHAM TO REBECCA BENTHAM

3 January 1752 (Aet 3)

Honour'd Madam
    I have been very much troubled with sore Hands, but the greatest Trouble was their preventing me thus long from writing to

---

[2] About 250 words omitted. Jeremiah's mother has just left on a visit to his aunt. He mentions Alicia's sisters Susannah and Deborah: the latter is Bentham's Aunt Deborah (d. 1769) mentioned several times in the reminiscences recorded by Bowring.
    [3] This seems to concern a miscarriage Alicia Bentham had just had in which case she would have gone to Andover to have her baby there. It is understandable that Jeremy would be told he might soon have a little sister.
    [4] 'Grana' is presumably Bentham's maternal grandmother, Mrs Grove. 'Tom' is Jeremiah and Alicia Bentham's second son, Thomas, baptised 17 December 1749: he appears to have died in early childhood.
4. [1] B.M. Add. Mss. 36524: 17–18. Docketed by Mary Bentham (?): '1752 Jan / Jer Bentham to his Grandmother.'
    Addressed: 'To Mrs Rebᵈ Bentham / at Aldgate / London.'
    Bentham wrote this letter to his paternal grandmother, Mrs Rebecca Bentham,

my dear Grand-Mama, indeed if you knew how bad they are still, you would be Sur-prised at my handling my Pen at all, having o[n]ly the use of my Thumb and the Top of my fore Finger, all the other Fingers of Each of my Hands being tied up together in a linnen Bag, otherwise I shod. say a Great deal more besides that I am

Your dutiful Grandson
Jeremy Bentham

P.S. My love to My Wife
Baghurst 3 Jan: 1752

5

TO JEREMIAH BENTHAM

20 December 1758 (Aet 10)

Sr.

According to your desire I have sent you the Verses which I promised you; I believe I had better not send 'em, 'till the Holi-

---

from Browning Hill, the home of his mother's family, when he was nearly four years old.

The (chronologically) next surviving letter which concerns Bentham is not here published. It is to Jeremy himself, then aged six, at Aldgate, from his father's first cousin, Mr Samuel Ray, in Kenton, Suffolk, dated 4 June 1754 (B.M. I: 13–14). Ray congratulates Jeremy on his recovery from his small-pox inoculation especially 'after the Loss of Master and Miss Clarke'. He hopes that he will soon come to stay at Kenton with his parents and grandmother. Mr Ray would visit them in Barking himself, but not having been inoculated as a child he fears catching small-pox on the way.

5. [1] B.M. I: 19. Autograph. Docketed by Jeremiah Bentham: 'Jeremy Bentham / Letter datd. Deans Yard / Decr. 20 1758.'
Addressed: 'To / Jeremiah Bentham Esqr. / at his House / in Crutched Friars / opposite Savage-gardens / London / Decr. 20th 1758.'
Jeremy Bentham was sent to Westminster School in 1755 at the age of seven. In his later life he always spoke of the school with dislike. He lodged at a boarding-house at 2, Little Dean's Yard run by Mrs Morell for Westminster boys. It is now one of the school houses, and is called Grant's.
In a letter (not published in this collection) dated 13 May 1755 (B.M. I: 15–18) Jeremiah Bentham tells his wife (who is at Browning Hill) that he has taken Jeremy round for an initial meeting with Mrs Morell and her sister, who 'seem mighty good sort of people'. They also called on a Mr Evans where 'Jerry had given our Entertainer a Specimen of his Proficiency in Musick by Playing a Sonata or two out of a Collection which Mr. Evans had by him of Handel's.' He also describes taking Jeremy some days later 'to Slaughter's Coffee House where we had an hour or two of french Chat, and Jerry was full of Spirits and attracted the Notice and engaged ye Conversation of almost every one there, and learned ye game of Polish[?] Drafts.' He mentions further French conversations and musical performances and goes on to say:
'The Secret is come out, and I can now account for your Son Jerry's *Inclinations*

8

days; when we can look them over, and I can have your Approbation of them.

I have told Wombwell[2] that I should only have a Man ⟨. . .⟩ for me without a Coach, and so our things could not be carried; he told me then that he would write home to Night for his Chariot to come for him and

Your affectionate
and dutiful Son
Jeremy Bentham

P.S. Turn over leaf and you will see my Verses. pray give my duty to my Mama and Grandmama.

Ad Marchionem Caermarthen a morbo nuper redditum[3]

Jam Schola laetetur, jamque urbs laetetur & ipsa,
    Utraque diversis fit benedicta modis.
Altera, praesidium quod patronusque futurus,
    Altera, quod rursus Gloria magna datur.
Nam tenûere illum tristis contagia morbi,
    Per niveam expansa est pestis cutem.
Quod neque carorum multum anxia cura parentum
    Ipsius potuit nec prohibere malum.
Jam timor expansus pretiosae est undique vitae
    Grata haud perque Scholam fama vagata fuit.
Jam tristes vultús coeperunt esse; tuique[?]

to accompany you into Hamshire abating—he has owned the Change was owing to the Cold Water you threw upon 'em by telling him he Shod. be dipped every Morning in Mr. Mulford's P⟨ond⟩ of Water—which he took such particular Notice of yt. I find like ⟨. . .?⟩ ⟨. . .⟩ it rise uppermost in his mind, and quench'd the *ardent* Fire with which he burned, so visibly, before, to see his friends at Baghurst.'

This letter of 13 May 1755 also refers to two other children of Jeremiah and Alicia Bentham: 'Nancy', i.e. Ann (1755–60) and 'Billy', i.e. William Woodward (1753–57).

One further letter from Jeremiah to his wife Alicia survives (B.M. I: 17–18). Its date is unknown and it contains no reference to Bentham.

The present letter is the first we have bearing the address of Jeremiah Bentham's house in Crutched Friars. It would seem, however, that the family had moved from Church Lane, Houndsditch, to Crutched Friars sometime in 1757, for the burial of Bentham's small brother William is registered at St Olave's, Hart Street, the parish in which Crutched Friars lies.

[2] John Wombwell, son of George Wombwell of Crutched Friars, London; b. 14 August 1748; educated at Westminster School; writer East India Company's Service (Bengal) 1775; paymaster of the Nawab of Oudh's troops under British officers 1779; d. 21 December 1795 (Barker and Stenning, *Record of Old Westminsters*, II, 1928). His father was a merchant.

[3] This poem is addressed to Thomas Osborne (1747–61), Marquess of Carmarthen, son and heir of the 4th Duke of Leeds (1713–69), and a Westminster schoolfellow of Bentham's. Though he recovered from this illness, he died at school of smallpox in 1761.

Nomen discipulis semper in ore fuit.
Omnes cognati multum coepêre vereri
     Ne talem perdant jam puerumque tui.
Quis nam prae tali haud potuit bonitate vereri
     Corpore cui tanta est gratia & ore decor?
Aetatem cui praeter inest sapientia talis,
     Cui matris pietas tanta, patrisque sui est.
Sed quid multa loquor? mirum est, ni stirpe creatus
     E tantâ, simili sit bonitate puer.
Namque bonum exemplar documentum exuperat omne
     Haec ambo ast unus continet ille simul.
Ergo jam merito multum Schola tota gavisa est;
     A morbô postquam gloria nostra redit.

Noster amice, hujus si das mihi nominis usum
     Accipe versiculos, aure favente, meos;
Nec malè quod feci spernas; me semper adesse
     Sollicitum credas proque salute tua. [4]

Bentham gave Bowring the following account of his relations with Carmarthen's family: 'Two sons of the Duke of Leeds—namely, the Marquis of Carmarthen, and Lord Francis Osborn, were among the Westminster scholars. The duke came once or twice to see them: the duchess came more frequently. She was the sister of the Duchess of Newcastle, whose husband was that foolish and ignorant duke who was the Minister, and who spent a large fortune in gross eating and drinking, and said he did so for the good of his country, and in the service of his majesty. One day, as the Duchess of Leeds was traversing the play-ground where I was amusing myself with other boys—one little boy amongst many great ones—the duchess called me to her, and said—"Little Bentham! you know who I am." I had no notion she was a great lady, and answered—"No Madam, no! I have not that honour." I found that some strange tale had been told of my precocity, and my answer was thought very felicitous; and, not long afterwards, I was invited to go home with her sons to the duke's. I was full of ambition; accustomed to hear myself puffed and praised; and my father was always dinning into my ears the necessity of pushing myself forward—so he hailed this visit as the making of my fortune. A short time before dinner, I was summoned up stairs to the duke's apartment, where was a physician, to whom he said:—"This is Bentham—a little philosopher." "A philosopher!" said the doctor; "Can you screw your head off and on?" "No, sir!" said I. "Oh, then, you are no philosopher"' (Bowring, x, 31).

Bentham's verses are printed by Bowring (x, 32–33, n.) though some of the readings there do not correspond to the present manuscript. The verses contain mistakes that are not surprising in the work of a ten-year-old schoolboy, and hardly merit full translation here. Their general sense is to call upon the School and City to rejoice at the recovery of Carmarthen, whose qualities are only what may be expected of a scion of such a house and fully justify general rejoicing. Carmarthen is asked to accept the trifling verses with the assurance of the writer's constant anxiety for his welfare.

[4] It is perhaps of psychological interest that the young Bentham has doodled in the margin of these verses as follows: 'Jeremy / Jeremy / Jerem / Jeremy / Je χριστος ὁ του θεου χριστος (actually 'Jeremy' is written many more times, and compendia are used for Greek letters).

6

To Jeremiah Bentham

10 July 1760 (Aet 12)

Honoured Sir

I expected that Dr. Markham[2] would have talked to me a good deal about my going to the University[3]; but as it happened he only asked me how I came to stay away and when I told him the reason, he went away and left me. I am very sorry to tell you, that Flood[4] came out of College the day before last, and he wrote last week to beg his Father to take him away from College for the Hardships were so great, he coud'nt bear them. he shammed out of College thinking not [to] go again 'till he had received an answer from his Father; but Dr. Markham having had intelligence how matters stood came to Mrs. Morell's[5] and fetched him to school, but behaved very kindly to him, and told him he should have all the

---

6. [1] B.M. I: 30–31. Autograph. Docketed by Jeremiah Bentham: 'Jeremy Bentham / letter datd. Deans Yard Westmr. July 10 1760.'

Addressed: 'To / Jeremiah Bentham Esqr. / in Crutched Fryers / London.' Stamped: 'PENNY POST PAID'.

Bentham's father, to whom most of his early letters are written, was now his only parent. His mother had died on 6 January 1759.

[2] William Markham (1719–1807); headmaster of Westminster School 1753–65; Archbishop of York 1777. Friend of Lord Mansfield and of Edmund Burke until the trial of Warren Hastings, of whom Markham was a supporter. It was his father's friendship with Dr Markham that decided Bentham's going to Westminster. At the conference with Dr Markham before his admission to the school Bentham was humbled by not knowing the meaning of 'genius'. Henceforward the word had a great emotional significance for him, which culminated in his discovery at the age of twenty that he had a genius for legislation. In the 1790's Bentham corresponded with Dr Markham, then Archbishop, concerning the Panopticon project, which required the purchase of Church property. For interesting comments on Markham, and a Latin Ode the eleven-year-old Bentham composed to him, see Bowring, x, 26–27, and 30.

[3] In June 1760 Jeremiah Bentham had taken his son Jeremy to Oxford to enter him for Queen's College (cf. Bowring, x, 36–37). He matriculated there on 26 June. He had previously won the right to a Westminster presentation to King's College, Cambridge, but was not sent there as ill-usage was apprehended for one so young (Bowring, x, 38).

[4] Jocelyn Flood (1746–67), son of the Right Hon. Warden Flood, Chief Justice of the King's Bench in Ireland, and half-brother of Henry Flood (1732–91), the great Irish statesman and orator. Jocelyn Flood went up to Trinity College, Dublin in 1764 and was M.P. for Callan in 1765. In Bowring's Memoirs he is referred to as 'Toulon Flood', but there seems to be no other basis for this form of his name, which is perhaps due to a misreading. He was Bentham's bed-fellow at Mrs Morell's, and, Bentham told Bowring, 'once spent two or three days with me' (cf. Bowring, x, 14 and 122).

[5] See letter 5, n. 1.

indulgences that cou'd be given to any body: however I am in hopes that his Father will have compassion on him, and take him away. Mr. Cowley[6] was with me on Tuesday and yesterday, and will be tomorrow with

Your dutiful and affectionate
Son
Jeremy Bentham

7

To Jeremiah Bentham

9 August 1760 (Aet 12)

Deans Yard Saturday August 9th 1760

Dear Papa

I am sorry I should have given you so much trouble by not answering your kind letter by Thursdays post; but, if you remember, you bid me write to you on Thursday or Saturday; and as I was pretty busy on Thursday, I thought it would be sufficient if I

---

[6] John Lodge Cowley, who taught mathematics to Bentham and later to his brother Samuel, was probably at this time on the staff of the Royal Academy, Woolwich, of which he became Second Master sometime in the 1760's. In 1768 he became F.R.S. and in 1773 Professor of Mathematics at Woolwich. Cf. also letter 28 at n. 4, and letter 92, n. 4.

7. [1] B.M. I: 32–34. Autograph. Docketed by Jeremiah Bentham: 'Jeremy Bentham / Letter datd. Deans Yard Augt. 9 1760.'

Addressed: 'To / Jeremiah Bentham Esqr. / at Tunbridge-Wells / Kent.' Franked: 'Wortley Montague,' Postmark: ' 9 AV'.

Edward Wortley Montague (1713–76), the splendidly eccentric son of the celebrated Lady Mary Wortley Montague, was M.P. for Bossiney, Cornwall, from 1754 to 1762. The Benthams may have known him through the Rev. John Forster (see letter 248, and cf. Bowring, x, 47).

Bentham spent much of his time with his mother's relations at Browning Hill (plans for visiting whom are discussed at the end of this letter), namely, his maternal grandmother Mrs Alice Grove, her son George Woodward Grove, her widowed sister Mrs Ann Mulford, and Bentham's aunts, his mother's sisters, Deborah and Susannah Grove. Bowring tells us of Bentham's great attachment to Browning Hill: '"It was my heaven", he used to say; "Westminster School my hell; Aldgate was earth, and Barking was paradise to me"' (x, 8). At Aldgate was his father's house, at Barking his other grandmother's house.

One of the attractions of Browning Hill was its large library. This consisted largely of the unsold stock of a brother of Bentham's maternal grandmother, Thomas Woodward, who had carried on business as a bookseller and publisher at the Half Moon opposite St Dunstan's Church in Fleet Street in the 1720's and 30's. 'He brought out Tindal's "Christianity as Old as the Creation" [1730]. He used to talk to Bentham of books and booksellers—of 'Honest Tom Payne', whose shop was then contiguous to the Mewsgate, and was a sort of gathering-place for the lettered aristocracy of the times. Woodward retired from business—was crippled and rich' (Bowring, x, 4).

12

did not write till today; or else, to be sure, if I thought that you would fully expect a letter from me by Thursdays post, I should not have been so disobedient as to have deferred it till now. Sam[2] has not wrote to you as he thought there was no occasion for him to write too; he has been to Mr. Metcalfe's,[3] but he was not at home, so he left your letter there. as you expressed when I saw you last some desire of knowing how Flood's affair went on; I have the pleasure to acquaint you, (I do not know whether you think I ought to be pleased) that he is to go away as soon as his Papa comes to England, which will be this Month. I will by your leave invite him to dinner on Wednesday or Thursday (for I do not know on which we break up) as I trust you will not deny me this one kindness at least, for if I have not a little of his Company then I shall not have any of it for a long time, and very likely never after as he will be gone to Ireland before the Holydays are over. I am very sensible, as I am sure I ought to be (do not stop here) of the kind regard you have to what you think may conduce to my pleasure, and shall be glad to go with you to Tunbridge especially as Stone[4] is to be there. I wrote a letter on Tuesday to my Aunt Grove[5] as you bid me to let her know the time of my breaking up, and to desire to let me know by an answer when it would be convenient for me to go there little thinking of going to Tunbridge with you, and must therefore write another to her to [un]say some things which I have said;

I am   Dear Papa
                 Your dutifull and obedient Son
                     Jeremiah Bentham

P.S. you see I have forgot my name.

---

[2] Samuel Bentham (1757–1831), the fourth son of Jeremiah and Alicia Bentham and the only one of their children apart from Bentham to survive early childhood, was born on 11 January 1757. For some account of him see the Introduction to this volume.

[3] Unidentified.

[4] A Westminster schoolfellow of Bentham's, who cannot, however, be identified from the published records of the school. According to Bentham, Stone was a son or nephew of the mathematician Edmund Stone (d. 1768). He was later secretary to the 3rd Duke of Dorset (1745–99), when Ambassador in France—a post the Duke held from 1783 to 1789. Bentham met Stone again on his return from Paris (cf. Bowring, x, 184; xi, 74).

[5] As Bentham's uncle George Woodward Grove seems to have been unmarried, this must refer to whichever was the elder of his two sisters, Susannah and Deborah.

13

8

To Jeremiah Bentham

30 August 1760 (Aet 12)

Browninghill Saturday August 30th 1760

Dear Papa

I arrived in good time at the inn on Tuesday morning, for I believe it was ¾ of an Hour after I came before they sat out: I believe I shall make you stare a little when you hear of one of the passengers: they were one Miss Norreys of Newberry,[2] Mr. Pointer that keeps an Inn there, and is intimately acquainted with Mr. Harris[3]; and Mrs. Vincent,[4] the famous singer at Vauxhall; who was going to pay a visit to her relations. she was pretty free in discovering herself, for she did not long wait before she talked about Mrs. Vincent as of herself and Miss Brent[5]; with whom she said she had had a quarrell; for the Girl was so insufferably proud there was no such thing as bearing her; however, she owned, the Girl was good natured enough: but at last they shook hands, and all was well again. At first I did not know what to make of her; for she intimated that she was in a publick way of life which I understood at first to be the Playhouse, but yet she talked of spending 3 Guineas in plays in one year and so I wondered how one that belonged to the play-house could talk of spending any money in Plays; and as she spoke her Husband's name quick, I thought she called it Finch. she is a good agreable woman, but talks rather too much in what great esteem she is had by ye world. one thing too in particular I dislike in her: she speaks very ill of her Father and Brother, and told us all, that they were both brutes: and proceeded to give us an account of the many obligations she had conferred on her brother, and how ungrateful he had been to her but these are

8. [1] B.M. I: 35–36. Autograph. Docketed by Jeremiah Bentham: 'Jeremy Bentham / Letter dated Baghurst in Hants Augt. 30 1760. Directed to me at Tunbridge wells in Kent.'

This letter describes his journey to Browning Hill. Probably he had returned to London for a night or so after being with his father in Kent, and had set out from there.

[2] Unidentified.

[3] The 'Quaker Squire' of the parish of Baughurst in which Browning Hill lay: cf. a letter from Bentham to his brother Samuel, dated 25 December 1806, to be published in a later volume; also Bowring, x, 24.

[4] Isabella (Burchell) Vincent (1735–1802), soprano singer, wife of Richard Vincent, junior, composer (d. 1766).

[5] Charlotte Brent (d. 1802), a well-known singer who had been a pupil of Arne and who later married the musician Charles Pinto.

circumstances which I think she might as well have passed over; and one would have thought that she might have been silent on that head on her own account, as well as her Fathers; especially as she owns, he is very fond of her. I am confident, if mine was ever so great a brute, and as unkind as he is kind and dear to me, yet from the consideration that he is my Father, I should think it my duty not only to provide for him and support him, but to love and honour him as much as possible; how much more therefore am I indebted to you, who have behaved to me in a manner so opposite to the foregoing? we all agreed not to dine at Maidenhead, which was the place the Newberry Machine dines at, but we walked on and had a very pleasant walk; and when we came to Reading we had some cold Beef and bread and cheese. I forgot to tell you, that Mrs. Vincent sang us *God save the King*, and *Britons strike home* in the machine. Mr. Pointer was very obliging too me, and invited me to his house, where he said I should have the best that Newberry affords. Miss Norreys is a plain good-natured-looking Country Girl, and lives with her Uncle from whom she had been absent at London a 12 month. I stopt at the 8 mile stone where I found Thomas with the Horses. my Aunt Grove would have wrote to you, if she had not wrote to you this day sen'night. our good friends at Browning hill and Mr. Pegment[6] desired their Compliments to you, and wish you would come down and fetch me, as you may be assured does

Your most dutiful and
affectionate Son
Jeremy Bentham

P.S. we are all well here and my Aunt Mulford is in as good Spirits as ever.

9

JEREMIAH BENTHAM TO CHARLES COOPER

13 October 1760

Crutched Fryars Octr. 13 1760

Sir

 Upon my Son's returning home from his Visit to take leave of Mrs. Morel and you, I found he brought none of his School Books with him, and it was not without some difficulty, and being more

---

[6] Unidentified.

9. [1] B.M. I: 37–38. Autograph. Docketed by Jeremiah Bentham: 'Copy Letter to Mr. Cooper about my Son's Books yt. had been taken out of his Book Case at Westmr. Datd. Octr. 13 1760.'

15

peremptory with him, than I had ever been upon any other occasion, that I got the better of his Reluctancy to tell me, yt. he had been plundered of 'em by some or one of the Lads, who had found means to open his Book case, tho' lock'd, and taken 'em out; I cod. not but think it a little extraordinary, yt. his property shod. be made a Ship wreck of, upon a presumption, as I suppose, of his not being to return to School again; but as I understand by him, yt. 'twas so notorious a transaction as to be the first thing ye Boys told him of, as soon as they saw him: I thought it proper for your Consideration whether some Notice shod. not be taken of it by way of Inquiry, for Example sake; for my own part, I had much rather my son shod. lose fifty times the number, indeed any Number of Books than add one to his own, by such improper means: Boys that cod. take advantage of their School fellows absence in such a manner, it is to be fear'd will improve but little in principle whatever they may do in Scholarship: and if such an Instance of indirect behaviour shod. be pass'd over unnotic'd, it cannot I shod. think be much for the advantage of the house where they are, but of this you are the best Judge. perhaps many of the Books might not be worth taking with him to Oxford, but if I shod. send his younger Brother to Westm.ʳ they might be of use to him; however it is not the value of 'em, but the regard I have for the order of the house in particular, and the School in general, that was my Induçement for giving you or myself any trouble upon this occasion.

The kind Treatment and Civilities my Son has met with in the Course of his Progress thro' Westmⁿ School, will ever be remember'd by me with the greatest pleasure and engage my warmest wishes for its Credit and prosperity. I am particularly to acknowledge your tenderness and Indulgence towards him, which I doubt not but he will retain a grateful sense of, as well as,

Sir

Your obedt. hble Servt.

J.B.

Bentham finished his time at Westminster in the summer of 1760. His father wrote this indignant letter to an usher at the school about the loss of his books. The recipient of the letter was Charles Cooper, son of John Cooper of Westminster; admitted to the school aged 7, June 1734; captain of the school 1744; Trinity College, Cambridge 1745; ordained priest 1754; became an usher at the school; D.D. 1769; subsequently prebendary, in succession, of York, Salisbury and Durham (*Record of Old Westminsters*).

Some of the missing books listed here seem to be the same as items in the list of books sent to Bentham at Oxford on 17 October 1760 (cf. Bowring, x, 36 n.). This suggests that Jeremiah Bentham's protest led to the recovery of at least part of what was missing.

P.S. If any of his Schoolfellows
had had a mind for any or all of
his Books I shod. have had no objection
to his giving 'em, where he thought fit.

Virgil. Delph. Edit.
Homer Odissey
Greek Testament
Euripides
Hebrew Psalter
   Grammar
Manuscript Diary
  of Hebrew Grammar
Greek Lexicon
Cæsar's Commentaries
Salust
Gradus
Peinax[?]
     etc. etc.

10

JEREMY BENTHAM TO JEREMIAH BENTHAM

29 October 1760 (Aet 12)

Wednesday Octr. 29th 1760

Dear Papa
  I did not receive your letter with the parcel till yesterday
night; and was surprised to see it dated as last Friday: for it was
left I suppose at Mr. Bowles's[2] by Mr. Malchair[3]: but I did not know
of there being one, till Mr. Bowles told me of it yesterday evening. I
begin now to live very comfortably having made several Acquaintance. one of them is Mr. Grisdale the Provost's Nephew[4] who is a

10. [1] B.M. I: 41. Autograph. Docketed by Jeremiah Bentham: 'Jeremy Bentham /
Letter dated Queens Coll Oxon / Octr. 29th 1760.'
 Jeremy Bentham went up to Oxford in October 1760. This is his first surviving
letter as an undergraduate.
 [2] Probably Oldfield Bowles (b. 1740). 'Among the persons to whom Bentham was
introduced at Oxford, was Oldfield Bowles, a gentleman commoner of Queen's College; a proud man, who received Bentham somewhat disdainfully. He was the patron
of a place where the Hell-Fire Club was held; a club somewhat characteristic of the
then state of Oxford. It was a club of Unbelievers, Atheists, and Deists, who pro-
fessed that, as they had a knowledge of their future destiny, it became them to prepare
for it; and they used, it was said, to strip naked, and turn themselves round before a
huge fire' (Bowring, x, 39).
 [3] It appears from letter 15 that Mr Malchair acted as Bentham's tutor in some
unknown subject.
 [4] Benjamin Grisdale of Maryport, Cumberland, matric. Queen's May 1760, aged
15; B.A. 1764, M.A. and Fellow 1767. For his uncle, the Provost of Queen's, see
letter 13, n. 6.

Scholar at this Colledge: and one Mr. Chambers[5] who plays very well upon the fidle. Mr. Pritchard[6] too, and I are pretty intimate. it was Mr. Cowper[7] that introduced me to the acquaintance of Mr. Chambers; and Mr. Pritchard to that of Mr. Grisdale, tho' he new nothing of him himself: which perhaps may seem strange to you. Mr. Pritchard called on me (on the Evening of the day that you went from Oxford,) to take a walk, as a beginning of a future Acquaintance, and by chance met with this Mr. Grisdale in the Quadrangle, and desired him to shew him my Chambers, so they both came together to me, and carried me a walking. I have been in Mr. Cowper's room for a day or two, while My Grate was mending; for he and I are very intimate.

Last night Mr. Aldersey[8] came to town, but did not lie in Colledge: but I was not so sorry at his coming, as I should have been at first: for that uneasiness soon wore off; and in two or three days time I did not care whether he came or no: he was very obliging (as I am told by the bedmaker) for I was not in the room when he came: and said he remember'd me very well, for he saw me when I was entered: so I am to go into another room till my own is finished. It has been painted and paper'd, tho' not with your paper as Mr. Jefferson[9] I suppose has told you. here indeed I am quite ashamed of myself, nor do I endeavour to exculpate myself, but must rely upon your goodness for pardon. tho' indeed the occasion of ye Mistake was this: the Upholsterer asking me whether I would have my room Paper'd then, I told him yes I believed he might: for I thought you had mentioned the sending of Paper from town only as a thing that might be done, and I did not care to be upon such

[5] Probably Jacob Chamber (or Chambre) of Kendal, matric. Queen's October 1757, aged 16; B.A. 1761. But possibly Thomas Chambers, of Studley, Warwicks., matric. Queen's 1755, aged 17, who apparently took no degree. For some amusing anecdotes about Chamber see letters B.M. I: 13 and 20.

[6] Not readily identifiable from the Oxford records. He was nephew to Jeremiah Bentham's friend, Dr Herbert Mayo: cf. letter 20 and n. 2.

[7] Probably William Cowper of Penrith, matric. Queen's October 1759, aged 15; B.A. 1763, M.A. 1767. He is subsequently referred to as 'Cooper.'

[8] Doubtless Samuel Aldersey of Queen's College who matriculated 1758, aged 16, graduated B.A. 1762 and died 1802.

[9] Jacob (or James) Jefferson (b. 1721), Bentham's tutor. Bowring describes him, on the basis of Bentham's conversation, as 'a morose and gloomy personage, sour and repulsive—a sort of Protestant monk' (Bowring, x, 37).

There is a letter (B.M. I: 39) from Jefferson to Jeremiah Bentham, dated 27 October 1760, explaining that Jeremy had arranged the papering of his room with the upholsterer's people without his knowing of it, and that he, Jefferson, was apparently the only person who knew of Jeremiah's intention of sending paper from London. He reports that Bentham 'appears very happy in his new situation'. See also letter 43, n. 2.

an uncertainty, as I thought it was. Mr. Jefferson lectures us upon Theoprastus's Characters and Grotius de veritate Christianæ Relligionis. this day the bells rang on account of Lord Leigh[10] being entered at Oriel Colledge. I have here sent you enclosed a Letter to Mr. Skinner[11] which if you approve of it, you may send to him, as you mentioned to me, in which if I have left out any particulars concerning myself that you would be glad to know, you may find them. I have wrote a letter to my Aunt Grove and have let her know I intend to write to my Cousin Mulford[12] very soon. excuse me, if you think my letter too short; for you know my letter to Mr. Skinner if you look into it will be as good as another from

Your most dutiful
and affectionate Son
Jeremy Bentham

[10] Edward, fifth Baron Leigh (1743–86). He was at Westminster while Bentham was there, and letter 11 suggests that Jeremiah Bentham was snobbishly urging his son to cultivate his acquaintance.

[11] Bentham once said to Bowring: 'I could, even now, if it were worth while, number up, to a certainty, all the visitors of an age approaching to my own, whom, down to the age of fourteen, I was ever allowed to receive at my father's house. There was Thomas Skinner, one of three or four sons of a clergyman who was a member of my father's clerical club: he was of Merchant Taylor's School; he was two or three years older than I, and twice or thrice he came to Barking' (Bowring, x, 14).

Skinner became a celebrated auctioneer and in 1783–84 was one of the Sheriffs of London, in which capacity he introduced several reforms including a more humane mode of hanging, 'the new drop', discussed by Bentham in *The Art of Packing* (Bowring, v. 118–19). The letter referred to here may be either to Thomas Skinner or to his father, the Rev. Thomas Skinner of Bishopsgate, vicar of Christchurch, Monmouthshire.

[12] John Mulford (d. 1814) was Bentham's mother's first cousin, the only child of John and Ann Mulford, for whom see letter 1, n. 5. In 1736, being then presumably at least fourteen, he was apprenticed to his father and served his time as a clock-maker. It was presumably in this trade that he carried on the prosperous business which, Bentham told Bowring, he abandoned before he was forty. In Bentham's early childhood Mulford lived in the parsonage at Baughurst, near Browning Hill.

Mulford's whimsical company was far more amusing to Bentham than that of his uncle Grove, and he took every opportunity of escaping to the parsonage. Mulford had been something of a rake, but in Baughurst his attentions were confined to a certain widow. It was a shock to the infant Bentham when the jeers of a Quaker farmer—i.e. Mr Harris (cf. letter 8, n. 3 above)—made him first realize the situation. Once Bentham met an illegitimate daughter of Mulford's 'borne down by poverty and premature old age'. In spite of all this, Mulford was a frugal man and inclined to religiosity. He had a store of odd knowledge which made him an interesting companion. He participated in chemistry experiments with the Bentham brothers in the 1770's. About 1760 he moved to Wargrave in Berkshire, and by the summer of 1765 he was evidently living at Steventon in Hampshire where Bentham often visited him. A number of letters survive which Bentham wrote to him and which will be included in later volumes of this edition. Mulford practised as an amateur surgeon and for this reason is often referred to in the correspondence as 'the Dr.' (For further anecdotes, see Bowring, x, 22–23).

19

P.S. pray do not forget my duty to my Grandmama,[13] and love to dear brother Samy who I hope together with yourself are very well, as I have been all this time.

11

TO JEREMIAH BENTHAM

6 November 1760 (Aet 12)

Queen Coll. Nov 6 1760

Dear Papa

I wrote on monday a short letter to you, only to acquaint you that I thought it needful to have mourning, since every body else are equipping themselves as fast as they can, and a good part are in mourning allready.[2] but Oh my Stupidity, I put it into my pocket with a design to send it, but as it was not then time I went about something else and forgot it; 'till this morning; when putting my hand into my pocket for something else, I pulled out the letter designed for you: I believe I was never much more vexed than I was then; just now I should say: for immediately as soon as I saw it, I sat down to write to you. Mr. Jefferson read some part of your letter to me, wherein you mentioned the mourning; and as I intended to write to you, he thought he himself needed not. I have not seen anything of Dr. Bentham[3] so as to speak to him; and I do not know whether it would be proper for me to go and see him without a more particular invitation; I shall not therefore 'till I hear from you. I remember you often seemed uneasy at the appre-

[13] After the death of Jeremiah Bentham's wife, his mother, Mrs Rebecca Bentham, seems to have taken charge of the household at Crutched Friars and of the four-year-old Samuel (cf. Bowring, x, 6, 17–18).

11. [1] B.M. I: 43–44. Autograph. Docketed by Jeremiah Bentham: 'Jeremy Bentham/ Letter datd. Queens College Oxon Novr. 6 1760.'
   [2] For the death of George II on 25 October 1760.
   [3] Edward Bentham (1707–76), second son of Samuel Bentham (1681–1733), vicar of Witchford, Cambs., and Registrary of Ely. Edward Bentham had been a canon of Christ Church since 1754 and was appointed Regius Professor of Divinity in May 1763. A virtuous, industrious, and plodding man, he published books on moral philosophy and logic. His connection with Bentham's family was direct but distant. Edward and Jeremiah Bentham were both in the sixth generation of descent from Thomas Bentham (c. 1513–79), Bishop of Lichfield and Coventry in the reign of Elizabeth I; but the two branches of the family had separated by, at latest, the early seventeenth century. 'The narrow allowance which Bentham got from his father, did not enable him to live without incurring debt at Oxford; and miserable he was when obliged to confess the fact to his father. Dr. Bentham . . . was the channel through whom the communication was made; and a remittance of ten pounds was sent to relieve the student from his embarrassments' (Bowring, x, 38).

hension that I should never know what to do with myself: but I can assure you, it is so far the contrary, that I can hardly find time for any thing; but what I cannot possibly do without. I have not been to see Mrs. Lee or Mr. Lee[4] yet; but intend to go to see them today. on Friday the King was proclaimed here by the Mayor, attended by the chief people of the several Occupations in this city, carrying flags in their hands, and some of the heads of Colledge's all riding on horseback amidst a great concourse of people. the proclamation was read before St Mary's where some other heads of Colledges and Drs. and all the noblemen in their robes stood upon a Scaffold erected for that purpose. it was read also at every one of the four gates of the City. as for myself, I got into Tom's Coffeehouse, where I saw all the Show without any crowding or trouble. I have not been to see Ld. Leigh, for I believe he is not now at Colledge: for my Acquaintance Burgh[5] knows nothing of him, nor has not seen him yet, tho' he is of the same Colledge and was very well acquainted with him at Westminster. We have lectures twice a day from Mr. Jefferson, at 11 o'clock in the morning, and 9 at night; except on Tuesdays and Fridays, (when we have publick lectures by the Greek Lecturer Mr. Hodgekin[6];) and Holydays. Mr. Jefferson does not intend beginning with me in Logic yet awhile: On Saturday we all received the Sacrament: upon which account we were Lectured in Greek Testament 3 days before, and as many after that day: to prepare myself for which awful duty, I read Nelson on the Sacrament[7] which Mr. Jefferson lent me; and intended to fast that morning; but it would not do, for I began to grow sick for want of victuals; and so was forced to eat a bit of breakfast with Mr. Cooper, with whom I have lived this 10 days.[8] we did St. Paul's Epistle to the Hebrews for lecture in Greek Testament which I found very difficult; and indeed it is allowed here to be the hardest Greek that there is.

I had much rather have my bedchamber Paper'd than my study for yt. looks pretty enough allready now the pictures are put up there but the bedchamber indeed looks very bad, and I think it would be well worth while to paper it: it was only against having Chints curtains yt. Mr. Jefferson spoke. I did not know whether

---

[4] Presumably Theophilus Leigh, Master of Balliol since 1726, and his wife (see letter 13).

[5] Thomas Burgh of Coventry, matric. Oriel October 1760, aged 18.

[6] Unidentified.

[7] Probably *The Great Duty of frequenting the Christian Sacrifice* . . . by Robert Nelson; 3rd edition, 1708, 13th edition, 1756.

[8] While his rooms were being redecorated (see letter 10, n. 4).

you would have all the rooms painted or no; so I have only my sitting room done.

I have sent you the only exercise we have done (inclosed) which Mr. Jefferson approved of very well. I intended making a Copy of Verses upon the Death of the late King; and, after that resolution was made, Mr. Jefferson spoke to me and desired me to do it: which confirmed me in my resolution; and 2 or 3 days afterwards it came out as a publick exercise for every body to do: and last of all your commands came to me, so that I have incitements enough to do it.

I have nothing more to add, than to tell you, that I am very well and happy (as I can be while unsettled) as I hope you and the family are at present. Pray give my duty to my Grandmama, and love to brother Sammy with a kiss, who I hope still goes on to improve in polite literature, as he used to do. Pray give my compliments to all my friends, and particularly Mr. Skinner and Dr. Owen.[9]

I will acquaint you in my next with some anecdotes concerning Mr. Chambers whom I mentioned to you, which I flatter myself will be as entertaining to you, as anything you can hear from,

> Honoured Sir
> Your dutiful and affectionate Son
> Jeremy Bentham

P.S. All the people at Queens are very sociable good natured men, except one whom my Aunt Grove told me she thought none of the wisest, and he is indeed a Dunce.

12

JOHN LIND TO JEREMIAH BENTHAM

17 November 1760

Coll. Ball. Oxon Nov: 17th 1760

Sir
        Tho' I staid in London a day or two after I saw you yet I was so much hurried that I could not again have the pleasure of waiting upon you.—

[9] Dr Henry Owen had been since 1750 rector of St. Olave's, Hart Street, the parish in which lay Jeremiah Bentham's house in Crutched Friars (Dr Owen also lived in that street). He was the son of William Owen of Dolgelly; matric. Jesus, Oxford 1736 aged 19; took the degrees of B.A., M.A., B.MED., and D.MED. From 1775 until his death in 1795 he was also rector of Edmonton.

12. [1] B.M. I: 45. Docketed by Jeremiah Bentham: 'Mr John Lind / Letter datd. Baliol College Oxon / 17 Novr. 1760.'

I spent an hour with your Son one morning in the last Week, very agreeably—He had rec'd a Letter from you, wrote since I saw you, which he propos'd answering that Day. Among other political Subjects the King's Death being introduced gave me an opportunity reminding him how fortunate he was in having it so soon in his power to make himself known; as I was sure, if he exerted himself, he need not fear, that his composition would be rejected.[2] —It seems he was thinking upon that very subject when I saw Him. —He is quite settled in his Room: and perfectly happy in an Academical Life.—He has stood the stare of the whole University: as his Youth, and the littleness of his Size naturally attract the

Addressed: 'To / Jeremiah Bentham Esq. / Crutched Friars / London.' Stamped: 'OXFORD'. Postmark: '18 NO'.

John Lind (1731–81) was a close friend of Bentham in the 1770's, when he was a well known political writer and unofficial minister for the Polish King. In 1758 he had taken deacon's orders. He graduated B.A. at Balliol in 1757, and M.A. in 1761. His improvident father, Charles Lind, a Colchester clergyman, was a friend of Jeremiah Bentham, who took charge of his financial affairs when, in the mid-seventeen-fifties, these became extremely involved. B.M. XXVII (Add. Mss. 33563) contains a large number of papers relating to these affairs which continued to occupy Jeremiah Bentham until at least 1774, three or four years after Charles Lind's death.

Later, Bentham's brother Samuel came to know two cousins of Lind's, both called Dr James Lind, and both (as though deliberately to confuse the historian) naval surgeons and medical authors. John Lind's father (Charles) was first cousin to Dr James Lind of Haslar (1716–94) and to Alexander Lind, father of Dr James Lind of Windsor (1736–1812). They were all descended from a Scotsman called John Lind and his wife Isabel (née Boyd). This John Lind had five sons, George (grandfather of James of Windsor and maternal grandfather of James Keir (1735–1820) the chemist), John (said to have settled and died in Poland), Robert, James (said to have returned from Poland in 1705, and father of James of Haslar) and Adam. Adam was a merchant, first in Edinburgh and then in London. Charles Lind, father of Bentham's friend John, was his son. (See *The Genealogy of the Families of Lind and the Montgomeries of Smithson* by Sir Robert Douglas, Bart., printed and it would seem completed by the younger Dr James Lind at his private press at Windsor in 1795.) When John Lind went to Poland in the 1760's he was evidently renewing a family link with this country. (For further details of John Lind's career see letter 99, n. 2. For James Lind of Haslar see letter 262, n. 2. For James Lind of Windsor see letter 206, n. 4.)

[2] The verses Bentham finally submitted are printed by Bowring (x, 41). Bentham gave Bowring the following account of the matter: 'Thirteen years had not been numbered by me when the second of the Guelphs was gathered to his fathers. Waste of time had been commenced by me at Queen's College, Oxford. Tears were demanded by the occasion, and tears were actually paid accordingly. Meantime, according to custom, at that source and choice seat of learning, loyalty, and piety, a fasciculus of poetry—appropriate poetry—was called for, at the hands of the ingenious youths, or such of them whose pens were rich enough to be guided by private tutors. My quill, with the others, went to work; though alas! without learned or reverend hand to guide it. In process of time, by dint of hard labour, out of Ainsworth's Dictionary and the Gradus ad Parnassum, were manufactured stanzas of Latin Alcaics, beginning *Eheu Georgi!* certifying and proclaiming the experienced attributes of the dead god and the surely-expected ditto of the living one, with grief in proper form at the beginning, and consolation, in no less proper form, at the end.'

Eyes of every one: However all enquiries after him will tend much to his Credit by convincing People that he has multum in parvo.

I beg my Compliments to Mrs. Westall[3]: And am,

Sir,
Your very Humble Servant:
John Lind.

13

JEREMY BENTHAM TO JEREMIAH BENTHAM

21 November 1760 (Aet 12)

Queen's Coll. Novr. 21st 1760

Dear Papa

I have been so busy for this last week about my Verses, that I have hardly stirred out in that time; which business was the reason of my delaying my letter. I think it was last thursday sen'night I was at Baliol to see Mrs. Lee[2]: at first I was shown into a good pretty genteel dressing room, where a Lady waited to receive me, whom I had not seen before. we talked together upon various subjects, such as Westminster, the University, the King's death, and the like. after a while, we went into that large Parlour, that they sat in, when you went there (I forgot to tell you that Miss Hodgekin[3] a young Lady, who you know, was there then, was ill, upon which I offer'd to go away; but they desired me to stay, telling me, that there would be company; for which reason I should stay, as they were to receive them.) in a little time Dr. Lee came in, and asked Mrs. Lee who I was; so she told him, and in the meantime a Gentleman came in whom they call'd Mr. or Dr. (I do not know which) Kennedy: I believe he is head of some Colledge or

---

[3] Mrs Elizabeth Westall was Jeremiah Bentham's cousin, though we do not know the precise relationship between them. It may be noted that Jeremiah Bentham's great-aunt Deborah, his grandfather's sister, married Samuel Westall in 1681. For Mrs Westall's will, under which both Bentham and his father were beneficiaries, see letter 106 below. Mrs Westall was also one of Charles Lind's creditors.

13. [1] B.M. I: 49–50. Autograph. Docketed by Jeremiah Bentham: 'Jeremy Bentham / Letter datd. Queen's Coll. Oxford. Novr. 21 1760. Recd. 24th'.

Addressed: 'To / Jeremiah Bentham Esq. / at Crutched-Fryars / opposite Savage-gardens / London.' Franked: 'Wortley Montague'. Postmark: '8 NO'.

A possible explanation of this postmark is that Jeremiah Bentham has coupled the wrong cover with this letter and docketed it accordingly. The cover of the letter here is separate, not, as in many cases, constituted by the reverse of the letter itself. Thus this cover may really belong to letter 11.

[2] See letter 11, n. 4.

[3] Unidentified.

other.[4] I am now in Mr. Chambers's room, (only upon a visit, for I am now got into my own Room) and as he is just stepped out, I take this Opportunity to write that that I promised about him[5]: which I could not do so well before, for fear, if he should by chance see what I am writing he might take it ill. he was a Scholar here at first, but is now a Commoner. after he had been here about a year, he grew a little disordered in his Senses, and was what I think people call Hypocondriac. he fancied once that the blood had all gone from his face, and that it was quite pale and wan on that account; he would take hold of his throat with his hands and squease it 'till he was almost throttled; and one day he tied a rope as tight as he could round his waste; and all this to get the blood up to his face; but after all this trouble he declared that it would not do, and that he was a dead Man. at last a Physician was sent for, but Chambers said it would not do, 'twas all over with him; he did not expect to live 2 hours longer: however, at last he recovered: Sometime after this, he and a Acquaintance of his a Scholar too being Confined to College for some Misdemeanor or another, one night being got a little tipsey as I suppose, and wanting to get out they went to a back door that looks into New-College-lane; a little lane if you remember by the side of Queen's; and from that door they wrenched off an Iron bar with ease, which it was thought 4 or 5 strong men could not have done; but they had the prudence after all, not to go out, for if they had, they would have been expelled ye. University certainly. however, the next morning the Provost[6] sent for Chambers, urging him to tell the truth, with a promise that if he did, he might find some favour: upon which he very ingenuously told him the whole affair. next the other was sent for, who for a long time stifly denied it, but it being proved clearly against him; he was turned out of the foundation; and accordingly put off his Scholar's Gown and put on a Battler's.[7] Chambers too tho' he was not ordered, yet as his Companion had been, thought he must too; and did so. but the Provost seeing him at the hall with his Battler's gown and apart from the rest of the Scholars, was surprised and sent for him again. Well, says he, Chambres, I though I had told you, that I would favour You on account of your ingenuity (ingenuousness I believe I should say) how came you to put on this

---

[4] No head of a college or hall of this or any similar name can be identified at this period.

[5] In letter 11.

[6] Joseph Browne, D.D. (1700–67), Provost since 3 December 1756. He was also at this time Vice-Chancellor, holding that office from 1759 until 1765.

[7] Battlers composed a rank of students below commoners and above servitors.

Gown? Yes Sir, says Chambers, but as you had turned off Hewson,[8] for the fault to which I was as much accessary as he, I thought I deserved Punishment as much as he. The Provost admired that, but told him that he was pardoned for telling the truth, and it would be better for Hewson if he had too. but at last he forgave them both, and restored them to the Foundation. About half a year ago Chambres having received a bank note of 3 ⟨. . .⟩ from his Mother (for his Father was not living) he made an Elopement from the College. the reason was, he did not like to be a Scholar, and indeed it is no very desirable thing; for the fellows are very absolute over them; and if it was not for the money and necessaries which amount to (I believe) not above 10£ a Year they would be no better off (for the time that they are Scholars, than even the Servitors[9]; and they too are paid by every Commoner so much a Year for their attendance at meals: besides a Scholar does not come to a Fellowship till he has been at College 15 or 16 years or more. for this reason Chambre not liking his situation, went to London with his Money, and there lived for some time very comfortably; but at last his Money being almost gone, he was forced to decamp, and go home having bilked his Taylor; in his journey he unexpectedly met with an Uncle of his, who carried him home, to whom he told his Story, and at last got leave to come and be a Commoner. he treated with the Vice-Chancellor from his own home and would not have come if he could not have obtained leave to be a commoner. You see I am stinted for room now, and therefore cannot write all that I would. I have received my Cloaths[10]; you will soon receive the Verses from

Your dutiful and affectionate Son, Jeremy Bentham

[8] Joseph Hewson of Wigton, Cumberland, matric. Queen's October 1756, aged 19; B.A. 1760, M.A. 1764.

[9] Students who paid reduced fees or none, and performed in return some menial services.

[10] Probably the mourning clothes asked for in letter 11. There is a letter from Mr Jefferson to Jeremiah Bentham dated 20 November 1760, in which he comments on Jeremy's having forgotten to send the letter asking for mourning clothes (B.M. I: 47).

14

To Jeremiah Bentham

26 November 1760 (Aet 12)

Queens Col. Novr. 26 1760

Dear Papa

I made my last letter imperfect, on account of my not having room enough to say all that I wanted; I find you had not received it when you wrote your letter. I received my Cloathes last Saturday sen'night and I suppose you concluded I had not received them, because Mr. Jefferson forgot to mention it when he wrote to you; as he told me he did, (upon the receipt of your letter.) Mr. Lind has been to see me, with the Cambridge Verses[2]; I was surprized when he came into the inner Quadrangle, and asked me whether my name was Bentham. (for I was just going into my room) Pray who is this Mr. Lind?[3] he is not sure the Son of that rascall that won't pay his debts, whose tythes you went to receive, when we were at Mr. Hall's.[4] I asked him to come up into my Room, and he did accordingly, and staid about an hour and a half with me. as I was coming home from Dr. Lee's who should I meet in the street but Dr. Burton?[5] he stared at me, and I stared at him for a little while, for I did not know him to be Dr. Burton, tho' I knew his face very well; till at last he spoke to me; "so little Bentham, (says he) how do you do, I saw you to day when I was walking with the Vice-Chancellor, but did not know you; I hope you intend to come

---

14. [1] B.M. I: 52. Autograph. Docketed: 'Jeremy Bentham / Letter datd. Queen's Coll. Oxon / Novr. 26 1760.'

[2] Verses written at Cambridge on the change of sovereign. See also letter 15.

[3] Cf. letter 12.

[4] Unidentified.

[5] Dr John Burton (1696–1771) was a first cousin once removed of Dr Edward Bentham (see letter 11, n. 3). According to the D.N.B., Edward Bentham's father, the Rev. Samuel Bentham, vicar of Witchford (c. 1681–1732/3), had Burton educated at Ely. Samuel Bentham, however, was not, as there stated, Burton's mother's cousin, but his own first cousin, and it seems possible that his education was in fact provided for by his uncle, Samuel Bentham (1653/4–1728/9), canon of St Paul's, Westminster, and Ely. Burton was a scholar of Christ Church Oxford and was admitted a fellow in 1723. He introduced the study of Locke into the schools, and acquired a great reputation for zeal. In 1733 a fellowship at Eton was bestowed on him. He was vicar first of Mapledurham (Oxfordshire), then of Worplesdon (Surrey). He published a large number of sermons and Latin tracts. A controversy with Dr William King led to the latter's fierce attack *Elogium famae inserviens Jacci Etonensis: or the praises of Jack of Eton commonly called Jack the Giant*. He and Dr Bentham are referred to in the Memoirs as examiners when Bentham won a Westminster place at King's College Cambridge (see Bowring, x, 28 and letter 6, n. 3).

to Dr. Bentham's, I dare say he will be very glad to see you.'' by
that I knew that it was Dr. Burton; so I thanked him, and all that:
the Sunday following after Church as I was setting with Mr.
Cowper[6] in his room, somebody knocked at the door, and when
it was opened I perceived 'twas a Servant in livery; as these People
are not very common in Oxford, I could not imagine what he
wanted; but he soon cleared up the Mystery, by telling me that Dr.
Bentham gave his Compts. to me and would be glad of my Company
that day to dinner; so I dressed myself up as well as I could, and
went there; we walked about in the Garden 'till dinner was ready;
but the Dr. seeing that I had pumps on, gave me a long harangue
upon the danger of wearing them in this weather, and told me I
should get cold if I did not get shoes. when I went away he made me
a present of some Reflexions on Logick,[7] written by himself; and
told me, he should be glad to see me at any time to drink a dish
of Tea; and that they drank Tea at 5 o'Clock. pray tell Sam not to
direct to me Master, when he writes to

Your dutiful and affectionate Son
J. Bentham

Pray give my duty to my Grandmama.

15

TO JEREMIAH BENTHAM

4 December 1760 (Aet 12)

Queens Col. Friday Dec. 4 1760

Dear Papa
     I think we have been at cross purposes with one another in our
letters for some time, occasioned I must confess, by a neglect of
mine to write to you hitherto as often as I should have done: for as
soon as you have sent your letter, you have received mine, and then
sometime after you have wrote me another letter chiding me for not
writing to you, and a day after perhaps you have received another
from me, and so on. both the letters that you wrote me, came at

<hr>

     [6] See letter 11.
     [7] *Reflections on Logic with a vindication* by Edward Bentham, first published 1740,
2nd edition 1755.

15. [1] B.M. I: 54–55. Autograph. Docketed: 'Jeremy Bentham / Letter datd. Queen's
Coll. Oxon / Decr. 4 1760.'
     Addressed: 'To / Jeremiah Bentham Esqr. / at Crutched-Fryars / opposite Savage
Garden / London.' Stamped: 'OXFORD'. Postmark: '8 DE'.

once, but no Mr. Skeates[2] along with them. all our Verses were shewn up last Monday sen'night or fortnight I think it was, but I shewed up mine to Mr. Jefferson 2 or 3 days before; he liked them very well, and seemed pleased. all the Verses are to be given up to the Provost, who is to chuse which he thinks best, or if he has a mind, none at all. but I can neither acquaint you when they are to be printed, nor who amongst us make them: tho' I believe most do. I Have seen Chambre's Verses and Cooper's; they are both very good Copys of English Verses; I will get them both for you if I can; tho' don't depend upon't: the Cambridge Verses to be sure are not extraordinary considering the rank that a good many of the Composers held in that University. I wonder how you can think of my verses being published, when amongst so many there must necessarily be a number of much better Scholars than I, and whose Verses would be printed rather than mine. I should have done Greek if Mr. Jefferson had not hindered me; (and indeed had begun and gone on some way) telling me that as I was not so much Master of that Language as of Latin; I had best not do it in Greek, but in Latin; so I was forced to obey, for these Fellows will have their will: or else I believe I could have done it as well in Greek as Latin, and then it might have stood some chance of being published.—t'other day (night I should say) I forget what day; Miss Harris[3] from Baghurst with Miss Goldstone[4] and Mrs. Flowers[4] her Sister, came to Oxford; and sent to me from King Charles's head Inn, to let me know that my friends at Browning hill were well: I asked the Man that brought it, (he seemed to be the Hostler of the Inn) when they went out of Town? he told me the next Morning at 9 'o'Clock; I sent word back by him that I would wait on them the next Morning: for I could not well go that night, as I had something of the Headake. accordingly the next Morning I went, and got to the Inn at about quarter after 8; but when I came to enquire after them, I was told that there had been three Ladies there, but that they were gone some time.—Mr. Malchair[5] was to have been with me Monday sen'night but could not on account of the illness of his Wife but was last Wednesday and do. sen'night; all the other times

---

[2] Denham Skeet (son of Denham Skeet, of Whitechapel, London, gent.), matric. Balliol 3 December 1760 aged 18; B.C.L. 1767 D.C.L. 1772. The letter in question may have been either from the father or the son. The son seems to have travelled between London and Oxford rather often, and to have carried letters between Bentham and his father.

[3] One of the daughters of Squire Harris of Baughurst: cf. letter 8, n. 3.

[4] Unidentified.

[5] It is unclear what Mr Malchair was teaching him: cf. letter 10.

which are the Mondays Wednesdays and Fridays of every Week; I flatter myself I shall improve much under him, as he is a very good Master. Mr. Jefferson says that I should have two or three more bands.—Pray give my Duty to Grandmama and a kiss to brother Sammy from

Your dutiful and
affectionate Son
Jeremy Bentham

P.S. You would have received my Letter sooner if it had not been for Mr. Godsalve[6] that came to see me while I was writing to you, and drank Tea with me.

16

To Jeremiah Bentham

16 December 1760 (Aet 12)

Queen's Coll. Tuesday Decr. 16 1760

Dear Papa

I take the opportunity of Mr. Skeate's going to town to write you a line or two: he called upon me this afternoon, to ask me whether I had any commands to London, for that he was going there early tomorrow morning: I asked him to stay and drink Tea with me; but he could not, for he told me he was going this afternoon to Dr. Hunt[2] who is Professor of something, the Oriental Languages I believe (but that you know best) so I told him I would trouble him with a Letter to you.—he told me he should be glad to see me, when he comes to Oxford again, which will be in about a Month hence. I am greatly at a loss for Bands; since I can have but 3 one Week and 2 another, (for the Washer-woman comes every Saturday with the clean things, and Monday for the dirty ones) which is by no means sufficient; for I ought to have at the least 4 a week: so I wish you would send me that band which was found in the Coach, as soon as you can; unless you intend that I should come down in a day or two's time; and indeed now I may come any

---

[6] John Godsalve of Westminster, matric. Christ Church June 1759, aged 18.

16. [1] B.M. I: 60–61. Autograph. Docketed by Jeremiah Bentham: 'Jeremy Bentham / Letter datd. Queen's Coll. Oxon / Decr. 16 1760.'

Addressed: 'To / Jeremiah Bentham Esqr. / at Crutched Fryars / opposite Savage-Gardens / London.'

[2] Thomas Hunt, F.R.S., F.S.A. (1696–1774) had been Laudian Professor of Arabic since 1738 and Regius Professor of Hebrew (and Canon of Christ Church) since 1747.

30

time, for the Term is out: there were three bands made me when I stood for College; I wonder what's become of those:—I want some Green Tea too, for since nobody here drinks Bohea, mine's all gone, except enough to make breakfast for two People; and there are several whom I have breakfasted with or drank Tea, whom I should ask: and I would not get any here, for it is so dear, that what I have would sell for 16 or 18s. a Pound. I want some other things too, which yet I can do without till I come to London, by borrowing.—I am glad to hear from you that my Cousin Mulford is to spend the holidays with us; tho' I shall not much care whether he does or no, if he spends such a Week with us as he did last time.—I often amuse myself with anticipating the pleasure of meeting at first with my Friends; but none so much as Mr./and Mrs./Skinner[3]; my esteem and respect for whom, I think I can compare very properly to that of my Lord Clarendon when Mr. Hyde for Mr. Selden. I imagine myself too just returned, finding you and my Grandmama and dear little Sammy sitting by the fireside when I come in, and his little Heart exulting and crying Brother Jery is come.—I suppose he often asks you where I am, and what I stay away for? and suppose I should come home, what harm will it do? or what then? Yet I do not wish to go home, with that longing which I used, when I was at School; arising from a kind of discontentedness of the place I was in, and the want of a great many conveniences, etc. I have sent you a little something* that we had for our last Exercise, not that I think it remarkably good, but that I think it may possibly amuse you, and with the hopes that it may not be disagreable, as it comes from

Your dutiful and affectionate Son
Jeremy Bentham

Pray give my duty to my Grandmama who I hope is well as well as Sammy. I have just now thought of something that I wanted to say: I think I may as well Carry up with me my light brown Cloaths, since they are too little for me now, and will be much more so when we go out of Mourning; and they will make a very good suit for one of your poor tenants.

*Nemo satis credit tantum delinquere, quantum
Permittas.—Give an Inch and he will take an Ell.

Oscula cum rapuit formosâ a Phyllide Battus,
Praedanti ignovit Nympha benigna dolo.

[3] The parents of Thomas Skinner (see letter 10, n. 11).

Attamen ulterius juvenis cum posceret audax,
Nec donum acceptum diceret esse satis;
Discedas, apage; tibi nam sanè æneus est frons:
Quod bona sum, nunc improbus, (inquit,) eris.[4]

17

To Jeremiah Bentham

21 December 1760 (Aet 12)

Queen's Col. Saturday Dec'r 21st 1760

Dear Papa

Although you had not received my Letter when you wrote to me, I suppose you have by this time. since you are so kind as to give me my choice of the day of my going to town, I have pitched upon next Monday for the day, for the convenience of having the Company of one of my Acquaintance of this Colledge, who was formerly of the Charterhouse; he lives while at London, at an Uncle's of his, at Cheapside. I have been to take a place at Kemp's[2] to day, and also to Mr. Jefferson to ask leave to go home, and intend to go to the Provost to day with a Latin Epistle, which we all carry him when we ask leave out: it only consist of a little form not consisting of above a line or two. You may tell Sammy that I will come morrow-day; and as morrow day will come so soon, I here conclude with the assurance that I am

Your most affectionate
and dutiful Son
Jeremy Bentham

I am very glad to hear my Grandmama is so well: pray give my duty to her.

---

[4] 'Nobody believes it sufficient to offend only as much as you allow. Give an inch and he will take an ell. When Battus stole some kisses from the lovely Phyllis, the kindly nymph forgave the plundering trick. But when the bold youth asked further favours, and said the gift he had received was not enough "Depart! Away! Really you have a brazen face: because I am a good girl" says she "you would now become a cad."'

17. [1] B.M. I: 62. Autograph. Docketed by Jeremiah Bentham: 'Jeremy Bentham / Letter datd. Queen's Coll Oxon / Decr. 21 1760'. (21 December was a Sunday.)

Addressed: 'To / Jeremiah Bentham Esqr. / at Crutched-Fryars / opposite Savage garden / London.' Stamped: 'OXFORD'. Postmark: '22 DE'.

[2] Kemp's was one of the regular stage-coach services between Oxford and London.

18

To Jeremiah Bentham

3 February 1761 (Aet 12)

Queen's College Tuesday 3d. 1761

Dear Papa

I wrote a Letter or at least part of one last Night, but being fatigued and not finding any of my Acquaintance I sat down to it so melancholy, and made it such a Melancholy Letter I was resolved to day I would not send it: I do not know when I wished for your Company so much as then; or when I have been so low-spirited: but a good Night's rest brought me to rights again.

Far from going to Oxford alone, we had one more in ye. Coach than our Complement; and I being in the Side where there was three, and in the Middle, was pure ⟨. . .⟩ Our Company were, one Mr. Benham or Benhall, who I guessed by his talking much of the Duke of Marlborough and his Affairs to be a Steward or some such thing to him; and A Sadler and his Wife and Sister who lived at Woodstock, and took places for the top of the Coach; and when Mr. Benhall and I came in, offer'd to go out of the Coach where he was with his Wife and Sister; but being known to this Mr. Benhall he was detained within not very much to my Satisfaction as it crowded me, but as it was not disagreeable and inconvenient to me, I thought I might as well not oppose it, as nobody else did. We were pretty chatty, but as I did not remark any thing extraordinary in them, I do not give any particular description of them.

The Oxford Verses came out it seems on Saturday; I have seen them, and read a good many of the first, and amongst the rest those of Lewis Bagot[2], which are reckoned very good, but as you will see them through Dr. Owen's means, I need not mention much concerning them[3]: I have got a Cough, which I believe I caught of you,

---

18. [1] B.M. I: 70–71. Autograph. Docketed by Jeremiah Bentham: 'Jeremy Bentham / Letter datd. Queens College Oxon / 3d Febry. 1761.'

Addressed: 'To / Jeremiah Bentham Esqr. / at Crutched Fryars / opposite Savage-gardens / London.' Stamped: 'OXFORD'. Postmark illegible.

This is one of the few letters of this period which hint at Bentham's unhappiness at Oxford, as recorded in his conversations with Bowring (cf. x, 39).

[2] Lewis Bagot (1741–1802) son of Sir Walter Bagot, Bart., of Blythfield, Stafford-shire, Westminster School 1748–57, matric. Christ Church 1757; B.A. 1760, M.A. 1764; Dean of Christ Church 1777–85; Bishop of Bristol 1782, of Norwich 1783, of St. Asaph's from 1790 till his death (*Rec. Old Westminsters*).

[3] The best verses written by Oxford students on the accession of George III were published. Bentham's verses had not been successful (see letter 12, n. 2).

if there is any such thing as catching Coughs; for tho' it has encreased considerably since I have been here, yet I think I had it a
little before when I was in Town. You may depend upon receiving
every week 20 Pages of Tully[4] if not more from

Your dutiful and
affectionate Son
Jeremy Bentham

19

To Jeremiah Bentham

15 February 1761 (Aet 13)

Sunday 15th Febry. 1761

Dear Papa

I send you enclosed my Translation[2] as I promised you and
shall continue it every Week and send it you this day as being the
last of the Week, for I think I need have at least a whole Week to
do it in, for I am got to a very hard part, and deeply immersed in
Philosophy; for a proof of which you need only read the Original at
your leisure before you read my Translation, and if you get to a
hard passage you may then look in for information, or to see
whether I have rendered it right. You see I have wrote the greatest
part very small, upon consideration that if I was to write as I commonly do, it would be so large, that the Expence would be much
greater, than I have made it by this means. tho' I say it is difficult,
and all that, do not imagine that I desire to have any of it taken off,
or that I shall be unwilling to keep my contract, for if it was 3
times as much I would do it, as I promised I would, and you would
like it: I flatter myself You will think I have hit off some of the
difficult parts not unhappily, and be convinced that what I say is
not of mere Idleness, and dislike of the Business I am about. I
expect to begin Logic tomorrow together with 4 more of us, and
with that, together with my Translation, I think I shall have
employment enough, One thing I forgot to desire is, that You

[4] In addition to his college work Bentham had regularly to send his father trans-
lations from Cicero.

19. [1] B.M. I: 72–73. Autograph. Docketed by Jeremiah Bentham: 'Jeremy Bentham /
Letter datd. Queens Coll. Oxford / 15 Febry. 1761.'
    Addressed: 'To / Jeremiah Bentham Esqr. / at Crutched Friars / opposite Savage-
garden / London.' Postmark: '16 FE'.
    [2] An instalment of his translation of Book I of Cicero's *Tusculan Questions*.

34

would not make any Alteration in my Translation except there be
any manifest mistakes in the use of the particles, etc., etc. for there
may be various lections, and what is in my book, (which I should
have told you, I found was one of the loose volumes of Tully which
you sent me) may be different in yours. I can add no more at
present, as I am just going to drink in company with an old Schoolfellow, who is come to see one of my intimate Acquaintance, except
that my Cough is almost though not quite well, and that you shall
receive in the middle of the Week an account of some very particular things, which will, I presume, surprize you as much as they
have done

Your dutiful and
affectionate Son
J. Bentham

P.S. pray give my Duty to my Grandmama, and love to Sammy,
who I hope is well, tho' in Petticoats still.

20

To Jeremiah Bentham

4 March 1761 (Aet 13)

Queen's Coll. Wednesday
March 4th 1761

Dear Papa
    Your letter which I received yesterday gave me a great deal of
concern to find you so angry with me tho' justly for a fault which I
indeed was guilty off, but not willingly: for I would have wrote to
you as I promised if it had not been for a deep cut in my finger
which I gave myself while I was mending a pen to write to you
with, just where I hold my pen; so that I could not hold it well
enough to write intelligibly; indeed you write to me nothing but
bad news; but I hope you will send me better next time; for it
concerned me vastly to hear poor dear Sammy was so ill. I hope I
have justified myself as to not writing to you in all this while; as to
the Translation I have been forced to omitt sending to you, I
make up the deficiency of that, by sending you if I can 40 pages this
week instead of 20, and the same number next which will just do.

20. [1] B.M. I: 74–75. Autograph. Docketed by Jeremiah Bentham: 'Jeremy Bentham /
Letter datd. Queen's College / Oxford / March 4 1761.'
    Addressed: 'To / Jeremiah Bentham Esqr. / at Crutched Fryars / opposite Savage
gardens / London.' Stamped: 'THAME'. Postmark: '5 MR'.

35

however you may think me idle, I fancy when you understand how much business I do you will alter your opinion. for what with logic, Geography, Greek Testament, Tully de Oratore and this translation, I think I shall have pretty well enough to do. at 10 o'clock we go to lecture in logic and as we can never get the bedmaker scarce to come to us till about half an hour after we come out from prayers and we must get by heart some Logic and look it over etc., and after we have come from lecture which lasts above an hour generally a good deal, we must have our hair dressed and clean ourselves and at half an hour after 12 dine, so that that takes up all the morning almost, besides Geography at 4 o'clock on Thursday and exercise on Saturday morning (tho' indeed those two days we have no logic lecture) and the classics at night. As you seemed not against my borrowing a harpischord and even learning some time hence, I thought it would not be amiss to buy a Spinnet as I could have one very cheap; and have accordingly bought one of Mr. Pritchard Mr. Mayo's[2] nephew who if you remember was at his chambers when we drank Tea there for 33 shillings besides 6d. for the carrying it to my Chambers, and 2s. 6d. for putting it in tune, which altogether made up 1. 16. if you do not approve of this purchase, I can sell it again for a shilling more than it cost me, to another Person. what I promised to give an Account of to you that was so extraordinary, is this which I shall tell you, tho' perhaps you may have heard of it from other hands: there is one Hawes[3] here that has a parish Church in this Town and belongs to Magdalen-hall who has lately imbibed the Methodistical doctrine and is become a famous preacher, has gained over a great many gownsmen to his opinions of other Colleges a few, but particularly Queen's and amongst them my friends Chambre and Cooper, and Grisdale the Provost's Nephew. these are such Fanaticks that they are much more Enthusiastical than the Methodists at London: one day I asked Chambre to take a tune upon the Fiddle together as we used to do often; but he truly was weaned from the pleasures and Enjoy⟨ments of⟩ this life, and however innocent that diversion might ⟨be⟩ he had lost all

---

[2] Herbert Mayo (*c.* 1723–1802), was a fellow of Brasenose from 1740 till 1765; B.A. 1742, M.A. 1745, B.D. 1762, D.D. 1763. In 1764 he became rector of St George's in the East, and for the last three years of his life was vicar of Tollesbury, Essex (a benefice, incidentally, held in the seventeenth century, by Bentham's great-great-grandfather, Randolph Croxall). According to Bowring (x, 35) Mayo had "recommended that Bentham should be sent to St. John's, as being celebrated for logic". For his nephew, Pritchard, see letter 10.

[3] Thomas Haweis (1734–1820), member of Magdalen Hall and curate at St Mary Magdalen, from which position he was eventually removed by Bishop Hume for his Methodist sympathies.

relish for such things, and had set his mind ⟨to⟩ those of a more important nature; only he ⟨. . .⟩ play tunes and sing Watt's hymns[4] together ⟨. . .⟩ ⟨. . .⟩ of the brotherhood with audible voice and str⟨ong emo⟩tion; and everything that they do now, is for ⟨the glory of⟩ God. Pray give my duty to my Grandmama ⟨. . .⟩ is ⟨. . .⟩ and love to poor dear brother Sammy ⟨with⟩ many kisses, who I hope I shall here is got ⟨. . .⟩ ⟨. . .⟩ ⟨. . .⟩ next letter, which would give the greatest ⟨. . .⟩ to

> Honoured Sir,
> Your most dutiful
> and affectionate Son
> J. Bentham

21

To Jeremiah Bentham

8 March 1761 (Aet 13)

Queen Coll. March 8th. 1761

Dear Papa

I am forced to send you this time an excuse for not sending you my translation instead of the thing itself: but as I shall make it up the succeeding weeks, and can give you the reason for my not having time to do it, I hope you will excuse me this time. Mr. Jefferson had set Mr. Cooper and I a great deal of Caesar's Commentaries to translate into Greek Prose which is more difficult to me in proportion than Verse; which I told Mr. Jefferson: but tho' I was sure it was so, yet I could not then account for it to Mr. Jefferson who thought it very strange that it should be so; but I have since thought of a reason, which is this: I having read chiefly Verse authors in Greek, could form my manner of Versifying and collect my words out of Homer etc. besides Verses give one a greater licence of expression, and if one cannot express one's Thoughts (or the Sense of the Author) in one way, one is more at liberty in Verse to alter the words so as the Sense may be the same, and even to alter the thought in some cases: than in Prose: and the

---

[4] The hymns of Isaac Watts (1674–1748) were first published in 1707.

21. [1] B.M. I: 76–77. Autograph. Docketed by Jeremiah Bentham: 'Jeremy Bentham. Letter datd. Queens Coll. Oxon March 8 1761.'

Addressed: 'Jeremiah Bentham Esqr. / at Crutched Friars / opposite Savage-garden / London.' Postmark: '[. . .]MR'.

Latino-Graecum of the Dictionary is so bad, that I can scarce ever find a word suitable to express the meaning I want. I have received a Letter from my Aunt Grove dated Turville Court,[2] wherein she says she would have come to see me here at Oxford, if the Horses had not been engaged. To hear poor dear Sammy is better, would give the greatest pleasure to

Your most dutiful
and affectionate Son
Jeremy Bentham

Pray give my duty to my Grandmama

22

To Jeremiah Bentham

15 March 1761 (Aet 13)

Queen's Coll. Sunday March 15 1761

Dear Papa

I have sent you inclosed 20 pages of my translation; and intend sending you 40 pages next week which will finish the book de contemnendâ morte which is a great deal longer than any one of the rest: Dr. Bentham came to see me in my Chambers to day and explained to me that part that I have marked in large brackets which I was forced to paraphrase upon a little as you see, for in some places as the Dr. says, the Latin cannot so cleverly be expressed in English, without some circumlocution: before the Dr. explained it to me, I was forced to leave room to put it in afterward, and go on. I should have told you that I have been to dine with the Dr. and Mrs. Bentham who sent for me last Sunday sen'night; they were very civil, desired I would come often, and so forth: and Dr. Bentham this time sends his Compliments to you. I received your letter on Sunday evening with Floods[2] inclosed in it; which indeed I think a very strange one. I am going to have an old Schoolfellow to drink Tea with me by and by who is just entered at Christchurch, and is to have a studentship given him by Dr.

---

[2] The residence in Buckinghamshire of Mr John Osborne (for whom see letter 64, n. 4), a friend of the Browning Hill household.

22. [1] B.M. I: 78–79. Autograph. Docketed by Jeremiah Bentham: 'Jeremy Bentham / Letter datd. March 15th 1761'.

[2] See letters 6 (including n. 4) and 7.

Bentham.[3] I hope poor Sammy is better, and you and my Grand-mama both well, as is

Your dutiful and affectionate Son
J. Bentham

23

To Jeremiah Bentham

25 March 1761 (Aet 13)

Wednesday March 25th. 1761

Dear Papa

Having had several interruptions from my Acquaintance just as I was writing my letter to you, I could not send you my Translation on Sunday as I intended: for one day Mr. Skate[2] came to drink Tea with me, another Mr. Godsalve, and another a Westminster acquaintance that I believe you never heard me speak off, so it does not signify mentioning his name. I find this part of Tully in several places extremely difficult, so that a page or perhaps 2 or 3 lines, will take me up as much time to translate as 4 or 5 of his other works, and indeed all the Tusculan questions in general, are the hardest Latin I ever met with: not so much because the construction is difficult, tho' that is none of the easiest, but frequently when I have got the Syntax of it it is some time before I can make head or tail of it: this often happens when 2 Sentences are joined by some sort of conjunction: when each seems to have nothing to do with the other: for tho' I could translate each of them literally, yet till I have found out the Relation they bear to one another, and by what means the Sense is connected, there's no such thing as making an intelligible Translation.—I long to hear how poor dear Sammy does, whether he is recovered from his Illness, and hope I shall as soon as you have received this letter. I have lately had a very lucky accident which tho' it kept me up a day or two, yet is of great

---

[3] Before Bentham went to Oxford, his father 'applied to Dr Bentham for a studentship; but got for an answer that his patronage was engaged. Afterwards, he spontaneously offered one to Bentham; who was so humbled by neglect and annoyance, and so desponding, that, after consulting his morose tutor, Mr Jefferson, he declined the favour which the Doctor proffered' (Bowring, x, 38).

23. [1] B.M. I: 80. Autograph. Docketed by Jeremiah Bentham: 'Jeremy Bentham / letter datd. Queen's Col. March 25 1761.'

[2] Presumably Denham Skeet: see letter 15, n. 2.

service to me: that Tooth which had several bits of it broke out and was as I complained to you so extremely sore being very troublesome I with my fingers pulled it out having plucked up a good courage: besides there were 2 other Teeth 1 of which had a young one growing out by the Side of it; I pulled them both out myself: however my Face swelled: before I pulled the Teeth out one or two of them aked very bad, so that with that and the Swelled face, which succeeded to the aking: I was forced to keep up: when Mr. Jefferson asked me what was the matter with me, and I told him, he told me aeger was Latin for idle: for when we are indisposed, and on that account do not attend Chapel and Lecture, we are put down in the books, such an one aeger: but Mr. Jefferson when I have not been well before that has suspected that it was idleness that made me keep up; which indeed I do not think is using me well; and I told him I thought 'twas very hard that I could never be believed by him when I said any thing: and this [has] often been ⟨the⟩ case in other things, tho' I have brought several circumstances to corroborate it. I am sure it could not be from Idleness that I kept up for then I studied a great deal harder than at another time, as I had nothing else—pray do not mention this tho'. Pray give my duty to my Grandmama.

I am
    Dear Papa
Your dutiful and affectionate Son
    J. Bentham

P.S. I have sent you 20 pages,[3] tho' I have wrote it very small and close, that it might not take up much Room.

---

[3] Of his translation of the Tusculan Questions. See letter 24, n. 1.

24

To Jeremiah Bentham

29 March 1761 (Aet 13)

The Tusculan Questions
of
Marcus Tullius Cicero
in
Five Books
Translated into English
by
Jeremy Bentham
Commoner of Queens College Oxon
1761
A° Aet suæ 14°

Hond. Sir!

By what I have already sent you of my Translation of the first Book of Tully's Tusculan Questions, you find, I am deeply immersed in Philosophy, the Part which I have now inclosed will finish that Book, which I must confess, is, in several places, extremely difficult, so that a page or perhaps two or three lines has taken me up as much time to translate as four or five of his other works; and indeed all the Tusculan Questions in general are the hardest Latin I ever met with, not so much because the Construction is difficult, tho' that is none of the easiest, but frequently when I have got the Syntax, it is some time before I can make either Head or Tail of it. This often happens when two Sentences are joyned together by some sort of Conjunction, when each seems to have nothing to do with the other, for tho' I cou'd translate each of 'em literally, yet till I have found out the Relation they bear to one another, and by what means the Sense is connected, there's no such thing as making an intelligible Translation. Tho' I say it is

24. [1] B.M. I: 83–84. Autograph.

Heading of his translation from Cicero, followed by introductory letter to his father. His autograph translation of the first book is in B.M. I: 85–120, consisting of instalments sent to his father at different times. Letter 27 shows that he continued the translation, but apart from a fragment of Book v in B.M. XVII: 132–137, none of the later part seems to have survived. It will be noticed that Bentham has incorporated in this 'dedicatory epistle' some passages from letters 19 and 23.

difficult don't imagin I am unwilling to go through with what I have undertaken, for if it were three times as much I shou'd have no thoughts of declining it, since I have set about it, and find it is agreeable to you, and flatter myself you will think I have hit off some of the difficult parts not unhappily. But shod. this Essay of a Translation have nothing else to recommend it, your goodness however makes me happy in thinking it will not be altogether unacceptable to you, as it comes from

> your dutiful and affectionate
> Son
> Jeremy Bentham

Queens Coll: Oxon
March 29th 1761

25

To Jeremiah Bentham

29 March 1761 (Aet 13)

Sunday March 29th 1761

Dear Papa

I have sent you 21 pages of the Translation: which just finishes the 1st. Book; as I am a little straitened for time, I must defer writing a long letter till the middle of next week, when you may expect to hear more from

> Your dutiful and
> affectionate Son
> J. Bentham

I long to know how the country Air agrees with poor dear Sammy. I suppose you have heard from my Grandmama by this time.

25. ¹ B.M. I: 81. Autograph. Apparently written after letter 24 (a copy of which follows it). Docketed by Jeremiah Bentham: 'Jeremy Bentham / Letter datd. Queen's Coll. Oxon / 29 March 1761.'
Addressed: for / Jeremiah Bentham Esqr. / at Crutched Fryars / opposite Savage-gardens / London.' Postmark: THAME'. Stamped: '30 MR'.

26

To Jeremiah Bentham

22 April 1761 (Aet 13)

Dear Papa

I am afraid you begin to think it long since you heard from me last; and indeed I am angry with myself that I did not write to you sooner; but will make amends by beginning the second book and sending you part of it next Sunday. What you mentioned in your last concerning Mr. Mayo's[2] Nephew, I find to be but too true; for his behaviour is so impertinent and childish, that I have tried to drop off his acquaintance entirely, but can hardly get rid of him, whether I will or no, he forces himself so upon me. he is known all over Oxford for Impertinence and Impudence; for if he happens to meet with any body at any of his Acquaintance's Rooms, he will go and see them next day, or invite them to come and see him. some time ago he was at Billiard-table, (where by the by he games very high) where was also a Gentleman of our house, who labours under an Impediment in his speech, when talking of speaking French, that Gentleman said that he understood a little of it, or had a good mind to learn it, or some such thing: You, says Pritchard, understand French; You can't speak your own Mother Tongue yet. I leave you to make reflections upon this behaviour of Mr. Pritchard's, which I fancy you will, not very favourable to him. I have been at Mr. Disney's[3] lodgings which are not in the College, but in a house adjoining, who upon reading your letter, gave me the 25s: I asked him to drink Tea with me. but he told me he was afraid he could not have time, as he was very busy in doing Exercise for his degree; he called upon me yesterday and told me, that he had taken it the day before. If you would let me know how poor

---

26. [1] B.M. I: 124–125. Autograph. Docketed by Jeremiah Bentham: 'Jeremy Bentham / Lr. datd. Queens Coll. Apl. 22d 1761'.

Addressed: 'To / Jeremy Bentham Esqr. / at Crutched Friars / opposite Savage-gardens / London.' Stamped: 'OXFORD'. Postmark: '23 AP'.

[2] Some one has tried to delete the name 'Mayo' and later 'Pritchard', but with the assistance of letter 20 they can easily be made out.

[3] Perhaps Matthew Disney of St John's College, matric. 1748, aged 18; B.A. 1752, M.A. 1756: he took his B.D. degree in 1761.

dear Sammy does, for I long to hear, you would give great pleasure to

Your most dutiful
and obedient Son
J. Bentham

I received the Sugar and Tea last week, this day sen'night.

Wednesday April 22d.
1761

27

To Jeremiah Bentham

25 May 1761 (Aet 13)

Monday May 25th 1761

Dear Papa

I have sent you 10 pages of my Translation,[2] and likewise have filled up the gap that you complained of in your last; you must know I had asked Mr. de Salis[3] my next door neighbour with whom I am now well acquainted (who is now a Batchelor and Fellow-Commoner, and has read the Tusculan Disputations) to explain the meaning of that passage, as I had given it over after a great deal of Study myself, but he could not, no more could another Batchelor of Arts of my Acquaintance, and so I went as my last resource to Mr. Jefferson, who after pretty much consideration explained it to me to the same effect as I have put down on the back of my translation. I have inquired about that Epitaph on beau Nash by Dr. King,[4] but find it is not to be had at the booksellers, but have borrowed it of Mr. De Salis to transcribe it for you, and will send it

27. [1] B.M. I: 126. Autograph. Docketed by Jeremiah Bentham: 'Jeremy Bentham / Letter dated Oxford / May 25 1761.'

[2] Of Cicero's *Tusculan Questions*. See letter 24.

[3] Henry Jerome de Salis (*c.* 1741–1810), son of Jerome de Salis of St George's, Hanover Square, matric. Queen's June 1757, aged 16; B.A. 1761, M.A. 1766; became a clergyman and chaplain-in-ordinary to George III; Count of the Holy Roman Empire, F.R.S., F.S.A. 'There was a gentleman commoner, who took to me a little— De Sellis, a Swiss. His chambers were underneath mine. He took in the Annual Register, which had then just appeared. I was a child; he a man; so we had few ideas in common: but the Annual Register delighted me' (Bowring, x, 40).

[4] Dr William King (1685–1763) was Principal of St Mary's Hall from 1718 till his death. His 'Epitaphium Richardi Nash' appeared in 1757. (See *Political and Literary Anecdotes*, pp. ix and 249, by Dr William King, first published in 1818.) See also letter 14, n. 5.

44

you this week, or next if I can, for it is a very long one: I am just going to Lecture, and have only just time to send you these few lines from

Your most dutiful and
affectionate Son
Jeremy Bentham

Pray give my duty to Grandmama.

28

T O   J E R E M I A H   B E N T H A M

12 June 1761 (Aet 13)

Friday June 12th 1761

Dear Papa

It was with great pleasure that I received your last letter, as it gave me such a surprizing account of dear Sammy's improvement, which is so great, that it quite astonished me when I read your account of him, as he could not spell above 10 or 15 words at most when I went away from home, and those monosyllables: I long to see him in his breeches, which I dare say become him extremely well.[2] Mr. Jefferson has had a very bad disorder in his hand much worse perhaps than Mr. Blankley[3] represented, but it is well now, so that I suppose he will write to you soon: as he now comes down stairs, which he has not done this long while. he had two or three Abscesses

---

28. [1] B.M. I: 128 and 132. Autograph. Docketed by Jeremiah Bentham: 'Jeremy Bentham / Queen's Col. June 12. 1761.'

[2] Samuel was almost four and a half then.

[3] A neighbour of Jeremiah Bentham's in Crutched Friars, or so it appears from some comic verses composed by Bentham and quoted by Bowring (x, 42) from a manuscript in the father's hand, dated Crutched Friars, 29 January 1761, which has not come down to us. Blankley seems not to have been at Oxford, as his name does not appear in *Alumni Oxonienses*. The verses are:

> I'm asked to see his ape, by neighbour Blanckley:
> I'll go—but, fear a truth, I'll tell you frankly,
> Lest he should strip the creature of his rug,
> And in his skin impose himself for pug;
> For had he but the skin, there needs no more:
> In genius, manners, phiz—he's pug all o'er.

> IN AMICUM MEUM, STANYFORDUM BLANCKLEY, ET SIMIAM EJUS:
> Visere Blanckleianum accersor Cercopithecum;
> Ibo; sed hoc metuo (non etenim absimile est)
> Ne forte illudat vestitus pelle ferinâ
> Ipsumque ostendat se mihi—pro Simiâ:
> Pelle sit indutus; præsto sunt cætera cuncta;
> Ingeniumque, et mos est Simialis et Os.

See also letter 31.

45

in his arm and hand which he was forced to have lanced, the pain of which threw him into a Fever. — I am very glad to hear of Mr. Cowley's[4] good fortune, which I am sensible is no better than he deserves, and propose to myself great pleasure as well as improvement in taking a trip over to see him at Woolwich. I should be glad to know of him when you see him whether there was any Satellite that attended Venus in her passage over the Sun, as some of our people thought they saw one—now I am mentioning that, I cannot help letting you know how by a piece of I hope not unwarrantable boldness I got a sight of Madam Venus in her transit, through the College Telescope.[5] you must know the College had not long ago a present of a Telescope, but that whatever belongs to the college far from being free for the use of all the individuals, belongs only to the fellows. instead therefore of letting the under-Graduates have the use of the Telescope, the Fellows had it entirely to themselves, so that we had no hopes of seeing this remarkable Phænomenon which it was allmost impossible we should ever have an Opportunity of seeing again in our lives as it will not happen again this 160 years and more. but I and two others of my Acquaintance, thinking it unreasonable that we should not see it as well as the rest of ye. College, at about ¼ after 6 stole up the common-room stairs and marched up to the leads where the fellows had brought the Telescope for the convenience of observing the Phænomenon. there we found only Dr. Dixon[6] and a Master of arts of his hall, by good luck, as the Fellows were gone to prayers, who very obligingly offer'd to shew it us, but unluckily the Sun just then happened to pop his head under a cloud, and we could not get to see it again 'till the Senior Fellow Mr. Knaile[7] came up thither, who seeing us there behaved civilly enough, as he could not then very well turn us out again. (I should have told you that there was among us three one who had just taken his batchelor's degree, which was of some service to us in our enterprize) and then came in the whole posse of Fellows from prayers; however we got a sight of it at last; and then went down triumphantly and told our Acquaintance of it, and that put some others upon going, and at last they all went,

---

[4] Cf. letter 6, n. 5. We do not know what 'Mr. Cowley's good fortune' was.

[5] It is said that the difficulty there was in observing this transit of Venus at Oxford led to the founding of the Radcliffe Observatory in 1772 (cf. C. E. Mallet, *A History of the University of Oxford*, iii, 125).

[6] Dr George Dixon (1710–87), Principal of St Edmund Hall, which office was in the gift of Queen's College.

[7] William Knail of Whitehaven, Cumberland, matric. Queen's 24 March 1728/29, aged 16; B.A. 1734, M.A. 1737; Headmaster of Rugby 1744–51; Fellow of Queen's 1751, B.D. 1759, D.D. 1762; d. 1765 (cf. letter 60 at n. 4).

for which they may thank us. when we looked thro' the Telescope, Venus looked to be considerably broader than a Crown-piece but we could see it plainly with Glasses blacked over the Candle which we had done so to prevent the brightness of the Sun hurting our Eyes; and I even saw it with my naked Eyes I am very positive, tho' some people won't believe me, when the Sun was a little obscured with a cloud. we are just gone through the Logic Compend,[8] and have been twice in the hall, but we go in three times to see the manner of it before we begin to dispute, which will be next Wednesday; I have reason to hope I shall be an overmatch for those of my class in that way.[9] I have sent You my bills, of my own Transcribing, for Mr. Jefferson's hand is so bad he could not do it himself; he has been putting if off from week to week he tells me in hopes that his hand might be well enough to do it, but he sees no likelyhood of it yet a while. Pray give my duty to Grandmama, and love to dear Sammy, and be assured that I am

Your dutiful and
affectionate Son
J. Bentham

Dr. Dixon gives his Compliments to you and all his Friends.

29

Sperne Voluptates, Nocet Empta Dolore Voluptas

27 June 1761 (Aet 13)

Despise Pleasures, every pleasure is injurious that
is purchased (in its consequences) by Regret.

Among all the follies and pursuits of mankind nothing surprises me more, my fellow Collegiates, than that Men should think of attaining the highest felicity by those means, which, instead of producing

---

[8] *Logicae Artis Compendium*, 1618 (and many later editions), by Robert Sanderson (1587–1663), Bishop of Lincoln.

[9] In the course of the four years' residence required before taking the B.A. degree students were required to take part in a certain number of disputations in Grammar or Logic. These were known as the Disputationes in Parviso (*Oxford Statutes*, *Tit.* VI, § 1, Ch. 3).

29. [1] B.M. I: 122v⁰–123. This is Bentham's translation of a Latin essay by himself: the original Latin is in B.M. I: 121–122r⁰. It is presumably the declamation mentioned at the beginning of letter 30 as having been already sent to Jeremiah Bentham.

This, the earliest essay in moral philosophy by the great hedonist, is remarkable both for its similarities and its dissimilarities to the work of his maturity. Morality is already seen as an affair of calculation, but there is a loftiness of sentiment dangerously redolent of the principle of sympathy and antipathy.

Pleasure, are, on the Contrary, frequently attended with pain and Misery; for it seems unworthy of Man, possessed as he is of that noble faculty of Reason, who discerns the consequences of things, understands their Causes, and, by comparing things with one another, can choose the good and avoid the Evil: yet Beasts, that are actuated by mere sense alone, can guard against and fly from things hurtful, and know how to shun things that are attended with future pain as cautiously as they wod. the venemous bite of a Viper. But Man, who, on account of his rational facultys, boasts of his Excellence above the Beasts, greedily covets, ardently longs for, and stupidly pursues those very things the wiser Brute flys from and avoids. O blind Infatuation of Men that despising the Council of Reason, their best guide, drives 'em headlong into certain and manifest ruine: Is this to excell the Beasts? Is this your so much boasted Wisdom? for shame! this is madness itself: to abuse the best and most precious gift of the deity by means so mad, so base, so impious, but this appears with still greater certainty when we turn our Eyes towards the objects of men's pleasures and delights; the Life of the Voluptuary is one continued scene of Madness, while he gives himself up entirely to the deceitful Allurements of Pleasure, not only not avoiding but eagerly meeting, of his own accord, the Snake that lies hid in the Grass: instead of Joys he is preparing for himself cares—instead of Happiness—pain. Why shod. I call to mind the adulterer who seeks his supream felicity in parties of Leudness and nightly Debaucheries? Why—the Glutton who, devoted to the pampering of his Belly, consumes his pretious time in satisfying a voracious appetite? But why him, who seems to place his highest joy in spending whole nights at the accursed gaming table, to the utter ruine of his fortune, his health, and reputation—the consequence of which is greivious Remorse, Sleepless nights, and ragged poverty? Why the Miser whose Sole aim is to heep up useless Riches, without regard to right or wrong; but this kind of Madness is obvious to every one since he is heaping up golden Treasures for himself which however wod. be worse than death for him to make use of; But why, I say shod. I recount these foolish pleasures when One much more ridiculous, much more infatuating, and much more irrational as yet remains unnoticed. Drunkenness of all false pleasures the most fallacious! This certainly argues the folly of men to the highest degree, who while they make an ill use of the Sweet Gift of Bacchus, foolishly drown in Wine their boasted reason, without which, nothing is grateful, nothing is pleasant; altho the Moderate use of the Grape Enlivens the Soul, and relieves it under goading cares—yet the Excess of it has surely nothing that's good, nothing that's pleasant. Wine destroys the fairest beauty and spoils the strongest Constitution yet this is called a mighty pleasure—but to every cool and dispassionate Judge it will appear sufficiently manifest, how great is the unhappiness that is frequently the attendant upon drunkenness: No sooner is any one heated with Wine, but his Limbs become heavy his tottering feet refuse to perform their accustomed offices, his Tongue stammers, his speach is broken, his mind and reason are suspended—his Eyes swim with moisture, he grows horribly noisy, then bitter qualms ensue, to this loathsome vomiting succeeds, and Grievous Headachs—till, at length, he becomes stupid and insensible throughout. This is the whole of the Drunkards pleasure—which no one surely in their Senses will say has any claim to happiness, for when once deprived of that divine particle within us our reason, I can't conceive any thing more miserable, any thing more unhappy than Man: But reason in a drunkard is so far buried in Wine that he knows not what he says— what he do's—what he sees. In what then does the happiness of Drunkeness consist—it certainly renders man inferior to the beasts. If this be a pleasure then it is a pleasure that is unworthy of the very beasts themselves—Despise therefore pleasures my fellow collegiates—but of all pleasures chiefly that of drunkeness, for as it is unworthy every man, so, more especially, is it a disgrace to a Gentleman, but above all to a Scholar.

habita in Aula Coll. Reg. Oxon Bentham 27 Juni; 1761.[2]

30

To Jeremiah Bentham

30 June 1761 (Aet 13)

Tuesday 30 June 1761

Dear Papa

    I have sent you a Declamation I spoke last Saturday, with the approbation of all my Acquaintance, who liked the thing itself

---

[2] Supplied from the Latin version.

30. [1] U.C. clxiii: 1. Docketed by Jeremiah Bentham: 'Jeremy Bentham / Letter datd. Queen's College Oxford / June 30 1761.'

    It is suspected that this letter belonged to Bowring's private collection of which C. K. Ogden was at one time the owner, and was presented or sold by him to the College. The relevant documents have been destroyed by fire. It has some notes on it

very well, but still better my Manner of speaking it. even a Batchelor of my Acquaintance went so far as to say, that he never heard but one speak a Declamation better all the time he has been in College. which indeed is not so much to say as perhaps you imagine; for sure no body can speak worse than we do here, for in short 'tis like repeating just so many Lines out of Propria quæ Maribus.[2] I have disputed too in the Hall once and am going in again tomorrow, there also I came off with Honour, having fairly beat off not my proper Antagonist but the Moderator himself: for he was forced to supply my Antagonist with Arguments, the Invalidity of which I clearly demonstrated. I should have disputed much oftener, but for the Holidays or Eves that happened on Mondays, Wednesdays, and Fridays: and besides we went 3 times into the Hall before we disputed ourselves, that we might see the Method: indeed I am sorry that it does not come to my turn to dispute every disputation day, for, for my part, I desire no better sport.—I wish you would let me come home very soon, for my Cloaths are dropping off my back, and if I don't go home very soon to get new ones, I must not go down stairs they are so bad, for as soon as one Hole is mended, another breaks out again: and as almost all the Commoners either are gone for the Vacation or will be gone in a day or two's time, very little business will be going forward; pray give me an Answer very soon, that I may know whether I am to wear Clothes or go in Rags. Pray give my duty to my Grandmama, and love to dear Sammy, and represent the woeful condition of one who is nevertheless

Your dutiful and
affectionate Son
J. Bentham

I should be glad to know your's and Mr. Skinner's Opinion of Higgenbroccius.[3] Pray see if you can make out this thing which is strictly true here.

in Ogden's hand. It was the only juvenile letter published by Bowring (x, 42) and apparently the only one of which he knew. On his own copy of *Works*, Volume x, now in the British Museum, he has noted at the end of chapter II: 'It is to me a subject of great regret that so little remains of Bentham's early correspondence with his father and family. He believed that the letters were destroyed wilfully by his mother-in-law, and his suspicions added not a little to the severity of judgment with which he visited that lady.' (It seems from this that neither Bowring nor Bentham knew that the contents of B.M. I survived.)

   [2] These are the opening words of a doggerel mnemonic on the genders of Latin nouns found in Lily's *Latin Grammar*. The phrase was used to signify the merest rudiments of Latin.

   [3] Presumably a reference to some comic Latin verses about Oxford. These are

Nostra parva Ursa non solum est sus vel, sed etiam oportet ego.[4]
Pray excuse my not writing over my Declamation.

31

TO JEREMIAH BENTHAM

6 July 1761 (Aet 13)

July 6th 1761

Dear Papa

I have just now taken a place in Kemp's Machine for Fryday,
and hope to meet you and Mr. Blankley at the Pack-horse at
Turnham-Green that Evening. I have had a sad misfortune since I
wrote to you last, namely the loss of my other Pocket book in much
the same manner as I lost the t'other. as I was walking with one or
two of my Acquaintance a good deal below Christ-church not far
from Friar Bacon's Study, which place tho' perhaps you do not
know, there were two Men a quarrelling, and a Multitude of black-
guard gathered about them, and some few Gownsmen, and it being
a narrow part of the Street, for it grows narrower and narrower,
and there it was that somebody stole it out of my Pocket; I did
catch hold of a Finger that was very near it, but being stronger
than I, the owner of it pull'd it away before I could turn round.
Indeed 'tis very strange that I should lose two pocket-books in that
manner, and one of them too in Oxford, where there [are] scarce
any Mobs, or Pickpockets but they whom we know and find to be
so, and who can do it safely without fear of being punished; I am
afraid for all you see it was none of my Fault, you may think me
careless. I would have sent Mr. Blankley's Verses, but they were in
my pocket-book, as was the account of Mr. Malchair.[2] I do not
mean the Verses on the Monkey,[3] for those I have not done nor
can do. Dr. Owen left his Name in my Room, but not his Quarters,
and when I went to Jesus, they told me they knew no such Person,

published in the 1806 edition of a humorous account of Oxford called *A Companion to
the Guide and a Guide to the Companion: being a Complete Supplement to all the Accounts
of Oxford hitherto published*. The verses are headed 'Carmen Introductorium Pietati
Oxoniensi Praefigendum Auctore Gerardo Higgenbrocio, etc., etc.' They are not
published in an earlier (1762?) edition of the work.
    [4] Our small beer is not only sour but also musty.

31. [1] B.M. I: 130–31. Autograph. Docketed by Jeremiah Bentham: 'Jeremy
Bentham / Queens Coll. Oxon / 6 July 1761.'
    [2] See letter 15, n. 5.
    [3] Perhaps some verses he had promised on Blankley's ape (see letter 28, n. 3).

and Dr. Edwards[4] was gone to London. I have nothing more to add, than that Mr. Jefferson plaguing me about doing Homer, I did above 3 books and a half in 2 days besides a good deal of other business, and that I am

Your most dutiful
and affectionate Son
J. Bentham

32

To Jeremiah Bentham

13 September 1761 (Aet 13)

Sunday, September 13th 1761

Dear Papa

Agreable to my Aunt's intimations that I should set out for London soon that you might take a place for me to see the Crownation as every body calls it;[2] I have tarmined and come to a solution to let you know that I intend to be in town on Wednesday next in the Newberry Machine if there is room, if not, in one of the Bath one's, as it is not convenient here to take a place for me at Newberry: it being uncertain whether you will be in town to send the Chariot for me and my things, or indeed if you could do that which Coach I should be in; you may if you please take a ride to Turnham-Green to meet me, and in case you should, I will stop there and enquire: if not, I will take a Coach from the Inn we stop at to Crutched-Friars—

My poor Grandmama continues very ill, for these many days she has altered a great deal for the worse, tho last night again she has had a very good night, but these weak efforts of Nature only serve to prolong the disorder not to destroy it.—my Aunt has received a letter from the Widow.[3] you can't expect any news from this

---

[4] Probably Edward Edwards of Talgarth, Merionethshire, matric. Jesus 1743, aged 17; B.A. 1747, B.D. 1756, D.D. 1760.

32. [1] B.M. I: 132. Docketed by Jeremiah Bentham: 'Jeremy Bentham / Lr. datd. Baghurst Sept. 13 1761.'
Addressed: 'To / Jeremy (sic) Bentham Esqr. / at Crutched-Fryars / opposite Savage gardens / London'. Postmark: '14 St'.
For Browning Hill near Baughurst see letter 7, n. 1. It is his maternal grandmother who is ill, and his paternal grandmother to whom compliments are forwarded at the end.
[2] The coronation of George III took place on 22 September 1761. For Bentham's later recollections of the event, cf. Bowring, x, 42.
[3] Probably a letter from the widow Mulford to Aunt Grove (see letter 8, n. 1); but 'the Widow' may refer to John Mulford's mistress (cf. Bowring, x, 23).

Quarter surely, or if we had any, it would only surfeit you, as you have so much publick News, but I who hear scarce any, hope when I come to London to devour enough to satisfy the rapacious Maw of

Your dutifull and affectionate Son

J. Bentham

Comps. etc. from every body wait on you and my Grandmama.

33

To Jeremiah Bentham

21 November 1761 (Aet 13)

Sunday Novr. 21 1761

Dear Papa

I need not tell you what a Comfort your kind letter was to me; you may easily imagine it revived my Spirits not a little, as it gave me such a convincing proof of your kindness, which I can never sufficiently requite. the best Testimony I can give you of my gratitude I have given by accompanying this with 20 pages of Tully, to whom I am now perfectly reconciled having got over the book that was most difficult of all.—My fellow-Traveller and I were a good deal crouded in the Machine, there being 4 in it beside ourselves, 2 of whom had placed themselves in the inside tho' they had taken places on the out Side, but as it rained very hard when we set off, they prevailed upon the other passengers to let them stay in. there was a brother Queen's Man in the Coach, who being remarkably fat and bulky crouded the side where he sat very much. I went to see Wheatly[2] the next day after I got to Oxford, and found he had in that little time made severall Acquaintance, with whom he seem'd to be free: I press'd him to come and see me, but he has not been anear me yet.—by your saying that Martha brought you my letter from Barking,[3] I find either that my Grandmama did not receive my letter till Tuesday, or that you were not

---

33. [1] B.M. I: 134–135. Autograph. Docketed by Jeremiah Bentham: 'Jeremy Bentham / Lr. datd. Queen's Novr. 21 1761.' (21 November was a Saturday.)

[2] William Wheatley, son of William Wheatley, Esq., of Erith, Kent, matric. Magdalen 16 November 1761, aged 18. Presumably an acquaintance of the Bentham family.

[3] Apparently a letter directed to his grandmother at Barking which he expected his father to see there. It seems that his father was often there on Mondays, but on this occasion stayed at his Crutched Friars house to be with 'his Club', presumably some small regular gathering.

at Barking on Monday, as you were to have been with your Club.
now I talk of Clubs, I should be glad to know how our Club does,
I call it our's, because I hope when I come to town, to be re-
admitted an honourable Member of it; I can assure you Papa, I
thought of you last Fryday with a good deal of pleasure, which
however was accompanied with some regret, that I could not be
present. pray remember me next meeting to Mrs. Holmes[4] and Mrs.
Abbot[5];—I find Mr. Jefferson thought I meant a Gentleman
Commoner's Gown, as also did Mr. Mores[6]; whom I met going up
in a Machine, as I was coming down hither; Mr. Jefferson told me
he intended waiting upon you to dissuade you from my having it,
upon supposition of it's being a Gentleman Commoner's Gown:
but I have explain'd to him my meaning, and he has no objection
to it. it is very cheap, being but 2s. 6d. a Yard, and costs less than
Prince's Stuff, and yet is I think a good deal handsomer.[7] I will
send you the Gown tomorrow sennight by Kemp's Machine with
some more Tully, 'till when I am

Dear Papa
Your dutifull and
affectionate Son (in good Spirits)
J. Bentham

Pray give my duty to my Grandmama, and love to dear Sammy
boy.

34

To Jeremiah Bentham

6 December 1761 (Aet 13)

Dear Papa
    I hope you will excuse my having sent you but 15 pages of my
Translation instead of 20 I intended to have sent you, having met
with some hard passages which made me lose a good deal of time,

---

[4] Unidentified; but cf. letter 37, n. 1.

[5] Jeremiah Bentham married Mrs Abbot five years later. For details about her cf.
letter 67, n. 1.

[6] Possibly Edward Rowe Mores (1731–78), the antiquary, who arranged and
calendared the archives of Queen's College (*D.N.B.*).

[7] Gentlemen commoners paid higher fees than other commoners (that is, students
not on the foundation), and had certain privileges including a distinctive gown.
Jefferson presumably thought that Bentham was aspiring to this status. Prince's
stuff is a corded material used then for B.A. gowns.

34. [1] B.M. I: 136. Autograph. Docketed by Jeremiah Bentham: 'Jeremy Bentham /
Queen's Co. Decr. 6. 1761.'

and time is pretious with me whatever you may think, as I have no time at all in the Morning except Thursday for this business and but little in the afternoon on Tuesdays and Fridays: I have 36 pages left to do which I hope to get done next week as I shall have a great deal more time than I have had yet, on account of an Examination of the Scholars which lasts Monday Tuesday and Wednesday which exempts us from the lectures and disputations which otherwise we must attend on those days except the Night-lectures which I believe we must attend notwithstanding. these Examinations are when one of the Scholars /the Senior/ is made Taberdar,[2] on which occasion he and the rest are locked into the hall from 9 in the morning till dinner, and from dinnertime to prayertime, which time they are employed in doing Themes etc. and while they are in the hall there are no Lectures that the Scholars may not lose the benefit of them.

I hope you received the things that I sent you safe: if you would be so kind as to favour me with a line it would much oblige

Your dutifull and
obedient Son
J. Bentham

Sunday Decr. 6th 1761

35

To Jeremiah Bentham

12 December 1761 (Aet 13)

Dear Papa

I send you inclos'd the last 36 Pages of the Tusculan disputations, which I doubt not will give you pleasure, as it does me to think my labours are at an End, which I hope are not in vain. you must needs think I studied pretty hard, to do 6 pages a day besides the College-Exercises which however as I told you, were not so many this week as they used to be, else I think I could hardly have done so much.

I hope my dear Papa, I have not done any thing that you are displeased at, I have not heard from you since the Wednesday or Thursday after I came to Oxford; above three weeks ago.

[2] A term used at Queen's College for a category of senior scholars from the gown they wore (*N.E.D.*). Bentham was not a scholar.

35. [1] B.M. I: 137–138. Autograph. Docketed by Jeremiah Bentham: 'Jeremy Bentham / Queen's Coll. / Decr. 12 1761.' (12 December was a Saturday.)

Wheatly goes to town on Friday the 18th the next day after the last in term, so that if you please I may take that Opportunity to go with him, as he said he would wait till then for me, but was obliged to be in town by next day, otherwise he would have gone the 15th or 16th: I hope you will send me a line by next post, whether I may go or not then: but as I hope to be in town before the week is out, I will conclude with professing myself

Your dutifull
and affectionate Son
J. Bentham

Sunday Decr. 12 1761

My duty to my Grandmama and love to my dear Brother.
> Accipe quos mitto, studii, Pater optime, fructus;
> En tibi longi operis, denique finis adest.

36

To Jeremiah Bentham

21 December 1761 (Aet 13)

Dear Papa

I received your letter that you sent me on Monday,[2] and finding that you did not approve of my going home till Wednesday, I was entirely indifferent about it, as it was the same whether I went a week sooner or later: but as Wheatly seemed desirous of having my Company, I could not help telling him that I would ask your leave to go that day, not thinking that you would have any objection to it.—I have been to wait on Mrs. Lee, and was received very obligingly. Mrs. Bentham[3] has been for some time at Hedding-ton about two Miles with her little boy for the recovery of his health; for he has been very ill. I have taken a place in Bew's Machine[4] that inns at the Bull in Holborn and gets there by a little after 5. as I shall see you so soon, I have nothing to add but

---

36. [1] B.M. I: 139–140. Autograph. Docketed by Jeremiah Bentham: 'Jeremy Bentham / Queen's Coll. Decr. 21. 1761.'

Addressed: 'To / Jeremiah Bentham Esqr. / at Crutched Fryars / opposite Savage-gardens / London.' Postmark: '22 DE'.

[2] The present letter was written on Monday 21 December, his father's letter on Monday 14 December, and the Wednesday referred to is 23 December.

[3] Wife of Dr Bentham (see letter 11, n. 3): her maiden name was Elizabeth Bates. The little boy who was ill would be either Thomas (1758–1803)—cf. letter 70, n. 5 —or Edward, who seems to have died young.

[4] One of the regular stage-coaches between Oxford and London.

my duty to you and my Grandmama and love to dear Sammy, and that I am

Your dutiful and
affectionate Son
J. Bentham

Queen's Coll. Decr. 21 1761.

37

To Jeremiah Bentham

12 January 1762 (Aet 13)

Dear Papa

My Grandmama thinks that maid you mention'd to her in your letter will not do, and would not chuse to have so young an one, and would otherwise have one that understood something in the Kitchen, finds that they expect as much wages as they that can do more; as to Betty she goes on pretty well at present. she does not doubt but that there will be maids enough offer themselves in a little time. upon opening the Packet my Grandmama found all the tea was gone, and therefore desires that when you come you would bring some with you. the Doctor is gone to Town, and will not come home till Thursday, so that I can do nothing till then. Your dutiful Son

J. Bentham

Tuesday 12th Decr. 1762.

37. [1] B.M. I: 154–155. Autograph. Docketed by Jeremiah Bentham: 'Jeremy Bentham / Barking 12 Jany.[?] 1761.'

Addressed: 'To / Jeremiah Bentham Esqr. / at Crutched Friars / opposite Savage-gardens / London.' Stamped: 'PENNY POST PAID'.

Jeremiah has composed the draft of a letter to his friend Mrs Holmes upon this letter.

The date on the postmark is illegible. 12 January 1762 was a Tuesday, and this dating seems best to explain the divergent dates given by father and son.

'The Doctor' is unlikely to be John Mulford though he is often referred to in this way elsewhere as he was a cousin on Bentham's mother's side.

38

TO JEREMIAH BENTHAM

5 February 1762 (Aet 13)

Queen's Febry. 5th 1762

Dear Papa

I hoped to have had the pleasure of hearing from you before now; but as that could not be, I flatter myself I shall not be disappointed of an Answer to this, when it comes to hand. I have the Satisfaction of telling you that I go on briskly in Homer, doing generally a book in two days, which is no very inconsiderable thing, to do exclusive of the College business.—You cannot expect a long letter from a place so destitude of Novelty as this is, all the news there is here is that the College is not only as full as it can hold but even fuller, there having come 3 or 4 in the little time that I was absent, one of whom his name is Peirs, whose father is a wholesale Grocer in London[2]; which puts me in mind of my wants, which I hope you will be so kind as to supply; you may guess I mean Tea and Sugar; or else I must be forced to get some here at half as much again as you can get it me for; I have been forced to live upon my Friends this 2 or 3 days. Pray give my duty to my Grandmama and love to brother Sammy, and fullfil the expectations of

Your dutiful and
affectionate Son
J. Bentham

39

TO JEREMIAH BENTHAM

1 March 1762 (Aet 14)

Queen's March 1st 1762

Dear Papa

I received your letter of the 23d, and find that you was of opinion that I should have sent to my Tutor to let him know I was

---

38. [1] B.M. I: 141. Autograph. Docketed by Jeremiah Bentham: 'Jeremy Bentham / Lr.—Queens Coll. 5 Feby. 1762.'
   [2] Richard Peirs of Queenhithe, London, matric. Queen's January 1762, aged 18.

39. [1] B.M. I: 142–143. Autograph. Docketed by Jeremiah Bentham: 'Jeremy Bentham / Queens Coll. Oxon / March 1762.'

not well, but that would not signify much, as he might have seen that in the books where I was put down aeger, and so might the Provost too; however as I am very well now, it does not signify. I could not help wondering at my own Stupidity, when I read that your letter which put me in mind that I had not acquainted you with my having given Mr. Jefferson the bank-Note, however, I can so far satisfy you that I was not so neglectfull in delaying giving it to him, as I have been in mentioning it to you. I shall do this week the first publick Exercise in the Schools that I ever did, that is answer under-Batchelor,[2] which is to dispute with another under-graduate for two or 3 hours sitting under a determining Batchelor, who is to take up the Cudgels in my defences, if there be occasion, which exercise can be done only in Lent. this Week too I shall finish Homer, having already killed Hector, and have only a few odd matters to do, before I finish my Poem. being straightened for time, I must conclude sooner than I intended, with desiring my duty to my Grandmama and to yourself from

Your dutiful and affectionate Son
J. Bentham

P.S. I will write to you at the End of the Week to let you know how I come of in the Schools.

40

To Jeremiah Bentham

10 March 1762 (Aet 14)

Dear Papa

    I beg your pardon for not writing so soon as I promised in my last, but what with my business in the Schools, and what with Acquaintances dropping in in the Afternoon upon me, I was always interrupted. on Fryday I went up for the first time as Respondent, since which I have been up twice as Opponent, this day for the 3d. time, and on the 24th shall go up again as Respondent.[2] it is very uncomfortable work, as we stay an hour and a half or more in the Cold; the Fees are $\frac{1}{2}$ a Crown each time. I have finish'd Homer's

---

    [2] This exercise was a disputation upon three questions, usually on Logic.

40. [1] B.M. I: 144–145. Autograph. Docketed by Jeremiah Bentham: 'Jeremy Bentham / Queen's College Oxon / March 10 1762.'

    [2] In the disputations the Opponent attacked a thesis which the Respondent had to defend.

Iliad, and also the Ethic Compendium[3]; I think of looking over the Odyssey, as I intend to be examined in it, good part of which I read at School. Mr. Jefferson began Natural Philosophy with us yesterday, but whether we shall improve much or no I can't tell, as he has no apparatus; but to day Dr. Bliss's[4] Lectures will begin, which I hope I may attend his next Course, which will be next Year: Dr. Smith[5] also begins his Course of Anatomy to day; and as he will have the Man that is to be hanged here to dissect, I imagine a good many will attend him.—As the time will soon come for me to go out of Mourning[6] I must beg you to be so kind as to send me my Silver Shoe-buckles and knee-buckles and buttons if you can find them; I have great Notion You put them into your Bureau. pray give my duty to my Grandmama and love to dear Sammy, and Comps. to all Friends that Enquire after

Your dutiful and affectionate Son

Wednesday March 10th   J. Bentham
1762

P.S. I find the answering under Batchelor to be very easy, as 2 out of the 3 times no Proctor came into the School.

41

T O   J E R E M I A H   B E N T H A M

1 April 1762 (Aet 14)

Queen's April 1st 1762

Dear Papa
    Since my last I have been agreably surprized with the arrival of two friends at Oxford; I think it was this day sen'night that Mr.

---

[3] *Ethices Compendium in Usum Juventutis Academicae ... Cui accedit Methodus Argumentandi Aristotelica. Oxonii*, MDCCXLV. This was not the first edition. It is an elementary textbook on moral philosophy intended for undergraduates, with short chapters such as Caput III *De summo Bono, sive de eo in quo consistit felicitas*. Bentham refers to this book in the *Deontology* as the Oxford Compendium, e.g. in Chapter x, 'Virtue Defined', where he gives page references. This suggests that he still had his old copy of it in old age.

[4] Nathaniel Bliss, son of Nathaniel Bliss of Gloucestershire; matric. Pembroke 1716, aged 15; B.A. 1720, M.A. 1723; Rector of St Ebbe's, Oxford, 1736; F.R.S. 1742; Savilian Professor of Geometry 1742–65; Astronomer-Royal 1762–64.

[5] Cf. Bowring, x, 40. John Smith of Maybole, Ayrshire, matric. Balliol 1744, aged 23; B.A. 1748, M.A. 1751, B.MED. 1753, D.MED. (from Magdalen Hall) 1757; Savilian Professor of Geometry 1766–97. For his anatomy lectures cf. *Boswell's London Journal*, ed. F. A. Pottle, London, 1950, 245.

[6] Perhaps for his maternal grandmother (see letter 32).

41. [1] B.M. I: 146–147. Autograph. Docketed by Jeremiah Bentham: 'Jeremy Bentham / Letter datd. Queen's Col. Oxon / 1st April 1762.'

Pemberton[2] and Miss Harris[3] came to the Cross Inn in their way from Birmingham to Oxford; just as I was going to Breakfast, there came a boy with a Note from them to tell me that they should be glad to see me there, and that they shou'd stay about an hour; remembering how short their hours were, I went there without staying a moment to put on a clean shirt, of which I had some occasion; and found them at breakfast: I sent my duty to my Aunts by them, and Compliments to my Cousin whom I understand they intended to call upon at Walgrave.[4] —I hear by a Winchester Man of this College that Sam Gauntlett[5] the eldest of those we saw there is come to enter of Trinity, but will not reside here this long while; there is also a brother of Miss Ralfe's[6] come to enter at the same College; it seems that and New College are both as one; each consisting chiefly of Winchester Men.

I have begun this week to work hard at Herodotus, and I read every 10 pages at least, that I may finish this week the book I have begun, which is the longest of all by much: henceforward I shall be able I hope to do a book every week; by which means I shall have read the whole by June; I forget whether I told you in my last, that there are 9 books, bearing the names of the 9 Muses. the 1st Clio, the 2nd Euterpe, the 3rd Thalia, the 4th Melpomene, the 5th Terpsichore, the 6th Erato, the 7th Polyhymnia, the 8th Urania, and the 9th Calliope.

Pray give my duty to my Grandmama and love to poor dear Sammy; I was in hopes of hearing how he did before now, but I hope you will let me know soon, which will give great pleasure to

Your dutiful and
affectionate Son
J. Bentham

I have enclosed my last Saturday's exercise, hoping it may afford you some entertainment.

[2] Unidentified.

[3] Cf. letter 15, n. 3.

[4] John Mulford (see letter 10, n. 12). 'Walgrave' is presumably Wargrave in Berkshire, where Jeremiah Bentham's friend George Darling was parson (cf. Bowring, x, 39).

[5] Samuel Gauntlett: son of John Gauntlett of Winchester, matric. Trinity March 1762, aged 17, but transferred to New College (cf. letter 46); B.A. 1767, M.A. 1771, B.D., D.D. 1794. Warden of New College 1794, till his death in 1822. See also letter 52, nn. 2, 3.

[6] Bentham seems to have been mistaken as to the college of matriculation, for William Ralfe of Durley, Wiltshire, matriculated from Brasenose on 3 April 1762: he is presumably the William Ralfe (b. c. 1744) who in 1766, when he was living in Winchester, married Samuel Gauntlett's sister, Anabella (b. c. 1751).

42

To Jeremiah Bentham

7 April 1762 (Aet 14)

Queen's April 7 1762

Dear Papa

I received your packet on Friday with a great deal of pleasure; tho' not from Mr. Mayo but from Mr. Prince the bookseller,[2] who waited on me himself with it, and told me that it was in a parcel to him. what you tell me is indeed great news; altogether I should think you and my Grandmama must have a very troublesome time of it for a great while.[3] it gave me a great deal of pleasure to hear that my Grandmama and brother were both got so well; I am glad you intend to send him to School, as he must necessarily make a greater Progress there than at home; only I am afraid my Grandmama will not know what to do without him.[4] when I come home again I shall find a very great alteration, I may almost say revolution, in the family, such an one has not happen'd since I have made a part of it: I should be very sorry if you should be forced to have chambers at one of the Inns of Court, than which I think, nothing could be duller.

Mr. Skeet is so good as to trouble himself with this, ⟨he and⟩ I are pretty much acquainted; I have discontinued Wheatly's[5] acquaintance, he's rather too much of a buck for me.—being in a reading humour to day, I have done 26 pages instead of 10 I allott for every

---

42. [1] B.M. I: 148–149. Autograph. Docketed by Jeremiah Bentham: 'Jeremy Bentham / Queen's College / Oxon Apl. 7. 1762.'

Addressed: 'To / Jeremiah Bentham Esqr. / at Crutched Fryars / opposite Savage gardens / London.' Franked: [?]'Wilson'. Post Office stamp illegible.

[2] Daniel Prince of New College Lane (see James Woodforde, *Diary of a Country Parson*, i, London, 1924, 12, 21).

[3] Probably the news that his father was to leave Crutched Friars. He seems to have taken temporary quarters while looking for a house (see letter 43). He found one in March 1763 and moved by May (see letter 47, n. 2). The two interim addresses we have are the house of Richard Clark (see letter 44, 15 July 1762) where he may have stayed some time, and 'in Broad Street / London.' (Address on B.M. I: 162, from Mr Jefferson, Bentham's tutor, dated 29 March 1763, unpublished; see letter 47, n. 4).

[4] Samuel 'was first placed at Mr Willis's private boarding school, then at Westminster School at the age of six' (*Life of Sir Samuel Bentham* by his widow M. S. Bentham, London, 1862, 1). The present reference is to Mr Willis's school (cf. letter 50 below). B.M. XVII: 215 is an account for school fees due to John Willis, 13 January 1763.

[5] See letter 33, n. 2; also letters 35 and 36.

day, but have not given myself time enough to say all I would, but am obliged to profess myself sooner than I intended,

Your dutiful and
obedient Son
J. Bentham

My duty to my Grandmama and love to my dear brother. the buttons you were so good as to send me are very pretty.

43

TO JEREMIAH BENTHAM

21 April 1762 (Aet 14)

Queen's Wednesday 21st April 1762

Dear Papa

I am glad to find you have fixed upon a lodging to your liking; a business which I apprehended wou'd have been attended with a great deal of difficulty, from what I had heard from you of the scarcity of lodgings in town. I am pleased to find my Verses are acceptable; which indeed I was not without hopes of, from the kind partiality with which you are wont to judge of my little performances.—I can also acquaint you now with a great event in my turn; I have changed my rooms for some time; and should have acquainted you with it before, but Mr. Jefferson told me I had better stay and see how [I] liked the rooms I am now in; which accordingly I have done, and being perfectly satisfied with them, which by the by I was not wth. the others, I now apply to you for your consent; which I have not much doubt of, as I like those so much better, and the rent is 1£ a year cheaper than that of the other. the considerations which induced me to change were these; first that my former rooms smoked very much; 2ly. that the tables and chairs in them were allways covered with dust, so that as soon as ever they were rubbed the dust would come on again; the reason of which I can't imagine; 3dly that the wet came in one side and spoilt part of the paper; 4thly that they were very dull and melancholy; etc. besides many small inconveniences, such as a very bad stair case and dark as pitch at night; a long way to go up; being detached from the quadrangle so that I often could not hear the Clock, or the trumpet for dinner, as I was setting in my room,

43. [1] B.M. I: 150–151. Autograph. Docketed by Jeremiah Bentham: 'Jeremy Bentham / Queen's Coll. Oxon 21 Apl. 1762.'

and other things; all which things are remedy'd in this I have at present. the Gentleman I exchanged with, was fond of retirement, which made him like mine preferable to his own, but however he says he finds it rather dull now and then.[2]— I spoke to Dr. Dixon lately, he very obligingly ask'd after you, (consider, 'twas a Fellow of Queen's did this!) and desired me to accompany with his Comps. the affectionate duty of

Your obedient Son
J. Bentham

P.S. Duty to Grandmama and love to the dear little Woodford Scholar.[3] Mr. Jefferson has a disorder in his foot as bad almost as that he had in his hand some time ago.

44

TO JEREMIAH BENTHAM

15 July 1762 (Aet 14)

Dear Papa

I received your letter of the 8th instant, which indeed did not give me so much pleasure as your letters usually do, as it dissappointed me of my expectations of your coming hither; tho' indeed considering the uncertainty of human affairs, (and especially of yours,) I did not entirely depend upon it. I had put my Room in as good order as College Chambers will admitt of, which is not extraordinary; we have such bad attendances. I enquired of Skeet last

---

[2] The following passage from Bowring, based on conversations with Bentham is of interest: 'On one occasion his father got into a long and angry dispute with a paper-hanger at Oxford, about papering Bentham's room; and it ended in his sending paper down from town. This brought upon Bentham the ill-will of the Oxford paper-hanger; who found many ways of saying and doing, and causing others to say and do, unfriendly things. The chamber which was the origin of the misunderstanding, was a very gloomy one. It looked into the churchyard, and was covered with lugubrious hangings. Bentham's fear of ghosts, and of the visitations of spiritual beings, was strong upon him; and the darkness of the chamber and its neighbourhood added to his alarms. But he was enabled to effect a change with another student, and got two guineas, in addition, for his thirdings, on account of his better furniture' (*Memoirs*, x, 39). For the paper-hanging dispute, see letters 10 and 11.

[3] Samuel Bentham. John Willis's school (cf. letter 42, n. 4) was presumably at Woodford in Essex.

44. [1] B.M. I: 152–153. Autograph. Addressed: 'To / Jeremiah Bentham Esqr. / at the Old South Sea House / London.' Stamped: 'OXFORD.' Postmark: '16 IY'.

This is the address of Richard Clark, with whom apparently Jeremiah Bentham was staying. For Clark see letter 62, n. 1.

Sunday whether Mrs. White[2] was come to Oxford; but he could not tell me; however we agreed to go to the Master's in the afternoon together. as I was returning from Baliol I met the Master himself; who told me Mrs. White had been there a Week, and ask'd me to dine with them; but I could not accept of the invitation, as I was engaged to Dr. Bentham's; I intend to wait on them to day.

Mr. Pickering with his two Sons Toby and Joe[3] have been here these two or three days, and go out of town to morrow. he told me he would call on me, but he has not yet.—as you gave me choice of any day next Week I have pitch'd upon Monday, 'till when I am

Your dutiful and
affectionate Son
J. Bentham

Queen's Coll. Oxon.
Thursday July 15th 1762.

45

To Jeremiah Bentham

24 January 1763 (Aet 14)

Queen's Col. Janry. 24th 1763

Dear Papa

I arrived here o' Tuesday evening in good condition, having made use of Mrs. Palmer's[2] recipe for Sickness, (a Sheet of Paper to be applied to the Stomach); tho' it is probable that Anticacchetic[?] received no small assistance from imagination. notwithstanding the Clocks were striking 5 when I got to the Inn, and the Watchmen going their Rounds, you little imagine how near I was missing my passage, the Coach having been gone about 5 minutes when I got

---

[2] Cf. letter 2, n. 6.

[3] Probably Joseph Pickering of Great Queen Street, Lincoln's Inn Fields, father of John Pickering who matric. Hertford, May 1760, aged 18, and became a barrister of Lincoln's Inn in 1766. Of the two other sons mentioned here one, also Joseph, matric. Christ Church, November 1764, aged 16, and also became a barrister of Lincoln's Inn; but he abandoned the law for the church and died in 1820 as perpetual curate of Paddington.

45. [1] B.M. I: 156–157. Autograph. Docketed by Jeremiah Bentham: 'Jeremy Bentham /Lr. datd. Queen's College Oxon / 24 Jany. 1763.'

[2] Unidentified: at a much later date a Mr and Mrs Palmer are found among Jeremiah Bentham's friends (cf. letter 131 and n. 3), but there is no way of knowing whether this is the same Mrs Palmer.

there, for in all probability Mr. Brown's[3] Man suppress'd the Sequel, as it could not afford a very striking specimen of his Wit. the Coachman had left Word he would wait at the White Horse Cellar; so thither we trudged, John having previously declared, he knew his Way; for my part I knew not a Step. When we had walked about a Mile and a half or more, we came to a Square, which to his great Surprize, and to my Great Vexation, we found to be Lincoln's-Inn-Fields, instead of Leicester-Square, which he intended to have made his way. I had little Hopes then of overtaking the Coach, but to leave nothing untried, resolved to continue my Walk, and accordingly beyond expectation found the Coach there waiting. there were in it two Men and a little Boy; the former of which got out at Hounslow and left the latter to pursue his Journey throughout; at Salthill took up a Passenger who proved to be a brother Westminster and Oxonian, and at length got here at 5 o'Clock; so now here I am, settled in my Monastic life for 6 Months, during which time, I do not, with some Sons, promise to renew my Studies with greater Application than ever, when, God knows, they have far different intentions, but content myself with assuring you that I will always continue to be, what I hope I have hitherto been

Your dutiful
and affectionate Son
J. Bentham

46

TO JEREMIAH BENTHAM

15 March 1763 (Aet 15)

Tuesday March 15th 1763

Hond. Sir

Hitherto I have waited in Expectation of a line from you, as you promised at parting; but as I imagine you may have forgot that promise, I write this to put you in mind of it. —Since you left Oxford it has been put beyond all doubt that there is to be some publick Affair this next Act; but whether an Encænia or a Publick

---

[3] William Browne was a friend and fellow-attorney of Jeremiah Bentham's often mentioned in the correspondence. He seems to have acted for Jeremiah Bentham in various property transactions (cf. B.M. I: 3). He and his wife Jane (née Vernon) are mentioned in the will (84a below) made by Bentham in August 1769: at that date Browne was resident in Lamb's Conduit Street, Holborn.

46. [1] B.M. I: 158–159. Autograph. Docketed by Jeremiah Bentham: 'Jeremy Bentham / Lr. datd. Queen's Col. Oxon / 15 March 1763.'

Act[2] is not yet known, but will be determined by Vote in the Convocation House as is said, in a little Time: whether we are like to
be honoured by their Majesty's presence, you can tell I suppose
better than we; tho' I suppose it can hardly be known yet. An
acquaintance was telling me last night that Mr. Jefferson had made
him a kind of an Offer of speaking in the Theatre; which very much
surpriz'd me, as he is but very lately come to College, nay even
since the long Vacation, and a Person nothing very remarkable as I
know of for either Rank or Abilities; which they generally are, that
attain to that honour. a Resignation has lately happened at New
College, which secures to my Friend Gauntlett his Election; a thing
which he had not any hopes of half a Year ago; but there have
happen'd more Vacancies this Year than ever were known before;
the Fellowships there are very good, besides a great many Livings
the College has.

We have gone through the Science of Mechanics with Mr. Bliss,
having finish'd on Saturday; and yesterday we begun upon
Optics; there are two more remaining, viz: Hydrostatics, and
Pneumatics. Mr. Bliss seems to be a very good sort of a Man, but
I doubt is not very well qualified for his Office, in the practical Way
I mean, for he is oblig'd to make excuses for almost every Experiment they not succeeding according to expectation; in the Speculative part, I believe he is by no means deficient. I have no more to
add at present, but my wishes that this letter may be productive of
another in return, and that I am

Your dutiful and
affectionate Son
J. Bentham

P.S. Grievances. No shirts to my back. No good shoes to my Feet.
My new Tablecloths full of holes.

---

[2] An Encaenia is the usual June commemoration of founders and benefactors; an
Act was an event occasionally held in July in which public disputations were held for
two days. The last Act ever held was in 1733.

47

T O   J E R E M I A H   B E N T H A M

24 March 1763 (Aet 15)

Queen Coll. March 24th 1763

Hond. Sir

I received the favour of yours on Friday, and am very glad to find by it, that you are likely to suit yourself with a house so much to your liking[2]; for my part, from the description you give me, and the idea I have of it, I really think it must be very pleasant and convenient; I should be glad to hear that you have taken it, of which I can only draw a probable conclusion from your *data,* as you have not expressly mentioned it. as to what you say about the King's not coming hither, I do not much like it so would not willingly believe it; neither indeed do I think it follows from what you tell me. you say the King will go to Hanover, ergo he will not to Oxford: negatur Consequentia, those two matters are not irreconcileable; Lloyd's evening clears it up very ingeniously: "we are credibly inform'd (says that Author of unquestionable veracity) that *their* Majestys intend shortly to honour the University of Oxford with a Visit for a few days, after which his Majesty will proceed in his journey to Hanover."[3]—as Mr. Samuel Bentham begins dispensing his Epistolary favours so soon, pray be so kind as to put him in mind that he has a nearer Relation, to whom a letter would not be less acceptable—but I have some news to communicate in return for yours: on Sunday Mr. Jefferson sent for me, and acquainted me with his receipt of a letter from you; in answer to which he told me, that he would use all his Interest with the Vice-Chancellor that I might speak in the Theatre, but yt. it depended upon myself, for that I must produce something extraordinary, (that was his ex-

47. [1] B.M. I: 160–161. Autograph. Docketed by Mary Bentham: '1763 J.B. to Jeremiah B.'

[2] By May (cf. the address of letter 50) Jeremiah Bentham had moved into this house which he at first rented from a Mr John Leech (see letters 59 and 188) until the end of 1764 when he bought it (letter 59). At least it seems fairly clear that the house he then bought was the one he had previously been renting.

The house was in Queen's Square, Westminster, near Petty France, and was subsequently known as Queen's Square Place (cf. the address of letter 86 for the first use of this name). It was the house which Bentham eventually inherited, lived in for many years as the Hermit of Queen's Square Place, and died in. In the garden stood a house in which Milton had once lived. Both houses disappeared in the 1870's to make way for a block of flats known as Queen Anne's Mansions.

[3] In point of fact George III did not visit Oxford until September 1785.

pression) in which case I might be pretty sure of succeeding, otherwise I could not; and that I should not speak of it, 'till it was determin'd, for fear I should miscarry; in which case it would be better to have nothing said about it: so I beg you would not mention it.[4] I think of taking for my subject, Dunkerca deleta; now there is a Poem in the Musæ Anglicanæ entitled, Dunkerca delenda, whence I may mention a Comparison between the then ineffectual and the effectual demolition of it, which will be Compleated no doubt before the Encænia.[5] I am at liberty to make upon any publick occurence that has happened since the beginning of the late war. but more of this another time. I began on the Harpsichord last Tuesday, since which I have had 3 lectures, and can play 2 Tunes. I had for ye. first lecture the first strain of a Minuet set me, and the second the remainder; the third I had a whole tune set me, and can play it now; Mr. Hayes[6] of whom I learn, comes to me again tomorrow morning: what with Philosophical and Musical lectures, I have not much time upon my hands at present; but the former will be finish'd on Saturday. the next time you hear from me, I shall let you know of my having wrote to my Aunt till when I am

Your dutiful and
affectionate son
J. Bentham

I forgot to mention that among *my* 10 Shirts, 1 is my brother's, another quite a rag, and 1 or 2 not much better. My love to my dear Brother.

[4] In a letter dated 29 March 1763 (B.M. I: 162) Mr Jefferson tells Jeremiah Bentham that he will do all in his power to promote Jeremy's speaking at the Encaenia, but that he must not be too hopeful as young gentlemen of rank and quality will doubtless have the preference.

[5] In March 1763 the terms of the Peace of Paris, which ended the Seven Years' War, were announced: they included the demilitarization of Dunkirk.

The poem Bentham refers to, 'Dunquerca Delenda', was by Charles Shuckburgh, (1694–1752), son of Sir Charles, second baronet, half-brother of Sir John, third baronet, and father of Sir Charles, fifth baronet. It appeared in *Musarum Anglicanarum Analecta* . . ., vol. III, Oxford, 1717, 98–100. This volume, evidently a supplement to the third edition, London, 1714, was not included in later editions, but was clearly one of the three volumes of the *Musæ Anglicanæ* which Bentham took up to Oxford in 1760 (cf. Bowring, X, 36, n.). Shuckburgh, matric. Queens' March 1710/11, presumably wrote on this theme apropos of the Peace of Utrecht, as Bentham did half a century later on the occasion of the Peace of Paris.

[6] The Hayes were a notable Oxford musical family. William Hayes of Magdalen was Professor of Music from 1741 till 1777, and it seems likely that Bentham's tutor was one of his sons: Philip Hayes (d. 1797), who succeeded his father as Professor in 1777, matric. Magdalen May 1763, aged 26; William Hayes (d. 1790), later a minor canon of St Paul's, had been a chorister at Magdalen from 1749 to 1751 and was a clerk there in 1764–65.

48

To Jeremiah Bentham

4 April 1763 (Aet 15)

Hond. Sir

I am to acknowledge the receipt of your favour of the 2d Instant, and to express my obligations to your learned friends, (whoever they are) for their promises of assistance,[2] but cannot thank them by name, 'till you or they, think fit they shall be no longer incog. Mr. Jefferson as usual discourages me as much as he can, and whenever we meet (which is not very often) expresses great anxiety least you should be angry /with him/ if I don't succeed; I should not have mentioned this had it not been his particular desire. I met him t'other day in Walking in the Cloisters, he asked me whether I had thought of a Subject: I said yes, and told him what it was: he did not seem pleased; he said there was a Copy of Verses on the same Subject as mine in the Musae Anglicanae; I answered, that could be no prejudice to me, as I have a greater diversity of matter to work on than that Author could have, from what has happened since the time he wrote in: besides, supposing the subject to be entirely the same, there was no necessity why I must transcribe out of that Book. I asked him whether he had any other objection? No. whether he could recommend to me any other subject he thought more proper? No. well, I must do as I pleased, he did not know what to say to it.

Mr. Bliss finish'd his Course of Lectures Saturday sen'night; he will begin another the beginning of next term. I have been sadly plagued about Examination; I had prepared myself, and was to have been examined on Saturday; but one of the Masters went out of Town and prevented Me.[3] I have executed your Commands in writing to my Aunt, and am

Your dutiful and
affectionate Son
J. Bentham

Monday April 4th 1763

---

48. [1] B.M. I: 164–165. Autograph. Docketed by Jeremiah Bentham: 'Jeremy Bentham / Letter datd. Quns. Coll. Oxon / April 4 1763.'

[2] In preparing verses to be read at the Encaenia.

[3] The examination for his B.A. degree, which was oral and public.

49

To Jeremiah Bentham

18 April 1763 (Aet 15)

Hond. Sir

I have waited for some days to have my Examination passed, before I wrote to you, which after a good many disappointments, is at length happily accomplished to day; that being over, I shall now set down with all diligence to the main affair[2]; which I could not do, 'till I had eased myself of that I mention. I had a very numerous audience, the seats were cover'd with people, besides a good many that stood in the body of the place: I was up for near an hour together, which was nearly as long again as the usual time. I hope I have acquitted myself tolerably well; and am pretty certain, if I have not gain'd credit, that at least I have not lost any. Tuesday or Wednesday last, the same day the Proctors were made, it was debated in Convocation whether we are to have a Publick Act or an Encænia; but was carried by a very great majority for the latter: as I believe now we have no hopes scarcely of the King's coming here. there was a great number of People by the Convocation-house to see the Colleges the Proctors belonged to, walk in Procession, and to know the debates and determination of the Convocation, about a matter of such importance; a great number crowding in to the Convocation-house, they were all turn'd out, upon which there began a kind of a riot, 2 or 3 especially, who knocked at the Convocation-door as if it were one of the Masters who wanted admittance, and when any one open'd the door, set up a laugh and hiss: one of them in particular cry'd out, if you will give the Porter a penny, he will let you in, (now there was a Master of Arts that came to the door) so the next it was open'd, he flung in some half-pence at him: after which some of them flung in some half-pence at him.—the post going out this moment, I am obliged to conclude myself,

Your dutiful and
affectionate Son
Jeremy Bentham

Queen's Coll. April 18th 1763.

49. [1] B.M. I: 166–167. Autograph. Docketed by Jeremiah Bentham: 'Jeremy Bentham / Letter datd. Queen's College Oxon / April 18 1763.'

   [2] The 'main affair' was preparation of verses for the Encaenia.

50

TO JEREMIAH BENTHAM

6 May 1763 (Aet 15)

Friday May 6th 1763

Hond. Sir

I am to acknowledge the Receit of your favour of the 21st last; at which time I had already rec̃ved the 6 Shirts of Mrs. Roberts[2] you were so kind as to order me; they fit me very well; and it was a very seasonable supply. My examining Masters whose names you were desirous of knowing, were Messieurs Chandler[3] and Newbolt[4] of Magdalen and Mr. Crablan[5] of Brazen-nose: my Friend likewise was examin'd with me: his Books were, Gr. Testament, Horace and Sallust; mine, Demosthenes, Anacreon and Tusc. Disps. — I have fix'd upon the Havannah[6] for the Subject of my Verses: I think I have settled my Plan: and have made some progress in the Execution of it: with all due deference to the respectable Opinion of Mr. Johnson,[7] I must own, the Conquest of North America did not suggest to me any Thoughts whereon to lay the Foundation of a Copy of Verses; I think I could better execute a prosaïcal Narration; and excuse me, Sir, if I likewise take the liberty to say, that I am no better able to find Matter on the subject of the Manilla's. I have not heard a Syllable from the Provost about this Matter: may be it is not intended I should speak; so I beg you would not be too

50. [1] B.M. I: 168–170. Docketed by Jeremiah Bentham: 'Jeremy Bentham / Lr. datd. Queen's College Oxon / May 6th 1763.' Docketed by Mary Bentham: 'Censures S.B.'s early entrance at Westr.'

    Addressed: 'To / Jeremiah Bentham Esqr. / at Queen's-Square / near St James-Park / Westminster.' Franked: 'Frank / J. Phillips.' Stamped: 'OXFORD'. Postmark: '7 MA'.

    The letter was presumably franked by Sir John Phillips, M.P. for Pembroke 1761–1802.

    [2] Unidentified.

    [3] Richard Chandler (1738–1810), classical antiquary and traveller, matric. Queen's 1755, demy of Magdalen 1757, B.A. 1759, M.A. 1761, Fellow of Magdalen 1770.

    [4] John Monk Newbolt of Winchester, matric. Christ Church 1754 aged 15, transferred to Magdalen, B.A. 1758, M.A. 1761.

    [5] James Crablan of Manchester, matric. Brasenose 1756, aged 16, B.A. 1759, M.A. 1762.

    [6] Havana was taken from Spain in August 1762 after a long siege. It was restored in the Peace of Paris proclaimed March 1763. Bentham had apparently given up the idea of writing on Dunkirk.

    [7] Bowring (x, 41) reports that Dr Johnson was shown the Ode Bentham wrote in 1760 (see letters 12 and 15) on the accession of George III and pronounced it a 'pretty performance'. Possibly Bowring was confounding that poem with the present one, or possibly both poems were submitted to Dr Johnson.

Sanguine in your Expectations; I have found since that what my Acquaintance said seemingly to me in Earnest about his having had the offer to speak, by his own confession was not true: it was very ridiculous in him to affirm it so seriously as he did: besides there is a Rumour there will be no Encænia this Year after all: Dr. Neblett Warden of All Souls[8] told a Gentleman of this College, that a letter had been recẽd from the Chancellor; desiring the Encænia might be put off if possible till next Year: as soon as there is any certainty about it, I will let you know. Yesterday being Thanksgiving day we had very grand doings here. The Vice-Chancellor read prayers, in the Course of which we had Purcell's Deum[9] perform'd by a band of Musick in the Organ-loft as well as the other Services: after which we had an excellent Discourse from (you may guess whom when you are inform'd that the Vice Chancellor had the appointment of the Preacher) Mr. Jefferson; his Text was out of Solomon: " When a Man's ways please the Lord, he maketh even his Enemies to be at peace with him." I perceiv'd by his discourse he is rather a friend to Lord Bute[10] than otherwise: and even allmost apprehensive of a civil War if the present factious Disposition in the Nation should continue. the whole Service was concluded with Handel's Coronation Anthem[11]; in the Evening we had Fire-works play'd off; the expences defray'd by Subscription. I was very much surprized to hear you had enter'd Sammy at Westminster; I should have imagined it might have been as well if he had continued at Mr. Willis's 2 years longer, from the observation I had made at School, that Boys that were enter'd there at the Beginning seldom turn'd out so well as those that had continued some time at a private School: it being better they should receive their first Impressions, at places where there is not much danger of their being bad ones; but as it is allready done, and past recalling, that it may be for the best, is the earnest wish of

Your dutiful and
affectionate Son
J. Bentham

P.S. In your letter I found 2 pieces of paper, cut in a particular

[8] Stephen Neblett, Warden from 1726 to 1766.

[9] Purcell's setting of the *Te Deum* was first performed in 1694.

[10] John Stuart, third Earl of Bute (1713–92), a representative peer of Scotland, favourite of George III, had recently resigned as first Lord of the Treasury. His widespread unpopularity turned partly on the belief that he and the King hoped to introduce a more despotic régime.

[11] One of the four anthems composed for George II's coronation on 11 October 1727.

manner, the meaning of which I should be glad to know; I enclose one for information.

51

To Jeremiah Bentham

22 May 1763 (Aet 15)

May 22nd Sunday afternoon $\frac{1}{2}$ after 4

Hond. Sir

Mr. Jefferson has this moment very much surprized me, by communicating to me the contents of your letter, by which I find you have not rec͠ed mine, which I wrote the very day after I received your's. I have this instant had repeated assurances, from the Person to whose care I committed the Letter, a Person whose word I have no reason to distrust, that she did actually put it in to the post; and it is possible you may have receiv'd it by this: whether you do or not, I hope from your paternal tenderness and experienced justice that you will not be angry with me, for a miscarriage that you must be sensible no caution of mine could prevent: and be assured that what I say is strictly true. what I said in my former letter was, that I could not have leisure at this time to accept of your kind Invitation, for a reason you may guess at, but which no more than my grateful sense of the favour you design'd me, I have not time to express, being at this Instant obliged to leave off by the Post setting out.—I am

Your dutiful and
affectionate Son
J. Bentham

51. [1] B.M. I: 171. Autograph. Docketed by Jeremiah Bentham: 'Jeremy Bentham / Letter datd. Queen's College Oxon / May 22d 1763.'

52

To Jeremiah Bentham

2 June 1763 (Aet 15)

Hond. Sir

Since my last I have had an extraordinary piece of news from Winchester, which was communicated to me by my friend Ralfe, who is lately recovered from the Small-Pox, which he took from Inoculation, and has had it as favourably as he could possibly wish. it is that Carew Gauntlett[2] will soon be married to Miss Ralfe, a match which her friends do not greatly approve of, especially as the Old Lady[3] will not give them a single farthing, tho' she cannot but be sensible it is a very advantageous match for her Son in point of Fortune, but she never liked him. they are to have the house Mrs. Saunders[4] lives in, and intend setting up the Wine-Trade[5]: they have had already great promises from severall quarters: so that it is to be hoped they may do very well, as Mr. Gauntlett is very diligent and clever at his business. this Ralfe had not directly from Winchester but from a Guardian of his that lives in Town: another thing is, that Miss Louisa Gauntlett is married to one Mr. Kirby,[6] a Clergyman with a good living, and severall thousand pounds besides: so that I am now deprived of both my Wives.

I am this day become Senior Commoner, by the Person next above me putting on a Civilian's Gown. the privileges of the Senior Commoner, if they can be called so, are the dinner when there is a Gaudy, and the taking cognizance of any faults the College Servants may be committ, or any neglect they may be guilty of; such as sending in bad commons, a deficiency of Knives and Forks etc., which it is the business of the Senior to complain of to the Fellows,

---

52. [1] B.M. I: 172–173. Autograph. Docketed by Mary Bentham[?]: '1763 June / Jʸ Bentham.'

Addressed: 'To / Jeremiah Bentham Esqr. / at Queen's Square / near St. James's Park / Westminster.' Stamped: THAME'. Postmark: [. . .] IV'.

[2] A brother of Samuel Gauntlett (cf. letter 41, n. 5). The Carew Gauntlett who matriculated at Oxford in March 1790 aged 23 was presumably a son of this marriage, his father being described as Carew Gauntlett of Winchester.

[3] Mrs Mary Gauntlett, the widowed mother of Carew and Samuel.

[4] Unidentified.

[5] John Gauntlett the father had kept the George Inn at Winchester.

[6] A license for the marriage of Lancelot Kerby, aged 24, and Louisa Gauntlett, aged 24, was obtained on 24 April 1763. The bridegroom was the son of Cranley Thomas Kerby of Winchester and matriculated at Trinity, Oxford in April 1753.

Bentham's joke about losing his two wives suggest some degree of intimacy between the Benthams and these Winchester families.

or lay a fine on them, which we call sconsing. I mention'd in my letter which did not come to hand how kind I took it of Sammy, his writing; and how much pleased I was to see the proficiency he has made: as for his playing on the Fiddle, I lately made a copy of verses which bear some relation to it, which I will send you by my next, and hope he may not be affronted upon hearing the contents, as I can ⟨ass⟩ure him they were made, before I knew any thing at all of his learning.—I hope it will not be long before I send you my Verses for the Theatre, and in the mean time am

Your dutiful
and affectionate Son
Jeremy Bentham

Thursday June 2nd
  1763

I have no more Franks.

53

T O   J E R E M I A H   B E N T H A M

19 June 1763 (Aet 15)

Sunday June 19th 1763

Hond. Sir

    I have succeeded about the affair of Mr. Latton better than I could have hoped for: I spoke yesterday with the Gentleman I mention'd to you in my last, by the means of a person of this College who is very intimate with him: he told me, the person in question was either his Great-Grand-father, or Great-Great-Uncle, but who was his heir, he could not then well tell, but would let me have his Pedigree very soon: he has a Curacy near Oxford, and is backwards and forwards very often. he will be at the Encænia no doubt of it, and then perhaps you may be chuse to talk with him yourself.[2] I am just come from Dr. Bentham's, the Dr. himself was not at home, but Mrs. Bentham was so obligingly as to say, she should be very glad to see my Aunt, and that it will be by no means inconvenient; she seems very sorry she is oblig'd to part with her

53. [1] B.M. I: 174–175. Autograph. Docketed by Jeremiah Bentham: 'Jeremy Bentham / Lettr. datd. Oxon June 19 1763.'

    [2] What 'the affair of Mr. Latton' was is not clear—presumably a case in which Jeremiah Bentham was professionally engaged. Henry Latton, son of William Latton of York Buildings, matric. Wadham March 1755, aged 17, B.A. 1758, M.A. 1762, was probably the gentleman with whom Bentham had spoken.

house and Garden,[3] as there is so little or no Garden to their new house, and her whole delight seems to be in one. you were very kind to think of sending me my watch; but the Seals are damaged very much by rubbing against each other. I hope you have receiv'd my letter of Fryday with my Verses[4]: you will find in this, Sammy's Epigram; I am,

Your dutiful and
affectionate Son
J. Bentham

Difficilia quae pulchra

Pollenti harmonicâ forte auscultaverit arte
    Si puer, attentâ captat in aure sonum.
Ex hoc nutricem solers atque impiger urget,
    Nempe dari citharam vult sibi: vult, et habet.
Quin bis sex obulûm pretio testudo paratur
    Fucato variis picta colore modis.
Discordes chordas fidibus votoque potitus
    Per totam torquens cursitat usque domum.
Parce, puer strepitu; tua nam sunt organa facta
    Non satis affabrè, nec satis apta manus.[5]

54

To Jeremiah Bentham

22 June 1763 (Aet 15)

Queen's Coll. June 22nd 1763

Hond. Sir

Just now Mr. Jefferson has informed me that the time for carrying in the Verses is fixed for next Saturday, and that after that day none will be accepted on any account, so that it is absolutely

---

[3] On Edward Bentham's appointment to the Regius Chair of Divinity.

[4] Apparently not extant.

[5] If a boy shall by chance have overheard the powerful harmonic art, he tries to catch the sound with attentive ear. Thence cunningly and persistently he urges his nurse; he certainly wishes for a harp to be given him, he wishes it—and has it. Yea indeed, a lyre is procured at the price of twelve obols, painted with coloured dyes in various ways. Once possessed of his lyre and his wish he rushes everywhere through the whole house torturing its discordant strings. Spare the din, boy; for your tools were not designed carefully enough, and your hand does not perform expertly enough.

54. [1] B.M. I: 176. Autograph.

necessary for me to have mine by that day; so that I must beg you will be so kind as to get them out of the hands of your learned revisers: the Persons that are appointed Inspectors, are Messrs. Wheeler[2] of Magdalen, and Stinton[3] of Exeter Colledges: what gives me encouragement is, that I find, that is not absolutely necessary for the Compositions to be quite perfect, as these Gentlemen are appointed to correct and amend as well as mark the faults.

As to the objection you are pleased to make, of my Verses ending improperly, if you will forgive my presumption in entertaining sentiments of the matter differing from those you have expressed, I will venture to offer two or three things to your consideration. 1st that, excepting the 6 or 7 lines whereof Velasco[4] is the subject, all the rest are to the honour of the Britons: 2ly, I cannot think there is any impropriety in concluding the whole with the most remarkable circumstance in it, for such I think that action of Velasco's certainly was, especially since as I imagine the close is the best exprest of any part of the Composition, which it allways should be if possible: 3dly, I cannot help being of opinion that Velasco's courage was more *conspicuous* than either Pococke's or Albemarle's,[5] at least it was more poeticall (si ita dicam.) 4thly in regard to the conclusion you propose, I must beg leave to observe that your method seems to me prolix and extensive for a close, nay would even suffice as a subject for a Composition of itself: and likewise that a regular and prosaïc Narrative is to be avoided as much as possible, which I am afraid allready /as it is/ I have not done sufficiently: this is what I humbly beg leave to submitt to your consideration; but as I am not so presuming as to depend upon my own judgment in opposition to a Father's, I have begun a conclusion of about 10 Lines or thereabouts, the design of which is to shew that the taking of the Havannah made the peace as far as the Spaniards were concerned, and to exhort the English to give up the

[2] Benjamin Wheeler of Oxford, matric. Trinity November 1751, aged 18; B.A. 1755, M.A. 1758, Fellow of Magdalen, B.D., 1769, D.D. 1770, Professor of Poetry 1766–76; Sedleian Professor of Natural Philosophy 1767–82. He succeeded Edward Bentham as Regius Professor of Divinity in 1776. Appointed a Prebendary of St Paul's on 21 July 1783, he died the following day.

[3] George Stinton of Ilfracombe, matric. Christ Church 1748, aged 18; Fellow of Exeter 1750–67, B.A. 1754, M.A. 1755; F.R.S., F.S.A. 1776; d. 1783.

[4] Don Luis de Velasco was governor of the Moro, the Spanish fort at Havana. He refused to surrender the fort even when the British attack (July 1762) which ended the long siege was evidently successful, and was killed in the battle.

[5] Sir George Pocock (1706–92), K.B. and Admiral of the Blue 1761, commanded the naval force at Havana. George Keppel, 3rd Earl of Albemarle (1724–72) was commander-in-chief of the British forces at the siege.

power they had by that means of possessing themselves of the Spanish mines, on account of their pernicious consequences we see allready exemplified in the possessors of them, especially as in return Florida is our own, and Portugal is freed from it's approaching ruin, and moreover that commerce will afford it us by a more peacefull method.[6] the Commemoration will begin the 5th of July. I am sorry you have ordered me a second mo⟨ur⟩ning Coat, as I have not a Wastecoat fit to wear with it. I am in great hurry

Your dutiful Son
J. Bentham

I shall have finished my Conclusion to morrow

55

To Jeremiah Bentham

29 June 1763 (Aet 15)

Hond. Sir

I am sorry to acquaint you that I have not succeeded; upon my not receiving Mr. Johnsons Criticisms[2] on Saturday, I was obliged to give my verses up to Mr. Jefferson as they were, and tell him how the matter stood: upon which he thought it was best to stay 'till the next day before he carried them up, in expectation of my receiving them then, as I did; but when they came, they did not answer our expectations: we expected Mr. Johnson would have altered the mistakes as well as pointed them out, especially as we had so little time before us: however, I corrected them myself as well as I could. on Monday there was a final meeting to determine who should be speakers: but Mr. Jefferson was so dissatisfied with my Verses, that I allmost question whether he gave them up. I do not believe he has done me much service except railing at me, which he has done pretty plentifully. he told me in the morning just before the meeting, that if my Verses had been ever so good I should have had very little chance, but that as it was I had none at all. but since that, I do not know why, he has altered his note a little, and become a little more gracious. I believe you will receive a letter from him

---

[6] Bentham was arguing in support of the Peace of Paris proclaimed in March 1763, which restored Havana to Spain. In return Spain ceded East and West Florida to Britain and restored all territories taken from Portugal.

55. [1] B.M. I: 178–179. Autograph. Docketed by Jeremiah Bentham: 'Jeremy Bentham / letter datd. Oxon / June 29 1763.'

[2] See letter 50, n. 7.

soon; but more of this when I shall have the pleasure of seeing you, in expectation of which I remain

> Your dutifull and
> affectionate Son
> J. Bentham.

Wednesday June 29th 1763

I hope you will excuse my bad writing, which is occasioned by a Cut in my finger. I have received the Coat you sent me.

56

To Jeremiah Bentham

28 August 1763 (Aet 15)

> Browning-hill August 28th 1763

Hond. Sir

A fortnight being elapsed since we parted, I thought you might not be displeased to hear that both your Boys were well. the youngest of the said Boys, gives his Duty, and desires me to acquaint you, that he is able to give entire Satisfaction in regard to his Holiday's Task. The eldest of the aforesaid, was on Saturday sen'night sent express to Wargrave on a blind horse to fetch Mr. Mulford; as was judged necessary seeing that the said Mulford, as usual, was tardy in the performance of his repeated promises of visiting this Habitation. I was to have returned the same day, but upon the repeated assurances Mr. Mulford gave me, that he would accompany me on Monday, I acquiesced in staying for him: however it was not till Wednesday afternoon that we got here. we are not to have his Company long, now we have got it, for I think he intends setting out the middle of this Week on his return.—and further your said Informant sayeth not, saving that the Compliments &c. of all Friends here accompany the humble duty of

> Your affectionate Son
> J. Bentham

56. [1] B.M. I: 180–181. Autograph. Docketed by Jeremiah Bentham: 'Jeremy Bentham / Letter datd. Browning Hill / Augt. 28 1763.'

Addressed: 'To / Jeremiah Bentham Esqr. / at Queens Square / Westminster.' Postmark: '29 AV'.

The two Bentham brothers were staying at Browning Hill with their maternal uncle George Grove. Samuel was then six and a half. Their maternal grandmother whose house it had been was probably now dead (cf. letters 7, n. 1 and 40, n. 6). For Mr Mulford see letter 10, n. 12.

57

TO JEREMIAH BENTHAM

5 December 1763 (Aet 15)

Queen's College Decr. 5th 1763

Hond. Sir

I arrived here between 5 and 6 in the afternoon on Thursday, without having experienced the Sickness which of late had been my constant attendant on a Journey, but did not find any thing in readiness when I came, the Bedmaker not having been able to get into my Room; however I managed as well as I could, and got half a Bed with my Friend Poore.[2] I have been 2 or 3 times to Mr. Jefferson, but had not been able to meet with him in his Room 'till this Morning, so as to deliver him the Note: his Recet for which I herewith inclose. Mr. Jefferson I hear to day is going to be inoculated: the Small Pox rages here terribly tho' not yet so bad as it has done; a month or two ago I am told there used to be buried three or four every day with it: amongst the rest the Woman at the Coffee-house where you were has lost her Husband. Gauntlett spent the Evening with me on Saturday, and I with him Yesterday: there is a great Bustle at New-Colledge, (where I should have told you he is now very happily situated) about the Election of a Warden of Winchester in the Room of the late Dr. Goulden; besides that the Warden of New-College is expected to die every day. the Election will come on next Week: there is one will have a Vote, that has left Winchester School but a fortnight or 3 Weeks, and is come in Fellow upon the Death of Mr Prince. The Candidates are Mr. Sare the

---

57. [1] B.M. I: 182–183. Autograph. Docketed by Jeremiah Bentham: 'Jeremy Bentham / Letter datd. Queen's Coll. Oxon / Decr. 5 1763.'

Bentham had now satisfied the requirements for proceeding to the Bachelor's degree, which he took formally in 1764. Bowring tells us that in November 1763 he began to eat his commons in Lincoln's Inn. He had been admitted to the Inn on 26 January 1763, while still up at Oxford (*Records of Lincoln's Inn*, i, 453), though he did not occupy chambers there until 1769 (cf. 84a, n. 2). At the same time he began to attend the Court of King's Bench, where his father had secured a student's seat for him. He returned to Oxford in December in order to hear William Blackstone lecture as Vinerian Professor of English Law (cf. Bowring, x, 45).

[2] Edward Poore, son of George Webb Poore of Devizes, matric. Queen's December 1761, aged 16; B.A. 1765, M.A. 1768; Barrister of Lincoln's Inn, 1772 (cf. Bowring x, 40, and 123.) The friendship continued into the 1770's when both Bentham and he were at Lincoln's Inn. Poore shared Bentham's interest in mechanical inventions and later gave Samuel some help in bringing his inventions to the notice of influential persons (see letters 96, 103, etc.). He became an F.R.S. at a date after 1768 and before 1772.

Proctor, Mr. Hayward, Sub-Warden, and Mr. Lee: the former is reckoned to have rather the better chance.[3] My Friend Ralfe will go to Town in about 10 days time; he talks of calling on you: I desired he would, and told him I dared to say you would be glad to see him, I am

Dr. Papa
Your dutiful & obedient
Son J. Bentham

I would beg leave to trouble to convey a Line to Mrs. Abbot.[4]

58

E D W A R D   C R A N M E R   T O   J E R E M Y   B E N T H A M

19 April 1764

Queen's Coll. April 19th 1764

Dear Bentham,

I have receiv'd your letter, and with regard to the first and second articles of it, would advise you to be in Oxford the very beginning of the next term. The term itself is but 5 weeks long, and it is a very common thing to meet with many delays, about convocations, and I don't know what myself, before you can be admitted to your degree. If you stay to keep the law term, which I

---

[3] For this election cf. A. F. Leach, *History of Winchester College*, 1899, 380–1; also James Woodforde, *Diary of a Country Parson*, i, London, 1924, 33–4. The late Warden of Winchester was Christopher Golding (*c.* 1710–63), matric. New College 1729, B.C.L. 1736, D.C.L. 1758; Warden since 1757. The Warden of New College was John Purnell, Warden since 1740: he did not in fact die till 1 June 1764. The recently deceased Fellow was George Prince of Wootton, Hants, who had died on 15 November. The candidates for Winchester were George James Sale of London, matric. Hertford, 1747, aged 19, B.A. from New College 1752, M.A. 1756; Thomas Hayward of London, matric. Oriel 1748/49, B.C.L. from New College 1758, D.C.L. 1764, in which year he succeeded Purnell as Warden of New College (d. 1768); Henry Lee (*c.* 1721–89) of Shropshire, the successful candidate, matric. New College 1741–42 aged 21, B.A. 1745, M.A. 1749, B.D. and D.D. 1764, Warden of Winchester until his death.

[4] His future stepmother: cf. letter 67, n. 1.

58. [1] B.M. I: 184–185. Autograph. Docketed by Mary Bentham(?): 'Cranmer Oxon to J.B. Q.S.P. Preparation for Oxford Degree.'
  Addressed: 'To / Mr. ⟨Jeremy Bentham⟩ / in Queen's Square / Westminster.' Stamped: 'OXFORD'. Postmark: '[. . .] AP'.
  Edward Cranmer (1744?–1802) matriculated at Queen's the same year as Bentham, and also took his B.A. and M.A. in the same years. Cf. Bowring, x, 40. Sixteen years later the acquaintance was briefly renewed (see letter 378). This letter contains his advice to Bentham on the best time for taking his B.A. and gives advice on the speech Bentham has to make on this occasion (perhaps in virtue of having been senior commoner). Cranmer later became rector of Quendon, Essex and vicar of St Bride's, Fleet Street.

see by the almanack does not begin till the ninth of May, you may probably come too late for your degree: but if you are here by the beginning of our term,[2] you may read your lectures, take your degree, and return to London time enough to keep the term there. This is my opinion of the matter, but, as a worthy gentleman of our acquaintance says, You must do as you please; if you dont like this you must take another method.

With regard to the last article of your enquiries, I have consulted Burleigh[3] and Stillingfleet[4] about it, and their advice is this. For the speech—*Exordium*. In congratulating yourself on the happy occasion of returning this public thanks for all favours—Next comes *General flummery*, or a panegyric on the college, and learned fellows belonging to it,—then *Particular flummery*. 1st to the Provost, commending his learning, his diligence, his conduct, in the offices both of Vice chancellor, and head of the college. 2dly to your Tutor, to whom your thanks and praises are particularly due for pointing out to you the way of attaining wisdom and virtue. And lastly conclude with good wishes to all in general.

A general dissertation on any Classick, divided into 3 parts, each part about half a sheet, will serve for your three lectures. Pope's preface to Homer, or Dryden's to Virgil, will give you a more adequate idea of the form of such a dissertation, than any specimen I can possibly insert in a letter.

Burleigh and Stillingfleet are the men to whom I have apply'd myself this month past, for a speech and set of lectures. Stillingfleet has given me his speech, and has promised to get me a set of lectures, but has not yet done it.

I am

Dear Bentham

Your affecte. friend

Ed.? Cranmer

[2] The Oxford term began on the 10th day after Easter, i.e. on 2 May 1764.

[3] Richard Burleigh, son of Rev. William Burleigh, of Chidton, Hants., matric. Queen's, July 1759, aged 18; B.A. 1763, M.A. 1768. Cf. also Bowring, x, 40.

[4] James Stillingfleet, son of Rev. Edward Stillingfleet of Wolverley, Worcs., matric. Queen's April 1759, aged 17; B.A. 1762; M.A. 1765. Rector of Hotham, Yorks, 1771–1826. His son, like his father and his elder brother, was a clergyman. Cf. also Bowring, x, 40.

59

JEREMY BENTHAM TO JEREMIAH BENTHAM

9 December 1764 (Aet 16)

Hond. Sir

    I received your favour of the 16th of last Month by the hands of Mr. Skeet, which as it gave me your opinion with regard to the affair of the Provost, made me congratulate myself that I had acted conformable to it. as for the Common-Room, I did not imagine you would take it so seriously as you did, I can assure you I meant far otherwise than you imagine, it was only their ⟨od⟩dity I imagined might divert you; for my part I had no reason to complain, as they then were, and still are very civil to me.

    I should have told you before, that Mr. Jefferson paid my Battels and Bills for this last Quarter out of his own accord, which somewhat surprized me, as he had no Money of mine in his hands, nor would ever before pay a bill without my signing: upon looking over the Articles I found Sponsion 10s. 6d. which upon my demanding an explanation he told me was for paying my Bills; that some People gave it him, and some would not, those were his words, but that he always pd. Mr. such an one's Bills naming him, and charged

---

59. [1] B.M. I: 186–187. Autograph. Docketed by Jeremiah Bentham: 'Jeremy Bentham / Lr. datd. Queen's Coll. Oxon / 9 Decr. 1764.'

    Addressed: 'To / Jeremiah Bentham Esqr. / at Queen's Square / near St James's Park / Westminster.' Postmark: '10 DE'.

    Bentham was now dividing his time between London where he kept the Law terms and Oxford where he was working for the M.A. and hearing the lectures of Bever and Blackstone.

    This is the only extant letter of 1764 by Bentham. In conversation with Bowring he recalled that in that year he had accompanied his father on an excursion to the North of England and later to France. 'He was delighted with a visit they paid to the chateau of the Prince of Condé at Chantilly . . . "I did envy the Prince" said Bentham, "his beautiful palace. I exclaimed, What a bliss to be a Prince! I was not much wiser than the ploughboy, who said his bliss would be to swing all day upon a gate, eating beef and carrots; or than a Justice of the Peace. who told me that his summum bonum was to grab for eels in the mud; and whom I once found tearing up Sanderson's Logic to ram into his fowlingpiece"' (Bowring, x, 47). They went the usual round of sight-seeing at Paris. Bowring remarks on the visit: 'France, as a country, left an unfavourable impression on young Bentham. The imitations of England appeared wretched; its gardens stiff and formal. But of the French, as a nation, he was always fond; their vivacity, courtesy, and aptitude for enjoyment, responded to all the tendencies of his own character. At Versailles, the beauty of the dauphiness charmed him. Most of the favourable impressions he received were from the people; but the backwardness of their agriculture, and of their domestic civilization, seemed strangely contrasted with the advances even then made by England' (ibid.).

that for his trouble. I desir'd an account of him, which he promised to give me, but has not yet: I shall go to him tomorrow or next day. —You acquaint me of surprizing Revolutions indeed in your Empire: they will be effected I suppose by the time I get home.[2]— Dr Blakistone[3] reads for the last time on the 17th of this Month—I am very glad you are likely to make the House at Queen's Square your own; since you were so kind as to express a satisfaction in it on my account, I will own, I always thought we should be "Felices nimium, propria haec si dona fuissent." the taking in of a Room of Mr. Leech's[4] would make a pretty addition to it. there has been another Sale here, at which I have bought 2 or 3 books—the Memoires of Philip de Comines[5] an historian/French/ of great authority, whom if you are not acquainted with, Mr. Clarke will give you an account of. he has got it in English, and it was on his credit in great measure that I bought it. 2 Vols 3s. also Tournefort's Voyages to the Levant 3 large Octavo Vols. 10.6. with many plates.[6] N.B. Tournefort was a famous French Botanist. Lastly an Italian book "Eneide de Virgilio Travestita["].[7] 1s.—I hope to hear from you what time you would chuse I should come home: if on any particular time; I suppose 3 or 4 days after we break up, if I may so stile it will be about the time: till when I am

Hond. Sir
Your dutiful and affectionate Son
J. Bentham

⟨Queen's⟩ Coll. Decr. 9th 1764

[2] Possibly a reference to alterations to be made in the house at Queen Square Place, which it appears his father was now to buy. Hitherto he had only rented it.

[3] Presumably a slip for 'Blackstone'.

[4] John Leech was Jeremiah Bentham's landlord (cf. letter 47, n. 2; also letter 188).

[5] Probably the edition by Denys Godefroy, published at the Hague in 1682.

[6] Joseph Pitton de Tournefort, *A Voyage into the Levant* (transl. J. Ozell), London, 1741.

[7] By Giovanni Batista Lalli, 1651 and other editions.

60

TO JEREMIAH BENTHAM

30 April 1765 (Aet 17)

Hond. Sir

I am much obliged to you for your intelligence in regard to the seeds, and can inform you on my part, that the Shoes you were so kind as to send me got here very safe, tho' some little time after you said you would send them. Dr. Bever[2] does not begin to read his lectures 'till the 21st of next Month, and as they continue above 2 Months, it will keep me some time longer here, than there would otherwise have been occasion. Dr. Blackstone[3] has deliver'd a paper about the University, in which after many Comp̃s and reasons for his taking this step, he declares his Resolution of reading 1 course more only, and that then he will resign his professorship. it is said, (but whether it is contain'd in this paper, I don't know, as I have not seen it,) that he will publish soon the 1st part of his lectures (of which there are 4) in one Vol. the price of which will be a guinea and a half: thus much is certain that it is almost all printed off: I mean the 1st part only.—the Provost is gone to Bath to try what that will do towards the reestablishment of his health: in regard to which his Drs. differed in their opinions; one said it would kill him, for that he would /could/ never bear the fatigue of the Journey; 'tother said it would cure him: whose opinion being strengthened by that of the Apothe-

---

60. [1] B.M. I: 188–189. Autograph. Docketed by Jeremiah Bentham: 'Jere^y Bentham / Lr. datd. Oxford / 30 April 1765.'

Addressed: 'To / Jeremiah Bentham Esqr. / at Queen's Square / near St. James's Park / Westminster.' Stamped: 'THAME'. Postmark: '1 MA'.

[2] Thomas Bever, LL.D. (1725–91). Fellow of All Souls; Judge of the Cinque Ports; lectured in Civil Law at Oxford; published works on jurisprudence, civil law, and the history of Roman legal polity.

[3] William Blackstone (1723–80), the famous jurist, was the first Vinerian Professor of English Law at Oxford (1758–66). The lectures he gave were the basis of his *Commentaries on the Laws of England* which he published 1765–69. He entered Parliament in 1761; became Solicitor-general to Queen Charlotte in 1763, and was knighted and made a judge in Common Pleas in 1770. He was concerned in drawing up the Hard Labour Bill discussed by Bentham in his pamphlet of 1778.

Bentham's *Fragment on Government* (1776) attacked Blackstone's views on sovereignty. The *Comment on the Commentaries*, which Bentham began in 1774, was first published in 1928 (ed. C. W. Everett). It is a more extensive critique of Blackstone's work.

Bentham told Bowring that the friends with whom he attended Blackstone's lectures 'both took notes; which I attempted to do, but could not continue it, as my thoughts were occupied in reflecting on what I heard. I immediately detected his fallacy respecting natural rights . . .' etc. (Bowring, x, 45).

cary prevailed: accordingly he set out o' Tuesday last, accompanied by one of the ffellows, his nephew, and his Housekeeper. it is said the College has great expectations from him, and that he intends to leave the bulk of his fortune to it: but he has a great many Nephews and Nieces that want it more. the Senior Fellow died about a week ago who never resided in College nor was permitted to take a living by the society, on account of his notorious bad Character for drunkenness:[4] and now Dr. Fothergill[5] is exalted to the superb stall or Alcove that answers to that where the Provost sits in Chapel.—Mr. Jefferson is going to take his Dr's. degree; he will be a great man then. very important news you will say; but such as I have, that give I unto you. but you have it all in your part of the World; pray what do people say of the Kg's. speech, and Almon's trial?[6] will it come on or no?—I forgot to mention that I have been doing Austins, an exercise for one's Master's degree, that one is obliged to do, on a summons from the Proctor, at a proper standing. it consists in disputing for 2 Hours in the Schools in the presence of the Proctor the whole time, and is therefore the least of a farce of any of the disputations in the Schools, at the rest of which the Proctors are only present occasionally, and sometimes not at all, as it may happen.—while your Garden is running to ruin, I am entertaining myself in the Physick Garden, to which for a shilling now and then, I have free ingress and egress. I cannot however be totally insensible of your calamities, in which indeed I myself have no small concern.—if you can excuse the trouble I give you, I should be glad to know exactly or at least as near as you can tell, how much the parcel of Seeds from Gordon's came to; and that within this fortnight, for reasons that shall hereafter be explained by

Your dutiful and affectionate Son
J. Bentham.

Queen's Coll. Oxon. April 30th 1765.

---

[4] William Knail, for whom see letter 28, n. 7.

[5] Thomas Fothergill, matric. at Queen's Coll. July 1734, aged 18; B.A. 1739, M.A. 1742, fellow 1751; B.D. 1755, D.D. 1762. He succeeded Dr Joseph Browne as Provost of Queen's on the latter's death in 1767, and was vice-chancellor of the University, 1772–75. He died in 1796 (see also Bowring, x, 37–38).

[6] John Almon (1737–1805), political journalist and bookseller, friend and supporter of Wilkes, was on trial for publishing a pamphlet called *Juries and Libels*.

61

To Charles Coleman

[?] Early May 1765 (Aet 17)

Μικρος Ὁμηλικι

Ου μεν γαρ ουδαμως, ω Δυσανθρακανδρε εμε τον σου μικροτερον εξονο-
μαζων ορθως ελεξας. τι γαρ ψυλλου και φθειρας τα περι ηλικιαν διαφερει;
ει/ αλλως τε και εκ του αρτι αυξηθηναι με λεγουσι, /ετι συνεχως αυξανομενον/
και αυξανομενον διατελειν. Συ δε πυγμαιε, και οίον αν τις ουκ Ανθρακανδρα
αλλα Ανθρακιδιον εξονομασειε, ποια προσωπα τοσουτους υβριστικους εις
εμε τους λογους αναρριπτειν ετολμησας; "αλλ᾽ οκνω μη περι σου τα
προσηκοντα λεγων, αὐτος ου προσηκοντας εμαυτω δοξω προηρησθαι λογους."
παυσαμενον ουν την μεγαλοτητα της οργης, εντρεπειν δει προς τα της σης
επιστολης μετριωτερα; ει μεν τι εξ ολου μετριον ἦ ονομαστεον. Και γαρ
εν αρχη γραφεις, ὡς τινες σεσυληκασι το περιστεροτροφειον, τό σαυτου
ειναι φασκων· εγω δ, ὡς απλως ειπειν εγηθεομην ακουσας, νομιζων
ούτως την αφορμην της ανοσιοτητος αφαιρεθηναι. τι γαρ ανοσιοτερον η
αισχροτερον η ει τις ιερευς ων το ιερειον αυτο ταις ἑαυτου αρπαγαις
και κλεμμασιν υποδοχην φωρων κατεστηκε; νυν δε ουκ εχοντι κλεπτειν,
αναγκη εστι καλως ζην. ταυτα ουν/ ἁ /επεπρακτο εν Στεφανοπολι/ διηγησο/·
δικαιον και τα εν Βουπορω συμπιπτομενα ακουειν. Επλαγη ὁ Πελλαιος ὁ
Κοινοβιου του ἡμετερου Επιστατης ὑπο παροξυσμου τινος παραλυτικου
ἡμερων γεγονοτων αμφι τας εικοσι και μιαν, και δεινον τι και επικινδυνον τα
πρωτα εξεφαινετο. αλλ᾽ ουκ ηθελε (ὡς εοικεν) ἡ τυχη, τουτο τω Φοθριγαλω
χαριζεσθαι· ταχυ γαρ ἀνεβαλεν, ὡς τε λιπειν το λεχος την ημερινην. εσχιζεσθην
δε γνωμαις τω ιατρω (δυω γαρ αυτω οντε ετυγχανετην) εφατην γαρ, ὁ
μεν, δειν πορευεσθαι εις Θερμας και εκει υδροποτην γενεσθαι· ὁ δε μη· ου γαρ
ανεχεσθαι ανασχησεσθαι την πορειαν, αλλ εφ᾽ ὁδου τεθνηξεσθαι. ταυτα δε
του πρωτου ἰατρου ενομιζεν ὁ Φαρμακοπωλης· νικησαντων δε τουτων, και
Πελλαιου (ὡς ακολουθον) Θερμαζε πεπορευμενου ηκον εκεισε επιστολαι
ἡμερων γεγονοτων τεσσαρων ἠ πεντε, ὡς διατελει συνεχως αναρρωννυ-
μενος. καταστρεβλωται ὁμως κατ᾽ ολιγον (ως φασιν) το καλον αυτου
το προσωπον· εξ οὖ φοβεροτερον τι βλεψειν εικος εκ τουτου και αξιωματι-
κωτερον. αλλα τι τουτων εχομαι; επειδαν ταχυ δὶα στοματος ελπιζω σοι
κοινωνησεσθαι· ελπιζω γαρ (αγαθη τυχη) Στεφανοπολινδε κομισασθαι
ἑκταιον η ογδοαιον απο ταυτης· τουτο δε σε αξιῶ και δεομαι (κι ποιων
ακολουθα. ισως αν συγγνωμης τυχοις) μη ειπειν τω Μουλφωρδω· οιομαι
γαρ λανθανων ελευσεσθαι /ερχομενος λαθειν/. ὁ δε Μουλφωρδος ουτοσι τα
δεοντα ανταποδιδοναι αει οκνωδης, απιστος, οφειλματων επιλησμονεστα-
τος, θεοις τε και ανθρωποις εχθρος. διο και οἱ, επευχομαι, μαρηνοιντο/
ξαιφνως/ τα σικυδια /μηδεν φυτον καλως συγχωροιτο/ γενοιτο δὲ ὁ Ρουηρος

και αυτου του δεσποτου απιστοτερος τελος δε λυπομενος, επι πεσοι δε ή
ταλαιπωρη ή καλυβη ενθα και ενθα περι τα ωτα, ταυτα παντα, και ει τι
τουτων δεινοτερον, επαραω. συ δε ευτυχοις και μηδαμως εκεινου τον τροπον
μιμοιο.

Translation

One Little Man to Another

My dear Coleman, you certainly did not speak with accuracy
when you said that I was smaller than you were; for what does size
matter, as between a flea and a louse? Especially since they say I
have recently been growing, and shall go on growing steadily. But,
you pygmy, fit to be named Coley rather than Coleman, what impertinence has made you dare cast up against me such outrageous
words as 'but I hesitate, for fear that if I say what ought to be
said about you, I may seem to have chosen words that I ought not
to use about myself'. Abating then the greatness of my wrath, shall
I turn to the more temperate parts of your letter? If indeed any
part of it can be called temperate? For you write, at the beginning,
that some people have robbed the dovecot, which you allege belongs
to you; well, to be quite frank, I am delighted to hear it, for it
seems to me that the opportunity for evil-doing has thus been
removed. For what could be more wicked or shameful than that a
clergyman, by his own robberies and pillagings, should turn his
very church into a resort of thieves? Those who lack the world's
goods must steal to live well. You have described your doings at
Steventon; now you must hear what has been happening at Oxford.
Browne the Provost of our College[2] was struck down about three
weeks ago by some kind of paralytic attack, and at first the
situation looked alarming and dangerous. But fate (so it seems) did
not wish to gratify Fothergill[3]; For Browne soon recovered enough

61. [1] B.M. I: 214–215. Autograph. Docketed: '176[?]. J.B. Oxon / to / Coleman
Steventon / Greek Letter'.

The Greek text is given exactly as in the manuscript (which is heavily corrected in
places and may be a draft) except for the extension of digraphs, and the adoption
in two passages of Bentham's indications of word-order. The accents and breathings
are those given by Bentham.

The recipient of this letter was most probably Charles Coleman, son of Charles
Coleman of Lyndhurst, Hants, matric. Trinity November 1754, aged 18, B.A. 1758,
M.A. 1761. He was evidently at this time parson of Steventon, where Bentham's
cousin John Mulford now lived. Charles Coleman was later vicar of Basingstoke, and
his son, also Charles, matric. St Edmund Hall 1807. Cf. also letter 71.

The present letter is undated, but its references to the illness of the Provost of
Queen's College show that its date must be close to that of letter 60, possibly a little
later.

[2] For Joseph Browne see letter 13, n. 6.
[3] For Thomas Fothergill see letter 60, n. 5.

to be able to get up during the day. His doctors (for there were two) disagreed one said that he must go to Bath and drink the waters; the other said no, he would not be able to stand the journey but would die on the road. The Apothecary agreed with the first doctor, so these two carried the day and Browne obeyed them and went off to Bath whence[4] we heard about four or five days ago that he is steadily recovering his strength. His noble countenance is said however to be a bit twisted, so he may be rather more terrifying and awe inspiring to behold in future. But why do I dwell on such matters? Since I hope to be talking with you face to face quite soon. For I hope (with any luck) to get to Steventon in six or eight days from now; but there is one thing I do ask and beg of you and that is (if you will be so kind) that you will not tell Mulford;[5] for I plan to come without letting him know. This Mulford is always sluggish about performing his duty, untrustworthy, very forgetful of his debts, an enemy to gods and men. Wherefore I pray that his cucumbers may suddenly wither that no plant may prosper for him that Rover may become even more untrustworthy than his master and may end miserably, that his wretched hovel may fall to pieces about his ears, all this and if there be anything yet more terrible than this, I lay upon him as a solemn curse. But do you fare well and in no respect imitate his ways.

62

To Richard Clark

14 May 1765 (Aet 17)

Dear Sir

As my dilatoriness in executing my promise will admitt of no excuse, I find I have nothing to do but to confess to you ingenuously

---

[4] The Greek text has εκεισε, 'thither'; this seems to be a slip for εκειθεν, 'thence' which the sense clearly requires.

[5] For John Mulford see letter 10, n. 12.

62. [1] U.C. CLXXIII: 37. Autograph. Docketed by Clark: 'Master Bentham's Letter dated Oxford May 14 1765.'

Addressed: 'To / Mr. Richd Clarke / at the Old South-Sea-House / in Old Broad Street / London.' Stamped: 'OXFORD'. Postmark: '16 MA'.

Bentham had few friends at this time, and it seems as if his father encouraged him to seek a companion in his friend Richard Clark (1739–1831) a successful young attorney. Clark and Bentham made a tour of the North of England together in the summer of 1766.

In 1776 Clark was elected as alderman, and in 1777 served as sheriff. He was elected Lord Mayor in 1784. In 1798, on the death of Wilkes, he was elected chamberlain of London, and next year was appointed president of Bridewell. He moved in literary circles.

the plain truth: there is a certain formality in breaking the Ice of a Correspondence, which notwithstanding the terms of freedom to which your condescension has admitted me might seem to render unnecessary, I must acknowledge has had such an influence over me, as to have frightened me into putting it off from time to time whenever I have had intention to attempt it. the truth is, I am not yet such a proficient in the art of Letter-writing, as to be able to sit down with ease to write upon *nothing*, which as it is, I believe, generally the principal subject of a first letter, so is it particularly here: for as to news, that I think can hardly be expected from a situation, noted, as mine is, even to a proverb, for dulness and uniformity. and tho' I seldom seem at a loss for more profitable conversation when in your company, yet as that cause no longer subsists, no wonder if the effect should cease accordingly. I will not however make any apologies further than that above mentioned; since if you are so disposed, you have means amply sufficient in your own hands to punish me, namely by silence: but in this particular, I hope you will consult rather magnanimity than Justice. if the former carries it, I should be glad to know the event of Mr. Tuffnell's trial; and would likewise take as a great favour any information you could give me in regard to that of Almon; at which, I dare say, if business permitted, you were present: for my own part, had I been to chuse, I had much rather have been there than at Lord Byron's.[2] Perhaps Business might supply you not merely with an excuse but a very substantial reason for refusing to gratify my curiosity in these particulars: but however that be, I hope you have not forgot your promise of giving me your company this Summer; previous to which you were to let me know the time, and acquaint me with my ffather's having rec̄ed the Balsam plants and Jerusalem Artichokes from Mr. Hawkins's;[3] which, as we then termed it, were to be the credentials to insure your reception—I cannot conclude this *nothing* without mentioning somewhat that

[2] On 16 April the fifth Lord Byron (1722–98) was convicted of manslaughter before the House of Lords. He had killed his cousin Mr Chaworth in a brawl. He was exempted from punishment by his privilege as a peer. We have not been able to trace Tuffnell's trial.

[3] John Hawkins (1719–89) was a man of humble origins who prospered as an attorney, married into a rich family, and established a literary reputation. In 1759 Richard Clark took over his business as an attorney in Austin Friars. Hawkins began work on his history of music about 1760, at the instigation of Horace Walpole. It was published in 1776 as *The General History of the Science and Practice of Music*. Hawkins was a friend of Dr Johnson (when Clark was fifteen he introduced him to Johnson) and wrote a life of him. He was knighted in 1777. He was then living in Queen Square, Westminster. See also letter 196, n. 2.

lately occurred to me in my reading, which tho' it strikes against
Milton, whom I know to be a particular friend of your's, and whose
integrity, I believe, you have hitherto esteemed equal to his learning, yet as I am convinced you are still more a friend to truth, you
will perhaps not be displeased to examine it. it is no less than a
heavy charge against him of falsifying and misrepresenting several
passages in Bracton the old lawyer: to whose life in the Biographia
Britannica, as they are much too long to insert here, I refer you for
particular's[4]—and am

Dear Sir
Yours obediently and affectionately
J.^y Bentham

Queen's Coll. Oxon
   Tuesday May 14th 1765

63

T O J E R E M I A H B E N T H A M

9 August 1765 (Aet 17)

Hond. Sir

Baghurst

I had the pleasure on my arrival here to find my two Aunts[2]
perfectly well; my Uncle is gone a Journey he was obliged to take
in consequence of his place in the Hawker's and Pedlar's Office[3]; but
is expected here some time next week. Mr. Mulford dined here last
Saturday se'nnight at which time he was just come off his Warwick-
shire expedition: he called, I understand at Oxford on his return.

---

[4] *Biographia Britannica; or, The Lives of the most eminent Persons who have
flourished in Great Britain and Ireland, from the earliest ages, down to the present times.*
(1747–66). Volume II (1748) contains the life of Henry Bracton (*c.* 1210–68), author
of a comprehensive treatise on the laws of England entitled *De Legibus et Consue-
tudinibus Angliae.* Milton is there said to have appealed (in his *Defence of the People
against Salmasius,* 1652) to passages from Bracton's work in justification of the trial
of Charles I, but to have distorted their sense by taking them out of context. The
question at issue was roughly: Is the King above the Law?

63. [1] B.M. I: 190–191. Autograph. Docketed by Jeremiah Bentham: 'Recd. 9th
Augt. 1765.' Also: 'Jeremy Bentham / Lr. datd. Baghurst / 9 Augt. 1765.'
   Addressed: 'To / Jeremiah Bentham Esqr. / at Queen's Square / near St. James's
Park / Westminster.' Postmark: '9 AV'.
   Written while on a visit to Browning Hill, home of his uncle George Grove.
   [2] Susannah and Deborah Grove.
   [3] G. W. Grove was one of the 'riding surveyors' of the Hawkers' and Pedlars'
Office in Gray's Inn Road. He held this position, with an annual salary of £100, from
1759 for over twenty years.

the Country every where hereabouts has been burnt up as much as with us: they have not even had near so much rain, as we had on Saturday and Sunday: butter is at 9d. per £ at Basingstoke. till we came to about Maidenhead yesterday the roads were perfectly sloppy: but all the way from thence there was not the least appearance of any rain. some Company came to breakfast here on Wednesday and carried my Aunt Grove with them the same day to Andover: where she staid till Saturday. but who they were I am not informed.—they have but little Paper here, and I forgot to take some down: I will therefore beg the favour of you to send me a Quire down by Sammy which will do equally as well. My Aunts desire their love and compliments, and are very sorry to hear of your indisposition; but hope soon to hear of your speedy Recovery, as does likewise—

Your dutiful and affectionate Son
J. Bentham

My Aunt would take it as a favour if you cou'd contrive to send her by Sammy the underwritten Articles:
$\frac{1}{2}$£ 10s. Tea: $\frac{1}{4}$£ 12s. do.: 1£ Bohea do.: 1£ Coffee.

64

TO JEREMIAH BENTHAM

10 October 1765 (Aet 17)

Hond. Sir
       The round of visitings etc. that I mentioned to you in my last has not been in the least interrupted since then: at that time one of the Miss Horgans[2] was here upon a visit to my Aunt for a week; since when, Mr. and Mrs. Darling[3] have spent a fortnight with us: and last of all, I attended my Uncle on Saturday sen'night to Mr. Osborne's at Turville Court, from whence we returned the Tuesday after with Mr. Osborne's Son (who is of Oriel College in Oxford) who

<hr>

64. [1] B.M. I: 192–192. Autograph. Dated by Jeremiah Bentham: 'Browning Hill. Baghurst Hants 10 Octr. He has also docketed it: 'Jere^y Bentham / Lr. datd. Baghurst 10 April 1765.' The postmark is very faint, but it seems to read: '10 OC'.
       Addressed: 'To Jeremiah Bentham Esqr. / at Queen's Square / near St. James's Park / Westminster.'
       [2] Unidentified.
       [3] George Darling, at one time curate near Andover, was parson of Wargrave, Berks. He won Bentham's affection, partly by showing him a solar microscope (cf. Bowring, x, 39).

left us but yesterday.[4] amongst all which engagements I have had no time to think of going, till now having talked with my Uncle and Aunt about it, they are both so kind as to say, it would be very odd for me to leave my own Relations to go and lay myself under an Obligation to other people, for such they think it would be, and would require some acknowledgement on your part. however that be, as I have no home to go to, I must lay under an Obligation somewhere, and tho' in general any one has a better title to reception from Relations than other friends, yet I have reason to think, Mr. and Mrs. Browne[5] would not take it amiss if I were to spend some little time with them, as you know there has been a little kind of Jealousy since our friendship with Mr. Clark; at least, I think they would take it ill if I were to go to the South-Sea-House without being at all with them. upon the whole I will attend your determination, and if I go to Mr. Browne's would be glad to know whether you have talked with them about it, and whether they have made me any sort of Invitation.—as to the literary Engagements you mention in your letter to my Aunt, I make no doubt of having fulfilled them by my return to London, notwithstanding that since the different Companies have been here, I have been continually called out to attend them somewhere or other: which tho' it has not, to be sure, much forwarded my advancement in learning, has considerably improved my health and skill in Horsemanship: for I not only am told, but can find by my cloaths, that I am much fatter than when I came down, which I dare say my frequent riding has contributed to as well as my good entertainment. I hope you will find less difficulty in reading these presents than I in writing; for the paper you sent takes this Ink but very indifferently; which of them is in fault, I know not, however at present I desire no more of them, than to assist me in ass⟨uring you⟩ that I am

> Your dutiful and affectionate Son
> J. Bentham

Compliments in abundance attend you from the different persons of your acquaintance I have seen lately: Love etc. as pr. last.

---

[4] John Osborne, sen. (d. 1775), was a bookseller who in 1753 bought the estate of Turville Court in the Chilterns. He was sheriff in 1759. He was named as administrator of the will made by George Woodward Grove on 28 November 1772, but died before Grove. His son, John Osborne, jnr., does not appear in *Alumni Oxonienses* and in the *Oriel College History* is presumed to have died young. In fact he died without issue in 1799, having married in 1781, and the estate passed to his married sister Letitia and her daughters.

[5] See letter 45, n. 3.

65

To Jeremiah Bentham

20 October 1765 (Aet 17)

Steventon Octr. 20th 1765

Hond. Sir

When your letter came to Browninghill, I was at this place, and did not go there till friday forenoon, at which time, my Aunt was gone to dinner to Mr. Mackreth's,[2] and my Uncle preparing to follow her thither, from whence he was to proceed to Whitchurch. upon communicating to him and afterwards to my Aunt your commands for my return, I found I could not conveniently be conveyed to the 8 mile stone at the time you appointed, and must therefore beg your acceptance of this letter instead of myself; but the beginning of next week they promise to send me. I had walked it hither from Browninghill on Wednesday, and returned there on friday on Mr. Mulford's Horse, and came back here again yesterday, which I should have done the same day I went, had it not been for the receipt of your letter, which occasioned me to stay to see my Aunt. both my Aunts were very much astonished at the unexpected account of More's[3] ill behaviour; but when I mentioned your hint to me about writing to Mr. Browne, we were at a loss to conceive of what a letter at this time could consist, or what could be the intention of it, unless it were to invite myself to his house, which would come rather more properly from him to me, than from me to him. We had a birth here the other day; Mrs. Plowden,[4] who was to have removed to Aldermaston this week, had mistaken her reckoning, and fell to pieces the last; it was a boy, but died the 3d. day after it

---

65. [1] B.M. I: 194–195. Docketed by Jeremiah Bentham: 'Jere[y] Bentham / Steventon / 20 Octr. 1765.'

Addressed: 'To Jeremiah Bentham Esqr. / at Queen's Square / near St. James's Park / Westminster.' Postmark: '21 OC'.

He was staying at Steventon with his cousin Mulford (for whom see letter 10, n. 12).

[2] Bob Mackreth (1726–1819) began life as a billiard-marker at White's. He married the daughter of the club's proprietor, Robert Arthur, and inherited the property in June 1761. He made a fortune, partly as a usurer. He sat as M.P. for Ashburton (1784–1802), and was knighted in 1795. In 1766 Bentham visited him at the large house he had bought at Ewhurst, but the friendship came to an end with an immoderate burst of laughter from Bentham while Mackreth was speaking French (see Bowring, x, 48).

[3] Not identified.

[4] Sarah Harris, younger daughter of Squire Harris of Baughurst (cf. letter 8, n. 3), had married James Plowden, then a lieutenant in the Navy, a member of the family from whom Mackreth bought the house at Ewhurst mentioned above at n. 2.

was born. I find there has been great changes in your Ministry as well as the King's; I am one of the Outs at present, but hope by Monday or Tuesday to be one of the Ins till when I am

Your dutiful and
affectionate Son
J. Bentham

Mr Mulford desires his Comps. and gives you joy of having gotten rid of your Magdalen unconverted.

66

To Jeremiah Bentham

24 August 1766 (Aet 18)

Monmouth Sunday Augt. 24th 1766.

Hond. Sir

Imagining you may by this time be fixed at Weymouth after finishing your business in Hampshire and Devonshire, and being obliged to make this day a day of rest by the rain which has fallen for the first time since we began our journey except a Shower at Oxford, I will take the Opportunity to make you the most grateful acknowledgments in behalf of myself and my fellowtraveller, for your kindness in obtaining the letter of recommendation from Mr. Browne and to acquaint you of our safe arrival at this place. our journey has been very delightful, and our feet and forces have held out hitherto extremely well: I mean our bodily forces: as for those of the pocket   *   *   *   *   *   *   *   hiatus valdè deflebilis—we could not leave Oxford 'till Saturday afternoon: but in the mean time I was so happy as to find Dr. and Mrs. Bentham at home and Mrs. Bentham was so kind as to give me a letter of recommendation to Mrs. Roberts wife of Dr. Roberts Physician at Ross in Hereford-

---

66. [1] B.M. I: 196–197. Autograph. Docketed by Jeremiah Bentham: 'Jere^y Bentham / Lr. to Weymouth datd. Monmouth 24 Augt. 1766.'

Addressed: 'To Jeremiah Bentham Esqr. / at Weymouth / Dorset / to be left at the Post Office.' Stamped: 'ross'. Postmark almost illegible—'27 AV'[?].

This letter was written while Bentham was touring with Richard Clark (for whom see letter 62, n. 1). Bowring (x, 54) describes what was evidently a later tour with Clark, which took place in 1770. On this occasion also the two visited Oxford, and Bentham told Bowring that he had to escape from a window to avoid marrying Dr Bentham's daughter; but this story may reasonably be doubted, since the only daughter of Edward Bentham of whom there is any record, Elizabeth (1760–1803), was only ten. Jeremiah Bentham appears to have been on holiday at this time with Mrs Abbot, whom he was to marry less than two months later.

shire,[2] which tho' unfortunately Mrs. Roberts was gone to Bath, proved of infinite service to us, as it introduced us to the Dr. who is an excellent Naturalist and Antiquarian, and whose candour and civility to us was equal to his learning. I met with a very cordial and polite reception from the fellows /with whom we dined in the hall/ and recēd my Exhibition from Mr. Jefferson tho' not till after several deductions which left me but 15£. 1s. 8d.. at ½ after 4 we left Friar Bacon's study in our way to Farringdon in Berkshire: the distance is full 18 miles. we got there at ½ after 9 myself indeed very much fatigued: for till within 2 or 3 miles we had walked at the rate of about 4 miles an hour. we made shift however to leave the place at 11 the next morning after taking a peep at the town and outside of the Church where tho' we spent some time in looking at the monuments we found nothing worth observation. between 4 and 5 we got to Fairford through Lechlade which is 10 miles and spent the remainder of the day in viewing the painted Glass for which the place is famous: by the way we regaled ourselves with 10 puffs and part of a vial of brandy which the Dr. had made up in packets, and Mrs. Bentham, deaf to all remonstrances, had with the utmost kindness crammed into my pocket. as soon as my duty to my father is paid, I shall offer my thanks to those valuable friends—to my Aunt I wrote yesterday from Ross in Herefordshire—from Fairford we continued our journey on the Monday to Cirencester which is between 8 and 9 miles stopping on our way at a farmer's who was brother to Mr. Bullock[3] an acquaintance of Mr. Clark's, and saw that evening the fine old Church at Cirencester, from whence we copied some ancient inscriptions. Tuesday we spent in admiring Ld. Bathurst's woods,[4] the usual way of visiting them is on horseback, but that we were above. on Wednesday we travelled on to Gloucester, breakfasting by the way with a Clergyman we had scraped an Acquaintance with, and dining at a pretty snug Ale-house at the summit of Burlip hill, from whence we had the most enchanting prospect my Eyes ever beheld. to Gloucester we got about 6 o'clock and there met Mr. Clark's beloved bags, which we had been obliged to send on thither with a few shirts: but as for the trunk we were forced to send that to Bristol and God knows when we shall see it again. there I

---

[2] Cf. Bowring, x, 46, where the meeting is dated to the 1764 tour with Bentham's father. (See letter 59, n. 1). The physician was probably John Roberts, son of Walter Roberts of Ross, matric. Balliol 1727, aged 18; B.A. 1731, M.A. 1734, B.MED. 1737.

[3] Unidentified.

[4] Oakley Park near Cirencester.

enjoy'd clean linnen for the first time since the Friday before. on Thursday, after dressing ourselves and spending a long time in taking a particular view of the Cathedral we sat out for Ross, not 'till 3 in the afternoon in a broiling Sun, dined at a Village about 6 miles in the way, and got to Ross about 10 at night. for the 3 or 4 last Miles we had a beautiful moon, and the Country the most romantic I had ever seen. from Ross one has a nearer view of the black mountains, which we saw from Cleve hill when we went with Mr. Reid to his living.[5] I should have been glad to have gone there now, but we found it would lie too much out of our beat. ⟨Friday⟩ and most part of yesterday we spent at Ross, and came away unwillingly ⟨in the⟩ afternoon, after a philosophical dinner at Dr. Roberts's. We got here ⟨in⟩ good time in the Evening after a most delicious walk which even exceeded that from Gloucester to Ross, as we had the River Wye to enhance the beauty of the prospect. the distance from Gloucester to Ross is 17 miles, and that from Ross hither 10 miles. as for the rest that we did, and the Castle that we saw, are they not written in the book of the Chronicles of the journey of Rich. Clark and Jere: Bentham?—as for our further intentions, I believe they will undergo some alteration from the lights communicated to us by Dr. Roberts; as I believe we shall find it necessary to leave the trouble we have occasioned to you and Mr. Browne ineffectual and to confine ourselves to Monmouth Sh. and Glamorgn. Sh. when we are got to Bristol, I will account to you for our intermediate proceedings unless Mr. Clark should then write which I believe he thinks of doing, and in the mean time desires to be kindly remembered to you. we will likewise beg you to present our best Compliments to Mrs. Abbot. and that she and you may enjoy all the pleasure and his Grace all the benefit of Canterbury you can wish for, is the sincere wish of Your dutiful and affectionate Son

J. B.

67

JEREMIAH BENTHAM TO JEREMY BENTHAM

7 October 1766

I shd. have answer'd my dear Jerry's agreeable and Entertaining Letter to me at Weymouth, while I was there, if I cod. have

---

[5] Presumably on the tour he made with his father in 1764 (see letter 59, n. 1).

67. [1] B.M. I: 198–199. Autograph. Docketed by Bentham: '⟨From⟩ My Father. Letter on his Marriage.'

concluded with any certainty where to direct to him; and at the arrival of Mr. Clark's to me, I was gone with a Party of Ladies and Gentlemen to the Isle of Purbeck, to see that most antient and confessedly most respectable Piece of Ruins in the Kingdom, Corfe Castle; upon my return back to Weymouth I had reason to think you were both decamp'd from Bristol. I am much pleas'd with the account Mr. Clark has given me of your friendly Reception at Mr. Vernon's which I must own far exceeded my Expectation; and you may assure yourself, my dear Jerry, I shall not be wanting in making my acknowledgements to Mr. and Mrs. Vernon[2] for their Civilities to you whenever I have opportunity—I came home Thursday the 18th, and was glad to find by Mr. Clark when he return'd that you got to Browning Hill before your Aunt sat out for Bath, and that Mr. Clark was so well pleas'd with the Entertainment he met with among our friends at Browning Hill and Steventon, and have no doubt but that they were equally pleas'd with him. Your Aunt's Absence is an unlucky Circumstance for you, however it was better for you to continue in Hamshire than to come up to Town, as things are Circumstanc'd at present, since you cod' have no Bed at home, on Account of the new Building and the General Repair, which makes it very troublesome and Disagreeable being here but which I hope will pay me in the Satisfaction I flatter myself with the Enjoyment of in Consequence of it. Since my Return, I have been greatly engag'd in preparing for the approaching Change of my Condition, but not so engag'd in that as to be unmindful of my dear Jerry, for whom I have been anxious to provide, as far as my Ability will extend, a decent and comfortable Situation of Life and to Intrust him with the means to that End independant of every Consequence that may possibly happen to myself, and for that purpose I have already made and Executed a Deed of Gift whereby I have Convey'd to your Uncle Grove In trust for you, in

Addressed: 'To / Mr. Bentham / at Mr. Grove's / at Browning Hill / near Basingstoke / Hants.' Postmark: '7 OC'. Forwarded: 'To / Mr. Bentham / near Queen's Square / Westminster.'

A week after the date of this letter, on 14 October 1766, Jeremiah Bentham was married to Mrs Sarah Abbot, as he announces in a letter to Richard Clark (U.C. CLXXIII: 38). Mrs Abbot (d. 1809) was the daughter of Jonathan Farr of Moorfields, citizen and draper of London, and the widow of the Rev. John Abbot, D.D. fellow of Balliol and rector of All Saints', Colchester. Letter 68 and note 1 thereto explain the circumstances under which the present letter was received.

[2] Bentham and Clark had visited the Vernons in Bristol (cf. Bowring, x, 46, where, however, Bentham has confused the 1764 tour with his father and the 1766 tour with Richard Clark). They seem to have been the parents of Mr Browne's wife (cf. letters 71 and 213).

regard you yourself are under Age, my Estate at Eastwood, and such Part of the Estate at Barking as is let to the Malster, both which are let to good Tenants at £103 a year, and which I propose shall be paid to you from this last Michaelmas. I have likewise with the Assistance of Mr. Clarke been all over Lincoln's Inn and both the Temples to get Chambers for you, and have luckily met with a Set which tho not large, are yet very neat and very pleasantly situated in Elm Court No. 1. and which front the Inner Temple Lane where you have a full View of the Garden that has a Fountain Constantly playing, and as the Chambers were compleatly furnish'd, and the furniture to be dispos'd of I got Mrs. Abbot to give me her opinion of 'em, and indeed there is an Elegance in the furniture from their being so well adapted to the Chambers, that she was much pleas'd with 'em; and at her Recommendation I have actually bought all the furniture and paid for em, at the Valuation of £70—which I was the rather inclin'd to do as by purchasing the furniture I reduced the Rent of the Chambers to £21 a year which wod. otherwise have been £35 and which would have been too much for you to Pay. As I propose to Paper the Upper Rooms here and to put a Bed in the Room where your Books were, I have removed your Books to your Chambers, where there are two handsome Sash Book Cases to Receive them; so that when you come up to Town you will find a Set of Chambers compleatly provided with every Convenience ready for you, and nothing that I can think of wanting for your Accommodation, and now I have plac'd you in such a Situation; surely I may claim every Return that might be expected from a Child for whom I have ever shewn the tenderest regard; I thank God I have hitherto had no reasons to Entertain the least apprehensions of a disappointment; and as you have every encouraging Circumstance to quicken and animate your Endeavours to qualify yourself for the Profession you are design'd for; I hope you will make so good a use of your Time, before you can be called to the Bar, by persevering in a regular Course of Study at your Chambers, and by a constant attendance upon the Courts of Justice, as to enable yourself to make every proper Return[?] to your friends that may employ you, by being really useful to them, which you must be sensible is the surest means of continuing their good offices—and consequently of building your own fortune.

In the Resolution I have taken to change my Condition ⟨. . .⟩ ⟨. . .⟩ my happiness to do it, with one, that has given the Strong⟨est⟩ ⟨. . .⟩ of her regard for me and my Connections that any one ⟨. . .⟩ by not desiring any Part of my fortune besides what she ⟨. . .⟩ ⟨. . .⟩ in common with her own while we both live ⟨. . .⟩ ⟨. . .⟩ Consideration of which (if there needed any other, th⟨. ⟩ ⟨. . .⟩ of the generous and obliging Temper and disposition w⟨. .⟩ ⟨. . .⟩ Abbot shews upon every occasion /when there is any the least Claim to her Friendship and regard/ will I hope meet a suitable Return from you; and it is with pleasure⟨. . .⟩. ⟨I⟩ can assure you that she has frequently expressed much Satisfaction, in your obliging behaviour to her. And as I have all the reason in the World to promise myself a faithful disinterested and agreable friend and Companion in her for the Rest of my Life, I hope it will prove an inviting Circumstance to you, to come oftener here from Inclination than Duty. We shall have a Table and Bed ever open to receive you. We propose this day Seven-night for the Day of our Marriage, and that the Ceremony shall be perform'd by Dr. Smith, the Master of Westmr. School[3] either at St Margarets or Westmr. Abbey. Immediately after which we shall set out, for a few Days, upon a Journey to Suffolk, which is a Part of the Country Mrs. Abbot has never been in as great a Traveller as She has been; since our Return from Weymouth we have had a very pressing Invitation (from a Gentleman and Lady of her Acquaintance we met with there) to Lechlade a Town you passed thro' in Gloucester-shire, but we have declin'd going thither till next Summer, when we may have time to make another Visit besides still further at Abergavenny. upon our return from Suffolk we shall be in Abingdon Street, Sammy and all, till this House is fit for us, and there Mrs. Abbot will receive her Visits upon the Occasion. I shall have a Suit of Cloathes made for you, against you come up, which you may do any time, ye. latter end of this or the beginning of next Month. I imagine you find an agreable House at Mr. Mackreth's[4]—with my sincere respects to Aunt Mulford and your Uncle and Cousin, believe me ever

My dear Jerry
Your affectionate Father
Jer^h Bentham

Oct 7th 1766

P.S. I have given the Deed I have Executed for you into ye hands of Mr Clark to be delivered to your Uncle when he comes to town.

---

[3] Samuel Smith (*c.* 1732–1808) was headmaster of Westminster School from 1764 to 1788.

[4] Cf. letter 65, n. 2.

68

JEREMY BENTHAM TO JEREMIAH BENTHAM

16 October 1766 (Aet 18)

Queen's Square
Octr. 16th 1766.

Hond. Sir

Yesterday evening I arrived here from Steventon, and not being willing to interrupt the general joy for the happy event, of which I was soon inform'd, I sat out immediately for the S;S; House, but finding Mr. Clark was gone to Twickenham to spend some time, I went to Mr. Browne's, where by a happy temerity I possessed myself of that letter which I shall preserve with reverence as long as I live, as the most important testimony of the affection of the kindest of Parents. the surprize however with which I was struck, and the agitations I underwent, before they were so agreeably suppress'd may be better imagined upon a recollection of the various circumstances, than express'd; my apprehensions suggested to me the having heavily offended by my stay in the Country which was longer than by what I mention'd to Mr. Clark I had given reason to expect, longer indeed than it would have been by a fortnight, had it not been for the kind violence put upon me by Mr. Mulford, who detained me during that time a half willing half unwilling prisoner. but now, upon understanding your pleasure in that particular supposing me to be still in Hampshire, and not knowing where to lay

---

68. [1] B.M. I: 200–201. Autograph. Docketed by Mary Bentham[?]: '1766 Octr. 16. J.B. Q.S.P. Congratulations on marriage.'

Addressed: 'To / Mr. Bentham.'

Bentham did not know of his father's marriage until the day after it took place, 15 October, when he came up to London from Steventon, where he had been staying with his cousin Mulford. He went to Queen's Square Place, where he learnt the news, presumably from the servants. His irritation at not having been informed was increased by his uncertainty as to where his father intended him to live henceforth. His friend Clark was out of town, and there was no one with whom he could discuss the matter. Letter 67 from his father had evidently missed him through being directed to Browning Hill after he had left there for Steventon. It was re-directed to Queen's Square and Bentham possessed himself of it when he called at the house of his father's friend Browne. This set some of his doubts at rest; but thinking it would be difficult for him to study at Queen's Square Place at this time, and perhaps with a resentful feeling that it was no longer his home, he returned forthwith to the doubtless sympathetic Mulford. Concerning all this his father shows some understanding and real concern in a letter to Richard Clark dated 'Abingdon Street Monday 20 Octr. 1766 (U.C. CLXXIII: 39) and thanks Clark and 'my good friend Mr. Hawkins' for an invitation to Twickenham (the home of John Hawkins) which they have sent to Jeremy. (For Hawkins see letter 62, n. 3.)

my head, nor seeing a possibility of studying were I to remain here, which I can't by any means dispense with doing, and which I have done assiduously during the extra time spent at Mr. Mulford's, I have taken the resolution, which I hope will meet with your approbation, of making an attempt to return thither to morrow morning or rather to night, however impatient to pay my duty to both my parents. but as that happy time is still at *some* distance, I cannot delay 'till then my sincerest congratulations on the auspicious event, attended with the most ardent wishes for your mutual felicity: which as far as I may say without presumption, carry with them a security of their completion. and may you, for it is hard if a disinterestedness in deed should not be returned by at least a disinterestedness in thought, and I have examined my heart and can truly say I wish it, may you, if that should be an addition to your happiness, be blessed with a family of other children; and I will be their father whenever they and I shall be so unfortunate as to want that loss supplied.

Your description having greatly inflamed my curiosity of taking a peep at my Chambers[2] before my departure, and having a commission to execute for Mr. Mulford that way, I went this Evening to satisfy it, and Mr. Jones[3] was so good as to shew me the way: I luckily found the Bedmaker in the Rooms cleaning them: but if my expectation was raised by your account how much was it exceeded by the apartment itself? the elegance of the fitting up perfectly surprised me, and I could hardly forbear crying as the children do, is all *this* mine, and *this* too? indeed I had almost said, that after creating me such powerful inducements to stay at home, you did well to engage me to this, by making it the residence of a Lady, for whom inclination ever inspired me with the highest esteem and respect, when I little thought it would become my duty: and permit me to boast that, that lady, whom I will now for the first time call by the endearing name of mother, was *my* first acquaintance: and that if *you* have known her better, *I* at least have known her longer.

being just going to set out for Piccadilly I have time to add no more, than to beg your excuse for the badness of my pen, strictly and metaphorically, owing to the hurry and distraction I am in, which I can account for no other way than from being whirled

---

[2] The chambers his father had taken for him in the Middle Temple (see letter 67).

[3] Of several possible identifications the most likely seems to be Thomas Jones, third son of Robert Jones, bookseller in the Middle Temple, who was admitted to the Middle Temple on 6 June 1764.

round in the general vortex; and to acquaint you and my Mother, which I am enabled to do with pleasure, that Farr[4] is mended to day very considerably, and lastly to assure you with the utmost gratitude that I am and ever will be

Your's and her dutiful and affectionate Son
Jeremy Bentham.

69

To Samuel Ray

Early 1767 (Aet 18)

Had my father in reality conceived any such resentment as you apprehend, for which I am satisfied he has little reason and less inclination, the pretence of adopting it would but ill justify me in the breach of those obligations of gratitude and affection by which I am bound to you. but it was your kindness to accompany a gentle admonition with the suggestion of some excuse however in-

---

[4] Mrs Abbot had two children by her former marriage, who now came to live at Queen's Square Place.

The elder was John Farr Abbot (1756–94); Westminster School from 1763 till 1770 or later; admitted to the Inner Temple; Clerk of the Rules in the Court of King's Bench; F.R.S. 20 June 1793; married, 13 July 1786, Mary, daughter of Thomas Pearce; died 22 September, 1794 (*Record of Old Westminsters*).

The younger was Charles Abbot, Speaker of the House of Commons and 1st Baron Colchester (1757–1829); educated at Westminster, Christ Church and Lincoln's Inn; Vinerian Scholar in 1781 and subsequently Vinerian Fellow at Oxford; joined the Oxford Circuit in 1783; F.R.S. 14 February 1793; Clerk of the Rules in the Court of King's Bench 1794 to 1801. In 1795 he entered Parliament under the patronage of the Duke of Leeds. He concerned himself with practical improvements in legislation, and in his first session obtained a committee to enquire into the manner of dealing with expiring laws. In 1796 he married Elizabeth, daughter of Sir Philip Gibbes, Bart. In December 1800 he introduced the first Census Act. He was Chief Secretary for Ireland in 1801–02, being appointed by his friend Addington. From 1802 till 1817 (when he was created Baron Colchester) he was Speaker of the House of Commons. 'He was a Tory of the Sidmouth rather than the Pitt school' (*D.N.B.*). (See also *Alumni Oxonienses* and *Record of Old Westminsters*.)

69. [1] B.M. I: 212–213. Extremely rough autograph brouillon. It is docketed, probably by Mary Bentham, thus: 'probably 1767—J.B.—Cousin Mulford praising highly his mother in law'. The date given here as '1767' looks more like '1787', but the third figure is hard to read, and the topic indicates early 1767.

Lady Bentham's docket is evidently mistaken: the letter is apparently to Bentham's cousin the Rev. Samuel Ray, who lived at Kenton in Suffolk, for he enquires after Mrs Ray. A letter survives which this gentleman wrote to the infant Bentham in 1754, congratulating him on his recovering from inoculation for the smallpox (B.M. I: 13, 3 June 1754). It is dated from Kenton. The Rays were relations of Bentham's paternal grandfather, and a member of the family paid for the education of Jeremiah Bentham (see Bowring, x, 3, 25).

104

sufficient. I have now indeed but too much reason to accuse myself of backwardness, as I had before of forwardness in obtruding that book upon you without any previous introduction or apology: which however I should not have done, if I cou'd with any conscience have detained the honest old Messenger any longer. the truth is, that seeing you take a pleasure in those pursuits I thought it might afford you some entertainment to peruse an account of that System which had made so much noise and occasioned so great a revolution in the Botanical world. the impetuosity of youth not allowing me time to reflect that tho' it had enabled me to scramble through that long ambages of hard words, the inducement might not be sufficient to operate upon my Cousin whose experienced years could teach him to make a proper estimation of the importance of the object, and the trouble in attaining it. My passion which was then at it's height is now considerably abated; and I am content at present to consider that as an occasional amusement, which before I made rather too principal a study. It is with pleasure I can confirm to you the favourable account you are pleased to say ⟨you⟩ have heard of my father's choice, and from the best authority: for such in this case is that of a Son-in-law, who is but too often the last person to do it justice. I began to be acquainted with her shortly after my own Mother's death: as soon, or I believe, a little sooner than my father: for some years there has been the strictest intimacy between the two families: she always had my esteem in the highest degree: and it cost me but little to improve that esteem into respect, when the voice of duty required it. since their marriage she has ever behaved to me and my Brother to speak in a word, in the same manner, (making an allowance for the difference of ages) as to her own Children, whom she tenderly loves. they form together a little Triumvirate, in which, very differently from the 2 great Cabals distinguished by that name, there reigns the most perfect harmony. For some time I had seen the necessity of having a place wherein to pursue my studies apart from the interruptions of a family, and sollicited my father to provide me with Chambers in some Inn of Court: upon his marriage he complied: and I am now settled by his bounty in a neat Apartment in the Middle Temple prettily furnished in a pleasant situation. Pardon my dwelling so long on the affairs of our family which from the kind concern you have ever shewn for it's welfare, I thought would not be entirely uninteresting, and may I be permitted to express how great would be my thankfulness for the satisfaction now and then of hearing from your self, of your health and Mrs. Rays. that you may not want the means of doing

it, if you should ever be disposed to favour me so far, tho' I would
not urge it at the expence of your ease and against your inclination,
I will subjoin a di⟨rection.⟩ in the mean time believe me to be with
all sincerity and affection your respectful humble Servt. and Cousin.

70

To Jeremiah Bentham

22 February 1767 (Aet 19)

Hond. Sir

You have begun I suppose by this time to expect an account
of my having taken my degree[2]; that ceremony is not yet performed, but will I hope in about a fortnight's time: the cold I mentioned to you in my last stuck by me and harrassed me a good
while, and incapacitated me a good deal for business: but has now
happily left me.

I called several times at the Master's of Baliol, but could not
meet with Mrs. White at home till the day before yesterday. Years
have made some alteration in her since I saw her last: their weight
has made her bend; and her hair is as white as snow: she seemed
however, perfectly chearful: and her eyes so good, as to permit her
to employ herself in needlework. the eldest Miss Waldoe was there,
who has taken the prænomen of Mrs., and the youngest Miss Leigh—
the eldest you know has been married some time: I did not see Mrs.
Leigh, and therefore wou'd not enquire after her, imagining she
might be dead. not having seen or heard any thing of that family
for a considerable time, I was afraid of making any enquiries.[3] the
old Gentleman, who is as hearty as ever knew me perfectly well,
and enquired after you and my Mother, whom it seems he had
known at Abingdon: they had heard of your marriage from Dr.
Parker.[4] the old lady seemed glad to see me, and Miss Leigh gave
me a general invitation. I am not certain whether I should have
gone had it not been for a Message Mrs. White sent me by Tommy

---

70. [1] B.M. I: 202–203. Autograph. Docketed by Jeremiah Bentham: 'Jeremy
Bentham / Letter datd. Oxford 22d Febry. 1767.'

Addressed: 'To / Jeremiah Bentham Esqr. / near Queen's Square / Westminster.'
Stamped: 'TETSWORTH'. Faint postmark: '23 FE'.

[2] His M.A. degree.

[3] The Master of Balliol was Theophilus Leigh (cf. letter 11, n. 4). Mrs White had
also visited him in 1762 (cf. letter 44); Miss Waldoe was her niece (cf. letter 2, n. 6).

[4] Unidentified.

Bentham[5] who went there one day to play with a little boy that was there, that she wondered I had never been to see her.

I received a letter from my Aunt yesterday in which she mentioned the having received one from you: she is so kind as to say she will defer her going to Town till my return: tho' all the roads are so bad about Browninghill that she cannot stir out; and would therefore think London at present the most eligible place. Poor Parson Hudson[6] it seems is like to die, if he should, the Lord have mercy on his helpless family of a wife and eight daughters.

Since my last my All Souls friends are come to College: I have called upon them there and their situation in respect to chambers and every other convenience seems very enviable: all the books of that noble library are entirely at their command to take if they please into their rooms.

I was at the Musick-room last Monday night, and plaid there; pray tell Mr. Clark who has often enquired of me about it that the Musick is very orthodox, more so than much that is plaid in London: I could have wished to have wrote to him before this time: but 'till my mind is disburthened from the weight of my present engagements it is as much as I can do to comply with what duty demands from

Your affectionate Son
Jeremy Bentham

Sunday Feb 22d. 1767

71

To Jeremiah Bentham

4 March 1767 (Aet 19)

Hond. Sir

Since my last I find that a formality observed in the College will retard my taking my degree sometime longer: next Sunday is appointed for our taking the Sacrament; and it seems that 8 days before and as many after, there is never any business done in the hall: so that I cannot read during that time the two lectures that

---

[5] Thomas Bentham (1758–1803), son of Dr Edward Bentham (cf. letter 11, n. 3); matric. Christ Church December 1772.

[6] Unidentified, but perhaps parson of Baughurst in view of the context.

71. [1] B.M. I: 204–205. Autograph. Docketed by Jeremiah Bentham: 'Son Jeremy / Oxon / 4 March 1767.'

Addressed: 'To / Jeremiah Bentham Esqr. / near Queen's Square / Westminster.' Stamped: 'OXFORD'. Postmark: '5 MR'.

remain for me to read. that will delay me 'till Wednesday in next week and Thursday and Saturday are days on which declamations are spoken: Friday then being the only day in next week on which I can read my lectures, I shall not have finished them 'till the Monday after. It will then be uncertain on what day a Convocation will be held by which degrees are conferred. On Monday next Mr. Hornsby[2] will begin his course of Natural Philosophy: he has it seems made several Improvements and additions to this course, which will render it completer than any of the former ones, either of his own or his predecessors: if it meets with your approbation, I should like extremely to attend: as I should hope to make much more advantage of it now, than I could at the time I attended before. I went then, I must confess, chiefly to see the pretty things: I should now go with other views. As he will read every day, the Course will last no longer than a Week, it will not therefore keep me much longer than I should otherwise have staid: and as I attended a course with Mr. Bliss, I should be admitted upon the same footing of paying a Guinea as those whose second it is with the present Professor. as I mentioned something of this before I left Town and you seemed not to disapprove of it, to save you the trouble of writing if you should not be disposed, I will take it for granted I have your permission if I hear nothing to the contrary before Monday: though a positive would be much more acceptable, than such a negative authority.—I was examined on Friday last. the little Parson Coleman[3] who happened to come to Oxford to preach before the University, was one of my Examiners. I tried to get Masters from All Souls: but there are none it seems of that rank now in College: out of 15 or 16, there are but 4 or 5 Seniors, Drs. and the rest, either Batchelors or Undergraduates—My six Lectures in the Schools, vulgarly called Wall lectures, are likewise over.

Your Intelligence of the Revolution in the Vernon family,[4] as you might well imagine, surprized me exceedingly: as to the behaviour of the old Brute, it is no more than one would expect: I am however extremely glad to hear that Mr. and Mrs. Browne have not withdrawn their countenance and affection from their unfortunate

---

[2] Thomas Hornsby (c. 1733–1810), Professor of Astronomy and Reader in Experimental Philosophy since 1763; matric. Corpus Christi February 1747, B.A. 1753, M.A. 1757. He became the first Radcliffe Observer in 1772 and Radcliffe Librarian in 1783. He was Sedleian Professor of Natural Philosophy from 1783 till his death.

[3] Charles Coleman, for whom see letter 61, n. 1.

[4] The Vernons were a Bristol family whom Bentham visited in 1766 (cf. letter 67, n. 2). We have no further information as to the 'revolution' here mentioned.

Sister; whose error can be deemed unpardonable only by those who pass a relentless censure upon offences against mere worldy prudence, who at the same time would slightly regard or even be guilty themselves of the most flagrant ones against Religion and morality.

The Frank you were so kind as to send me enclosed. I have received, and return you all due thanks and am

Your dutifull and affectionate
Son
Jeremy Bentham

Oxon. March 4th Ashwednesday 1767

72

TO RICHARD CLARK

26 March 1767 (Aet 19)

My dear friend

I have hitherto deferred writing to you reserving that pleasing employment in store as a refreshment after the labour of Academical exercises: but as my advancement to that pinnacle of honour which was the object of them has been hitherto retarded by the intervention of several accidents, to which these things are liable, I must lose no time in mentioning a Scheme that has just occurred to me, which if I were to delay any longer it would be too late to propose to you. My father has probably informed you of my attending a Course of Natural Philosophy which will continue till Saturday se'nnight the 11th of next Month. now if you could so contrive your affairs as to run down for 2 or 3 days between this and then, you might have an Opportunity which if I know you at all will not be unacceptable of being present at them as long as you stay. The three or four last concerning the nature and properties of Air may be very well heard separately from the rest and from one another: if you were to come 3 or 4 days before the conclusion, we might return ogether. tho' I could hardly expect this should be sufficient to incline you to take such a journey, if it were the sole inducement, yet I hope when added to the other considerations we have so often discuss'd, it may prevail with you to stretch a point if it should not

---

72. [1] U.C. CLXXIII: 40. Autograph. Docketed by Clark (?): '26 March 1767. Mr. Jeremy Bentham's letter.'

Addressed: 'To Mr. Clark / at / the Old South Sea House / Old Broad Street / London.' Faded postmark.

be totally incompatible with your engagements. if I am not mistaken, it will not be much wide of the time when you thought you
should probably have some little leisure. If this should find you
much engaged, I will not insist on requesting any other answer than
a bare yes or no, but that I hope you will not deny me. in the mean
time it may be some satisfaction to you to know that Dr. Roberts
received our letter, and acknowledged it by Mrs Roberts to Mrs
Bentham in an obliging manner.[2] Pray remember me with all respect to Mr. and Mrs. Hawkins, and tell Mr. Hawkins that I have
executed his commission, and am ready for any other he shall
please to entrust me with. Know likewise by me, and grieve with
me for the general concern of mankind that Mr. Harrison's[3] project
for discovering the Longitude which was thought to have been
accomplished is come to nothing. That his timepiece in the 2
several trials that were made of it by sending it to the West Indies
performed what was designed was owing to an artifice: it has since
been found while remaining in England to have gone extremely
irregular. the artifice he made use of was this: he had never pretended that it would go exactly true, but if the variation were uniform, it would be the same thing, as it might be easily allowed for.
in order to make it appear so he calculated what the degree of heat
would probably be at the latitude to which he was to go, and applying to his timepiece an artificial heat equal thereto, he observed
what the variation amounted to. I think it was a second lost in
every 24 hours: he therefore just before the Ship was to sail gave
that in to the board as the rate of variation, and declared he would
abide by it: accordingly at the conclusion of the voyage the irregularity of the variation was found to be very small, and considerably
within the limits prescribed by the Statute. during all this time he
would never trust it out of his own Custody: he even carried his
precautions so far, as to desire that he might have notice whenever
a Gun was going to be fired, on which occasions he used to set it on
his lap and shield with his Coat from the violent concussion of the
Air. he also kept it on his lap whenever there was a high Sea. the

---

[2] See letter 66, n. 2. The Mrs Bentham in question is the wife of Dr Edward Bentham of Christ Church.

[3] John Harrison (1693–1776), a mechanician, who devised various important
improvements in horology. In 1713 an Act had been passed offering large rewards
for various degrees of improvement in the methods of determining the longitude. In
1735 Harrison constructed an instrument for this purpose for which he obtained £500.
Throughout his life he constructed various improved time-pieces of this kind, obtaining various rewards and campaigning for larger ones. He was known as Longitude
Harrison.

reason of which precautions was, the axes of the wheels being so exceedingly small to diminish the friction, that the least shake would have been liable to have broken them. so that that imperfection alone would have been sufficient to have rendered it unfit for general use. but after the performing the last voyage, when as an ultimate test it was placed for 4 months in the hands of the Professor[4] at Greenwich, it was found to go so very irregular that a good watch made upon the common principles would have done almost as well. the whole account of this affair was communicated to us by the Professor on Tuesday at the conclusion of his lecture. If I should be so happy as to see you here, I will beg the favour of you to take the first and last 2 or 3 words of my Froissart and Caxton's Polychronicon[5] that I may supply the deficiencies from some library ⟨. . .⟩ ⟨. . .⟩

Your's sincerely and affec⟨tionately⟩
J. Bentham

Queen's Coll. Oxon
    Thursday March 26th 1767

tomorrow if nothing farther happens to prevent me I think of taking my degree.

73

To Jeremiah Bentham

27 March 1767 (Aet 19)

Queen's Coll. Oxon. Friday March 27th 1767

Hond. Sir
    I have just time to acquaint you with my having taken my degree this morning which several accidents had conspired hitherto to put off: be pleased to excuse my abruptness, as I have but just time to seal this up before dinner, after which I shall go up with the fellows into the Common Room, and from thence immediately to Mr.

---

[4] Presumably Thomas Hornsby (see letter 71, n. 2.)

[5] Caxton's edition of John Trevisa's translation of the *Polychronicon* of Ranulphus Higden was publishd in 1482, with subsequent editions in 1495 and 1527.

73. [1] B.M. I: 206–207. Autograph. Docketed by Jeremiah Bentham: 'Son Jeremy / Lr. datd. Oxon 27th March 1767 / of his having taken his Degree of Master of Arts.'
    Addressed: 'Jere.ʰ Bentham Esqr. / Queen's Square / Westminster.' Stamped: 'OXFORD'. Postmark: '28 MR'.

Hornsby's lectures which will take up all the intermediate time between this and the going out of the post. I am

Your dutiful and affectionate Son
J. Bentham

Dutifull respects to my Mother.

74

To RICHARD CLARK

2 April 1767 (Aet 19)

Thursday April 2d. 1767

Dear Sir

I reꞓed your letter last night and am exceedingly rejoiced at the hopes you give me of your Company. the Lectures finish sooner than I expected—they conclude on Thursday next. so that then I shall be at liberty to return with you: but do not stint yourself as to time if you can help it. the weekly concert is of a Monday: as there are several foreigners that attend the lectures who are not gownsmen, and it is a common thing to introduce people who are not subscribers, I make no doubt of obtaining the like liberty in your behalf. I am obliged to you for the extracts from my books, and will do what I can towards compleating them, as you desire, before you come. I have met with the following works mentioned in the Catalogue of Bodleian Manuscripts.

De Musicâ continuâ & discretâ cum Diagrammatibus per Simonem de Tustude. Anno 1351|—Metrologus liber the planâ Musicâ. /bound up together/ |Compositio consonantiarum in Symbolis secundum Boëtium.| Joannis de Muris musica. |Gilbertus de proportionibus fistularum ordinandis.|—Tunes set in Old French and Spanish.[2] I mention this that you may communicate it to Mr Hawkins, who if there should be some of them that he has never heard of might be glad to know something about them. the first article I have looked at. it is written on Velom in rather an obscure

---

74. [1] U.C. CLXXIII: 41. Autograph. Docketed by Richard Clark: '2d April 1767. Mr. Jeremy Bentham's Letter.'

Addressed: 'To / Mr. Clark / at / the Old S: Sea House / Old Broad Street / London.' Postmark: '3 AP'.

Written from Oxford. Apparently he no longer had a room in college, but lodged with a Mrs Bull.

[2] Apart from the last ('Tunes') these works are identifiable in Volume I of the *Bodleian Catalogue of Western Manuscripts.* The vertical strokes in the text have been added by the editor to make the punctuation clearer.

112

hand and full of diagrams which are drawn confusedly in inks of different colours. in it I observed the words long, breve and semibreve, and notes down so low as the quaver. I think too there was a distinction of bars. I had not time for any very minute inspection as I only looked at it for about half an hour this morning; I convinced myself however that the date was as expressed in the Catalogue. it was with some trouble that I could make it out being full of abbreviations. if Mr. Hawkins should be desirous of being made further acquainted with this or any other of the books I mentioned I will beg you to bring down with you a book of court hand, which will assist me in making out the abbreviations. there may indeed be several other treatises of Musick in the Library besides those. there is one in the Catalogue of printed books by Johannes Faber Stapulensis. 4r.[?] libris. As it is uncertain by what conveyance you will come, I cannot propose any Scheme for meeting you: the only way therefore will be to direct the Coachman to set you down at the end of Magpy' lane opposite St Mary's Church, and the first house on the left hand is Mrs. Bull's where I lodge and where there will be room to accomodate us both. I am called off suddenly and am therefore obliged to subscribe myself

Yours sincerely and affectionately
J. Bentham

75

To Thomas Gwatkin

7 April 1767 (Aet 19)

Quod ad te non antehac scripserim, Gradûs petitio fuit in causâ: scilicet, non potui nisi improvidentiae /reus/, ea quae voluptatis esset quantumvis exoptata, necessariis negotiis anteponere: Jam, cum ejus negotii finem viderim, ex eo quod mihi reliquum est

---

75. [1] B.M. I: 210–211. Autograph. Docketed: '176[?]. I.B. Oxon / to / T. Gwatkin / Latin / Facienda for Degr.'

Thomas Gwatkin, the recipient of this letter, was the son of Thomas Gwatkin of Hackney, matric. Jesus 1763 aged 21. Evidently he had not pursued the regular course of study at Oxford, since Bentham's letter is largely concerned with the requirements Gwatkin would have to fulfil for his degree. In the event Gwatkin received his B.A. by decree of Convocation on 21 May 1778, and took his M.A. from Christ Church on 23 March 1781. He seems to have been one of Bentham's closest friends in the late 1760's and is mentioned in the will (84a below) Bentham made in August 1769. Subsequently Gwatkin went to America and was employed as tutor to the children of Lord Dunmore, Governor of New York and Virginia (cf. letter 138).

otii, non possum melius aut libentius insumere, quam ut sermones apud urbem de commercio epistolarum motos meâ culpâ intercidere non sinam. Verum metuo ne admotis statim oculis ubi chartam hanc Latinis oblinitatam litteris, tecum cogitaveris quid sibi vult molestus iste, qui se cum suâ barbarie interpellat? ut igitur me arrogantiae opinione liberem, ne in veluti[?] in certamen litterarium videar provocasse, habeo, id quod res est confiteri, in hoc me magis mihi ipsi quam tuis temporibus consuluisse. cum enim quadantenus in votis sit aliquam qualemcunque in Latinâ lingua facultatem adparare, reputabam, non mediocri id fore adjumento, si uti possem auxilio viri alicujus eruditi, qui necnon hujus modi consuetudinum inire non fuerit dedignatus. Vides, quam bellum ludimagistri coner tibi obtrudere: verum & id tibi prospectum sit, magistralis esse ordinis qui tuus cupit esse discipulus: Aut si hoc non valeat, at certe valebit apud te autoritas amici communis viri gravissimi Joannis Hawkins[2], qui me tibi, te mihi commendavit, ut mutuam hanc necessitudimem susciperemus. Neque tibi id omnino nisi mihi ipsi illuserem visum est displicuisse: praesertim cum acceperim ex Clerico nostro[3], percontatum te qua ratione litterae ad nos pervenire possint. Quare & eo nomine excusatum habeas cum adverteris id tantum me fecisse, quod in hâc re aequum est pro utriusque nostrum aetate, ut quae intellexi tua proposita anteverterem. Mandata tua quae ad gradum pertinent, ea quâ potui diligentiâ, exsecutus sum: dolet vero me non posse renuntiare quod tuis rationibus commode respondent. Quae enim ad gradum capessendum requiruntur sunt duo; Temporis praestituti completio, & eorum quod aiunt barbarâ voce exercitia versus: Hoc quod te non tangit, non nimis severe exigitur: Illud est, quod te urit in quod omnis pene vis legum incumbit ambienti. Gradum Baccalaurei in Artibus prius asservandi sunt ad minimum termini undecim citra eum quo quis quod aiunt matriculatus fuerit, eumque quo gradum suscipiat: de duobus aliis sine molestia dispensatum est: de tertio non sine[?] formulâ quâdam quae 40 circiter solidis constabit. Ad horum terminorum autumnalem & hybernum asservandos requiritur 28 dierum commoratio, ad vernum 21, ad aestivum 14. miserum est, Tempus non posse comprimi sicut aër, & in spatium angustius

Gwatkin's father was first cousin to John Hawkins (cf. letter 62, n. 3), through whom Bentham probably made Gwatkin's acquaintance (see Percy Scholes, *The Life and Activities of Sir John Hawkins*, 1953, p. 3).

Bentham's Latin dating is not wholly clear, but Tuesday 7 April 1767 seems to be the date he intended.

[2] See letter 62, n. 3.

[3] I.e. Richard Clark, for whom see letter 62, n. 1.

adigi. Quod si ullis iacturis[?] fieri potuerit[?] profecto hae non de-
fuissent: Post susceptum Baccalaureatum nihil ultra est, quod
multum exhibeat modestiae: duodecimo termino Magistratum licet
ambire, in quibus annumeratur is quo quis priorem gradum sus-
ceperit, sex quocunque modo datur transilire et quattuor igitur
tantumodo sunt asservandi, forsan et tres sufficiant tantum, verum
ubique intelligendum velim, non de tempore sed de sola commora-
tione dispensari. paene tramitem, inito calculo brevissimum com-
peri. At mehercule praeceptor tibi tribuendus est: scilicet, qui
moribus tuis prospiciat qui tibi Maronem aut Flaccum explicet: qui
quot sint praedicamenta edicat: qui denique mox cum adoleveris,
quo pacto triangulum aequilaterum sit describendum, doceat; quibus omnibus rebus tu tantopere indigeas. Insuper pro his tantis
beneficiis, octo aurei sunt ipsi annumerandi. verum ad id quod
attinet ultro pollicitus est mihi, meus qui fuit[4], si Reginensibus
velis te adscribere, aut parum aut nihil eo nomine accepturum.
pudet me profecto ejus qualiscunque sit dignitatis, quam tu eum
appetas, non possis nisi tantâ interpositâ morâ molestiâque ob-
tinere. qui de penu tuo depromere possis quantum sufficerit tribus,
ut modum servem hominibus qualibuscinque instruendis, quo
deinde ad capessendum magistralem gradum felici omine mitteres.
neque me putares adulari si nosses quantula nonnulli eruditione qui
omnia ista examina subeamus. expecto mox Clericum nostrum, qui
a me saepe efflagitatus tandem promisit se huc paulisper diver-
surum hodie: quanto cum studio tu licet conjicias, qui noris, quae
nostra familiaritas: eisdem ille litteris quibus me de proposito tuo
certiorem fecit valere nuntiavit Joannem Hawkins cum suis. Post
aliquot dies una Londinium concedimus. Vides quam longam con-
scripserim epistolam: tu vellem propositum exemplar sequare: &
si errata quae deprehendisses nisi vetet numerus inter rescribendum
adnotaveris, hebebis gratiosissimum discipulum.—puto patrem his-
toriae nostrum jamdudum perlectum placuisse: cum tu non sis ille,
apud quem liber inchoatum haereat[5]. Vale, meque inter tuos
numera. Dabam Oxoniae 7va.[6] Idus Aprilis die Martis 1767

Translation

The reason for my not having written to you before was the taking
of my degree; for naturally I could not, without being guilty of

[4] I.e. Jacob Jefferson, for whom see letter 10, n. 9.

[5] This presumably refers to a copy of Herodotus lent by Bentham to Gwatkin.

[6] Bentham apparently wrote '8 va' and then corrected the figure to a 7 without
changing the 'va' to 'ma'.

imprudence, put pleasure, however greatly desired, before necessary business. Now that I have seen the end of that business, I cannot employ the leisure I have at my disposal as a result better or more agreeably than by seeing to it that the discussions we began in town about exchanging letters do not come to nothing through my fault. I am afraid, however, that as soon as you cast your eyes on this letter, all filled with Latin characters, you will think to yourself, what is this troublesome fellow after, disturbing me with his barbarity? To avoid giving the impression of presumption, therefore, in case I should be thought to have thrown down a challenge, as it were, to literary combat, I must confess the true state of affairs, which is that in this matter I have considered myself rather than your convenience. For being somewhat desirous of acquiring a certain facility in the Latin language, I thought it would be of no small assistance if I could avail myself of the aid of some learned man and one too who should have condescended to institute a custom of this kind. You see how I am trying to thrust a schoolmaster's contest upon you: but do not overlook the fact that it is one of master's rank who wishes to be your pupil; or if this is not good enough, you will surely accept the authority of our common friend, that gravest of men, John Hawkins, who recommended us to each other with a view to our mutually supplying this need. Nor, unless I deceive myself, did this seem to be disagreeable to you: especially since I have heard from our friend Clark that you have been enquiring for means of sending letters to me. For this reason too, hold me excused on that account when you understand that I have done what is just, considering our respective ages, to anticipate what I understood to be your intentions. Your commissions in regard to the degree I have executed with all the diligence I could: I am grieved, however, to be unable to report that matters correspond completely with your reckoning. Two things are required for taking a degree; the completion of the prescribed period of time, and a series of what in their barbarous jargon they call "exercises". The latter, which does not affect you, is not over-strictly enforced. It is in respect of the former, which does worry you, that almost the whole force of the law falls upon the candidate. Before the degree of Bachelor in Arts at least eleven terms must be kept, not counting that in which one has matriculated, as they call it, or that in which one takes the degree: the two others are easily dispensed with, the third only by means of a process costing about forty shillings. Of these, to keep the autumn and winter term twenty-eight days' residence is required, for the spring term twenty-one, and for the summer fourteen. It is sad that time cannot be compressed like air and forced into a smaller space. If that could be done by means of any omissions these would indeed not have been wanting. After taking the Bachelor's degree, nothing further is required save great sobriety of conduct: in the twelfth term one may proceed to the Master's degree, including in the reckoning the term in which one took the first degree; of these six may be passed in any manner whatever, so that four only need be kept, or perhaps three may suffice; but throughout I would have it understood that the dispensation relates not to the length of time but solely to residence. I have, I may say, after making the reckoning, discovered the shortest route. But by Hercules! you must provide yourself with a tutor—to keep an eye on your conduct, of course, and to explain Virgil and Horace to you; to make known to you how many predicaments there are; and finally, when presently you have grown up, to teach you how an equilateral triangle is to be described—all of them things of which you stand in such great need. Besides, for all these great services eight guineas are to be paid over to him. But as far as that goes, the man who was my tutor has voluntarily promised me to take little or nothing on that account if you are willing to become a member of Queen's College. I am indeed ashamed of any distinction, be it what it may, which you cannot obtain when you desire it without first enduring so much delay and trouble—you who could produce from your own resources enough to teach three—not to exaggerate—three men of any kind whatever, whom you might then send up to take the Master's degree with happy prognostications. Nor would you think I was flattering you if you knew with how little learning some of us take all these examinations. I expect our friend Clark shortly, for after frequent urging on my part he has at last promised to come here today to stay for a little while; you can guess how eagerly I look forward to it, for you know how close our friendship is. In the same letter in which he informed me of your plan, he told me that John Hawkins and his family were well. After a few days we go together to London. You see what a long letter I have written: I should like you to follow the example I have set; and if when replying you noted the mistakes you may have detected—unless the number is too great—you will have a most grateful pupil.—I suppose you have now read and enjoyed my copy of the father of history; for you are not one with whom a book once begun hangs fire.

Farewell, and count me as one of yours. Oxford, Tuesday 7 April 1767.

76

T o   R i c h a r d   C l a r k

5 August 1767 (Aet 19)

My dear Friend

The length of Time that has elapsed since our separation, tho'
it has reminded me that I can no longer defer the taking up my pen,
has afforded me nothing to employ it on. that is to say, I have no
Marriages, Deaths, Births, nor Burials to inform you of; no trips
to Races or Assemblies, not so much as a visit to Sr. Charles's, or
Mr. Belmour's, from whence to take occasion to give you an
account of the Company, together with the Compliments of the
Ladies. My time on the contrary has glided on in a pleasing, tho'
uniform tranquillity: I might indeed have told you that I have
spent the greatest part of it between this place, Mr. Mackreth's at
Ewhurst, and Mr. Mulford's at Sherborn; but to me such an account
of passing time, tho' not unfrequently given, conveying no Idea but
that of locomotion, would seem extremely insipid. I will rather tell
you, that in my Uncle's library, which you know consists in great
measure of odd Volumes, I have met with the 3 first Vols in 12mo.
of Burnet's Hist. of his own times, which come down to the Revolution, and which my Uncle says, is the extent of the 1st Vol. of
the Folio Edition.[2] I have read it with great delight, and the
greater, for that it promises to be the means of drawing our political
Sentiments still nearer together. more, yea much more could I say
on this subject, but that my pen which is as diabolical as your's are
divine, will not permit to contract my type.[3] it was with great
regret, that when I came to the third Volume of the History I found
the thread of it prematurely cut short. I had nothing left for it, but
to betake my self to Locke's Essay: which has it⟨s⟩ place likewise
in the Collection of un-uniform Volumes. that you know is ground
not to be galloped over; I am accordingly yet on my way in the
first. Poor Ld. Coke, being of a gross habit of body and no good

76. [1] U.C. clxxiii: 42. Autograph. Docketed by Richard Clarke: 'Aug. 3d. 1767.
Mr. Jeremy Bentham's Letter.'
    Addressed: 'Mr. Clark / at / the Old South-Sea House / Broad Street / London.'
Stamped: 'reading'. Postmark: '6 AV'.
    The earlier part of the letter was written from Browning Hill. The later part is
written at the house of a neighbour, Mrs Noyes, whom he was visiting with his aunt.
    [2] Burnet's *History*, 12mo., vol. i–iii: of the edition published in six volumes at
Edinburgh in 1753.
    [3] The diabolical pen has forced him to write in a very large hand.

traveller,[4] did not make his way hither from Mr. Mulford's till this day: having been every day uncertain where I should be the next. My Aunt is planning Expeditions: but I own I am not fond of quitting this place, which you need not be told is the seat of my affections. thus far I had written, when I was called off by a Summons to prepare for a Journey to this place, which is the residence of Mrs. Noyes, whom you saw at Browning-hill. I have not informed any body of my writing to you, as I have no room for Compliments: which if I had, I presume would have been universal: let it suffice that very tender Enquiries have been made after you by this family. I cannot however omit, that every body at Browning-hill has repeatedly expressed to me how great would be their satisfaction to see you there. ⟨from what⟩ you told me, I have likewise not been without my hopes: let me know whether I may be yet permitted to entertain them. if you do not repent of your undertaking to give me an abstract of Priestly's account of the Electrical Kite,[5] direct to me at the Rev Mr. Hill's at Sherborn[6] near Basingstoke which is the place of Mr. Mulford's residence. I can no more, but to assure you, which yet I hope is almost unnecessary, that I am

Your's sincerely and affectionately

Jere[y]. Bentham

pray let me know if your intentions to go to Winchester still subsist.

Southcot near Reading Aug. 5th 1767

77

To Richard Clark

28 August 1767 (Aet 19)

My Dear Friend

I have rec̄ed your Letter with the extract, and am much obliged to you for the trouble you have given yourself, as well as pleased

---

[4] The reference is to either the *Reports* or the *Institutes* of Sir Edward Coke, chief justice of the Common Pleas and subsequently of the King's Bench, 1606–16.

[5] Joseph Priestley's *History and Present State of Electricity, with original experiments* was published in 1767 and had been reviewed in the *Critical Review* for May.

[6] The parish is properly Monks' Sherborne. Some rather unflattering comments on the incumbent are given in Bentham's letter to Samuel of 25 December 1806 (referred to in letter 8, n. 3). Cf. also letter 81.

77. [1] U.C. CLXXIII: 44. Autograph. Docketed by Richard Clark: 'Augt. 28 1767. Mr. Jeremy Bentham's Letter.'

Addressed: 'To / Mr. Clark / at the Old South Sea House / Broad Street / London.' Postmark: '31 AV'.

Presumably written at Browning Hill.

with the hopes of seeing you so soon. If I should not, I intend to return to London the 2d. week in next month, and proceed immediately to Suffolk. but if you have any project to propose, let me know it, and I will adjust my Scheme, to coincide with yours. if words are not very deceitful there is nobody here but would be happy in seeing you. if you should go through Parliament Street you will oblige me in buying Webb's Catalogue of Seeds, to bring down with you. it is a small Pamphlet and takes up no room. if not, it is of no consequence. I am your's

sincerely and affectionately
Jeremy Bentham

Friday Aug 28th 1767

78

To Jeremiah Bentham

26 September 1767 (Aet 19)

Kenton Saturday Septr. 26th 1767

Hond. Sir

I arrived here late last night after a sickly passage as far as Copdock, where I was met by my Cousin's Man with a very handsome pair of Horses, and found the roads good much beyond your expectation, owing it seems to the neighbourhood and attention of two Justices of the Peace, Mr. Chevalier[2] and Mr. Capper.[3] amongst the Passengers of the Coach, was one not of the smallest size, who was going upon a visit to Mr. Middleton's, of Crowfield Hall,[4] where he will no doubt meet with a warm reception: the Gentleman is no other than a fine fat Turtle. I write this in the morning, and

---

78. [1] B.M. I: 208–209. Autograph. Docketed by Jeremiah Bentham: 'Jeremy Bentham / Ld. datd. Kenton Suffolk / 26 Sepr. 1767.'

Addressed: 'To / Jeremiah Bentham Esqre. / Queen's Square / near St James's Park / Westminster.' Postmark: '30 SE'.

Bentham was staying at Kenton in Suffolk with his cousin the Rev. Samuel Ray. Apparently Clark and Bentham had visited the place together on some occasion.

[2] Probably Temple Chevallier (c. 1732–1804), Magdalene College Cambridge 1749, B.A. 1753, M.A. 1756; perpetual curate of Aspall and rector of Kedington and Wratting Magna, all in Suffolk.

[3] Francis Capper, second son of Francis Capper, Bencher of Lincoln's Inn (d. 1764), Westminster School 1742, matric. Christ Church 1753, aged 18, B.A. 1757, M.A. 1760; rector of Monk Soham and Earl Soham from 1759 till his death in 1818; author of The Faith and Belief of every sincere Christian.

[4] William Middleton (d. 1775), whose family had close connections with South Carolina: his wife was Sarah, daughter of Morton Wilkinson of that colony, and his younger son died there in 1785.

have not yet seen any of the Mickfield Family,[5] but may perhaps before I send it away, my Cousin William[6] being expected to dinner. Miss Sally Ray[7] is gone upon a visit to Diss: but I found two other young Ladies one of whom is a daughter of one of the Rays, and the other a Miss Allen sister to a person who married one of the daughters of Mr. Ray of Woodbridge.[8] the great dearth of all kinds of fruit has extended itself hither as well as every where else, and the winter was uncommonly severe: the two beautiful Cypresses we so much admired, as well as several other trees, were destroyed. I am a little surprised to hear of several Gentlemen of Oxford hereabouts: Mr. Capper was of Christ Church, and there is another of that College, whom I remember at Westminster School, that lives at Debenham, a Mr. Forrester.[9] Mr. Chevalier, it seems, has managed well in the comfortable State of Matrimony: he had not, I believe been many weeks married when we were here last: since when he has had 4 Children, 2 of which are dead, and a 5th is expected. Old Mr. Bacon[10] died very rich: it is said here that besides his estates, he left 60,000£ in Money.

My Cousin and Mrs. Ray both enjoy very good health in the main: yesterday indeed he had some Symptoms of an approaching fit of the Cholick, but he is better today: he now and then gets on Horseback and takes a little exercise: they both desire their best Respects to you and my Mother. I have now told you all the News I must therefore proceed to assure you what I hope is not so, that I am

Your dutifull and affectionate Son
Jeremy Bentham.

[5] The family of William Ray (c. 1708–79). Samuel Ray's younger brother. He was a prebendary of Wells from 1745 till his death. Cf. B.M. I: 13 (unpublished, but see letter 4, n. 1) where Samuel Ray refers to 'my Brother and Sister of Mickfield'.

[6] Presumably a son of the Rev. William Ray (cf. n. 5 above).

[7] Presumably a daughter of the Rev. Samuel Ray.

[8] Thomas Ray (d. 1773), headmaster of Woodbridge School from 1736 till his death: perhaps a brother of Samuel and William. His daughter Lydia married Loder Allen on 10 February 1765 (Suffolk Parish Registers: Marriages, II, ed. W. P. W. Phillimore and others, 1912, p. 84).

[9] Perhaps Henry Forester (c. 1743–1819), son of Paul Forester (c. 1693–1761), canon of Christ Church; Westminster School, King's Scholar 1757, Christ Church 1760, B.A. 1764, M.A. 1767.

[10] Nicholas Bacon died at Shrubland Hall, Coddenham, Suffolk on 22 April 1767 (Gentleman's Magazine); he was a brother of the scholar and critic Montagu Bacon (1688–1749).

79

To Jeremiah Bentham

12 July 1768 (Aet 20)

Chertsey Monday night
12 July 1768

Hond. Sir

You will expect to hear accounted for how I came not to breakfast with you as I intended; for that purpose I must give you the history of my proceedings—When I left you, I went to Mr. Tatischef,[2] who expressed great concern at having forgotten the appointment he had made with me for Thursday last, and particularly when I told him I should not see him again; and seemed extremely desirous of a direction to me in the Country, I promised to write to him from thence soon—I staid there but a short time, and then went to drink a dish of Tea at the Coffee House—it was then necessary to have my hair tied up that it might last when I could not have the opportunity of a Barber. when that Jobb was accomplished, I sat out for St. Paul's Church Yard with 4 pr. of old Shoes in my pockets and a bundle of a dozn. Arrows between my coat and my back to have them stowed in a vacant space in a double fiddle case I had making there. I had likewise to go to a Booksellers a contrary way to the former to make sure of a book that I feared would otherwise have escaped me. The things I had to send were so various, and the cases I had to send them in were so various likewise that it took me up no small time and trouble before I could perfectly adjust the contained to the containing— when that was at length accomplished there was not a crevice in any that would hold a handkerchief—You will wonder how all this abundance of employment could arise—you are to know then, that besides the Cloak bag, the Arrow-case, and the double Fiddle case at St. Paul's Church Yard, that were to be sent to ~~Oxford~~ Hampshire, I had a parcel to dispatch to Norfolk, and another to Oxford—

79. [1] Keynes Collection, King's College Cambridge. Autograph. Docketed by Jeremiah Bentham(?): 'Jeremy Bentham / Letter datd. Chertsey Surry / 12th July 1768.' (12 July was in fact a Tuesday.)

Addressed: 'To / Jeremiah Bentham Esqr. / Queen's Square / near St. James's Park / Westminster.' Postmark: '13 IV'.

Bentham spent some time in Chertsey in 1772 also. He probably stayed with Richard Clark, who appears to have had his country residence there: cf. the reference below to 'Mr. C.' and n. 4.

[2] One of two Russian brothers whom Bentham had met through the Rev. Mr Forster (see letter 248, nn. 4 and 5).

be it however as it may, after another call at the Coffeehouse for
some Supper, for running about all day long and packing had made
my hunger such as not to be resisted, it was $\frac{1}{2}$ after 12 before I went
to bed, and my labour not brought to a conclusion: as I had ordered
myself however to be called at 4 yesterday morning, I thought I
might still have done time enough to reach Richmond Park by
breakfast. I got up the instant I was called, and fell too again.
I then thought it would be prudent in order to prevent such an
accident as happened when my Books came to town after I had put
in one of the Bales of Cloth which were very heavy into the round
Arrow case to bind it round all over as tight as I possibly could with
strong packthread. in short after putting my house in order, locking
up teachests etc. disposing of my straggling books, putting on Shirt,
hair dressing, spatterdashes buttoning on which being new took me
near an hour and made my fingers so sore I feel it now, and writing
directions for the Laundress it was $\frac{1}{2}$ after ten and more before
I could set out—it was then evidently too late to think of visiting
Richmond—I breakfasted at the Coffee House and left the Temple
exactly at $\frac{3}{4}$ after 11. when I had walked 2 or 3 miles I began to
consider I had no great time to spare even tho' I had determined to
go directly to Twickenham—it was you know a very hot day: I kept
on however a pretty brisk trot, now and then with my book in my
hand, and had the happiness of getting to Mr. Hawkins's[3] door the
instant the Clock struck three—I rung—a Maid Servt. came to the
door—'Is Mr. Hawkins at home, pray?' 'No, Sir, he sent word
yesterday that he should not come 'till tomorrow to dinner.' this was
an occurrence I was not prepared to expect: I had little acquaintance
of the /remainder of the/ way, and secure of getting intelligence there,
I had not bestowed a thought about it. while I was endeavouring to
recollect the course of the Country, I sauntered, as I soon came to
consider, the contrary way to the Common, which was the right;
I was then turning to pursue the right way, when perceiving the
maid still staring after me, I did not care to betray my irresolution
and perplexity, and therefore endeavoured to strike out a way to
the Common by the back of Mr. Hawkins's and the other houses in
the Row. after a pretty many turnings and windings I found myself at last at Strawberry Green where was a direction post pointing
the way to Hampton. I knew *that* to be in the way and went on
about a mile, but beginning to feel rather faint and weary I was
tempted by the sight of a delicious Hayrick not far from the water,

[3] See letter 62, n. 3.

to sit and repose myself—I staid there two hours, I dined upon Epictetus's Morals which I had in my pocket. I do not know that I was any thing to signify less contented than if I had found Mr. H. at home just setting down to a fine piece of roast Beef. upon quitting my retreat I walked a considerable time before I came to Bushy Park, which I crossed, and then found myself in Pays de connoissance—when I got to Hampton[?] it was too late for dinner, and too soon for Tea, considering the walk I should have afterwards. at Sunbury there was ne'er a publick house above the rank of an Alehouse. Shepperton was almost at home—so that at last I got to ⟨Chertsey⟩ at 9 very tired very hungry, and very thirsty, not having eat or drunk since Breakfast—Mr. C.[4] came soon afterward, and with him Supper, neither of which I was sorry to see, especially the latter—to day I have been working very hard in both the Gardens—to morrow I set off as proposed, but without seeing Mr. Hawkins to my mortification.

But the principal business of this letter, I must not forget, the dimensions of the Chimney /in the Parlour below./ are as follows—Height 4F.–11.—Width 4F.–21.—Depth 1F.–91.—the Study has a Bath Stove—the 2 Chimney Pieces above are 2: 10—3: 1—1: 7. the Garden I have not measured but Tom has got the dimensions exactly.—When you send Thomas for Burrow's Reports,[5] I could wish you would let him on his return take to Mr. Tatischef at Mr. Forster's[6] the small pamphlet that lies upon them: it is an account of the designs of Dr. Bray's Associates.[7] this Ink is Chertsey Ink, and most villainous Stuff; so bad that I fear my censure on it will scarce be legible—it will I hope just enable me to subscribe myself, which it is my aim to be

Dear Sir, Your dutiful and
affectionate Son
Jere:ʸ Bentham.

[4] Someone (Jeremiah Bentham?) has annotated the manuscript thus: 'Alderman Clarke'.

[5] *Reports of cases adjudged in the Court of King's Bench, since the death of Lord Raymond* by Sir James Burrow (1701–82). Only the first (published 1766, covering the years 1756–58) of the five volumes had so far appeared.

[6] For Forster see letter 248, n. 1.

[7] *An Account of the Designs of the late Dr. Bray with an account of their proceedings* (1764) by John Burton (for whom see letter 14, n. 5). Dr Thomas Bray (1656–1730) vicar of St Botolph, Aldgate and commissary to the Bishop of London for Maryland, was founder of what became the S.P.C.K. He concerned himself with the conditions of negro slaves in the West Indies and North America. His work was carried on by a group known as 'Dr Bray's associates for founding clerical libraries and supporting negro schools'. Dr Burton was a strong supporter of their work.

80

TO JEREMIAH BENTHAM

21 July 1768 (Aet 20)

Browning-hill Thurs. July 21st 1768

Hond. Sir

I hope I have not outstayed your expectations of hearing from me from hence; the Ground required some time to be surveyed before I could be qualified to make my report. the conversations could not be introduced all at once, from whence those particulars were to be collected whereof you desired to be informed—sorry I am that the report which I have at last to make should be so un-favourable to all our wishes. I have perceived marks of a mutual aversion which I fear is too firmly established to be removed by any endeavours of mine, or any one else; it had it's root in the clause of the Deed of Partition by which the Essex Estate is to go to my Uncle if Mr. Mulford should have no issue. to speak the truth, it is not to be wonder'd at, that my Uncle knowing Mr. Mulford's caprices, and not knowing what inducements he might possibly have to make a different disposition of it, should be very sollicitous to prevent his making such an one as would be prejudicial to him-self: at the same time it is not more to be wondered at, that Mr. Mulford should be very uneasy at having his hands tied up. no reconciliation therefore can be expected, till Mr. Mulford can be satisfied that his own conduct was a sufficient justification for Mr. Grove to require and Mr. Mulford to consent that he should be controlled in the disposal of what he looked upon to be his own: and whether that it is ever like to be the case, I leave you to judge. the current of the resentment is from Mr. Mulford to my Uncle, and

---

80. [1] B.M. I: 216–217. Autograph. Docketed by Jeremiah Bentham: 'Fils Jeremy Bentham / Lr. datd. Baghurst Hants / July 21st 1768.' Docketed by Mary Bentham(?): 'Projected tour to Buxton etc.'

Addressed: 'To / Jeremiah Bentham Esqr. / Queen's Square / near St James's Park / Westminster.' Postmark: '25 IY'.

The death had recently occurred of Ann Mulford, the widowed mother of John Mulford, and sister to Bentham's (deceased) maternal grandmother. Bentham's account to Bowring (x, 24) of the disposal of her estate seems to be somewhat in-accurate. Apart from minor bequests, her will—made as long ago as 1752—directed that her estate be divided equally between her son John Mulford and her nephew (Bentham's uncle) George Woodward Grove. It was presumably difficulties over the division of the estate that caused the ill-feeling between the two cousins referred to in the present letter; and it is perhaps significant that the widow Mulford's will was not proved until 26 November 1768, at least four months after her death.

from my Aunt[2] back to Mr. Mulford. what my Uncle's feelings are, I know not with any certainty; what his right hand does, you know he keeps it from his left. I have never heard him mention the least word about the matter. I am inclined to think he surveys it with the same phlegmatic indifference he does, or appears to do every thing else—that temper of his, at the same time that it does not admitt of any extraordinary flights of benevolence, serves effectually to keep any resentment if he forms any, from appearing; tho' I must say I have always had reason to believe benevolence predominant. My Aunt's Death has no share in producing this discontent, but only in discovering it: Mr. Mulford now intends (and the Devil, I believe, if he was so disposed, could not keep him from it) to throw off the mask which he had kept on for his Mother's sake—as to the Will it was made in 1752, and with Mr Mulford's knowledge, who had, as soon as made, a Copy of it.

I am sorry poor Sammy must unavoidably lose his Country-house this Summer; we shall not however be deprived of it for the future as I expected. my Uncle tells me he intends to continue this house, that my Aunt may have a place to come to in the Summer, for in Winter she will be chiefly at Bath, and that there may be a place, as he says, where we may all meet: Mr. Mulford mentioned among the rest. his business he says fixes him to Whitchurch, but he is not fond of it, and thinks to retire here in his old age.

My Uncle has very kindly told me he intends giving me 10 Guineas for mourning; but as I have mourning of my own, he makes me the Offer, which you may imagine I cannot refuse of taking me with him in his journey to Buxton and whatever expence should be incurred beyond he will take upon himself: my Aunt indeed claims to take upon her her share of the extraordinaries. They propose setting out the beginning of next week; but as they are to make several visits in their way, at Southcot[3]; at Turville Court,[4] and 1 or 2 other places in Buckinghamshire, I am to meet them at Northampton. we all go on horseback—Aunt and all. Mr. Mulford will lend me his horse: he still talks of going to Exeter, but has agreed to let me off; if he should not set out time enough for me to return to meet them. I do not imagine he will go, however there is still a bare possibility of that journey too. My Aunt is still but low, there will be no great festivity I doubt in our peregrination, it will be a kind of a solemn progress; however I shall have the oppor-

[2] Presumably George Grove's sister Deborah.
[3] This was the home of Mrs Noyes: cf. letter 76, which is dated from there.
[4] The home of John Osborne, for whom see letter 64, n. 4; also letter 21 at n. 2.

tunity of seeing the Peak and the different Mines, which will be no small satisfaction. when we get to Buxton, which my Uncle proposes to make his head quarters for about a fortnight, we are not to confine ourselves there, but to make excursions 30, 40, or 50 miles if there is any thing worth seeing.

When you (I speak in the Dual Number) have perused ⟨this I⟩ could wish you would burn it; least at any distance of time it should chance to fall into the hands of any of the persons mention'd in it. such an event, as you may conceive might hereafter chance to happen; for which reason this precaution will I hope not appear entirely frivolous.

I am Hond. Sir
Your dutiful and affectionate
Son
Jeremy Bentham

I shall set out I imagine to meet my Uncle and Aunt in about 3 weeks from this day.

81

To Richard Clark

26 July 1768 (Aet 20)

I must not quit this station wherein you imagined me fixed, without acquainting you how Fortune has disposed of me. my Uncle has made me an offer (which I could not well refuse, neither indeed should be disposed to do it, since tho' the company is rather insipid, there will not be wanting I imagine, 'agreable circumstances,' to make the Scheme palatable) to take me with him and my Aunt upon an expedition to Buxton-Wells in Derbyshire, whither he is sent by his Physician for the benefit of his health. I shall thereby not only have the opportunity of satisfying the passion I have in some degree in common with Mr. Calcot,[2] of fathoming altitudes in the two opposite senses of the word, by climbing the mountains and penetrating the mines of that romantic Country, but the wish likewise

81. [1] U.C. CLXXIII: 45. Autograph. Docketed by Clark: '26 July 1768. Mr. Jeremy Bentham's letter from *Whitchurch*.'

Addressed: 'To / Mr. Clark / Old South Sea House / Old Broad Street / London.' Postmark: '27 IY'.

Written from his uncle George Grove's house at Whitchurch, Hants. It appears from letter 80 that Browning Hill was to be temporarily vacated.

[2] Unidentified.

127

that I have entertained of seeing that uncommon collection of
natural curiosities assembled at the Peak, in which I must be
countenanced by all those to whom admiration is a source of entertainment. I leave you to judge how many tacit wishes I have formed
if that can be called a wish, where accomplishment is not in the
least expected, of having you for a partaker of my satisfaction, and
a companion in my Journey. I might add,[3] if it could have any
effect, that my wishes are not the only ones in the company.—My
Uncle and Aunt propose to set out next Monday: I shall follow
them in about a week, in order to come up with them at a friend's
house not far from Northampton where they are to make a visit.—I
had the pleasure a few days ago of making one in a very agreable
little musical party with a Nephew of Mr. Hills who is Minister of a
parish about 7 or 8 miles from the 8 mile Stone from Reading across
the Country beyond Englefield House,[4] and a neighbouring Clergyman, at the house of the former. the one played thorough Bass on
the Harpsichord extremely well, and the other the fiddle, who had
just such a superiority over myself as not to be a painfull one, and
as I would wish for the sake of the musick—We played some fine
Musick, and of sterling orthodoxy—Corelli was not forgotten. I am
in hopes of a repetition of the entertainment at Mr. Hill's before I
go on my Journey. this has put me in mind to request of you to send
me by a conveyance that has offer'd itself if this letter comes time
enough to give you the opportunity and you can do it without inconvenience a double suit of Strings for a fiddle (except the 3d. and
of that only one) and if you can spare me in order to enrich our
Stock either Bononcini[5] or Handel's Sonata's till my return about
the latter end of Septr., I shall be obliged to you; at the same time
strictly enjoining you on pain of being thought guilty of a breach
of friendship not to send it unless you can do it without apprehension
of being in want of it yourself. I am called off instantly and forced
abruptly to subscribe myself,

Your's

Jeremy Bentham

To be sent on Thursday as soon in the day as convenient, and
left at Mr. Reynolds Hatter opposite St. Dunstan's directed for me
to be left till called for.

Whitchurch 26th Tuesday

---

[3] MS, 'bad'.

[4] Mr Hill's parish was Monks' Sherborne: cf. letter 76, n. 6.

[5] Giovanni Bononcini (1670–1755).

82

To Jeremiah Bentham

26 July 1768 (Aet 20)

Hond. Sir

I take the liberty of requesting your assistance in furnishing us with some articles we have occasion for in our expedition; the plan of which as to the outset is now pretty well settled—on Monday my Uncle and Aunt propose to set out directly for Turville Court, and from thence to Mr. Shippam's[2] near Northampton: so far my Aunt will ride double: they are then to send back to Baghurst for her Mare, and I am to return with the Man to meet them there, from whence we shall proceed the rest of the way together. My Aunt has a mind to have a Net to throw over the Mare to screen her from the Flies which would be very troublesome to her now in the hottest time of the Year: she would therefore take it as a favour if my Mother would purchase her one and send it down on Friday, if possible, by the Exeter or Salisbury Coach, or any other that goes that road, to Basingstoke to be left at the Post House: as some of them set out very early, it should be sent to the White-Horse Cellar over night. she would have it of white Thread, of the size fit for a Horse not quite 14 hands high. if there is any difference in the make of them. she leaves the choice to my Mother: only I know she would avoid finery as much as possible, as that was at first an objection with her to the having it at all. I should likewise be glad if you could spare me either of Ogilby's engraved Maps of the roads, and buy me besides the last edition of the small pocket Book of the roads not engraved, which is called Ogilby's, with the Map of England in it.[3] it is to be had, I imagine, at any Booksellers. I would further beg, if it could be done without inconvenience, that somebody might call at Mr. Reynolds's the Hatter in Fleet Street, and ask if there be any thing left there for me, not sooner than 9 in the evening, if

82. [1] B.M. I: 218–219. Autograph. Docketed by Jeremiah Bentham: 'Jere^y Bentham / Letter Whitchurch 26th July 1768.' Docketed by Mary Bentham(?): 'Preparations for Buxton Journey.'

Addressed: 'To / Jeremiah Bentham Esqr. / Queen's Square / near St. James's Park / Westminster.' Postmark: '27 IY'.

[2] Unidentified.

[3] The most recent editions of these publications were: (1) *An actual survey of all the principal roads of England and Wales*; . . . Improved and corrected by J. Senex. 2 volumes, London, 1719. By John Ogilby. (2) *The Traveller's Pocket Book; or Ogilby and Morgan's Book of the Roads, improved and amended*, 2nd edition, corrected [1761?].

possible, that if there should be, it may be put up with the other things. in that case it may be perhaps as well to send them to the Bel Savage whence there is one Coach at least sets out that goes through Basingstoke. if this last can not be done with entire convenience, it is not of indispensable necessity.—My Uncle desires his Compliments—Yours Dear Sir dutifully and affectionately

Jeremy Bentham

Whitchurch Tuesday July 26th 1768

I could wish to know that you have received my two former letters.

83

To Richard Clark

16 August 1768 (Aet 20)

Derby August 16th 1768

I will treat you with a Letter, but it must be but a short one being as usual like the french prints, all of a flutter. but in truth, I have set down as soon as I could, and the Post is going out in less than half an hour. I set out from Baghurst last Sunday sen'night to meet my Uncle and Aunt at Mr. Osborne's Turvill Court in Buckinghamshire about 7 M. from Henly. from thence we have successively visited 1. Tame 2. Aylesbury, Buckingham, 3. Stony Stratford, 4. Northampton, Higham Ferrers, 5. Kettering, Northampton, Leicester and this place, whither we are just arrived. I might have mentioned some intermediate places, or omitted most of these, our stay having been but transitory at those marked with Numbers. at Aylesbury they have been so mad as to set up a flag with 'Wilkes and Liberty' over the Town hall, notwithstanding I have been informed he is so much in debt there, that he is no great favourite. about Buckingham we staid part of 2 days one of which was taken up with seeing Stow. I bestowed on it a second review with great pleasure, it being so long as 8 or 9 years ago since the first, when I was not of an age to make very important remarks. I was however almost out of patience with the female strictures and my Uncles phlegm[?] finding fault with the most minute and almost

83. [1] U.C. CLXXIII: 46. Autograph. Docketed by Richard Clark: 'Derby. Augt. 16. 1768. J. B.'s letter.'

Addressed: 'To / Mr. Clark / Old South Sea House / Broad Street / London.' On cover (in Jeremy Bentham's hand?): 'to be forwarded Mr. H. or J.[?] B.' Postmark: '18 AV'.

inobservable parts, inattentive to the whole, incapable of relishing the classical beauties, giving the preference in each particular to some other place without remorse in presence of the Gardener. Then did I wish—who did I wish for? even for my companion and my own familiar friend. Stony Stratford we came to only in our passage to the house of a friend of my Uncle's, Steward to Ld. Spenser. he took us with him on Friday to Althrop,[2] through Northampton, his Ldp's. seat where we spent the day and night besides, and had therefore full leisure to view the pictures which are numerous and some very good particularly one the particular observation of which flattered my Vanity as a judge of Painting which I never knew I was before any more than of elegance of Stile in the Arabic, being told afterwards it was reckoned the finest Vandyke in England. it was a whole length of Russel Earl of Bedford and Digby of Bristol—in one.[3] the rest of the furniture inadequate, situation of the house wretchedly gloomy, Gardens none, Park in the true strait line taste, and that as wretchedly applied as possible. at Higham Ferrer's we arrived Saturday staid Sunday at the house of another friend of my Uncle's brother to the former, Steward to Ld. Rockingham whose Borough that is—their names Stripton. I believe there is not so beggarly a Corporation Town in England, no trade, every ⟨thing⟩ dead, the houses ruinous. Leicester is a town well worth an antiquarian's curiosity. my Uncle and Aunt came from thence early this morning, I staid after them some hours to satisfy mine which I did pretty effectually: but the result of it I have not time now to communicate, but will shortly. In return for this I must send you to Paternoster Row to enquire for an account of the Isle of Man published within this year or two by I know not who.[4] If you meet with it send it to me as soon as possible to Buxton unbound and 2 bass and 2 treble strings of Whitaker's.[5] Adieu my dear Friend

J.B.

---

[2] John, 1st Earl Spencer (1734–85), had his seat at Althorp in the parish of Brington, Northants. Cf. Bowring, x, 46, which indicates the visit to Althorp, Matlock, Buxton, etc., in 1764, but it seems clear that Bentham's account to Bowring confused several tours.
   [3] This portrait is of William Russell, Earl and later 1st Duke of Bedford (1616–1700), and George Digby, Earl of Bristol (1612–77), Bedford's brother-in-law.
   [4] Probably Charles Searle's *Short View of the Present State of the Isle of Man*, 1767.
   [5] Maurice Whitaker, musical-instrument maker, music printer and publisher, carried on business near the Royal Exchange.

84

To Richard Clark

29–30 August 1768 (Aet 20)

Manchester Augt. 29th 1768.

Uncertain how soon I may have another opportunity, I will steal a short half-Hour to dedicate to you. my last dated this day fortnight (15th) carried on the thread of my travels, I think, to our arrival at Derby. the next day we forced our passage through the Clouds and got to Buxton. What we did there, during the 7 days which was the time of my continuance and the sights that we saw, and the Mountains that we traversed, and the Holes that we crept into, I shall not now relate. I shall confine myself to account for the date of this present Letter. I had all along in my thoughts the Scheme of getting a Furlow when we should have staid some time at Buxton, concluding that the time necessary for my Uncle's health would be more than sufficient for the satisfying my curiosity at Buxton and the places adjacent. Upon proposing it to my Uncle and Aunt, they consented without that reluctance which I expected from the cautious and apprehensive Temper of them both. I sat out therefore on Wednesday last in the forenoon, alone, 'the World before me and providence my Guide.' Heaven however, whether it disapproved of my enterprise I know not (though from the success I have met with in every subsequent stage of it, I must conclude it *then* vented all it's displeasure if it had any) more than 'some few sad drops' wept, yea, and in such plenty, that after enduring the violence of it's affliction for an hour, the continuance of it any longer became a matter of indifference. from Buxton to Macclesfield is 10 Miles over what is called a Turnpike road, where the object seems to have been to improve upon (I mean to heighten) Nature's original ruggedness. I arrived at the Inn just as the Landlord was setting down to dinner with 3 or four other travellers; of quality I may say without taking too much upon myself, somewhat inferior to my own. I have risen however during the course of this peregrination, I can assure you greatly superior to those adventitious distinctions. nothing I find smooths the way to sociality like previous solitude.

84. [1] U.C. clxxiii 47: Autograph. Docketed by Richard Clark: 'Manchester / Stockport / Augt. 29. 30 Sepr. 1768'.
Addressed: 'To / Mr. Clark / Old South Sea House / Old Broad Street / London.' Stamped: 'STOCKPORT'. Postmark: '5 SE'.

this consideration now it occurs reconciles me to the want of you, when

(Cheshire)
Stockport Aug. 30

An *agreable circumstance* just at that instant occurring has occasioned that 'Hiatus nunquam satis deflebilis,' I do not mean to you so much as to the Booksellers of the next Century who may be so fortunate as to become possessed of the inestimable Treasure of our Correspondence. do what I can to retrieve it the thread of the discourse, alas! is inevitably lost. I can only find in general that I was pleasing myself with reflecting how much better I was without you than with you, which being a discovery I had just made, and which I thought might be of use to recur to on occasion, if any qualms of friend-sickness (a Name for a disorder not taken notice of in the Dispensatory but which I formed by analogy from Mother-sickness) should come across me. For when my travels were with you, though I might see the 'Urbes hominum multorum', yet as for their manners, the knowledge of which can be gained no otherwise than by mixing among them, I might have remained as great a stranger as to those of the Antipodes, if you had not sometimes forced me out into the wide Ocean of Society.—But now I can assure you I am a perfect Ulysses. Forgive me, I have been betray'd into this Latinity, by a frippery Classical Letter of Dr. Burton's to Dr. Bentham[2] containing a Paneygyrick on the Archbp. of Canty. that is now lying before me in Ms. How should I come by that? say you. that is an Aenigma that remains to be solved. let it suffice that I am now writing amidst the confusion of Mrs. B's tongue, which did it not utter the dictates of a benevolent heart would be absolutely intolerable. but I cannot find it in my heart to keep you in suspense—I will anticipate then to inform you that I am now writing from the House of one of the Dr's. Brothers who has within these 2 months been ⟨. . .⟩ to a Benefice in this Town[3] (17 miles from Buxton ⟨. . .⟩ ⟨. . .⟩ the Dr. etc. are also on a visit. I have also met with a College acquaintance. throw me any where, you see, I can fall upon my Legs as well without as with you. But this agreable circumstance? that is a Stock I must beg leave to keep in hand to pay you for intelligence from Guilford, where you went no doubt at the time of the Assizes: and which I must desire you not to dismiss from your thoughts, or in Mr. Collyer's words not to take the peg out, till

[2] See letter 11, n. 3.
[3] This was Thomas Bentham (*c.* 1714–90), sixth son of Samuel Bentham, vicar of Witchford. He was vicar of St Peter's Stockport from 1768 until his death.

I come to catch what drops. But 'Dic aliquid de tribus Capellis' you may very well say. I have travelled over this enormous length of Paper and but 10 Miles of Road: yet as I have room for no more without taking another Sheet, I may e'en as well send away what I have written as it is. I shall go from hence to Matlock to morrow, to meet my U. and A. whither I should desire you to write, but find that your's cou'd not reach that place in time. I must desire however I may find a Letter at Baghurst in 10 days or a fortnight. by which time at farthest we shall have returned. in which I may hear of the requests in my two last letters, which I suppose did not come to you time enough to be fulfilled, and are now become immaterial. Vale.

84a

WILL OF JEREMY BENTHAM

24 August 1769 (Aet 21)

I Jeremy Bentham of Lincoln's Inn[2] Student of the Law do make this my last Will and Testament. I give unto my Mother-in-Law all my Jewels save as hereafter excepted—unto John Farr Abbot eldest Son of my said Mother-in-Law, five Pounds in money—unto the Revd. Thomas Gwatkin, twenty Pounds to be paid him within one Month after my decease—unto Richard Clark now of the Old South-Sea House, all such Books relating in the

84a. [1] B.M. Add. Ms. 36652: 9. Autograph.

This will, made by Bentham about six months after he came of age, was apparently sent by him, some two months before his death, to Southwood Smith, who quotes briefly from it in a footnote to the printed text of the lecture he delivered over Bentham's remains on 9 June 1832. At the top the 84-year-old Bentham has written the following note: '5th April 1832. Of the persons in this Will named no one being now alive my decease will suffice to deprive it of all effect, without need of cancelling.'

The inclusion here of a document not forming part of the correspondence seems warranted in view of the singular dearth of letters illustrating a crucial phase in Bentham's development. For the ten years from 1764 (when Bentham was sixteen) to 1773 we have fewer Bentham letters than for the three years he spent as an undergraduate at Oxford. For 1769 itself only one letter survives. Yet, Bentham himself told Bowring, '1769 was to me a most interesting year . . . Montesquieu, Barrington, Beccaria, and Helvetius, but most of all Helvetius, set me on the principle of utility. When I had sketched a few vague notions on the subject, I looked delighted at my work. I remember asking myself—Would I take £500 for that sheet of paper? Poor as I was, I answered myself—No! that I would not' (Bowring, x, 54).

The will does throw some light, not only on Bentham's friendships at this period, but also on his interests and on the movement of some of his ideas. Notes have already been given on most of the persons mentioned.

[2] Bentham had removed from the Temple to Lincoln's Inn some time after his twenty-first birthday on 15 February. Bowring, in a manuscript note on page 68

whole or the greatest part thereof to the Laws and Antiquities of Great Britain and Ireland whereof he shall not be possessed of a Copy either in the same or any other Edition or Language at the time of my decease—I further give him all such other Books as either have no date, or are of a date prior to the year one thousand six hundred whether bound separately or together with other Treatises; in which last case I will that he have the whole Volume. I give unto Charles Abbot youngest son of my Mother-in-Law such of my Books of Law and Antiquities as Richard Clark shall have duplicates of in manner abovementioned. Of the rest of my Books printed or Engraved Maps Tables and Charts, I give unto the Revd. Thomas Gwatkin sixty Volumes at the choice of the said Thomas Gwatkin: the remainder I give to my Brother Samuel Bentham.[3] I further give unto my said Brother all my Music Books and Musical Instruments—also my Gold Watch with its appendages. I further give to the said Thomas Gwatkin all such Instruments and apparatus belonging to the Mathematics or any branch of Natural Philosophy or Natural History, as, if any, I shall be possessed of at my decease. I give unto William Browne now of Lamb's Conduit Street Holborn Attorney at Law two Table Spoons marked with my name at length, as also the Engravings of illustrious Englishmen published by Virtue and Houbraken[4]—and unto Jane, Wife of the said William Browne my yellow Diamond ring or else the Diamond Head-pin formerly the property of my deceased Aunt Deborah Grove,[5] at the discretion of my Mother-in-Law—I give unto George Woodward Grove my Uncle, John Mulford my Cousin, the Revd. Samuel Ray of Kenton and the Revd. William Ray of Mickfield both in the County of Suffolk my Cousins, a Gold Ring each in Token of remembrance. The rest of my personal Estate of whatsoever kind it be I suffer to return and do hereby give to my Father from whose bounty I received it the real estate which I likewise

of volume x of his own copy of the *Memoirs,* now in the British Museum, says: 'On his coming of age a small property fell into his hands which had been bequeathed to him by his Grandmother Grove and which his father applied to the purchase of the Chambers set up two pairs of stairs and for which he paid the sum of £402 six shillings'. (In the preceding sentence Bowring mistakenly dates the move to Lincoln's Inn to the year 1771.) Bentham retained these chambers until he went to Russia in 1785.

[3] Samuel was then twelve and a half.

[4] *The Heads of illustrious persons of Great Britain engraven by Mr. Houbraken and Mr. Virtue* . . . —i.e. Jacobus Houbraken (1698–1780) and George Virtue (1684–1756)—was published in 1747, and a second edition in 1756.

[5] Deborah Grove had died at the beginning of the year, or perhaps at the end of 1768, her will being proved on 21 January 1769. In addition to her watch and jewels she left Bentham £50 and the reversion of £100 in the event of the death of her brother George Woodward Grove without issue.

possess by his favour being by the terms of donation to return to him of course—as to my body my will is that it be buried by the rites of the Church of England, or the rites of any other Church, or no rites at all at the discretion of my Executor, so that the funeral expenses do not in any wise exceed forty shillings. but it is my Will and special request to my Executor that if I should chance to die of any such disease as that in the judgment of my said Exor the art of Surgery or science of Physic should be likely to be in any wise advanced by observations to be made on the opening of my body, that he my said Executor do cause my said body as soon after my decease as may be to be delivered unto George Fordyce[6] now of Henrietta Street Covent Garden Dr. of Physic; or if he should decline to accept the same, then to any other Dr. of Physic or Surgeon so to be dealt with and to be kept by such Dr. of Physic or Surgeon for such time as such Dr. of Physic or Surgeon shall think proper. and this my Will and special request I make not out of affectation of singularity, but to the intent and with the desire that Mankind may reap some small benefit in and by my decease, having hitherto had small opportunities to contribute thereto while living.[7] Lastly of this my first and, to this time, only and last Will and Testament dated the 24th day of August 1769 I do make the abovementioned Richard Clark sole Executor. This Will being all of my handwriting is written upon this one and no other Sheet of Paper— Jeremy Bentham

85

TO SAMUEL BENTHAM

14 September 1769 (Aet 21)

My dear Sam

I write to you in great haste rather to apologise for not writing, if I may say so without an Iricism, than having time to write to any

---

[6] Dr George Fordyce (1736–1802) was a celebrated physician and chemist of the time. A Scotsman, trained in Edinburgh, he established in the 1760's a great reputation in London as a lecturer on medicine and chemistry. Bentham told Bowring: 'I made acquaintance, before I was of age, with Dr. Fordyce, in consequence of his lectures on chemistry; and I once gave him and (Chamberlain) Clarke a dinner in Lincoln's Inn. Dr. F. was, I think, at that time, the only chemical lecturer, and was very poorly attended' (Bowring, x, 133). In 1776 Fordyce was made F.R.S. He published many scientific papers. Samuel Bentham married his eldest daughter Mary in October 1796.

[7] This sentence was quoted by Southwood Smith in *A lecture delivered over the remains of Jeremy Bentham, Esq. . . . on the 9th of June, 1832*, London, 1832, 4.

85. [1] B.M. I: 223–224. Autograph. Docketed: 'I.B. Septr. 14th 1769.' Also in pencil; 'Charta Chymica.'

other purpose. the course of conveyance between us is so precarious, that though I answer'd your's as soon as 'twas possible for me and you replied to mine as soon as 'twas possible for you, your last letter did not get to town before yesterday, nor to my hands before this morning. and now it has got to my hands it is at a time when unfortunately I cannot pay that attention to it I cou'd wish and would have done had I not been under an engagement for the remainder of the day of long standing. while I am now writing there is actually a Gentleman in the room upon a first visit to me, of whom I have begged permission to retire to my desk for a few minutes to give you as many lines. and it is necessary for me to send my letter by this very night's post, otherwise I foresee it will not reach you before Papa and Mama get to Kenton and you are fetched away. It is that consideration and no other that prevents my complying with your request for supplying you with Music; another Holidays, since I know your wants, and your opportunities, they shall be supplied, and seconded.

I cannot sufficiently express my sense of the kindness, which I am so happy to learn you meet with from all our friends: kindness, I cannot say unexpected towards you, because so amply experienced by myself. thank them for it on my account, in the best words you can devise: they shew it you, I make no doubt, for *your own* sake; but they could not in any manner confer a more sensible obligation on me.

The paper on which I write this, and on which I wrote the last is of a peculiar kind, newly invented: it was for this reason I desired you to save it. it is called in the advertisement by the pompous title of the Royal Charta Cymica; for every thing must be royal to recommend it. the peculiarity of it is; you may make a mark on it with any *Metal* except Iron, like that made with a Black Lead pencil upon any other paper.

Adieu, dear Sam I have 150 other things to say, which I must reluctantly suppress for the reason above-mentioned.

Your's affectionately
J.B.

Sepr. 14th Thursy. 1769.

Addressed: 'To / Mr. Bentham / at the Revd. Mr. Sl. Ray's / Kenton / Suffolk.' Postmark: '14 SE'.

This is the first extant letter from Bentham to his brother Samuel, then a twelve-year-old Westminster schoolboy. For Samuel Ray, with whom Samuel Bentham was staying, see letter 69, n. 1. Bentham, probably, was writing from his chambers in Lincoln's Inn.

86

To Jeremiah Bentham

15 September 1770 (Aet 22)

Rue de Seine
Petit Hotel d'Angleterre PARIS Thursday Septr. 15th 1770.

Hond. Sir

I am at length arrived at this place after meeting with a variety of adventures, pleasing and disagreable; mixing with a variety of characters, admirable and contemptible; and undergoing a variety of fatigues which would have killed some people, but seem rather to have mended *my* health than impaired it—It is a great happiness however that those of my adventures which have been of the unpleasant kind have left no such consequences behind them; and being singular to me however common in themselves, are now become pleasant in the recollection how much soever otherwise in the sufferance—I had once intended to give you a minute detail of my progress from my setting out to my arrival in my first letter; but I find it upon a little reflection to be impossible; and that I should then be spending all my time in writing my history when I should be acting it—let it suffice for the present that I sat out from London this day sennight with Mr. Clark in his Titiwhisky; got to Brighthelmston at noon on Friday, embarkd on board the passage boat on Saturday between 7 and 8 in the evening, after parting with Mr. Clark in the morning—arrived at Dieppe on Sunday about noon, and at this place yesterday about the same time, on Horses, Asses, in Boats, Chamber Pots,* and a floating kind of Black Hole, which in Calcutta must have infallibly have been attended with the consequences of it there. out of this time, I spent the greatest part of a day at Rouen, the pleasantest, most stinking place I have ever seen.

Expences, thanks to my good fortune in joining with a Frenchman though unfortunately in English company have been hitherto

* *Pots de Chambre* a kind of 2-wheeled 2-horsed voiture, clumsy to the most exquisite perfection.

86. ¹ B.M. I: 229–230. Autograph. Docketed by Jeremiah Bentham: 'Son Jeremy Lr. datd. Paris 15th Sepr. 1770.' (15 September was in fact a Saturday.)

Addressed: 'To / Jeremiah Bentham Esqr. / Queen's Square Place / Westminster / Londres et Angleterre.' Scrawled in pencil on cover in another hand(?): 'Henry Foley[?] Ships.'

This was Bentham's second visit to France (see letter 59, n. 1 for the first visit).

moderate enough—about 3 Guineas and a half I think have brought me here, five or six and twenty shillings of which I left behind in *dear dear* (to write it twice for the two different senses to which it is equally competent) England. I have got a very respectable apartment with a bed in it however, which the best, you know, may have in them without disgrace, for 9s. a week—with a good natured talkative Landlady, and I already have good reason to believe an honest one, tho' settled at her house but an hour or two, not young and handsome enough to give you much uneasiness, nor yet too old to cease to be agreable—don't let the name of her house mislead you, for she never in her life pronounced a syllable of English.

I have not yet been able to wait on the French Gentlemen to whom I have recommendations; but I have not lost my time by falling in with some Scotch Gentlemen, who have and will give me very useful advice in respect of purchases and accommodations. each of these hints which I have given you may and I hope will one day furnish me with the subject of a distinct Chapter: but I must now go to a supper which is waiting for me of Wine at 10d. a large Bottle, Peaches (bought disadvantageously after the Market was over) at about 3 farthings apiece, and bread, notwithstanding the reported and indeed actual scarcity, a penny loaf for 5 farthings notwithstanding (again) my boasted economy I foresee I must be extravagant in dress, and come back to you with my ears hanging down and my back as fine as a Horse to receive a lecture—time presses—Adieu therefore in french words but in very sincere English Sense, Monsieur mon cher and trés honoré Pere says

Your dutiful and affectionate Son
Jere.ᵞ Bentham

Remembrances where due and always preserved Dum studeo festinare obscurus fio.

Charles shall be provided for in a week.[2]

---

[2] Charles Abbot (see letter 68, n. 4).

87

TO RICHARD CLARK

16 September 1770 (Aet 22)

PARIS Petit Hotel d'Angleterre Rue de Seine
Friday morning Septr. 16. 1770.

If I had but a quarter of what I have to set before you, I believe you would fare the better—as it is, I believe, it will be with you as it is with people at a Lord Mayor's Feast, where too great Plenty often makes them go without a dinner—not to starve you quite however, though I cannot possibly find time to give you a Bellyfull, I have sent you a stay-stomach in the inclosed which I have left open. You will there find a Skeleton which you may dispatch to the person to whom it is directed, after you have picked the bones. I know you are apt to be squeamish at such a contrivance, but I can't help it—every thing that I have said to my father I should have to say to you again and how the deuce should I find time for copying it?[2]

Well, I begin already to find myself pretty much at home and have fallen in with tolerable alacrity to an arrangement of the time totally differing from my accustomed one, and not at all for the worse, I can assure you. I rise about the time I used to be falling into my second sleep—have my Hair divinified for the day—have finished my Breakfast perhaps by eight—dine between one and two—turn down my dish of Coffee about the time I used to be thinking of going to dinner—drink no Tea—and after a light but luxurious repast for Supper toss down my tenpenny Wine with all—all-most not quite as much goût as I used to do the infusion of that cursed Herb, which I must take to again, when it's more salutary substitute is to be had no more. The Author of "The six weeks Tour to Paris" is a Blockhead—as if every Englishman's Guts must necessarily be griped by the light wines because his were whimsical, and did not know what was good for them.[3] This is a sad hoggish Letter—but I introduce the mention of my meals to give you an Idea of the distribution of my occupations, not of those occupations themselves.

87. [1] U.C. CLXXIII: 50. Autograph. Docketed by Richard Clark: 'Paris. 16 Sepr. 1770 / Mr. Bentham.' (16 September was in fact a Sunday.)
    Addressed: 'To / Richard Clark Esqr. / at the Old South Sea House / Broad Street / Londres / Angleterre.' Postmark: 'SE 25'.
  [2] It seems that letter 86 was enclosed with this.
  [3] This work has not been traced.

I don't know whether I shall do any thing for you—it is a great question among the learned whether silk Stockings in France are in fact any thing to signify cheaper than in England—however with a little experience I shall be able to decide the controversy, and will act accordingly—there is every where in this city to be met with a two-legged Animal called a Savoyard—it seems to be something of the Cameleon kind in living upon Air, and taking all manner of shapes as that of colours—you give it 10 pence a week and it will clean your Shoes go errands, and do all manner of odd Jobs—if I can meet with a creature of this species that has any thing to distinguish him from the rest, I may possibly bring him over to put into your Menagerie. I don't know what else I can bring you over except Victuals, unless it be a little dog you could put into your breeches Pocket or a Parrot or a Marmozet or some such sweet pretty little Creatures. I should be very glad of your Company to dine with me whenever it may suit—I could treat you and any friend of your besides paying for my own dinner better and at a less price than I could dine for in London by myself.[4]

*   *   *

I have been with the person whom Elmsley[5] recommended to me for a Cicerone: I found him in a little nasty hole, half filled by a Bed stained with the Blood of many a Bug, making an Index to a Treatise of Architecture he is about publishing—he was very civil, and will be doubtless very useful to me—but I must finish in a violent hurry   J.B.

seal my Father's Letter with some strange Seal not your own. direct as above.[6]

---

[4] Eight lines following are carefully scrawled out.

[5] Peter Elmsley (1736–1802) was one of the foremost booksellers of the day. Bentham bought many books from him and later did a translation from the French for him. There are many references to him in the correspondence.

[6] At the end of the letter, someone—presumably Clark—has written the following: 'Peach Trees—mignion—gallande &c. to bear our climate attend to graft. 'a box of yᵐ.' For the subject of these jottings see the early part of letter 89.

88

To Richard Clark

1 October 1770 (Aet 22)

I give you one more letter, but I doubt the subject of it will turn out to be rather my own business than your entertainment. I want your advice upon the important subject of Cloaths. As I must soon at all events make up a Suit of Black to wear under my Gown,[2] I have thoughts of having it here of what they call Velours de Coton (Cotton Velvet) like our Manchester Velvets. It will cost here about as much as Cloth in England—the Manchester Velvets I believe something more—but I am told by Englishmen, and indeed I have often read and heard so before that the Black Dye, particularly upon vegetable matters as Cotton, which they use in England loses its colour very soon and turns rusty, but that that of France stands infinitely better. besides that sort of Velvet will last allmost as long again as Cloth, and looks handsomer. the fine Velvet would cost as much again and would be much too shewy to wear for such a purpose. this I am speaking of is in appearance just like the Manchester Velvet. Now all I want is your worship's opinion whether I can wear such a thing with common decency, and without being much stared at. Give me an answer as soon as you can that there may be time to make it, if such should be your pleasure, but consult my Father first if you should have an opportunity, and he should be returned. The proper lining what? how much a yard in England, and how many yards will it take? Wastecoat and Breeches of corded Silk for the Summer, (for all Velvet will then be too heavy) how much would they cost in all? Red Shag for lining a Winter suit fit for a Mylord—how many yards would it take and how much a yard? how wide the yard? answer me these questions.—I have bought you some stockings, but they won't save you above 2s. or 2s. 6d. a pair, in proportion to their strength.

I have not been without apprehensions of being obliged to return before I intended: /above/ about a week ago a Gentleman of my acquaintance was cautioned to keep himself in readiness to leave

88. [1] U.C. CLXXIII: 51. Autograph. Docketed by Richard Clark: Paris. 31 Sepr. 1770 / Mr. Bentham.'

    Addressed: 'To / Richard Clarke Esqr. / Old South Sea House / London Londres / Angleterre / Single Sheet / une seule feuille.' Postmark: 'OC 9'.

    Bentham has dated this 'Monday Sepr. 31st 1770'. Clearly the date was in fact 1 October which was indeed a Monday.

    [2] Bentham had been admitted to the Bar in 1769.

the Kingdom by a Secretary in our Ambassador's office, who told him at the same time that they had every thing of consequence there packed up ready to set off with at an hour's warning. I suppose our disputes with Spain are the occasion of these apprehensions.[3] but however that be, I have heard nothing of it since—let me know what is said about it in London if you hear any thing more than what is in the News-papers. If the Spaniards should break with us, the French ought to and certainly will join them, if they can possibly find money; but how that can be, the heart of man is scarce able to conceive, unless they can conjure down the Moon, and coin her into Ecus. Mr. Vanloo the Fr. King's Painter[4] has not been paid his Salary, this—I can't tell you how long till I have enquired again—In the midst of all their poverty they are building a most spacious and magnificent Edifice, between the 'Pont-neuf' and the 'College des 4 nations', for a public mint— It was the Hotel de Condé. Monsr. Pingeron[5] took me over it, and got me a sight of the model from one of the persons employed about it, who told us it was to cost 24,000,000 Livres, which you know makes a Million Sterling—but there certainly must be some mistake somewhere, for large as it is, and built all of stone, I cannot conceive how it should cost any thing near the money. it is upon the South Shore of the Seine, and fronts the River. the new buildings in the Place de Louis 15 that were on foot when we were here together are now nearly compleated, and very elegant they are: but after all, as far as I can find, no use is to be made of them now they are finished. Great part seems nothing but a Screen, and one can see through it. a few Soldiers are to be lodged in another part.

As I was sitting in the Caffé de Conti about a week ago a corner of Rue Dauphine Fauxbourg St. Germain directly opposite the Pont Neuf, who should come in but a Gentleman in plain Coat and Breeches and laced Wastcoat with a sword by his side, whom after a short stare I found to be no less a personage than Mr. Ross Gwatkin[6]—I accosted him and we enter'd into conversation—he told me he had been in Paris about a week—I asked him whether he was acquainted with the Language—he said, 'very little'. I

---

[3] Britain and Spain were disputing the possession of the Falkland Islands.

[4] Probably Louis Michel van Loo (1707–71).

[5] Jean-Claud Pingeron (1730?–95), after serving in the army of the King of Poland, returned to France and was attached to the royal office of works at Versailles. He translated into French Giacinto Dragonetti's *Trattato della Virtu e dei Premi*, Paris 1765; an English translation appeared in 1769.

[6] Ross Gwatkin, otherwise unidentified, is evidently a brother of Thomas Gwatkin (for whom cf. letter 75, n. 1).

believe I asked him then whether he was come on the design of learning it, or about business—he said *no, only upon a Tour of pleasure*, and that he should return to England in about a fortnight. he seemed in a little confusion at the sight of me, and I have not seen my Gentleman since. you have heard ⟨of his⟩ sudden disappearance from England without the knowledge of any ⟨of⟩ his friends, and that the bad situation of his affairs was the cause of it. Give my compliments to Mr. Hawkins and communicate the intelligence to him if you approve of it, and think it will answer any good purpose—for this I must desire you to consult your discretion—I think a Commission was taken out against him, and I do not know whether his Year is not expired—if so what he said about returning to England may be only a pretence—I told him about his Brother's going to America, which he had not heard of, and which he received with indifference enough. Adieu—what I had to say farther there is no room for—

Your's affectionately
J.B.

Paris—Petit Hotel d'Angleterre
  Rue de Seine Monday Septr. 31st 1770.

my sincere respects to Mr. Villion[7] when you see him; I have not yet made use of the Letter of credit with which he was so kind to furnish me—ask him if I can do any thing for him here.

Direct to me as above.

89

TO RICHARD CLARK

8 October 1770 (Aet 22)

Petit Hotel d'Angleterre Rue de Seine Paris Monday Octr. 8th 1770.
  Pox on the Man why does not he date his Letters?—I received your's last night; but it's not furnishing me with the means of computing the time within which I may expect to have an answer, throws me quite at Sea—It will be the greatest pleasure to me to

---

[7] Francis Villion was the Genoese merchant 'who helped cheer Bentham's Lincoln's Inn solitude.' He was dirty and mean, though not poor, but he was much attached to Bentham, who said that Villion 'studied chemistry for the love he bore me' (cf. Bowring, x, 131–133).

89. [1] U.C. CLXXIII: 52. Autograph. Docketed by Richard Clark: 'Paris 8. Octr. 1770. Mr. Bentham.'

Addressed: 'To / Richard Clark Esqr. / Old South Sea House / Broad Street / London / Londres / Angleterre. / Single Sheet. / Une seuille feuille.' Postmark: 'OC 15'.

144

execute these as well as every other commands of Mr. Dunn,[2] if I can hope to do it to his satisfaction: but I think I should not deserve well at his hands, if I were to make a purchase immediately from such an authority as this, which I thought would not answer, without first apprising him of my opinion, and taking his farther directions if time will permitt. I am satisfied that with regard to vegetables in general, the French Nurseries do not afford any thing like the Choice that is to be had in England: if Mr. Dunn has any particular reason for thinking that an exception is to be made with regard to Peaches, that alters the case. I have eaten a great number since I have been in France: but I have not observed them to be much better or worse than ours. In so small a number as Mr. Dunn can have occasion for, the expence of transporting will bear a prodigious proportion to the first price: I should imagine, by the time he could get them into his garden they would cost him twice or three times as much as he could get the best Trees for at a London Nursery—besides the navigation of the Seine is very tedious—at least the course by water is very long, as I had occasion to learn in my journey hither—so that with me, the danger of their not succeeding, added to the superiority of the price would overbalance the chance of their being better than the English ones. But perhaps the Mignon and Gallande are not to be met with in England: though I have some notion of having remember'd them there. perhaps after all Mr. Dunn may not grudge to purchase the satisfaction (which is neither an uncommon nor unnatural one) of having it to say that his Fruit came from France, at a rate which I should deem rather extravagant: I will therefore make all the enquiries in my power, and regulate myself by the result, in case there should not be time enough for me to have his further directions—I shall quit Paris either the 25th or 26th—if you write again, do not forget to tell me the number of trees he wants or at least the length of his wall—that number whatever it is must at least be doubled, to make allowance for those that may die in the passage.—So much for Peach Trees.

I have met with a most amiable French Man—but his History is too long to give you here—he is very desirous of having a Ticket in the English Lottery: he has addressed himself to several English Bankers for that purpose, but they have none. I will therefore beg the favor of you to send me one without fail by the next Post, if possible—you may get the money of my Father: give him to understand that it will be an advantageous method of getting money here

---

[2] Unidentified.

145

as it will save the expense of Commission: tell him I have not yet had recourse to either of my Letters of Credit—if he distrusts imposition, tell him I shall be sure not to trust the Ticket out of my hands till I have the money:—at any rate send the Ticket, if you sell my Books to pay for it. give me advice of the price, and the day you bought it.[3]

Give me your opinion, if you can with any tolerable certainty, of the following case—with the Authorities if any—enable me to give as good an account as possible.—there is a remote possibility you may be benefitted by it. *A* is the owner (Lessee for a long Term though at Rack Rent) of a House in London (that is in Dean Street Soho out of the Liberties and Customs) with a bit of ground behind it—he gives up part of it to Trustees B B of a Lutheran or some such Chapel to be built who build partly upon that, partly upon other ground. soon after their building is compleated *A* erects an additional building to his house, upon that part which remained— the lights to it are two Skylights like the Melon Glasses on the Bank. one of them comes /or rather was designed to come/ so near the upright window of the first erected building of B B, as to intercept part of the rays of light in their passage to it. for in passing through 2 or 3 media of Glass part of the rays must necessarily be absorbed or reflected, and so not transmitted. but nothing absolutely opake is interposed. I take it, that supposing it granted that the light of B B was materially a⟨ffect⟩ed, in point of Law this is a nuisance— and that whether it is or no might be subject of litigation before a Jury. for every obstruction however slight can never be deemed such—if it were no new building could ever be erected in London where the Houses are thick—if this should take up too much time, take no more notice of it than just to say so—Dancing I have not been to, nor shall—Country Dances are not practised in Paris, as I have been informed, and verily believe. I was on Friday at a Concert on Friday last where there were $\frac{1}{2}$ a doz: Fiddles 2 Viol[os]. a Bassoon 2 Horns and a Trumpet in a Room about the size of yours at the O.S.S.H.—and with a Bed in it: we made a most damnable noise, and split a thousand Crochets each into a thousand Shivers—

---

[3] Clark (it seems) has enclosed in the letter a slip certifying that a lottery ticket has been sent on his behalf to Mr. Bentham. It reads:

> 'Bot. for Mr. Richard Clarke   Octr. 16th 1770
> One Lottry. Ticket No. 14919 –   –   –   £13. 15. 6
>   Com. –. 6
>   £13. 16. –
> Made the above purchase and sent the Ticket (No. 14919)
> by the post in a Letter directed to Mr. Bentham at Paris.'

I shall go there again—God take you into his most holy keeping—
Farewell. I have written one other Letter besides that you answer'd
—you have it I hope by this Time.

90

To Jeremiah Bentham

18 October 1770 (Aet 22)

Petit Hôtel d'Angleterre Paris
Oct. 18th 1770

Honoured Sir

This will be deliver'd to you by a Gentleman[2] who will also at
the same time pay you the Sum of £43 Sterling (for which you will
be so kind as to give him a receipt on my account) being the equivalent, according to the rate settled by the Banker here, (Mr.
Thelusson)[3] for 960 Livres Tournois with which I accommodated
him. the history of the Transaction is much too long to give you
here: perhaps you may have it from himself. permit me to content
myself with assuring you in general that I did not do what I have
done without having all the reason to be assured of the safety of it,
that could well be imagined and taking proper measures to in-
demnify you in case of Accident—the punctual repayment of the
money will justify me eventually.

The familiarity with which I have lived with him here and the
degree of intimacy which I have contracted with him have let me
pretty much into the state of his affairs—he is a painter by profession and came to Paris chiefly to engage an engraver to engrave

90. [1] B.M. I: 231–232. Autograph. Docketed by Jeremiah Bentham: 'Son Jeremy
Bentham Lr. datd. Paris, 18 Octr. 1770.'
Addressed: 'To / Jeremiah Bentham Esqr. / Queen's Square Place / near the Broad
way / Westminster.'
[2] Evidently David Martin (1737–98), who 'offered to paint Bentham, who refused
the attention proferred, as he could not afford to pay the import duty into England'
(Bowring, x, 65–6). Bowring mentions a picture (perhaps a study for the portrait at
Christ Church) of Lord Mansfield which Martin gave to Bentham (x, 46). He was the
son of a schoolmaster in Fife, and had studied under Allan Ramsay the famous
Edinburgh portrait painter whom he had accompanied while quite young to Rome.
He had also studied in London at the academy in St Martin's Lane. When Bentham
met him he was at the beginning of a successful career both in England and Scotland
as an engraver and portrait painter. In 1775 he was appointed principal painter to the
Prince of Wales for Scotland. See also letters 144a and 300.
[3] George Thelusson, second son of Isaac de Thelusson (1690–1770) the resident
envoy of Geneva at the French Court, founded a large banking house in Paris.
Isaac's third son, Peter Thelusson (1737–97), was naturalized British in 1762 and
amassed a great fortune in England as a merchant.

from a portrait of his of Ld. Mansfield[4] with whom he is in great favour—you would soon discover him to be a Scotchman—I have scarce need to tell you that he is a Scotchman: but of a Character the very reverse of that which is generally attributed to his Countrymen, open, disinterested and unsuspecting—You will not find him a man of the very first rate abilities—but he is very far from being a fool, and has very considerable merit in his profession, thrives well and has travelled through many parts of Europe without exposing himself—He is withal, if I am not deceived a very worthy young man, and you will be so kind as to receive him as my friend—at the worst, my mother and you may satisfy your curiosity concerning me by his means as I have been but too much with him.

I must not forget while paper will permitt me to thank you for a very long and kind letter without Date which I received by the post of Saturday last—Your account of Farr[5] would have been a melancholy one indeed had it not been terminated ⟨by⟩ assurances of his amendment—I ⟨. . .⟩ ⟨. . .⟩ to hear that your journey in other ⟨ways⟩ has been so agreable to all parties concerned—mine shall without fail terminate at the period I assigned for it. by the first or the second of next month at furthest, I shall hope to embrace you till when accept of all affectionate and tender wishes for yourself my mother and my young friends of your dutiful Son

Jeremy Bentham.

91

TO JEREMIAH BENTHAM

5 November 1770 (Aet 22)

5th Novr.

Hond. Sir

I arrived at length last night too late for me to wait on you after 2 accidents impossible to be foreseen which happened one

---

[4] William Murray, 1st Earl of Mansfield (1705–93), was the most celebrated English judge of the time. He was the fourth son of the fifth Viscount Stormont, a Scottish peer. After an active career as an M.P. and a barrister (1742: solicitor-general; 1754–56: attorney-general) he became in 1756 Chief Justice of the King's Bench and Baron Mansfield. He was created Earl of Mansfield in 1776. The young Bentham admired him much as a reforming judge, but later saw his methods as inimical to true reform by legislation.

[5] John Farr Abbot the elder son of Bentham's stepmother: cf. letter 68, n. 4.

91. [1] B.M. I: 233. Autograph. Docketed by Jeremiah Bentham: 'Son Jeremy Bentham / Lr. upon his arrival from Paris. 5th Novr. 1770.'

Addressed: 'Jeremiah Bentham Esqr. / Queen's Square Place / Westr.'

after another to retard my embarkment. I thought it my duty to put a stop to the uneasiness I knew you could not fail to suffer on account of my unexpected delay by giving you this earliest intelligence of my arrival. I shall wait upon you at dinner.

Your's dutifully and affecty.

J. Bentham

92

To Jeremiah Bentham

3 September 1771 (Aet 23)

Hond. Sir

I sit down to pay my duty to you in a few lines on my return from your house where I dined with Mrs. Farr,[2] and took charge of the two letters herewith inclosed—others you will receive by the care of Mr. Hughes.[3]

I have the satisfaction to inform you of my having settled my

---

92. [1] B.M. I: 236–238. Autograph. Docketed by Jeremiah Bentham: 'Son Jeremy Bentham / Lr. datd. 3d Septr. 1771.' Two other dockets are probably in the hand of Lady Bentham, Samuel's widow, and read: 'For Appendix', 'S.B.'s thirst for knowledge and rising ambition.' In fact there is no appendix to her biography of Samuel and the letter does not appear in the book.

Samuel Bentham, with whom this letter is largely concerned, had, in August 1770, when aged 13, begun to learn shipbuilding under the instruction of William Gray, Master Ship-Wright of the Royal Dockyard at Woolwich, with whom he lodged for £50 a year, in addition to the fees for his training. On 11 January 1771, his 14th birthday, he was bound apprentice to Mr Gray (copies of the indentures are in B.M. XVII: 52–5). Jeremiah Bentham had expected Samuel to follow his brother from Westminster to the University, but had given in to Samuel's 'uncontrollable desire to become a naval constructor' (*Life of Sir Samuel Bentham*, 3). Samuel's position as a gentleman apprentice was somewhat unusual, and he was allowed time off for more general education.

Bentham's surviving letters for the period 1768–1771 certainly give little idea of the intense intellectual excitement of those years in his life. The end of 1770 had seen his first excursion into print. Three letters signed 'Irenius' were published in *The Gazetteer and New Daily Advertiser* on 3 December 1770, 1 March 1771, and 18 March 1771. The first, a letter 'To John Glynn, Esq., Sergeant-at-Law' concerning the pressing of sailors, is reprinted as Appendix III to *Bentham and the Ethics of Today* by D. Baumgardt, Princeton, 1952. The other two constitute a defence of Lord Mansfield against an attack by one signing himself 'Touchstone'.

Bentham's investigations in jurisprudence were diversified by experiments in chemistry, though these were a great expense for him on his income of £103 a year (cf. Bowring, x, chaps. III and IV, also letter 67).

[2] The mother of Mrs Sarah Bentham (cf. letter 67, n. 1).

[3] Unidentified: possibly Jeremiah Bentham's clerk (he is referred to in a note on one of the copies of Samuel Bentham's indentures mentioned above in n. 1).

Brother with Mr. Cowley[4]—Sam was so kind as to take a walk up to Town on Sunday morning to tell me of a Mortar-exercise that was to be performed yesterday, which he knew I was desirous of seeing and of which he had no other means of acquainting me. I had already allotted in my mind that day to go to Woolwich—We set out at day-break, and after breakfasting at Mr. Gray's and satisfying my curiosity went up to Shooter's-Hill upon being informed at the Academy that sickness had prevented Mr. Cowley's attendance there that morning. We found the poor mathematician in the agonies of a fit of the Gout, which had seized him in the Stomach with such violence, as to have racked him through a series of the most excruciating pains into a state of insensibility, succeeded by a short sleep, the departure of which had just plunged him into fresh Torments. Mrs. Cowley took us up into the Chamber where he lay, and whether it was owing to Company, or the course of the disease the pain ceased in a few minutes after our entrance. before we left him it had begun to make it's appearance in his Legs: All this he endured with a fortitude that shewed his philosophy was not confined to speculation.

We quitted him with some degree of reluctance on all sides upon the approach of dinner-time after a stay of 2 or 3 Hours: it was settled that Sam should go to him either at his house at the Warren or that on the Hill as it might happen 3 times a week; beginning with to day: and I left the entrance-money at my departure.

I had told you before that Sam's engaging in this course of Study would be not more the result of my persuasion than of his own wishes—he enters into it with a zeal proportionate to it's relation to that business which he loves as a source of present amusement, and esteems as a foundation of future fortune. I endevor'd to point out that relation in the course of our morning's walk; and to give him such a prospect of the introductory parts of the Mathematical Sciences as I was capable of giving, and he of receiving: he listened with an attention, which if I might believe him mitigated a Tooth-ach which he had upon him at setting out, and dispell'd entirely a weariness of which he complained soon after.

The day before some parts of experimental philosophy had been the subject of our discourse: we exemplified a few positions by some knick-knacks yt. I happend to have by me: and project after project was engender'd in the fermentation of promiscuous enquiry.

With all that calmness of his temper, which you have sometimes

---

[4] 'A distinguished master of mathematics, Cowley, of Woolwich Warren, was engaged to give Samuel lessons in that science, in which he made such progress as to write during his apprenticeship a treatise, which had the reputation of having exhibited unusual ability' (*Life of Sir Samuel Bentham*, 3: cf. letter 6, n. 6).

seemed to look upon as exclusive of active propensities he has an ambition which is not the less real, for not manifesting itself in ye. impetuousities of a hostile selfishness—he looks forward with an eye of desire to the future improvement of the scientific part of his profession, as a road to fame as well as fortune uninfested by competition; and leading by a necessity which he thinks happy through the avenue of perfect utility. he now looks back with a disdain which it would answer no end to discourage now the object of it is fairly abandon'd upon the counter[?] which he considers himself as having escaped—All this and more I learnt by neither appearing to him to act a part nor doing so.

As you appeared to entertain some doubt at first about the expediency of his immediate attendance upon Mr. Cowley; he looks upon your permission as a sort of conquest: and if I might take the liberty to advise it may be as well not to undeceive him at first by any sollicitous enquiries or exhortations: a sense of duty, may serve very well, when applied if one may say so to produce the passive effect of restraining irregularities: but pleasure when the Idea of it can by any contrivance be excited must succeed more powerfully as an active principle.

I have little room for any thing that concerns more peculiarly myself—A French Client 'tother day found me out during the time of general recess to whom I have given an opinion (and indeed drawn[?] the case from his stating[?] in that language which hereafter it may perhaps be some amusement to peruse.[5]

I met Dr. Smith[6] on Saturday with his little Boy as I was going to Queen's Square Place. I found he had already put a period to his Holiday excursions.

That you may enjoy with my Mother and Brothers all the pleasure that fine weather good health and variety of objects can afford is the continued wish of Dr. Sr.

Your dutiful and affectionate Son
Jere:^y Bentham

Tuesday
Septr.
3d. 1771

Mr. Clarke is not yet gone to Holland nor probably will be at all, business interfering.

---

[5] 'The first brief Bentham ever got, was from Mr Clarke; it was a suit in equity, on which £50 depended, and the counsel he gave was, that the suit had better be put an end to, and the money that would be wasted in the contest saved' (Bowring, x, 51). Possibly the reference here is to this brief.

[6] Presumably Dr Samuel Smith, headmaster of Westminster (cf. letter 67, n. 3).

93

TO JEREMIAH BENTHAM

21 September 1771 (Aet 23)

Lincoln's Inn Septr. 21st 1771

Hon'd Sir

It gave me great pleasure to receive the favor of your letter, a favor of which I began to despair, not apprehending your stay would be so long as it has proved: and to learn that your expedition has been so prosperous and so agreable in every respect to you and your's—I know not whether I shall not commence Traveller myself next week for a few days upon an occasion which you would never have thought of.—learn with surprize, that Mercury (excuse the Chymist) is fixed at last—Dr. Mulford has made a purchase (as I hear from my Uncle who had it from a friend of the aforesaid Dr's. at Basingstoke) of a House not far from Southampton—at a place that I think is called Totton—a House without prospect and without ground those sine qua nons without which hitherto no purchase was to be thought of: be it however what it may, I am determined to go and look at it: tho' he has not yet let me know of his being settled as we had agreed upon when he was last in Town: but he does not know of a circumstance which will confine me to get back to Town by the first of next Month—and as we never stand upon any sort of ceremony, any hole that he can get his head into I can put mine in too.

Mr. and Mrs. Browne are just returned from a little Tour which I chalked out for them on the other side of the water highly delighted with their expedition: as their time was limited to ten days it was but a short one—to Margate through Rochester Canterbury etc. from thence by the Coast to Dover from Dover to Calais St. Omers Cassel Dunkirk Calais again and so home—Monsr. le Brun is come home quite a French-Man—he rubbed up his rusty French and jabber'd away as he tells me with amazing fluency—their Voyage both ways was prosperous and expeditious—3 hours only, going—and six returning—Mrs. Browne you may imagine cruelly sick the first time of going on the water; but saved herself by lying a bed the second. I spent the last evening with them before their

93. [1] B.M. I: 239–240. Autograph. Docketed by Jeremiah Bentham: 'Son Jeremy Bentham Lr. datd. 21st Septr. 1771.'

Addressed: 'To / Jeremiah Bentham Esqr. / Bristol / To be left at the Post Office till called for.' Postmark: '21 SE'.

departure which was last Sunday sennight and furnished them as ample instructions as I could devise /and a letter to an acquaintance at Dunkirk who was very civil to them/—they have brought home with them one of Mr. Pym's daughters who with her Brother and two sisters had been a twelvemonth at a sort of a smuggling Merchant's at St. Omer's for education—a strange sort of a contrivance calculated only to get them out of the way, while the Father who you know is a strange creature was muddling out a wretched existence by himself at home.[2]

I received t'other day a letter from Sam full of Fractions Vulgar and Decimal, Roots Cube as well as Square—by what I can f⟨ind⟩ Master and Scholar are so well satisfied with each other that he goes to Mr. Cowley as often as the weather will permitt without much regard to days of which, if I understand him right, he had omitted but two in all the time from his beginning to the 18th the date of his letter—Mr. Cowley's confinement I suppose gives him the opportunity for the present of practising this extraordinary assiduity—It is very happy when these abstract Sciences, the stumbling block of so many, meet with so much alacrity in so young a boy to encounter them. My paper is exhausted before I am aware and I must conclude with a premature but very sincere assurance that I am Dear Sir

Your dutiful and affectionate Son
J. Bentham.

94

T O   J E R E M I A H   B E N T H A M

29 September 1772 (Aet 24)

Chertsey Tuesday morng. 29th Sepr. 1772

Hond. Sir
    I find myself prevented by the weather from paying my duty to you, as was my intention, to day; but tomorrow, if there should

---

[2] Mr Pym has not been identified.
94. [1] B.M. I: 241. Autograph. Docketed by Jeremiah Bentham: 'Son Jeremy Bentham Lr. datd. Chertsea 29 Septr. 1772.'
    Addressed: 'To / Jeremiah Bentham Esqr. / Queen's Square Place / near the Broadway / Westminster.'
    Bentham was probably staying again, as in 1768, with Richard Clark at Chertsey, in order to have a peaceful place to work (cf. letter 79, n. 1). This letter shows him at work upon the analysis of offences and punishments which would one day culminate in the *Introduction to the Principles of Morals and Legislation* and in the works edited by Dumont.

be any probability of rain, I shall make sure by getting into the Coach. At our interview, I hope to read in your looks a confirmation of the account that my Landlord has given me, that this Summer's campaign has answer'd perfectly to yourself, my Mother, and Brothers, in point of health and entertainment—till when I am

Your's dutifully and affectionately
Jere:^y Bentham

I have sent you a few passages from my Book which I have got Mr. Clark's Clerk to transcribe—The remainder of the Chapter of Offences Principal and Accessory he has with him in Town and has probably finished by this time—that of Theft I have not yet revised.

95

To Jeremiah Bentham

14 October 1772 (Aet 24)

Hond. Sir

It gives me great satisfaction to find that the small specimen which you have as yet seen of what I have in hand, has met with your approbation: that being the case, one great end of it is answer'd. Having occasion to say something to the Public on the subject of that abstruseness of which you take notice, and which I see, must /from the causes which you mention/ to a certain degree remain after all my efforts to clear it away, I will not anticipate any thing on that behalf at present—In the mean time, excuse the liberty I take in supposing that with regard to some parts that abstruseness may possibly appear greater to you in common with others of your former profession, than to men at large, as, besides having a new language to acquire, you have the old one to unlearn. As to myself, if I had waited till I had been immersed in the depths of practise, I am satisfied I should never have had ability, even if I had had inclination, to engage in the design.

The great point is, to conciliate the suffrages of the *Masters* of the *Science*, of those who, as the French expression is, give the '*ton*': which is not to be done, in an eminent degree, but by eliciting such Truths, as shall be both new and interesting, not only to others but to them. For such Truths one must often dive deep; they are not

95. ¹ B.M. I: 242–243. Autograph. Docketed by Jeremiah Bentham: 'Fils Jeremy / Lr. datd. Chertsey Surry Octr. 14 1772.'

    Addressed: 'To / Jeremiah Bentham Esqr. / Queen's Square Place / Westminster / Single Sheet.' Postmark: '16 OC'.

to be gather'd on the surface. Others I believe there will not be wanting, which may find easier access to popular apprehension, by touching upon some string of the affections: and these may help draw in the rest. With others, this may be a point of prudence, with me it is a matter of necessity—I cannot rest till I feel myself every where at the bottom—I cannot go on with what is *before* me, while I have any thing behind me unexplor'd—I feel myself to have acquired to a considerable degree that pleasing and uncommunicable sensation—Thus only can one hope to keep clear of those inconsistencies, into which I see my predecessors, (as far as I have predecessors) humble servants for the most part to Authority, and to one another, falling evermore.

Forgive me Sir, if I declare simply, and once for all, that till this great business is disposed of, I feel myself unable to think of any other—The *Will* is here out of the question. Whatever may be the case with others, I find it impossible with me to bring the powers of invention to a mechanical obedience to the good pleasure of that faculty—The sense of *necessity*, which may set them to work in some, strikes me motionless—I am in this respect like David; I can 'give no melody in my heaviness.' In the track I am in, I march up with alacrity and hope: in any other I should crawl on with despondency and reluctance—If I am not likely to succeed in a pursuit in which I am engaged with affection and with strong presentiments of success; much less am I where both are wanting: I mean situated as I am at present—any tolerable share of success in such an undertaking as mine, you are sensible, must needs work a considerable revolution.

It was, I own, a little disappointment to me, to find along with my Mss, and the Ten you were so kind as to send me, nothing in your hand. I rummaged them over and over, and thought there had been a mistake.

The News you tell me about the Barracks, is comfortable indeed—I hope that source of your anxieties will soon be stopped up—Down with the Red-Coats! Lord North and Liberty for ever![2]

[2] We do not know what Jeremiah Bentham's news about the barracks was, but the following passage from Bowring (x, 71–72) perhaps throws some light on the matter: 'I find, in the handwriting of Bentham's father (dated 1773,) "Verses by a young gentleman of Oxford, on the report of a design to make barracks for recruits of the building in St James's Park, adjoining to the garden of Jeremiah Bentham, Esq., in which is erected a temple to the memory of Milton, whose house it was, and where he lived when he wrote his immortal poem of Paradise Lost.

> Peace to these shades! where once our Milton trod—
> Where yet his spirit reigns, a guardian god!
> Far off let Mars his crimson standard rear—
> Divine poetic peace inhabits here.

I congratulate my Friend Charles[3] on his new Amours: in this, as in every thing else he undertakes, I am satisfied he will come off with éclat: let him pray stoutly, if not to Venus, at least to Aesculapius and Minerva, to be propitious to him.

I just now learn, that a neighbour who lives but a Door or two off has just had a practical Lecture on Criminal Law read to him, which is not much to his liking: some Rascals got in last night, and took every Apple out of his Garden*—I have fortunately housed the greatest part of my Landlord's—

With sincere respects to my Mother and Brothers, believe me to be

Dr. Sir   Your dutiful and affectionate Son

Jere:^y Bentham

Chertsey Oct. 14 1772.

I believe it will not be many days, before I pay one visit more to Town before the Term.

* The Common Law, you know, as it stands at present, is so complaisant to such Gentlemen as these, as to give them leave: I think there has been no Statute inflicting a Punishment for taking fruits; tho' there are for Trees and Roots—my Definition, would hook him in.

96

To Samuel Bentham

25 November 1772 (Aet 24)

Linc. Inn Wednesday Novr. 25 1772

Dear Sam

Your letter in spite of the indifferent news it brought, gave me great pleasure—I have just stolen a few minutes to tell you so,

> Where hireling troops, with wanton license stray,
> Milton's free spirit would disdain to stay.
> Hence then, stern god! and other mansions choose;
> Be those reserved for Milton and the Muse!"

' No doubt Bentham was the author of these lines. The adjoining of the barracks to his hermitage troubled him to the end of his days. His studies were sometimes interrupted by the cries of the soldiers who were flogged in the barrack-yard; and I have often heard him speak with the utmost indignation and horror of that most unnecessary penalty, whose infliction was so frequently called to his mind by the suffering of its victims.'

It seems in fact unlikely that Bentham was the author of the verses: 'a young gentleman of Oxford' would have been an inappropriate description of him in 1773.

[3] Charles Abbot: see letter 68, n. 4.

96. [1] B.M. I: 244–245. Autograph. Docketed: 'I.B. Novr. 25th 1772.'

Addressed: 'Mr. Sam: Bentham / at Mr. Gray's / Master Shipwright / at Woolwich.' Stamped: 'PENNY POST PAID'.

relying upon the situation which I am in, of having my thoughts pretty much occupied, for my excuse with you, who have so full an experience of such a situation, ⟨for not⟩ telling you so sooner—A Gentleman[2] happening to call upon me 'tother day with whom I am intimate and whom I believe you once saw at my Chambers, and the discourse falling upon our several families and relations, I pulled out the letter which was then in one of my pockets, without any thoughts of what happen'd and shew'd it him—He joined with us in our reflections upon the behaviour of the sleeveless Knight,[3] and told me, that, being upon good terms, as I knew, in Sr. Gilbert Elliot's[4] family, who is one of the Carleton-House Junto as it is called, and what is more to the purpose, Treasurer of the Navy, he would, if you thought proper, undertake for your Scheme in that way, to get it a fair hearing.[5]

I hear however from Mr. Townsend,[6] through the medium of my Father, that you have met with some encouragement since: if so, pray inform me of the particulars: if it is not so great as to supersede the advantage of the offer which I have been mentioning, let me know when you will come to Town, that I may engage my friend to give you the meeting—His name is Poore: He is deeply instructed in the Mathematics, and fond of viewing every thing that is curious under the article of Machines: you will find him perfectly qualified to understand, and disposed to assist you.

Adieu

Your's affectionately

J.B.

[2] Edward Poore. See letter 57, n. 2.

[3] Presumably the Captain Knight referred to in letter 99. 'Sleeveless' means *incompetent* or *idle*.

[4] Politician and man of letters (1722–77). Treasurer of the Navy from 1770 till his death. Cf. also letter 200.

[5] Samuel Bentham, then aged fifteen, had devised a pump on the chain and bucket principle which would pump out the bilge water with far less manpower than the existing system. The proposal was put before the Navy Board and rejected on two grounds, first, it would not work, second, no captain would put to sea without it, and the expense would be too great. It seems that a contract was to be made with a more influential party, namely Captain Bentinck (cf. letter 248). (See also the unpublished letters B.M. I: 246, 248, 250, 253.) B.M. I: 248, 250 and 252 are letters from Samuel to Jeremy on this topic. B.M. I: 246 from Samuel to his father 30 December 1772, reports the visit to the Navy-Office by the Bentham brothers and Edward Poore to inspect the pump, which was there for examination.

[6] Possibly James Townsend, mercer of Bishopsgate, alderman of London 1769, M.P. for W. Looe, 1767–74, for Calne, 1782–87. A prominent Whig leader in the City and an adherent of Lord Shelburne. His brother the Rev. Joseph Townsend (1739–1816) was a later acquaintance and correspondent of Bentham's.

97

TO JEREMIAH BENTHAM

15 May 1773 (Aet 25)

Hond. Sir

As I thought it would be more satisfactory to you to see the Act itself, and for us to consult together, than trust singly to my report of it, I have sent it you by the Bearer—This I take to be most conformable to the spirit of your commands—laying the enacting clause, and proviso (Postscript) together.

Your's dutifully and affectionately
J.B.
15th May 1773

I have taken this opportunity of returning the Annual Register. [*On cover:* Horace shall be brought.]

98

TO SAMUEL BENTHAM

20–26 August 1773 (Aet 25)

Friday eveng. 9 o'clock

Dear Sam

I have just received your letter. Your queries in it I will do my endeavours to answer as soon as I have an opportunity, probably

---

97. [1] B.M. I: 258–259. Autograph. Docketed by Jeremiah Bentham: 'Fils Jeremy. Letter datd. 15 May 1773.'

This was doubtless written at Lincoln's Inn, whence it was sent to his father by private bearer. The topic of the letter remains obscure.

98. [1] U.C. cxxxv: 2 and B.M. I: 260. Autograph. Docketed: 'I.B. Augst. 17th 1773.'

Addressed: 'To / Mr. Sam.[1] Bentham / at Mr. Gray's / Master Shipwright / in his Majesty's Dock Yard / Chatham / Kent. Single Sheet.' Postmark: '26 AV'.

This letter has survived in two parts: the first five paragraphs, now in University College, were evidently filed separately by Samuel Bentham because of their exclusively mathematical content. On this portion someone has written the date 'August 17th 1773.', while on the second portion has been written 'part of a letter Dated Augst. 17th 1773', but the letter was completed and posted on Thursday 26 August and had evidently been begun on the preceding Friday, 20 August.

The address shows that Samuel had removed with his master, William Gray, to Chatham. A friend of Samuel's called Burket had invented a fire-escaping engine (cf. letter 101). It was doubtless with this in mind that Bentham transcribed the advertisement from the *Gazetteer*.

tomorrow; in the mean time I will execute a design which your letter has revived, and which I formed soon after your departure: it is that of communicating to you a few considerations which I believe will perfectly obviate your scruples about taking the description of the parts of a mathematical figure from the accidental circumstances of its situation—I drew these up immediately in a form which I will now transcribe, and which I reproach myself very much for not having transcribed and sent to you before, as it would have put you *in possession,* as it were, of a very useful perhaps even necessary expedient which perhaps you may have been losing a good deal of time in endeavouring to steer clear of.

It is to be observed that of the three sides (better called *bounds* or *boundary-lines* for a reason that will appear presently) of a triangle, as such, there is no one in particular to which the name of *base* more properly belongs than to another: the *source from* whence that name is taken is never any other than the accidental circumstance of the situation of the figure with respect to the reader. And from this source the name may *well* be taken: since it is easy to conceive, that whatever station the reader may find it convenient to view the figure from that figure in itself must ever be /(still)/ the same.

The *purpose for* which it is taken is, to distinguish some one of the three that one means to speak of, from the two others which, at the instant, one does *not* mean to speak of: which two others are still, by Euclid, continued under the common (or twin[?]) appellation of the sides.

Now then, for whatever purpose, by whatever reason, and in whatever manner a man is justified in distinguishing any one of the bounds from the 2 remaining ones, for the same purpose, by the same reason, and in the same manner is he justifiable in distinguishing these 2 from one another—let them be so distinguished and call one of them the *right*, and the other of them the *left*.

So of the *Angles* call one the angle *to the right* (not *the right* angle for an obvious reason) the other, the angle *to the left;* and the remaining angle which is opposite to the base (boundary-line) the angle at the top (not the vertical angle, that being to be reserved for a *twin* name, ex. gr. the vertical angles).

Thursday eveng.

Extract from an advertisement in the Gazetteer of 28 July 1773.

Premiums given by the Society of Arts etc. dated April 14th 1773.

No 22 'Machine for preserving lives in case of Fire. For a Machine superior to any hitherto in use for preserving the lives of persons in case of fire; to be deliver'd the first Tuesday in Novr. 1773; the Gold Medal or £30.

N.B. Strength and cheapness in the Machine will be consider'd as part of its merit.

Compleat Books of Premiums may be seen at every Post Office in Great-Britain etc.'
Thus far the Advertisement.

I have no notion of a man's being precluded from a Patent by the acceptance of one of these Premiums. It is possible this may be a condition annexed to the granting of the premiums in some cases, viz: not to apply for a Patent—I mean for aught I know to the contrary—though I never heard of any such thing. This I am certain of, that the bare acceptance of such a Premium, if no such condition be enter'd into, cannot by Law disable a man from obtaining any Patent he might otherwise.

Thursday evening 26th
I wrote word by Tuesday's Post to my Uncle that we should be with him on Monday if the weather permitt, and to Mr. Mulford that we shall be with him some day the latter end of the week.
I shall therefore expect to see you on Sunday.

99

To Jeremiah Bentham

15 September 1773 (Aet 25)

Totton Wednesday Sept. 15 1773
Honoured Sir
I have taken up the resolution at last not to make the length of my neglect in not writing to you a plea, as is sometimes the case in matters of this sort, for omitting that duty altogether. I have thought to have had to congratulate you upon the acquisition of so

99. [1] B.M. I: 261–262. Autograph. Docketed by Jeremiah Bentham: 'Son Jeremy Lr. datd. Totton Hants 15 Sepr. 1773.'

Addressed: 'To / Jeremiah Bentham Esqr. / Queen's Square Place / Westminster.' Stamped: 'SOUTHAMPTON'. Postmark: '17 SE'.

This letter is written from Totton, Hants., where John Mulford had bought a house in 1771 (cf. letter 93). Bentham describes a visit Samuel and he had first paid to their uncle George Grove at Whitchurch, not far from the old family house, Browning Hill.

agreeable a companion at Matlock as Mr. Lind,[2] and intended to have taken that opportunity for a letter; but when the time came, he could not prevail upon himself to leave the scene at such a distance, while the fate of his friends the Dantzickers, continued yet in suspense, little as the probability was become, of his being able to render them any service.[3]

On Saturday fortnight Sam came up from Chatham: we intended to have sat out on the Monday: but as I happen'd to have no sleep the night before, I did not think it prudent to undertake an expedition so laborious as we proposed our's should be under such a circumstance. The next morning however (Tuesday) we sat out a little after 5 and got to Whitchurch between 8 and 9 after travelling 36 miles on foot, whereof 5 were out of the way, owing to one of those mistakes which, where it is possible, you know I always make.

[2] For John Lind (1737–81) and his family see letter 12, n. 1.

In the autumn of 1761, after taking his M.A. at Oxford, Lind, who had been appointed by the Levant Company as their chaplain at Constantinople, accompanied Henry Grenville, the newly appointed Ambassador, to Turkey. He was in Constantinople from March 1761 until July 1766; but the latter part of his stay was marred by a violent quarrel with John Murray, who had succeeded Grenville as Ambassador in 1765. Lind lost his post through 'being too agreeable to His Excellency's mistress' —though Murray's version of the affair was somewhat different (cf. P.R.O., S.P. 105/119, 110/87). Lind repaired in 1766 to Warsaw where he dropped his clerical title and became tutor to the king's nephew, Stanislas Poniatowski. He was soon noticed by King Stanislas, who made him governor of a school for cadets and a privy-councillor. Late in 1772 or early in 1773 he returned to England with a pension from the king. In effect he acted as his minister, though being a British subject he could not formally adopt the title. His anonymous *Letters concerning the present state of Poland*, attacking the 1772 partition, appeared in the latter part of that year and early in 1773. He was probably also the author of *The Polish Partition Illustrated*, a series of satirical dialogues published in several languages during 1773 and 1774 (cf. D. B. Horn, *British Public Opinion and the First Partition of Poland*, Edinburgh, 1945, 29–31.) He had many influential friends, including Lord Mansfield and Lord North, the Prime Minister. Lord Mansfield assisted in his admission to Lincoln's Inn, and he was called to the Bar in 1776. In 1775 he published *Remarks on the Principal Acts of the Thirteenth Parliament of Great Britain*, which included a defence of the Government's American policies. Bentham had helped him to compose it. On the outbreak of the American War Lind wrote *An Answer to the Declaration of the American Congress*, which won a pension for his sisters.

From 1773 Bentham and Lind were close friends. Lind gave Bentham reports of, and some entry into, the eminent society in which he moved. Bentham gave away the bride—Mary Welch—at Lind's marriage on 31 December 1774 at St. George the Martyr, Queen Square, Holborn. Lind died in Lamb's Conduit Street in January 1781.

Cf. *D.N.B.* and Bowring, x, 55–64.

[3] The 1772 partition of Poland by which Russia, Prussia and Austria obtained large slices of Polish territory was formally accepted by the reluctant Polish *seym* in 1773. Danzig was not among the spoils, but was now separated from Poland by Prussian territory. Lind's correspondence with the British Government about Danzig and other Polish matters is in P.R.O., S.P. 88/117.

We took the wrong road from Basingstoke, and so had to cross the country from Popham lane, through Steventon etc. to Overton.

I don't know whether it was before your departure that my Uncle had given us an invitation. He treated us with great civility and kindness: and owing to his pressing we staid till the Monday following (last Monday se'nnight) instead of one or 2 days as we had proposed. He entertained us (Sam in particular) with the sight of Mr. Portal's Paper-Mills[4]; and we were to have gone to Baghurst, to take a view once more of the old place, but could not get permission of the weather. Mrs. Riley was there, which I was pleased to find as I was afraid of his putting himself to the inconvenience of sending her away, and it was a kind of confidence that may serve for the future to banish a number of little disagreable reserves. She appeared in every respect as mistress of the house and once or twice according to Sam's observation, the words 'my dear', escaped her: but the apartments, as you may imagine, above stairs were distinct.[5]

On Monday sennight we got to this place—we made a day of it for the sake of shewing Sam what was to be seen at Winchester. The Dr. received us very cordially notwithstanding he had been to London for some days without calling on me not long before we quitted it: a behaviour which I should have construed as a repeal of the invitation, in any body but him. He is grown very religious, very recluse, very slovenly and very oeconomical. He has however made a present (or rather indeed a loan) to Sam of a variety of curious tools, to some value; and to me a sort of general offer (which probably will not amount to much except as a testimony of his disposition) of any that I will select out of about half of his books that stand apart from the rest, as he shall have less and less occasion as he intimates for any prophane books except medical etc.

I have taken advantage of the neighbourhood of Southampton to bathe every morning except one: which was indeed a principal inducement with me to this excursion, in hopes of improving the

[4] Joseph Portal (d. 1795), son of Henri de Portal (1690–1747), a Huguenot refugee naturalised in 1711, had succeeded his father in business as a paper-maker at South Stoneham and Laverstoke, near Whitchurch, where G. W. Grove had an estate. Portal had purchased the Laverstoke estate in 1759 and was high sheriff of Hampshire in 1765.

[5] Mrs Elizabeth Riley or Ragg was George Woodward Grove's housekeeper at Whitchurch, and his mistress, by whom he had two daughters, Ann (b. c. 1761) and Susannah (b. c. 1772). They later took the name of Grove and are both mentioned in their father's will. Ann Grove married Lloyd Williams, vicar of Whitchurch, and died sometime before 6 August 1788 (cf. B.M. XVII: 61, 255).

state of my health which for some time past has not been altogether what I could wish it. I find it thus far of service that it reestablishes my stomach *for the day* after it has suffer'd as it will do by my continuing in bed a few minutes after six: but I do not perceive as yet that it has done much towards giving such a permanent tone to the fibres as to prevent that effect's taking place. Sam threshes hard at Euclid, upon a new plan of my invention, and takes the opportunity of pressing me into his service. He desires me to tell you that he fears there is no probability of Capt. Knight's promotion. We both beg to be remember'd with all respects /and affection/ to my Mother and Far, whose amusements we hope have suffer'd no interruption by the Surgeon. The paper, which is the largest the house happens to afford, will just allow me to subscribe myself Dr. Sr.

Your's dutifully and affectionately
Jere:^y Bentham

We think to be in London by the end of next week.

100

To Granville Sharp

28 October 1773 (Aet 25)

Mr. Bentham presents his respectful Compliments to Mr. G. Sharp and returns him many thanks for the favour of his learned and ingenious publication.

Lincoln's Inn No. 6 Octr. 28th—73.

---

100. [1] MS. in the possession of Miss Lloyd Baker, Hardwicke Court, Gloucester.

Granville Sharp (1735–1813), philanthropist, pamphleteer, and scholar, is best remembered as one of the first campaigners against slavery. The publication he had sent to Bentham was presumably *Remarks on the opinions of some of the most celebrated writers on Crown Law, respecting the due distinction between manslaughter and murder*, 1773. There is no evidence of any further contact between Bentham and Sharp at this period, though Sharp is mentioned in a letter from Bentham to Sir James Mackintosh in 1806 printed by Bowring (x, 428). It seems likely that Bentham would have been critical of some of Sharp's work, notably *A Declaration of the People's natural right to a share in the Legislature*, 1774. The fact that Bentham was considered by Sharp to be a suitable recipient of his work suggests that already Bentham's interest in law reform was becoming known outside his own immediate circle.

101

To Samuel Bentham

4 November 1773 (Aet 25)

A thousand pardons I have to beg of you, my dear Sam, for this long silence; tho' I have thus much to say in apology, that you yourself have been in some measure the cause of it. Your first, however interesting, happen'd to be of such a nature as not to require an answer, except as to the Law-case, of which presently. On the other hand; your second required so much to be said to it, if I said any thing, that not willing to consider it by halves, I put it off till I could muster up resolution to fill as much paper as I foresaw would become necessary.

As to your *Case*—young gentleman—aw—hum—your case, I say, difficult and important as it is, I have however that regard for you and your friends, that nobody should be more ready to give you the information you desire, were it not for two ancient and fundamental maxims, which men of our profession never lose sight of. *The one*, which is for the use of our clients, is, that a Law opinion is to be depended upon in exact proportion to the fee that is given for it; so that seeing there was no fee (let me look once more—no—no fee at all given with your case, the kindest thing I could do by you, was, instead of giving you an opinion, which under such circumstances, even tho' *mine*, could not be depended upon, to give you none at all. *The other* which is for our own use, is, 'never to take promises for payment'. However, you may get a piece of paper, between your finger and thumb (you understand me) against I come into your part of the world, and I shall then you may be assured, Sir, be very ready to shew you any favour.

So much for the Counsellor—now brother again—At the same time with your 3d and last, came to hand a letter from Mr. Mulford, which being partly on business, I have been obliged to give the preference to in answering. We had scarce left the poor Doctor, when he was attacked by that very same nasty disorder that we all took so much pains to guard against—The Latin proverb 'Occupat extremum Scabies' which is commonly render'd 'the Devil' but on this occasion may be translated 'the Itch' takes the hindmost, i:e: him who is left behind, was verified in his person—The 21st

101. [1] B.M. I: 263–266. Autograph. Docketed: 'I.B. Novr. 4th 1773.'
    Addressed: 'To / Mr. Bentham / at Mr. Gray's / Master Builder / of the King's Dock Yard / Chatham / Kent. / Double Sheet.' Postmark illegible.

of last month, the day on which his letter is dated, was the very
first he says 'of his venturing to set himself down for sound.'
To add to this, he has another passage, which containing the history of your lost sheep, I shall transcribe for your edification.—
'Samuel found a coat and wastecoat wanting, but as you mentioned disposing of it before *my Boy*, he look'd mighty grave at
your departing without receiving it, as I thought: therefore in the
name of Samuel I took the liberty of presenting them to him.' So
far the Doctor: the reflexions upon this, I shall leave for *you* to
make, to save the trouble of communicating to you mine—I told
him in answer, that 'Sam would be very glad that his rags had
met with any body to whom they proved acceptable; particularly
as it was young Trusty, who however, I believed, was one of the
last persons to whom we should have thought *ourselves* to have
given them.'

I cannot enough admire the humane delicacy of your ingenious
friend: and as he appears to be one of that small and valuable
number of men in a community who are governed in the first place
by conscientious motives, and capable upon occasion of postponing
a benefit of their own to a greater benefit of their neighbour, I
shall venture to treat the question you proposed to me as a case of
conscience, without fear of being laughed at for my pains by him I
am writing *of*, should he happen to come to the knowledge of what
I say, any more than I am sure I shall be by him I am writing *to*.

Mechanical inventions are calculated for one or the other of 2
purposes: either 1st to compass some end that *was not* compassed
before: or 2dly, to compass one that *was*, at a less expence. This
expence is either 1st of *materials*, or,
2dly, of workmanship—so that the
saving to be made by an invention of
this last mentioned kind must be a saving either of materials or of workmanship. Of a saving of *materials* (whatever
may be the case with it in respect of
workmanship) an invention that I saw
a few days ago for making wheels out
of single pieces of timber, by *bending*,
may serve for an example; it taking no
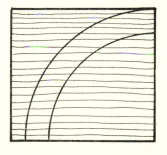
more than about $\frac{1}{3}$ of the wood that is necessary where each quar-
[ter] (or *felly* as it is called) of the wheel is to be cut out of a
solid parallellepipedon. A saving of *workmanship* is made either
at the expence of 1st the *Masters* (already in the business) *only*;

or 2. of the *Workmen* only: or 3d of both at once. It is made 1. at the expence of the *Masters* only, when the quantity of the commodity that *might be* vented if produced is so much superior to that *actually* produced (viz: before the invention) as that employment might be found for the same number of *Workmen* still: at the same time that the invention, being kept *private* is put in practise by the inventor on his own account, who by underselling the *Masters* can take the business out of *their* hands. It is made 2. at the expence of the *Workmen* only when the invention is made public but the quantity of the commodity in demand is limited, and the invention is of such a Sort, as to require either, 1. an entire *new* set of workmen to execute /so as to throw all the old ones out of employment/ or, 2 the *same* set, only in a less number, so as to throw a *few* out. It is made 3. at the expence of *both*, in the manner that you will see by laying the 2 first cases together. You see this 2d case divides itself into 2 others; the 1st of which was or at least was imagined to be that of Mr. Dingley's Saw Mill at Limehouse which was destroy'd some years ago by the Sawyers as you probably have heard (and £2000 given by Parliament to make good the damage)[2]—Mr. *Burket's* Invention I suppose would come under the other; if the business is executed not *solely* by men who like those in the *King's service* are provided for as I understand, work or no work, but in part by workmen *at large*; for I suppose that there would be nothing in his machine, whatever it is, but what could be done as well by the men at present employd in making Treenails by *hand*, as by any others: only that perhaps it might not find employment for them all. I leave it to your sagacity to supply a great many deficiencies in these observations that I may come to the point in question in reasonable time—You will naturally observe, for instance, that a saving of materials must of course include in it in some degree a saving of workmanship; viz: of that which is bestowed in bringing the materials from that state in which they are a part of or supported by the original soil (old Dame Tellus the universal mother) to that in which they are to be consumed.

　　Now then as to the *Workmen*; however it may be with an *individual* who may be expected to regard himself in the first place; to the *State*, which ought to regard every one of it's members (or if you please, the Government which ought to regard every one of it's subjects) with an equal eye, it ought ever, I think, to be a

---

　　[2] Charles Dingley, master of the saw-mills at Limehouse, d. 1769; described in the *Gentleman's Magazine* obituary notice (xxxix, 559) as 'a great projector'.

condition *sine quâ non* of it's acceptance of such a project to secure
a subsistence to all such persons as being thrown entirely out of
employment, would otherwise be deprived of it: for it can hardly
be, that the accession of happiness, comfort etc. (call it what you
will) to those to whose benefit the saving accrues, can compensate
the sum of the distress experienced by a number of workmen in such
a situation: and if the expence of this be objected, it may be
answer'd, that if the saving which is perpetual will not answer this
expence which is but temporary, to the Government which is not
limited as a private person is in it's ability to make advances, it is
not worth attending to, nor the plan itself, whatever it be, worth
adopting. You will further observe that though the *saving itself* is
perpetual, the accession of happiness which it produces can hardly
be reckoned other than *temporary*: for, in a little time, that burthen,
whatever it be, from which men were relieved by the saving, is
forgotten, and they relapse into the same state of mind in that
respect as they were in before. The persons to be benefitted by the
saving in this case (besides the person who is benefitted by the
profit of the business) are the nation at large, that is all the individuals indistinctly who compose it, who will be eased of so much
of their taxes as it amounts to. I need not tell you that it is impossible to form any tolerable æstimate of the quantity of happiness
that the saving, supposing the exact sum of it could be known,
would produce in this way. We are not however to conclude that
this quantity, because difficult to adjust, is unreal or inconsiderable. It will often happen that a person who at a given time can
bear his share of the taxes tolerably well, when it comes upon any
occasion to be ever so little encreased, is reduced to great distress:
and when this is the case with one, it must be so with numbers;
many more probably than would be thrown out of employment by
the saving. That great distress is often brought on numbers of
people by taxes is certain; and the cause of that distress must in
every case have a beginning *somewhere*, that is in the lessening of
their subsistence money by a *certain* sum. Not to mention that the
difficulty of finding a small sum of money will often prevent the
Government from setting on foot a scheme of public utility: and
so be a means of intercepting and preventing a quantity of happiness which to some persons or other would have accrued by means
of it.

From thus much that I have said you must be sensible that it is
not in my power to form a decided opinion for want of being
master of those facts upon which it would turn—I mean whether

the men who derive their subsistence from this business in the present state would be thrown entirely out of employment, or to what degree—and that for a long time probably, or a short one, and whether they are many or few. As the scruples you have alledged bear no reference to any persons under this description, I am disposed to hope that the subject is free from any scruples on this score, upon which supposition I cannot but heartily and strongly join with you in opinion that Mr. Burket will be very much wanting both to himself and to the public if he suffers his invention to perish.

As to the old Shipwrights, if the air blowing upon them (after their having lived in it the greatest part of their lives) should give them cold, he ⟨may⟩ make each of them the present of an umbrella. I cannot treat this objection, humane as it is, more seriously.

As to the Contractors, men of property, he must needs see that there is no one of them all, but is as much a rival to every other, as he can be to any of them.

For all undertakings which, like this, are supposed to be lucrative, there will be competitors; of whom some of course must be disappointed. Opposition he must look for from all of them, as being also of course, just as they expect and experience it from one another; with this difference indeed, that as his invention tends to take the business out of the hands of every one, as much as of any, it is but natural that against *him* they should all of them join forces. But none of them could be so unreasonable as to accuse him of any injury to them, nor could anybody else be so weak I think as to pay any regard to them if they did. One man is just the same /and no more/ to the public, as another man. If he is ready to do the work at an expence to the public *equal* to theirs, he has an equal right with them to be employed: if at a *less* expence, a *superior*.

If his invention does any thing like what he expects from it, in this respect, and those with whom it lies to determine are not wholly abandoned to sor⟨did⟩ and mercenary conditions, it must be adopted: because it being an invention the utility of which is demonstrable in pounds shillings and pence, there can be no pretence or subterfuge for not adopting it. The best and most satisfactory proof however of it's being of this kind, and what it would best answer his purpose to give, would be the offering to execute the work himself at a rate some considerable degree less, for example at $\frac{2}{3}$ of (that is $\frac{1}{3}$ less than) the price normally taken. This method of contract seems in every respect the best, both as a manifest and indisputable evidence of the fairness of the proposal, and as the least invidious and alarming method of acquiring that recompense for the invention which it deserves—To speak out— the Government would never think of giving any thing near so much at once, as a reward, as might be g⟨ained⟩ upon the computation you mention if it came any thing near the truth (⟨for⟩ I suppose it is a random one) in the way of contract. As to what he says about having his throat cut (the word 'deservedly' might as well have been spared) by Messrs. the Contractors, which doubtless is in joke, you may tell him in the same strain, that a man need not wish for a better cause.

But howsoever it be with *this*, there is another invention of his which you have mentioned, that I cannot by any means commend him for witholding so long nor excuse him, if he persists in witholding it any longer. I mean the Fire-escaping engine, as you term it: an invention that I might have alledged as an example of that class, the purpose of which is to compass some end (and few can be more important) *not compassed before*.

I must acknowledge to you, indeed, for my own part, that considering the matter at large, and antecedently to any particular knowledge of his contrivance, I have no great presentiment in favour of the utility of any engine for that purpose: since the making use of it upon any occasion will I think require a number of little circumstances to be aware of and operations to be performed which persons under that kind of distress which the invention is calculated to relieve cannot commonly be supposed to be in a condition to perform and to be aware of. If however he who knows best how this is, continues to be of opinion that it will answer in any degree a purpose so important, I think that if he delays communicating it to the public he is inexcusable. As to what you were once mentioning concerning his reluctance to take it out of the hands of that brute Allen, I could wish him to take himself a little to task, and consider what cause he can find to attribute it to other than indolence and a false modesty, and how he can reconcile to himself the sacrificing of his own and the public benefit together to such considerations. Put him in mind of the parable of the talents in the Gospel.

I had like to have forgotten to mention, that whether it be or be not in the nature of things for any contrivance to answer the purpose compleatly and effectually, nothing however should prevent him from being a candidate for the reward offer'd by the Society of Arts for the engine *best* calculated to answer that purpose as far as it *can* be answer'd.

If I should not have render'd myself sufficiently intelligible upon any of these points, let me know that I may do my endeavours to set it right. Adieu, my dear Sam, and judge from the length of this Epistle of my desire to make you amends for the silence which preceded it.

Your's ever affectionately

Jere:^y Bentham

My best Compliments to Mr. Gray—let me hear from you soon, and in my next I will send you some little intelligences relative to E.F.[3] I will certainly write to my Uncle about the paper to-morrow.

Thursday Novr. 4 1773
Lincoln's Inn. No. 6.

102

SAMUEL BENTHAM TO JEREMY BENTHAM

6 November 1773

Chatham Novr. 6th 1773

Dear Brother

I shewed Burket your letter and he admires your impartial way of reasoning very much but still persists in his determination of setting it aside. the only objection he makes to your reasoning is that you suppose other people to be as sensible as yourself, for instance he says if the contractors and other supposed injured persons were sensible men they would be sensible of the justness of his proceedings but as few are especially those poor men who would be put out of (at least that kind of) employment, and as a mans happiness is chiefly in his imagination they would think themselves much injured and therefore would be very unhappy but as I hope you will come down soon I will not trouble you to answer or my-self to write any more arguments concerning this scheme of Burkets, as there is no immediate necessity of having it solved but as to his Fire escaping engine I believe if I or you press him close he will

---

[3] East Florida. Bentham seems to have toyed with the idea of emigrating there; (cf. letter 104 and letter 122, n. 3).

102. [1] B.M. I: 267. Autograph.

By no means all the extant letters of Samuel Bentham to Jeremy Bentham are included in this edition. The interest of Burket's reported reply to Bentham's remarks in letter 101 on new inventions and unemployment seems to justify the inclusion of the present.

170

send for it as he intends writing to Allen soon out [of] pure friendship to let him know that a Model of his will be spoiled unless he sends for it away. I wish you would come soon viz in a day or two. and I will take care to get a whole quire of paper between my finger and thumb and then as opinions are in direct proportion to fees I shall hope to have justice done me. When you write again direct to me at Mr. Grays etc. of the King's Yard ~~Near Rochester and I shall save a penny or if the letter is double 2 pence.~~

Pliny's letters. Sailing Cruize, Ship [. . .?],
~~E. Florid. Catalog. steering experiments.~~
Steel yard. ~~Money Bank Note.~~
Burket 1000. Sailing Boat. ~~Description of machine to contract or extend drawings to bring or send.~~
Doctor Hammond[?] french. Burket not Rec'd[?] his Matters go to [. . .?][2] Guittar. Burkets Flowers from ⟨. . .⟩.

103

JEREMY BENTHAM TO SAMUEL BENTHAM

November 1773 (Aet 25)

Dear Sam

Of what Mr. Gray loses by your absence one way, he gains only a *part* the other—Your pay is 1s. 6d. pr. day—the cost of your board is but half that—This I know by my experience for I am lately become a Housekeeper—When we meet again I hope to give you a dinner—clean not as at the 3 Tuns—*and* plentiful, not as at Queen's Square—I have laid in a Stock of Apples, which your friend Mrs. Green[2] covers for me with a coat of rice—I hope to have your opinion that in that form by the help of a Julep of Wine and Butter, they make a very pleasant Bolus. For Meat I have a Machine by which upon occasion, I could dress anything myself without incessant watching, burning out my eyes or greasing my fingers.

You complain of the multitude of your Speculations upon

---

[2] This word carefully scrawled out. Final word in letter hidden by B.M. binding. At bottom of page some such words as '2 SR Burket composed'.

103. [1] B.M. I: 268–269. Autograph. Docketed: 'I.B. Novr. 1773'.
    Addressed: 'To / Mr. S. Bentham / at Mr. Gray's Master Builder / at his Majesty's Dock Yard / near Rochester / Kent.' Postmark: illegible.
    [2] Cf. letter 211, n. 3.

Euclid—clap them all down—it takes up less time than considering whether they are necessary or no—When you are in possession
of a certain quantity, by surveying them with this view, you may
collect them into genera, and so reduce the multitude of them, or
rather the space they occupy upon the paper, for the future. As
to your scheme of residing here, for about a fortnight at Christmas
it is easily compassable, or rather is concluded upon already—For
any further continuance, you know it depends neither upon you
nor me, but upon Queen's Square. There is one condition however
on which even its *commencement* depends, as far as it depends on
me. Think not that I will set eyes on you till you have finished the
2d Book—I am serious—you will not find my doors open till that
is done, though the time of your visit to Queen's Square should be
come.[3] If you have done it before then, I will pay you a visit, perhaps so as that we may return together—Mr. Poore has expressed
a desire of being better acquainted with you—I proposed to him
to go down to Chatham—he embraced it with pleasure—I thought
that was the best place you could see him at, where he might see
your curvator,[4] and Burkit's inventions—though I had rather in
point of present satisfaction be with you alone, I could not answer
to myself the letting slip an advantageous opportunity for you of
cultivating an acquaintance with a Gentleman who on variety of
occasions may be useful to you, and in your own way.

Mr. Lind is a member of the Society of Arts, and pretty constantly
attends—If upon comparing notes upon your curvator we should
think it worth while, I might probably get it introduced there by
his means—they will sometimes give a *bounty* either honorary or
lucrative, for an invention for which they have not previously
announced a premium.

I gave my father some hints tother day about your scheme of
being discharged from the yard previous to your going to Petersburg—he seemed not to relish it, from his inability to believe that
you would continue nevertheless in a capacity or at least in the
track of promotion. If however that difficulty could be overcome I
think he might be brought into it. Against you come, you must
therefore furnish yourself with proofs of this.

---

[3] In U.C. CLXXIV and CLXXV there is a large collection of papers on mathematical
topics exchanged by Bentham and his brother, largely about this time. They can
hardly be reckoned as part of Bentham's correspondence—apart from some fragments of letters which are included in the present collection—but they contain matter
relevant to Bentham's theory of fictions.

[4] An invention of Samuel's for measuring crooked timbers (cf. *Life of Sir Samuel
Bentham*, 5).

Why do I hear no more of Burkit's Fire-escaping Engine? is indolence (if such it may be called) his ruling motive? or is he industrious only to make things for the pleasure of thinking when he has made them that he has thrown away his time? You know how many pair of Stairs my Garrot is from the ground—If I should be burnt, for want of ⟨. . .⟩ it, my Ghost shall lead him a weary life.

Uncle. Ay, that was that I might not forget—I have received a letter from my Uncle dated 23d of this month in answer to one I had written to him as I promised—he talks of coming to Town in a fortnight from that time, and promises in the meantime to use his endeavours to get the paper, as you desire, and bring it with him.

Once more—The time within which the engine must be sent (if at all) for exhibition approaches fast—I think it is the 1st of Jany. but that you know by a former letter—If he will get it and send it or bring it to Town, I will speak to Mr. Lind and any other friend I may have in the Society—if not—why—there is nothing more to be said about it—And so, good night, my dear Sam, having filled his paper, says

Your ever affectionate Brother—Jere:^y Bentham

Mr. Gray was very well advised in not meddling with the Dutch Lottery Tickets—It seems to have been a trap laid for him by some villain: if he had disposed of them, and written word of it, his letter would have been full evidence to convict him—the penalty is (by Stat. 6. G. 2. ch. 35. § 29) £200—and a year's Imprisonment. If the postage is an object, I suppose he may have it back by the method you mention, but as to that can say nothing of my own knowledge.

104

TO SAMUEL BENTHAM

4 December 1773 (Aet 25)

Dear Sam

With respect to the 8th proposition and that only I grant you a dispensation. You must stay till we can combat it with united forces. It is abominable in Euclid because he does not know how to

104. [1] B.M. I: 270–271. Autograph. Docketed: 'I.B. Decr. 3 1773.'
    Addressed: 'To / Mr. Sam: Bentham / at Mr. Gray's / Master Builder / at his Majesty's Dock Yard / near Rochester / Kent.' 3 December 1773 was a Friday. Since Bentham dates this Saturday, 3 December, and the postmark is '4 DE', we may presume it was written on the 4th.

describe the figure himself, to throw the burthen of it upon other people.

I despatch this much without saying any thing more to set you at ease as much as is in my power and as soon as it is in my power— Your letter is but just come to hand,

Adieu.

A friend of Mr. Villions [2] has got several plans and estimates of portable Houses for East Florida as they call them at Carolina— That same friend wrote about 2 months ago to his friend one of whose letters we have got, making further enquiries so that we may expect to have an answer to it in 2 or 3 more ... Mr. de Braun [3] and Q.S.P. I find are upon pretty intimate terms—He paid a visit there on Sunday when I was there to dinner; but as there was a good deal of company besides I did not choose to make my appearance, happening to be en deshabille ... Mr. Villion tells me that the E.F. Indigo sells for a great deal more (I believe half as much again) than any other. A Paragraph that appeared there in the News Papers about a Month ago speaks of some late settlers as doing extremely well, and mentions sugar among the products. Our Ragamuffin Cousin [4] of the Navy Office (son of the Clerk) of whom all that any body has heard these 8 years is that he has done what is too bad to be told, did me this morning the very unexpected honour of a visit—He, as fortune would have it, has been lately in the 2 Floridas. According to his account the settlers do extremely well in E.F. but the country is not so healthy as the printed account would persuade one to believe, tho' more so than W. Florida. There is no knowing how much may be owing to intemperance and imprudent conduct—we shall know more particularly from Mr. Villions Friend's Friend.

Saturday Decr. 3d 1773
    Lincoln's Inn

I heard no more from our Cousin having every reason and extremely glad of an opportunity which happen'd to present itself

---

[2] See letter 88, n. 7.

[3] In letter 134 De Braun (or De Brahm) is again mentioned in connection with East Florida.

[4] This was Edward William Bentham (d. 1785), son of Edward Bentham (d. 1774) of the Navy Office. The elder Edward was the son of Bryan Bentham (d. 1748) of Sheerness, a brother of Jeremiah Bentham's father. The unsatisfactory relations between the 'ragamuffin cousin' and his father are referred to at greater length in a letter from Jeremiah Bentham to Samuel dated 18 December 1773 (B.M. I: 273).

of getting rid of him as soon as possible—I should be glad to have some further discourse with him, if it could be done without incumbring myself with a disagreable connection—I could tell you however a good deal more of him as it is if I had time,

Once more Adieu my dear idle brother

I had no particular reason for doubling my letters as I did.

105

To Samuel Bentham

28 January 1774 (Aet 25)

Lincoln's Inn Friday 28 Jany. 1774

My dear Sam

Your silence had begun to be a matter of some surprize to me; and is now of much more concern, since I have heard the cause of it. You frighten me with your Catalogue of disorders—From what you tell me of the ill health of the family, it looks as if they were owing to the place—If so, you had better leave it for a while, till the cause whatever it be is dissipated, and come back again to your old quarters—Putrid sore throats, by the bye, if that has been one of the complaints the family have had as well as yourself, are contagious—What advice have you? If you do not mend, let me know, that I may come down to you. Whatever you do, lie in bed as little as possible—Your habit of body is naturally relaxed; and lying in bed, which is sufficient to weaken persons in health and strength to a great degree, must have that effect in a much greater degree upon persons already weakened by a disorder. If you cannot support yourself in a common chair, the best thing is an easy chair, if it can be got, enclosed on all sides with a cushion at bottom, such in short if you remember as my Grandmother Bentham used to have in her Bedchamber.

I received your letter last night: and this afternoon went to the Glass Warehouse but found no body there. As I was not certain whether I should be able to go there tomorrow, I would not put off writing to you on that account.

Since you have gone I have made considerable additions to my

---

105. [1] B.M. I: 275–276. Autograph. Docketed: 'I.B. Jan. 28 1774'.

Addressed: 'To / Mr. S. Bentham / at Mr. Gray's / Master Builder at his Majesty's Dock Yard / near Rochester / Kent.' Postmark: 28 IA'.

175

abstract of Priestly's book on Airs but have not finished it.[2] Mr. Poore has told me as a great secret that Priestly since the publication of it, has made some very material discoveries, more singular and important even than his first—One of these is, that of 2 Airs, which being put together, unite, crystallise, and become a solid. He has some of this solid now in bottles, and will in due time exhibit the experiment before the Royal Society. Mr. P had this from one of the 2 Secretaries of the Society. It was with much difficulty that I could get him to tell me of it, as it is not intended in these cases that any body should know any thing of the matter, till the whole account comes to be published together. It is natural for men to wish themselves to have the ripening of discoveries, of which they have been at the pains to sow the seeds—After all, this phenomenon of 2 vapours concreting upon union into a solid, is not without examples: but those in question are two I suppose that were not known to do so before. Volatile Alkali disengaged from Sal-Ammoniac by Fixed Alkali in the manner I shewd you, if you remember, in the Tea Cup, is in a state of Vapour and accordingly not sensible to the eye, but only to the smell—The case is the same nearly with the Muriatic Acid (the other constituent element of Sal Ammoniac) which (I mean the Mc. Acid) is always flying off in fumes from the vessel which contains it—Hold these 2 near one another and the Sal Ammoniac which is extemporaneously regenerated by their reunion, crystallizes into little solid Atoms, which tho' exceedingly minute, are by their number render'd visible in the shape of a whitish fume or cloud.

My Father who called this morning, made so many enquiries after you, that I could not avoid shewing him your letter—You may imagine him very anxious to hear further particulars of the state of your health as soon as may be

Dear Sam
Your's most affectionately
Jere:^y Bentham

---

[2] Though here called a book, this is evidently *Observations on different kinds of airs* by Joseph Priestley, LL.D., F.R.S., published in the *Philosophical Transactions* for 1772, (Vol. LXII pp. 147–265). Later in 1774 it was published in an enlarged form as Volume I of *Experiments and Observations on Different Kinds of Air* (see letter 111, n. 2).

106

TO SAMUEL BENTHAM

4 March 1774 (Aet 26)

My dear Sam

You ask my Father whether I am alive—'tis a severe question. I cannot but be sensible of the reproach contained in it: I acknowledge the justice of it: and submitt myself to your forgiveness. One principal cause (I believe I must not say justification) of my silence has been, the looking upon your condition which if it had been possible, nothing should have been wanting on my part to alleviate, as that in which a person is little able to be studious of any thing but present ease, or to interest himself much in any persons or things but what exist in the narrow circle of his chamber.

This instant (since the writing of the word chamber) a letter from you is brought me. It gives me great pleasure to find by the ease, by the vivacity, by the precision of it, that however severe your late illness may have been it has left your spirits as well as your faculties, improved[2] (I can't write of one thing for thinking of another shame on my faculties) improved I was going to say, (if it be in the nature of any illness to have such an effect) rather than impaired.

'Dead or alive'? alive and alive like—'Sick or well'? so, so— plagued for some little time past with coughs and noseblowings and such like petty ailments. 'affronted or not'? affronted a little, till I heard of your being ill, about not seeing you and Burket—that is affronted *nisi* as we Lawyers say but *definitively* (am I? I think not— I am sure one should not be) without an explanation, or without knowing that no explanation can possibly alter the case, I never am.

'Priestly'?[3] Not much of Priestly, since you, for whose sake I was working upon him, have been peeping at the land where all things are forgotten—but I dare engage to have dispatched him by the time you have the apparatus put together. You must fit up 2 phials one with each sort of Athanor, and let me know how they answer.

Perhaps I may dabble a little that way myself—more especially as I find that the new Air from Phlogisticated Alkali is not obtainable with any heat that I think you can probably conveniently

106. [1] B.M. I: 277–280. Autograph. Docketed: 'I.B. March 4th 1774.'
Addressed: 'For Mr. Bentham.'
[2] 'improved' is substituted for a deleted word. It is to this that the parenthesis refers.
[3] Cf. letter 105, n. 2.

give—It must be a *white* heat—I dabble? but how you will say? with what assets? you may guess however from the colour of the clothes in the pocket of which you will find this letter—indeed probably *know* from some letter which you either have received or will receive from my Father—Our old Couzin[4] is at last departed— She has left me £100 besides 10 for mourning. My Father will get, besides the extinction of an Annuity of 7£ pr. year for her life, after all sorts of charges and deductions about 600£ more. She used to tell me she had left me her Gold Watch, but I have heard nothing of it yet, perhaps as my conversation with my Father about her affairs has been but short—If she has, you shall have a Gold one, either hers or mine unless you prefer *use* to finery: for your own I believe is better than either—perhaps your's might fit the case of mine—I believe I shall employ half of it (I mean the 100£) in the purchase of a modicum of Stock which would bring in 40s. a year: the rest I must sink in bringing myself even with the world, in the long-wished for Articles of furniture you have heard me speak of, and perhaps £8 or 10 in Natural Philosophy—

Friday morning—

Friday evening—I have seen my Father—I dined with him at Q.S.P. upon his return from the Funeral—Mr. Clark was there—I don't know whether you will have your Watch or no—appearances seem against you—I mentioned the affair to him, he acknowledged his knowledge of Mrs. W.'s *intention* but said there was nothing about it in the Will—and he had no notion of nuncupatory Wills against written ones—My Mother then put in a word—The old Lady had used to shew her a pair of Chintz curtains and tell her they were to be her's—but there was nothing about it in The Will, and so there was an end of them—I said upon that, if all parties were not agreed I had no more to say about it—She replied hastily that she did not want it for her part, she had one of her own—My Father then asked me what I could want with it. I explained to him my intentions—I suppose if I was to make a point of it I could have it—The 'parole must demur' for a while, as the watch is left at Woodford for a little time, while the Maids stay in the House.

I have just called at Ramsden's[5]—nothing done—he is a sad

---

[4] Cf. letter 12, n. 3 for Mrs. Elizabeth Westall of Woodford.

[5] Jesse Ramsden (1735–1800) was a celebrated inventor of mathematical and astronomical instruments. In May 1774 he published a description of a 'New Universal Equatoreal'. He had a shop in the Haymarket. He and Bentham about this time belonged to a philosophical (scientific) club with very distinguished members (see Bowring, x, 148 and letter 169).

man in that respect—but he assures me they will be both done next week—so they must be postponed till another conveyance—have sent your ruler—Buckmaster's[6] Boy waits—Adieu

March 4th 1774.
    Lincoln's Inn

                                    Your's ever affectionately
                                         J.^{y} Bentham

East Florida while I think of it—I met with a Gentleman yesterday at Mr. Lind's—a Mr. Barker a Captain in the Merchants' service[7] who has 3 Brothers settled there—He tells me it has been computed that since the acquisition of the Colony about £100,000 has been laid out in all by Settlers—that the last produce viz for a year sent to England was worth about 12,000£ and that it is now encreasing rapidly—That out of that £100,000 a considerable some has been sunk by the dishonesty or incapacity of Agents: that his Brothers in the course of 3 years flung away 600£ in that way, and nothing done—that since they have been there themselves they have laid out as much more as makes £3000 that the last (which indeed I believe was their first) crop of Indigo was 1000Lb weight which might sell here for about £350, That the Indigo is much superior to that of Carolina, and promises to be equal to the best which is the Spanish and used to come from the province of Guatemala (in Mexico I believe) the capital of which is lately destroy'd.

                                    107

                        To Samuel Bentham

                        5 April 1774 (Aet 26)

Dear Sam
    So much for the Boat—I have read what you tell me about the Boat, with as much satisfaction as any thing upon any subject you could have written upon—But what's become of the 'tres capellæ'—'Tres Capellæ' are three little Goats, but from the occasion on which they are mentioned in an epigram of Martials, are made to stand for the subject whatever it was, that one was

---

[6] Perhaps Walter Buckmaster, hosier of New Bond Street.
[7] Unidentified. See also letter 122 (5 October 1774).
107. [1] B.M. I: 281–282. Autograph. Docketed: 'I.B. April 5th 1774.'
    Addressed: 'To / Mr. Sam: Bentham / at Mr. Gray's / Master Shipwright / at his Majesty's Dock Yard / near Rochester / Kent.' Postmark: '7 AP'.

last upon. What we were last upon was the Air-experiments—The apparatus was to have been proceeded upon forthwith—Specimens were to have been fitted up, and your most obsequious elder brother and humble servant to command, was to have been commanded down by the time all was ready—A letter after a considerable time has come from your honour, and in the said letter, concerning the said apparatus, or concerning his said proposed-to-be-commanded journey your said humble Servant has heard nothing—To confess the truth, your said humble servant, being now as at all times a little upon the lazy order, is not sorry for the pretence—But you, Sir, may it please your projectorship, where is your consistency, your steadiness, your resolution? Where are the fruits of your gold, that you melted into Glass? Is the Glass to be melted into Pitch again to caulk your Boat with? You who blew so hot when the weather blew so cold, do you now blow colder, as the weather, Sir, blows warmer? Think, and if you regard not an epigram of Martial, hear a text of scripture. 'These things ought ye to have done, and not to have left the others undone.'

Alas! Samuel. Night is come, and I can write but very little longer—I don't know that either of us is a Sorcerer, that we are thus both stricken with blindness—You indeed with your spouting Dolphins and Water-Trumpets may be a conjuror, for aught I know—but I! what have poor I done? however so it is—for these 3 weeks past I have sympathized with you in your blindness—As the Candles have come my eyes have gone—It began with an Inflammation in my left eye seemingly from cold, with soreness and a trifling degree of pain—I put a salve to it a day or two after, of Mrs. Browne's prescribing which seemed to have taken off the other Symptoms—but left a weakness behind. My eyes (for I put it to both, as the right began to be slightly affected) felt very stiff and *astricted* the next morning (it was at going to Bed that I applied it) so I did not repeat it—Since then I have put sometimes Conserve of Roses between a Rag doubled, with a few drops of solution of Camphor in Spirit of Wine dropped upon it, sometimes the Conserve alone—It was the prescription (voluntary and gratuitous prescription) of a Physician a friend of Mr. Lind's. What efficacy it may have as far as I can judge, seems to depend entirely upon its mechanical properties. By it's glutinous consistence fit to retain moisture it applies itself closely to the eye, and covering it (the eyelid you are to understand is closed) prevents the water of the Tears from evaporating and leaving the mucilaginous matter in the form of a Gum which you know is troublesome by its hardness. It is the Air which it serves to exclude, that is the grand promoter you know of evaporation—But I am encreasing my blindness while I am giving an account of it. Every Candle in the Coffeehouse is surrounded with a thousand luminous circles in all the colours of the Rainbow— You talk of scraping and raking money together as if you were poor. Our riches here have made us as poor as poor can be—The Bank is locked up and my Father's Executorship has made him for this 3 weeks an absolute Beggar—I received the Guinea for you from the Dr.[2] before he left Town: but it is gone the way all other Guineas go with me—If you were to skin me alive, this instant you could not get it out of me—You would get just so much and no more out of me as you would out of a Cat viz that is to say the Skin. My Father's face is as long upon the occasion, as a reasonable man's arm.

Adieu mon Frere
J.B.

April 5th 1774

Ramsden is . . . but I won't swear—I must not send this letter, I believe till I can send you some fresh account of him.

108

To Samuel Bentham

19 April 1774 (Aet 26)

Pish—Troughs—What signify the Troughs? The Joiners are not to cut the corks to the Phials—are they? are *they* to fit on the Athanors? Paltry excuses—any thing may do for a trough for an experiment or two to try how things pay—take your Hat—or what should hinder your borrowing a wash-tub?

Pray Mr. Boat-builder how goes on Euclid? Is it the Joiners who are to translate Euclid for you, or do you leave him to translate himself?

Thus far I had written a day or two ago and left off—Tuesday Evening—Your second letter is come to hand—My dear Sam, it is impossible for me to satisfy your impatience especially when you assign no other reason for it than itself—I am now in the suds; and can not answer for getting out of them tomorrow—besides if I

---

[2] John Mulford (see letter 10, n. 12).

108. [1] B.M. I: 283–284. Autograph. Docketed: 'I.B. April 19 1774.'

Addressed: 'To / Mr. S. Bentham / at Mr. Gray's / Master Shipwright / in his Majesty's Dock Yard / near Rochester / Kent.' Postmark: '19 AP'.

can, I have an engagement—In the suds you will say—what's that? Not the properest of all expressions, but the 1st that comes uppermost—It's well you got the Tin as you did (though indeed I don't find you intend making any use of it) for I have eat up all you left me, and shall devour the Lord knows how much more before I have done. It is for the entertainment of those troublesome guests you have sometimes heard me speak of—I hope if they do not like their fare, they will shift their quarters. As to what you tell me about money I am vexed to hear of it, but don't know how to remedy it—I have enough to supply your wants could I but get at you—As my Father has bid you refer the Apothecary to him, there is no help for it—Could not you beg the favour of Mr. Gray to advance you what you want 5 or 6 guineas or so, and I will pay it to any person in Town he will please to appoint as soon as the answer comes to hand—I have ne'er a Bank note of £10 nor any thing in paper that would go, nor can get such a thing at this time of night, or I would send you—But I must go to bed—Good night—and patience is the wish

of Your affectionate Brother
Jere:ᵞ Bentham

Apr. 19th 1774.

109

To Samuel Bentham

25 April 1774 (Aet 26)

. . . the change of winds so frequent in that atmosphere, may perhaps by this time have brought about another—But why do I sit to write all this stuff, when I shall see you in a day or two—

> Now to—etc.
> all might majesty and dominion
> and so forth

Monday evening
  April 25th 1774

Jereᵞ Bentham

109. ¹ B.M. I: 285. Autograph. Docketed: 'I.B. April 25 1774.'
  Addressed: 'To / Mr. Sam: Bentham / at Mr. Gray's / Master Shipwright / of his Majesty's Dock Yard / near Rochester / Kent.' Postmark: '25 AP'.
  Only the last page of this letter is extant. The remainder was probably burnt according to instruction.

Letter last but one—'therefore if there are any faults excuse.' why do you write so? any body (I should be ashamed to shew your letter) any body I was going to say, would think I was your father or your Schoolmaster—But as much of that as you will to my father—I have told you so before, You neither think nor write respectfully enough to him—you don't say 'Sir' often enough—I saw your last letter You called him bluntly a Lawyer—you should have said 'of the profession of the Law' or somewhat of that sort—

Put all this into the fire—Dead men tell no tales.

I will get a definitive answer from Ramsden, so as to send you down a pair of Barnacles[2] either of his making or of some body else's by my Father.

You are to say nothing about my Father's intentions of coming to Mr. Gray.

110

TO SAMUEL BENTHAM

8 June 1774 (Aet 26)

p	l		
2	last	for 'numbers' read 'Mambres'	
5	3	for 'horrible' read 'terrible'	
7	14	for 'the Ass' etc. to 'her heels' read |	|

Dear Sam

What is above was not written for thy instruction: but seeing this was the first sheet I happen'd to lay my hands upon, I thought it meet to send it unto thee.

Dear Sam

I thought you had been dead: but seeing thou has now at length written unto me; my conclusion from thence is that thou art alive: at least (for I would not be too hasty) that thou wert so at the time thou wrotest the letter which I have received. 'The Lord giveth and the Lord taketh away.' and the Lord leaveth things as he finds them—he hath left them: blessed be the name of the Lord.

---

[2] Spectacles.

110. [1] B.M. I: 288–289. Autograph. Docketed: 'I.B. June 1774.'

Addressed: 'To / Mr. Sam. Bentham / at Mr. Gray's / at his Majesty's Dock Yard / near Rochester / Kent / Single Sheet.' Postmark: '8 IV'.

For the opening lines see n. 4 below.

Thou seest I have not drawn the same conclusion concerning thee which a certain man had once drawn concerning him from the like premises. It was the Almanack-maker *Partridge*. 'Verily he is dead,' said a man of God, whose name was *Swift*: 'for such stuff as this of his would no man alive have written.'[2] O Samuel, thou art slow to write: yet when thou dost write perhaps thou deservest not altogether to be so blasphemed.

Thou hast said unto me! It requireth much to answer thee: I write unto thee not in order, but as the Lord putteth words into my mouth: or, if it so please thee, into my pen.

A black colour still wanting, sayest thou? Burkit knoweth the solution of Silver in the water which is called Aqua fortis: and asketh he still after a black colour? The Acid of Vitriol, yea the Vitriolic Acid, doeth that which is required of it, in that it giveth the black colour: so I understand thee: but it faileth, in that it will not dry—I will tell thee, in what manner thou shalt make it dry; so at least it seemeth likely unto me: When thou has forced it out of the wood, yea out of the pores of the wood, as much as may be, by the heat of fire, thou shalt then apply therewith a few drops of the fixed vegetable Alkali in a weak solution: peradventure it will reach the whole of that which is contained within the pores of the wood, and neutralize it, that is cause it no longer to be Vitriolic Acid, but that other thing, which upon turning to the tables thou mayest see—Is it not written in the book of the tables which I have given thee, that thou shouldst learn them? As thy soul liveth, it will neutralize every part thereof whereunto it reacheth. Can the Aethiopian change his skin or the leopard his spots? verily I say unto thee the black colour, once taken, shall not depart from it, yea it shall not depart from the stick, untill that stick shall be no more.

Thou askest of me more bent tubes—O thou of little faith! hast thou tried any of those that thou hast, together with the rest of the utensils the mixing phials and the corks, and the glass necks that are to go into the corks, and the athanors that are to go in the same, and the store-phials that are to fit upon the glass necks by leather? hast thou tried all these things? then wherefore is it that thou dost not tell me?

What chuckle heads some people are to give themselves the world and all of trouble, and make one pay eight pence for nothing? —as if the same people who made the head could not put it in, O

---

[2] *A Vindication of Isaac Bickerstaff, Esq.,* . . . 1709: *Prose Works of Jonathan Swift,* ed. Temple Scott, London, 1897–1908, i, 322.

Samuel, thou and a pin have heads, tho' my poor stick has none!
Give me thy head, to put upon my stick; for it will well befit it.

Pshaw—here's the scrap of a letter has been lying in my Cabinet
any time this 4 or 5 days, and won't finish itself, if I wait till
Doomsday. I wish the cat could do it for me you should have her
for a correspondent—she makes legible marks enough sometimes
with her 5 fingers upon my papers—here now must I put by a
thousand things I have in my head (besides lice and maggots) to
go on writing nonsense to you—well I'll make an end of it.

Send me the stick (for which many thanks to Burkit) by the next
conveyance, of which give me notice by letter—Take care and cover
it up with a competent proportion of his Majesty's Royal Tow
(God bless him) together with Paper, Packthread etc.

Last Wednesday I was at the '*Arts*' for the first time of their
appearance and the last of their sitting, for this season and in that
room—They have been thinking of nothing for some time past but
removing.[3]

The White Bull[4] is in the press—almost out I hope by this time—
—You will see him come down to Chatham in a week or so, 'like
spirits bellowing on the ground', according to the sublime and
matchless simile of Mr. Theodosius or Mr. Varaner or Mr. somebody
else of your magnificent theatre at Rochester.[5]

As to visiting you, I cannot say any thing positive as yet—I am
to go in about a fortnight with Mr. Lind to spend a week at Colchester—I shall go on Horseback: I shall then see whether that sort
of exercise will do ⟨any⟩ thing for me.

Don't you expect petty coats some time or other in the summer.
I thought they were to have been with you before now. If you know
before hand of their coming, let me know—I may as well come
down to you then as any other time; provided always notwithstanding that there is room enough in your house to hold us all

[3] The Society of Arts, founded in 1754 for 'the encouragement of Arts, Manufacture, and Commerce', had occupied since 1759 premises in Little Denmark Yard
(now part of Exeter Street) opposite Beaufort Building in the Strand. In 1774 the
Society took possession of new premises in the Adelphi (cf. H. T. Wood, *History of the
Royal Society of Arts*, 1913). Bentham's father was a member of the Society and so,
according to letter 103, was John Lind.

[4] *The White Bull, an Oriental History from an Ancient Syrian Manuscript, Com-
municated by Mr. Voltaire. Cum notis editoris et variorum: . . . The Whole Faithfully
Done into English*. London: Printed for J. Bew, Pater-Noster Row. MDCCLXXIV.
This was an anonymous translation by Bentham of Voltaire's *Le Taureau Blanc*.
There is a 'Preface, which may just as well be read afterwards', by Bentham, a satire
on Biblical exegesis. This letter opens with a list of *errata* for the book.

[5] The reference is to *Theodosius; or. the Force of Love*, a tragedy by Nathaniel
Lee (1653?–92). 'Mr. Varaner' has not been identified.

without lying all one o'top of t'other as the pigs do; which I should not care for, unless I was to take my choice.

The Dr[6] has been in Town—he tells me of a Ship (that Ship you know we saw the 50 Gun Ship) that is to be launched next August, and invites you and me down—he is got thick, he says, with the Builder of her.

Well, here's an end of the paper, and so Good b' w' ye to you— Jere:[y] Bentham

Wednesday June 8 1774
All well at Q.S.P. but as
certain accounts are settling,
rather cloudy,

How far hast thou got in Euclid? give me a few details on that subject in thy next.

111

To Samuel Bentham

July 1774 (Aet 26)

Dear Sam

A line or two in haste—setting out tomorrow morning with Mr. Lind for Colchester.

I have sent you herewith a new publication of Priestly's: containing what you saw republished with additions. Nothing you will find done to remedy the disorder—The *essence* as you are pleased to term it, I cannot send you this time—Qu?—whether it will be worth while to finish it? Yes I believe it will: but then this new publicn. will require it to be enlarged.—[2]

[6] John Mulford.

111. [1] B.M. I: 296–297. Autograph. Docketed: 'I.B. July 1774.'
Addressed: 'For Mr. Bentham'.
The expedition with Lind to Colchester foreshadowed in letter 110 (8 June) was apparently postponed. In letter 112 (19–20 July) Bentham says that he returned 'on Sunday'—i.e. 17 July. Assuming that the visit lasted for the expected '10 days or a fortnight', the present letter must have been written during the first week of July.
Colchester was Lind's early home, his father having been a clergyman there (cf. letter 12, n. 1). His sisters, Mary and Laetitia, now ran a boarding-school there. Their considerable financial difficulties were somewhat eased when an annual pension of £50 each was obtained for them by Lord North in recognition of Lind's services to the government as a pamphleteer (cf. Bowring, x, 57, and letter 99, n. 2).
[2] The new publication was *Experiments and Observations on Different Kinds of Air* by Joseph Priestley LL.D., F.R.S., London 1774. It is dedicated to Lord Shelburne. Volume II was published 1775, Volume III 1777. *Experiments and Observations relating to Natural Philosophy* was published in three volumes (1779, 1781, 1786). In 1790 the two works were published together in three volumes. Bentham was making an abstract of an earlier version of it (see letter 105, n. 2).

The White Bull[3] too at last I have sent to pay his respects to you—The Preface all your humble servants—The notes likewise, except a hint or two for 2 or 3 of them—It's a sad wicked book you will perceive—You must keep it close; and not let it be seen by any body except in such an out of the way corner as your's you should chance to meet with one of us: and then you must use discretion—Remember the sage Mambrés[4] preaches up discretion—and whatever you do let it not be known for mine—

I am uncertain whether I shall find the time to say any more to you—if not, adieu—I shall stay at Colchester ten days or a fortnight—Upon my return I shall begin to think of paying you a visit—Mean time remember me tenderly to the ladies—If you want a pretence for a kiss, tell any body you please (I will trust to your choice if you deal fairly by me) that I beg to be admitted to pay my congratulations on her arrival by proxy, in the mean time until I can have that happiness in person—

The Stick-business must demur for the present—Mr. Lind's Stick has already been to the Merchant's for a Gold head: so there is no help for that.

Diacentric is a more significant word than Diameter but Diameter if you recollect is the word in use for the purpose you mention.

Chymical Dictionary[5] very naughty in the particulars you mention—that untidiness of nomenclature is a great vice—But do not the Synonymisms in some of my Tables remedy it?

112

To Samuel Bentham

19–20 July 1774 (Aet 26)

'Diacentric' you may keep: since you have a passion for it; any thing for a little peace and quietness. Now you *tell* me what you

[3] See letter 110, n. 4.

[4] A magician, guardian to the heroine of *The White Bull*, Princess Amasida.

[5] Possibly *Dictionnaire de Chymie*, 1766, 2 volumes, Paris. 2nd edition, revised and expanded 1778. By Pierre Joseph Macquer. This work is referred to later in the correspondence. James Keir (1735–1820) published a translation in two volumes (1771–76).

112. [1] B.M. I: 300–301. Autograph. Docketed: 'I.B. Augst. 1774.'

Addressed: 'To / Mr. Sam¹ Bentham / Mr. Gray's / Master Shipwright / The King's Dock Yard / Rochester / Single Sheet.' Postmark: '20⟨. . .⟩'

This letter can hardly have been sent so late as the 20 August, for letter 114 which seems certainly to belong to 1774 raises the possibility of a second visit to Colchester on 24 August. In fact it would seem to have been finished on Wednesday 20 July 1774.

want it for, I know—'tis the best way in the world of letting one. It will answer your purpose very well as a term inclusive of and superordinate to /more ample than (if you please)/ the proper signification of the word diameter; and as such capable of being put in contradistinction to it. A Diameter is a line struck /that passes/ δια through or across the figure in question viz. a circle: and which μετρενει [?] measures it; that is determines, and is determined in it's own magnitude by the size /magnitude/ of it. A Diacentric is a line that is struck through the figure viz: through the center of the figure, whether it measures it or not: it may fall short of the boundary of the figure, or stretch beyond it, or do both: viz. the one by one of its end, the other, by the other. Hence you get an *interior* part of it, and an *exterior*—When you have fixed your Circle in its position you may have a perpendicular diacentric, and an horizontal diacentric—you might have a superior Semicircle (or Semicircumference which is the base line that bounds the figure) and an inferior one—a right and a left—a dextro'rsum—(or right-handwise)—ascending (and so a *sinistro'rsum*) *oblique* diacentric, semicircumference and semicircle.

Tuesday morning.

I returned on Sunday from Colchester; much mended both in health and spirits—We went on horseback—If my Father will keep a horse for me, I shall live; otherwise I shall go the way of all flesh: and you will come in for the Assets. Be sure you don't let my Father keep a horse for me if you can possibly help it: it may put off your chance for years.

Wednesday morning.

I can't stand writing any longer—I have been considering with myself ever since I came home whether I should pay a visit to your worship. now immediately, or wait a while and compleat the Air Apparatus—well, I think I will go now—it will be impossible to settle what is wanting or the proper shapes of things (mixing tubes etc. for instance) without seeing with my own eyes—I will trudge down on Friday—unless it rains—if it does, then not till Saturday—if it does then too, not at all for this time. The Dr.[2] has written to invite us down to Totton. The Ship will not be launched till October: but he would have us come now while the weather's fine. Shall I go? hang it I don't know what to say to't—I feel an almost unsurmountable reluctance at the thoughts of stirring any where without Mr. Lind—and these peregrinations run

[2] John Mulford.

away with a mortal deal of money. It's such a monstrous long journey to Southampton—But it's time enough for these matters when we meet.

If I go down on Friday, I shall spend Saturday and Sunday with you, and return on Monday. On Friday tell Miss Whitehorn,[3] I hope to have the happiness to cast myself at her feet—If you want to be doing, you may cast yourself at the old lady's at the same time—It is but right you should be promoted when your humble servant and brother comes to take your place.—Not that I shall cast myself at any body's feet neither, if I am no better in sorts than I am now—I shall sit plump upon my —e — The virtue of the exercise begins already to evaporate.

Essence of Priestley? 75 pages done out of 105—I may bring with me perhaps what I have done—hang it, I can not raise up interest enough in my gizzard at present to carry me through the trouble of it—talking over it with you may perhaps give me a spur.

113

PSEUDO-VOLTAIRE (JOHN LIND) TO JEREMY BENTHAM

20 July 1774

Monsieur

Agrèez les remerciemens qu'un octogenaire vous fait d'une main tremblante. J'ai toujours rendu justice à la nation Anglaise, mais vous seul de tous les Anglais m'en avez rendu. Vous avez accueilli l'enfant de ma vieillesse: vous l'avez fait avantageusement connoitre aux Anglais: sans lui oter les graces dont on est idolatre chez nous, vous lui avez donnè la force que Nous ne nous donnons guere la peine atteindre. Mais Monsieur, la fiertè Anglaise parait meme dans vos bienfaits. En introduissant mon ouvrage aux

---

[3] Apparently the daughter of 'the old lady' mentioned below, Mrs Elizabeth Whitehorn, widow of Caleb Whitehorn, surgeon at Portsea (d. 1771), the sister of Samuel Bentham's master, William Gray (cf. letter 131, n. 1). We do not know whether Caleb Whitehorn was related to the first husband of Alicia Bentham (née Grove), Jeremy and Samuel's mother (cf. letter 1, n. 1). If there was a family connection it may perhaps account for the choice of William Gray as Samuel's master.

113. [1] B.M. I: 294–295. Docketed by Jeremy Bentham: 'Lind July 20th 1774 as from Voltaire.'

Addressed: 'A Monsieur / Monsieur de Bentham / A Londres.'

Lind pretends to be Voltaire writing to congratulate Bentham on his translation of *Le Taureau Blanc* and his introduction thereto (see letter 110, n. 4). Lind has written it in a comically shaky writing.

Anglais, vous lui donnez un avant-coureur qui l'a eclipsè. Vous vengez les torts que des ignorans lui ont faits; mais vous lui en faites un plus irreparable en le contrastant avec un rival qui lui est trop superieur. Je vous pardonne toutes fois ce triomphe. Comme gage de mon pardon je vous envoye mon portrait. Daignez l'agrèer et me continuez votre amitiè. Peutêtre saurez vous adoucir en ma faveur l'aigueur des Dames, et le fiel des savants Eveques Anglais.

J'ai l'honneur d'etre
Monsieur
Votre tres humble et
tres obeissant Serviteur
De V.

A mon chateau
  de Fernès ce 20
  Juillet 1774.

114

JEREMY BENTHAM TO LAETITIA LIND

Early August 1774 (Aet 26)

Well, there is no truth in woman say I, as a man says of course when he fancies he has found one thats false. one such however I have

---

114. [1] U.C. LXX. 1. Autograph.

This is the draft of a letter to Laetitia Lind or perhaps to Laetitia and her sister Mary (see letter 111, n. 1). It is written on the back of a page of manuscript headed 'INTROD. Law Common. What. Beginng.', which seems to belong to the *Comment on the Commentaries*. The dating is somewhat speculative, but it probably belongs to early August 1774.

Bentham (we believe) returned from a visit to Lind's sisters at Colchester with Lind himself on 17 July (see letter 111, n. 1 and letter 112). On this visit (we suppose) he first met and fell in love with Miss Polly Dunkley. Mary Dunkley (b. December 1757) was one of the five orphan children of Thomas Dunkley, surgeon, of Earls Colne, Essex, who died in 1767, his wife having predeceased him. His father, Joseph Dunkley, died in 1768, and the children's maternal uncle, Humphrey Carleton of Colchester, acted as their guardian.

The present letter seems to have been written shortly after this visit, referring as it does to Bentham's introduction to Miss Dunkley by Miss Letty Lind. The last paragraph suggests that Lind had visited Colchester not very long before 24 August, and this helps to fix the year. In the event Bentham and Lind did not revisit Colchester until about the end of October.

The earlier part of the letter apparently refers to some fool's errand on which Letty Lind had almost sent Bentham, but from which he had been rescued by Miss Lind, i.e. her elder sister Mary.

Bentham's love affair with Miss Dunkley was suppressed by Bowring, but his knowledge of it is shown by important manuscript notes in his own copy of the Memoirs, now in the British Museum. For these notes see letter 133, n. 1. The love affair led to great unhappiness. Bentham's father was implacably hostile to their marrying, presumably because the lady had no fortune. They very nearly did get married, but the affair was finally broken off in the course of 1776.

found, sure enough—its something more than fancy, Miss Letty! Miss
Letty, what will become of you. Have you forgot already what
your mama I am sure has told you many's the good time and oft—
of the fate of little misses who play with fire? Alas how cruelly
have you sported with my flames.

[*In margin:* There are certain pleasing experiments a man has
commonly /at least frequently/ made before he comes to that discovery: I mean that there is no truth in woman: /he has/ in that
there is something to console him: poor I. I have nothing to console me.]

I hope I should have had more prudence and philosophy; and
yet it's ten to one but what if Miss L. /kind ingenuousness/ had not
prevented me, [*In margin:* I have proof of it—in black and white]
I should have sallied forth upon the enquiry. I'll tell you what I
should have done—I did something like it /this as I was saying/
once upon a much less occasion—and afterwards I will tell you
that too[?]. There was a French merchant who had shown me some
civilities abroad.[2] He was to come to England some time afterwards. I asked him, and he promised to come and see me. He
called but as I happened not to be at home he left me his address
thinking it sufficient to mention such a house in Bell Alley. As it
happens there are 5 or 6 and twenty Bell Alleys in and about
London: I found the [. . .?] in the London Directory, and to get a
line conveyed to him, that he might not think I slighted him I
could think of no other expedient than sending a Penny Post letter
to every one of these places. One of my letters accordingly found
him out. 'Near or very near or just by Lincoln's Inn' I am not sure
which, but I should have looked again before I had done any
thing! said Miss Letty in her letter to Mr. Lind. At a Miss Ward's
/a Milliners/ she says in her letter to me. Let it be only *near*: that
can hardly mean farther off than half a mile. Well then to find out
this Mrs [*sic*] Ward what should I have done. I should have taken
out my map of London, and my compasses, and setting one foot in
Lincoln's Inn I should have swept a circle, with a radius answering
to half a mile. Within that circle beginning with Chancery lane
and so veering about regularly to the right and left till I came to
/reached/ the line I set out with taking[3] I should have gone putting
/pirking/ in my pretty face into all the Milliners shops high and
low I could get scent of, in Town—What a deal of execution I

[2] Presumably during his visit to Paris in 1770.
[3] The passage 'beginning . . . taking' is added in the bottom margin with no
indication of its place; but it seems to belong in this sentence.

should have done in my way! It's well for the Milliners Girls Mrs.
Ward turned out so soon to be a non-entity. What an escape too
has the public had—what a loss there would have been of a time so
valuable to it as mine must needs be!

[*In margin:*[4] A propos—this in a parenthesis—I happen'd to
drop in at a certain house on Saturday, the master not at home.
I found another person there, very busy putting up a letter.
apprehending from /a word or two dropt and/ some little significant
looks that I was a party not wholly unconcerned in it, the spirit of
impertinence seized me, and after a little struggle, I made myself
master.]

With respect to certain matters. As it would be my anxiety to
keep peace in families—especially where matters of such importance
are liable to come into dispute—I do hereby adjudge and determine, calling into my assistance all the elucidatory powers in-
herent in my profession—as follows. All that is /literally/ true in
these presents is the sole and lawful property of Miss Lind: if there
be any thing that is false/ or which there is [. . .?] otherwise shown/
it belongs naturally to Miss Letty [. . .?] [. . .?] [. . .?] [she] has an
indisputable right to it.

If any question should still arise, which I would not suppose,
what part thereof shall be severally and respectively so deemed: I
would recommend to call in Miss D. herself to be Umpire /Arbi-
tratrix/ and I do hereby most humbly and respectfully request of
her the said Miss Dunkley to take upon her that office. If /there
should be occasion/ she should condescend so far, I beg further
that she may sign her award and that I may see it.

I am glad however to find, I hope at least find, I have one true
friend at Court.

What Miss Letty says I find I am to interpret by /there is but
one rule for interpreting. It is/ the rule of contraries. For Miss D.'s
sake forsooth I should not have seen her half a dozen times more?
I understand—Tell me, then, Miss Letty, for you will not deceive
me, tell me as the most likely means of perfecting my cure, what is
it she has said of me? what expressions of ridicule and contempt has
she let escape her for the awkward being Miss Letty forced into her
sweet company? What sport has she made of this embarrassment?
It will /may/ be the best chance I have for purchasing lasting ease
at the expense of a momentary pain, If I was troublesome to her
'twas your doing Miss Letty, that's one comfort: and I have
smarted for it, she knows not nor would I tell her, how severely:

[4] It is not at all clear where this passage belongs.

/I am glad the good books I sent you have had so salutary an effect:/ You do well to make an abridgement /deduction/ of /two hours from/ your repose: 'tis the least atonement you can offer for the breach you have made in mine.

[5]You see what shifts /expedients/ I have fixed upon to chide ~~Miss Letty~~ that vivacity of Miss[?] L's[?] which notwithstanding it is tempered to the degree I cannot but acknowledge it to be with politeness, I stand so much in dread. something of this sort I was able to say, or she would have said it for me. When a man has said of himself the worst people can say of him, they hold their tongues. You know Friend Squire Sancho found it much more convenient[?] to lay the lashes on his own shoulders than to receive them from Don Quixote.[6]

[7]What Miss Lind said about her brother revisiting Colchester so soon as the 24th of August, I am satisfied was rather wish than expectation. I would gladly have seconded the request if I had seen any chance of its being complied with. Mr. L. expects his Uncle from Derbyshire very soon.[8]

115

To Samuel Bentham

5–9 September 1774 (Aet 26)

Charta Chymica? I have got some of it somewhere still—You know the use of it. It saves pencil: you write upon it with a *style* of any metal except Iron: the marks are not so subject to rub out as those of pencil: but then they are fainter.

To Southampton by water? that's a good scheme if practicable. It gives experience, saves charges, and the Boat will be very handy for the purposes you mention—Make haste, and if you can get it ready by the time you say, I will meet you at the Dr's. I must spend a week at Whitchurch before I go to Totton: my Uncle is to have a horse for me, borrow'd of Mr. Osborn: He talks of buying it. I

---

[5] This paragraph is in the margin, but seems to be the conclusion of the letter.

[6] This sentence is in another part of the margin but seems to belong to this paragraph.

[7] This paragraph is written upside down amongst some lines earlier in the letter.

[8] Lind's father was an only child so that this uncle must have been a brother or brother-in-law of his mother, whose maiden name was Porter.

115. [1] B.M. I: 302–303. Autograph. Docketed: 'I.B. Aug. Sept. 1774.'

Addressed: 'To / Mr. Sam: Bentham / at Mr. Gray's / Master Shipwright / of his Majesty's Dock Yard / near Rochester.' Postmark: '9 SE'. The earlier part of the letter was evidently written on Monday 5 September (see third paragraph).

must try whether I can beg it of him. begging is a trade I am not used to—Father excepted, I don't know that I ever begged the value of half a Crown of any body in my life. I believe I have told you that my Father undertook to keep a Horse for me if I could get one.

I was to go to Whitchurch on Thursday (*come*) sennight as my Grandmother used to say. I will put it off till the Monday following: I will stay at Whitchurch till the Monday after that (this day 3 weeks) by which time I suppose you would be able to meet me at Totton in the manner you proposed.

For '*each to each*' say '*each to its correspondent one.*' *Each equal to each* spoken of two pairs of any-things, is properly speaking *all four equal*. '*Either to either*', is to this purpose the same as '*each to each*'. I say to *this* purpose—for to *another* it is not. take an example. 'I have a pear and an apple: you have a pear and an apple: you shall have mine, *either* of them.' What do I mean by that? this. viz: you may have the pear, but not the apple: or the apple but not the pear: *which* you will, but not *both*. Had I said '*each*' of them, 'twould have been the same as if I had said '*both*'. On the other hand if I said My pear and my *apple* are *equal* to your pear and your apple, *either to either*, 'twould have been the same as if I said each to each: in which case they are all four equal taken separately: and therefore *both* mine taken together equal to both your's taken together: and therefore in short any two of the whole four equal to the remaining two.

The different effect of '*either*' in the two cases depends.[2]

In a Parenthesis—You never told me about the phials: Whether you received them—Whether they answer the purpose. the smallest are half-ounces—no—I believe ¼ oz. I thought you wanted some small: they are no cheaper than ounces or even I believe 2 ounces.

The Tables representing the Combinations[?] of the 3 Mineral Acids with the several other substances yet known (together with the manner of effecting those combinations) was transcribed for you into a thin book of the small 4to. form with a blue paper cover: surely you have it: Thomas sat up ⟨an hour⟩ or two extraordinary to finish it before you went.[3]

---

[2] Some words are crossed out here, and are illegible, but clearly the passage would be unfinished even with them.

[3] For Thomas (or Tom: surname unknown), Bentham's amanuensis, see also letter 140 (12 September 1775) at n. 6.

Friday. 9th

Alas! Sam it is but too true—The Sails must be *New* under the penalty you mentioned. That d—d Act (God forgive me) that you and I looked at together, is continued by another d—d Act (God forgive me once more) to the present time. The original act is 19. G.2. Ch. 28. § 11. The continuing Act 6 G.3. c. 45. § 5. 'Ship or Vessel' are the words, so that if your's is either a Ship or a Vessel, there is no help for it, *New* Sails must you have or none. But by the bye is the Boat your own? is it not in the King's Service—if it is, or you can contrive to make it so, we are safe again. For no Act extends to the King, unless he be specially named in it.[4]

I have called at *Wright's*[5] for your pencils, and have a promise of them for next week. I had him not send them to you: but to me, as I shall see you somewhere or other I suppose before it's long. He said somebody called about them when he was not at home about a month ago. do you know any thing of it?

The reason of the different effect of ('*either*') in the two cases instanced must be deferred to my next. Duty to my Father etc. How does the Chatham air agree with him? How do they like their quarters? Should they take Brighthelmstone in their travels they may not improbably meet with a Clergyman of the name of Downes.[6] He is a very agreable man, an Irishman; he has been some years abroad. If they think proper they may give my Compliments to him, by way of introduction. He is an old College acquaintance—I have lately spent some hours every now and then in his company.

[4] Neither of Bentham's references is wholly accurate. The 1746 Act is 19 Geo. II c. 27, of which § 11 provides that 'Every ship or vessel which shall be built in *Great Britain* . . . shall upon her first setting out, or being first navigated, have or be furnished with one full and complete set of new sails . . . made of full cloth manufactured in *Great Britain.* . . .' The penalty was £50. The continuing Act referred to by Bentham is 6 Geo. III c. 44, § 5 of which extended the provision to 1774. (It was in fact further extended to 1781 by an Act—14 Geo. III c. 80—passed in 1774.)

[5] Perhaps Wright and Gill, stationers, of Abchurch Lane.

[6] Probably the Downes with whom Bentham had attended Blackstone's lectures in 1763–64 (Bowring, x, 45): this was presumably Dive Downes, son of Robert Downes of Dublin; matric. Queen's College 4 May 1762, aged 17; B.A. 1766, M.A. of Trinity College Dublin 1771, LL.B. and LL.D 1776; Prebendary of St Patrick's Dublin 1775–94 and of Kildare 1775–94; died unmarried 1798.

116

To Samuel Bentham

16 September 1774 (Aet 26)

I wish you had been a little more explicit about the purpose for which you want the Cork Jackets—You have one for your self—whom else can you want one for—Your Crew all of them I suppose can swim—If for me,—a Guinea for a week's use, that is for a day or two's, which is as often certainly as we shall go out, is not worth while.

As to the Dr., flatter not yourself with the thoughts of his going upon any such expedition. It is true that with a Cork Jacket, there can be no danger: but that is an argument with those only who consult their reason. He you know has better counsel.

As to the Compass I am afraid to venture without further directions—What Diameter? in Brass or what other material? —Hung upon Gimbols (is not there such a way) or in what other manner? about what price? whereabouts I might as well have said as to price?

Bed—do you want Blankets and Sheets as well as the mattress?

I shall not go into Hampshire till Tuesday. This is Friday. You will receive this scrawl on Saturday—write on Sunday, I shall receive your letter on Monday time enough to execute your commissions if you persist in them.

'In a hurry'? why are you then? what's the matter with you of all men and boys in the world that you must always be in a hurry? —even I with all my indolence and *nonchalance* am not always in a hurry when I write—the length of my letters to you proves as much.

At the same time I received your letter, I reced one from my Father: serious and querulous, as usual but kind; concluding with the offer of a horse: so that now I shall be *horsed* at any rate—'tis the very best thing that can be done for me—My health I think of late has mended: 'tho not so much but that there is room for further

116. [1] B.M. I: 305–306. Autograph. Docketed: 'I.B. Septr. 16 1774.'

Addressed: 'To / Mr. Sam: Bentham / at Mr. Gray's / Master Shipwright/ of his Majesty's Dock Yard / near Rochester.' Postmark: '16 SE'.

Samuel had had a twelve ton vessel built under his direction, and partly by his own hands (see letter 248). Towards the end of September he sailed it from Chatham to Southampton. There he met Jeremy who was then staying with cousin Mulford at nearby Totton. Such at least was the intention, and it seems to have been carried out (cf. letter 120, n. 1).

amendment by the continued application of the same remedy—
Now is your time to enter your caveat against my equipment, or
you may stand but an indifferent chance for the monopoly of the
assets: at least for one while. If the 'master of things' denies you
that satisfaction you must content yourself as well as you can with
the sight of my hand every now and then (I mean the hand you
see now) to improve you in the cut of your letters, and of my
Chesterfieldian physiognomy so replete as it is with the graces
(you have heard doubtless by this time enough and enough about
the graces) to improve you in the carriage of your person. This
latter satisfaction if such it prove, you may expect the oftener, from
this arrangement.

Adieu Sam quoth he, who while he lives and breathes and *rides*,
without which perhaps he might not do the other, is ever affectionately your's—

My Father's letter I intend to answer tomorrow—Give him in
the mean time my duty if you see him, and my thanks.
Linc. Inn. Friday. 16 Sepr. 1774.

117

To Jeremiah Bentham

17 September 1774 (Aet 26)

Lincoln's Inn Saty. Septr. 17th 1774

Hond. Sir

I received last night your favour of the 14th I answer the
miscellaneous part of it first; because, to the introduction, my
answer, if any, I foresee will not be a short one.

Mr. Mulford's receipt for his year's annuity I have already: he
left it with me when he was last in town. It is dated July (as to the
month) but the *day* is left blank.[2]

Part of my time Mr. Clark, I suppose has given you an account of:
the rest, since you have been in the country I have spent in town. I

117. [1] B.M. I: 307–308. Autograph. Docketed by Jeremiah Bentham: 'Fils Jeremy.
Lr. dated Lincoln's Inn Septr. 17, 1774, directed to me at Dover on my Journey along
the Sussex Coast etc.'
Addressed: 'To / Jeremiah Bentham Esqr. / at Dover / To be left at the Post
Office.' Postmark: '17 SE'.
It may be guessed that in the letter which this answers Bentham's father railed at
him for the apparent aimlessness of his life. Jeremiah did not yet know of Miss
Dunkley but he knew that his son's life was not such as to realize any of the ambitions
he had had for it.
[2] We do not know to what annuity this refers.

thought to have been in Hampshire before this; but one little matter or other, not worth mentioning, has prevented me. My Uncle has been in Town, and is returned again, rather out of order. I am to wait on him on Tuesday. I have hired horses to go as far as Bagshot: Mr. Lind is so kind as to lend me his servant who will return with him the same day. From Bagshot (26½ from H.P. Corner) to Hartford-Bridge (35½) I shall walk alone. at Hartford Bridge my Uncle is to send horses to meet me. There I shall dine; and hope to sleep at Whitchurch (58½). My Uncle would have sent as far as to Blackwater (22½) but I chose rather to have 9 miles walk to diversify the exercise. There will be a good 50 left for riding. I want a little hard exercise to fatigue me. I have not been so well for years as I was the day I rode 40 miles with Mr. Lind on our return from Colchester and for some time after: ten of them after a Postchaise; an indisposition obliging him to quit his horse: I had not the least sensation of fatigue—I have engaged the same horse I had then; and that since has carried me to Chatham. The horses, my Uncle is to send, are, that he rides himself, and one he has borrowed of Mr. Osborn: as I understand him, on my account; tho' he said somewhat about purchasing of him; whether that was also on my account, is more than I can tell you as yet; be that as it may, if I like the beast I shall fix a coveting eye upon him, in spite of the commandment: the most judicious commentators are agreed that in such a case as mine, the word '*neighbour*' does not extend to *Uncles*. In the mean time, Sir, I am sensible touched by your kindness in authorizing me to equip myself at any rate. you have taken counsel it seems of the proverb, and satisfied yourself that a living *Avocat-sans-cause* for a Son, is better than a dead Attorney-General.

Lord Mansfield's trip to Paris occasions much speculation among the politicians: I have reason to think it had nothing to do with politics. He took with him, or rather he went with, his natural Son, Sr. Tho:[s] Mills; Mr. Moffat the East India Director, and his daughter: this daughter with £40,000, to her fortune is shortly to be married to Sir Thomas.[3] About 4 months ago Lord Stormont[4] was over here in London upon a furlow. Martin[5] the Painter met him one day at dinner at Lord Mansfield's. Lord S. was talking to

[3] Sir Thomas Mills, nephew of Lord Mansfield, married Miss Moffat of Cranburne, Essex, on 1 November 1774 (*Gentleman's Magazine*, xliv, 541).

[4] David Murray, Viscount Stormont, second Earl of Mansfield (1727–96) nephew of the first earl, was in the diplomatic service. In 1779 he entered Lord North's cabinet, and was later lord president of the council (1783, 1794–96).

[5] For Martin, see letter 90, n. 2.

Ld. M. about the Hotel he had taken at Paris: what the apartments were, and how he had furnished them. 'One' says he, 'is destined for your Lordship: that I shall say nothing to you of, till you see it yourself.' Lord M. upon that raised some objections to the journey: which Lord S. answer'd: and it was afterwards spoken of by Lord M. and the rest of the company as a matter that was at least designed tho' not absolutely concluded on—Unless therefore some matter of business had started up since then, which he has contrived to engraft upon his pleasure, you may venture, Sir, it should seem, to assure your friends, that you and Lord Mansfield have been travelling on the same errand: I hope neither of you will have lost your labour.

As for Sam, you need not tell me that he is busy, nor that he is happy: that he is busy I know from his own report: that he is happy I am full as well assured of as if he had told me so. Those who are busy (I mean when it is their hopes and not their fears that make them so) are always happy: witness my own happiness, when no discontents of those that are dear to me come across me to disturb it.

As this sheet is pretty well filled, I may as well fold it up and send it at all events: perhaps, Sir, you may receive another at the same time: if not, I shall probably pay my respects to you once more according to your other direction. Tell my Mother, pray, that I called at Q.S.P. about a week ago, I think it was, but forget the exact day: all well, particularly Mrs. Far. Thanks to her and 'the Brotherhood' (not the *holy Brotherhood* I hope) that you have got at your heels, for their kind remembrances: mine wait on them in return. I have just room, with much ado, to assure You that I am, Dear Sir, with all duty and respect, Your affectionate Son,

Jere:^y Bentham

118

To Samuel Bentham

19 September 1774 (Aet 26)

Bespeak a quantity of Iron-filings against we have occasion for it: now is the time, that we may not be at a stand for want of

118. [1] B.M. I: 311–312. Partly autograph, partly Villion's hand. Docketed (By Villion?): 'Villion vice I.B. Sepr. 19 1774.'

Addressed: 'To / Mr. Bentham / at Mr. Gray's / Master Ship Wright / of his Majesty's Dock Yard / near Rochester.' Postmark: '19 SE'.

For Bentham's friend Villion see letter 88, n. 7.

materials, when experiments occur to us that we wish to try. I shall want to make some examination into Air phlogisticated by Pyritic mixture. I do not recollect precisely, but I have a notion that, according to Priestly's experiments, Air phlogisticated this way is *not* dephlogisticated by vegetation. That the case in this respect is the same with Common Air phlogisticated by having decompounded Nitrous Air or by having served to *burn* anything: and in short that it is only when phlogisticated by respiration or putrid effluvia, that it is dephlogisticated by vegetation.

Along with my *essence of Priestly* you have *one or two* Sheets (I forget which, but I believe only one) containing heads for a Synopsis or Abridgement, of my own contriving, not extracted from him— let me have that; by bringing it with you, if we are to meet at Southampton; or by the first conveyance.[2] suppose you were to bring a book of Geometry to Mr. Mulford's, and as you go by Sea, where you will have Stowage in plenty, why can't you as well bring the whole Air apparatus, that we may figure away at the Doctor's. I have bought your Cork-Jacketts, they are to go to-morrow by the Brompton Coach, the Compass I hope will answer your purpose. it costs 12 Sh. I bought it at Gilbert's upon Ludgate hill; neither Martin nor Adams had any such thing, the Cork Jacketts cost £2. 3Sh. along with them you'll have a book upon ye. subject. I wrote to my father on Saturday, pray don't you think my hand much improvd. I was so affected by your reproof that I have been doing nothing else but writing Copys. In the hopes of producing something worthy your approbation. I hope I have succeeded. Lincoln's Inn 19 Sber. 1774

The writer hopes you will land at Southampton in your boat and not in your Cork-Jackett.

119

To Samuel Bentham

19 September 1774 (Aet 26)

Dear Sam

I have sent my letter to the post office, or else I wou'd have added a postscript to it. I must then write you a few words more by

[2] What precedes this is autograph, what follows is in Villion's hand—hence the joke about his improved hand.

119. [1] B.M. I: 309–310. In hand of Bentham's friend Villion. Docketed (by Villion?): 'Mr. Villion for I.B. Sepr. 19 1774.'

Addressed: 'To / Mr. Bentham / at Mr. Gray's Ship Builder / in his Majesty's Yard / near Rochester.' Postmark: '⟨. . .⟩ SE'.

way of brotherly advice, for I cannot but be exceedingly uneasy on your account, when I reflect upon the boldness of your enterprise. besides one good turn deserves another. you have very kindly express'd your concern, and the apprehension you are in for fear I shou'd fall from my horse; I cannot in return do less than tell you that I tremble for fear you shou'd fall from your boat, or your boat shou'd fall along with you God knows where.

It is not uncommon for some people to dream when they are awake. I am not yet gone to bed, but it is past 11 o'clock, which you know is my usual bedtime, what influence that can have upon me I don't know, but I know very well, that I see some times the boat with my dear brother in her, now upon the very tip top of a wave mountain-high, now, to the very bottom of an abyss deeper than a coal mine. I see nothing else but Scilla on one side, and Charybdis on the other, or as Jack Tar wou'd express himself, I see nothing but Godwin's Sands and Scilly Rocks. ah Sam take care what you are about, don't spread all your canvass, *chi va piano, va sano*, you are a bold enterprising young man, remember the fate of Icarus, he made a trial of his Skill in the air, you are going to venture upon an element as dangerous—but My good Genius— inspires me with a lucky thought, damn your Cork Jacketts I have hit upon something that will prevent the boat from sinking and will keep her a float in all weather with all her cargo. order directly upon the receit of this some of your people to quilt a large sail with cork. wrap up the boat in the sail, and then you may defy the fury of the waves. you understand me, you are to use the sail in the same manner as they use sometimes a common one to stop a leak. the Endeavour had recourse to that expedient upon the coast of New Zeland.[2]

don't neglect my advice: and remember that if phlogisticated air is bad, hidrosticated air is worse, if you take once a full gulp of it, it will be over with you.

Lincoln's Inn. 19 7ber. 1774.

[2] During Captain Cook's first voyage, 1769–71.

120

To Samuel Bentham

20 September 1774 (Aet 26)

I forgot to tell you last night what stay I proposed to make at Whitchurch and Totton respectively: but I cannot help thinking I told you in a former letter. At both together I propose to stay about a fortnight; much longer I cannot: the very outside of all will be three weeks. I have been engaged for months past to go and spend a few days with Mr. Lind at Colchester[2]: the letters from thence began to be pressing and reason were given why we ⟨should⟩ not make it much later. The first week I shall spend at Whitchurch: I shall then go over to Totton for another week: part of which I hope will coincide with the time of your being there. I shall return by the way of Whitchurch. Probably in the course of the week I shall allott to Whitchurch I may take a ride over and dine with Mr. Mulford.

A propos. The Dr. has got a burning Mirror, I have a notion: I am sure he had one: if he has not parted with it along with the other vanities. It would melt Lead. Do you recollect seeing it at

120. [1] B.M. I: 304. Autograph. Docketed by Jeremy Bentham: 'I.B. Sepr. 9 1774.'

Addressed: 'To / Mr. Bentham / at Mr. Gray's / Master Shipwright / of his Majesty's Dock Yard / near Rochester.' Postmark: '20 SE'.

On the cover is the following in Wilson's[?] hand:

'This letter came open to Lind. If you think your Brother has a determined resolution of *melting* me pray break into a thousand pieces the Dr's. damned glass—I wish to grow leaner, but I hate melting. It carries a nasty idea long with it. A good voyage to you! May your fame surpass that of the Argonauts.'

Bentham's date on this letter is not very clear, but he has definitely docketed it as above. In fact it seems to have been written on Tuesday 20 September 1774, for in his letter to his father dated 17 September (letter 117) he says that he leaves for Hampshire on Tuesday.

He was to spend a week with his uncle George Woodward Grove at Whitchurch. Early in the next week (beginning Monday 26 September) he was to move on to Totton near Southampton where his cousin Mulford now lived. There he hoped to meet Samuel who was to arrive at Southampton in his own boat (see letter 116, n. 1 and letter 118).

Apparently Bentham was at Southampton on Thursday 6 October, and returned to his uncle Grove at Whitchurch the next day (see letter 122). A few days after that he intended to return to London, hoping that Lind would meet him halfway in order to travel home with him. Shortly after that they were to go again to Colchester together. In fact letter 125 written on 14 November or earlier reports his recent return from Colchester.

[2] The phrase 'for months past' is slightly odd if Bentham in fact visited Colchester with Lind in July. One might almost be tempted to give a later date to letter 112. However letter 117 makes it clear that Bentham had gone with Lind to Colchester not so long before.

Totton? However if it be there twould be a rare opportunity for trying our burning experiments: as far as it can be done without Mercury. Venus without Mercury is a well known wish for a sentiment: but as for managing *Jupiter* without Mercury, it is what I doubt cannot cleverly be done, Jupiter, you may or may not remember is a name given by our quondam friends the Roman Poets, to the Air.

Letters come to Whitchurch 3 times a week, Wednesdays Fridays and Sundays. A letter from Chatham of the Wednesday would reach Whitchurch on the Friday.

Tuesday 21[?] Septr. 1774.

Swan Inn Egham (in Surrey) 10 o'clock, just breakfasted and jogging onwards.

121

To John Lind?

1 October 1774 (Aet 26)

I

Totton near Redbridge and 4 miles up the River from Southampton Octr. 1. 1774.

I arrived at this place to day at 2 o'clock it is 25 miles from Whitchurch: Winchester half-way, Mutton on the Table. Pudding just dismissed. For such is the order of precedence among the dishes at primitive country tables. Not that my Cousin was originally of the country: tho' in many articles he has assumed the manners of it.

II

⟨. . .⟩ me. I sat out on that account from Whit-
⟨church⟩. (no unwelcome excuse) by a rain so violent as
⟨. . .⟩ as many Coats as a Dutchman wears
⟨. . .⟩—another for his shield. Continued too, without
⟨. . .⟩ After all it was not that night (viz yester

---

121. [1] B.M. I: 313. Autograph. This MS is a piece of paper cut out from a letter, in order to preserve I. II is the other side, and the cutting has removed the first words of each line. The Roman numerals are not in the original.

Bentham was staying with John Mulford at Totton (see letter 120, n. 1). The letter is very probably to Lind.

⟨. . .⟩ they should, but the night before. So that
⟨. . .⟩ undergoing a sousing in the attempt, Oh had it been
⟨. . .⟩ ⟨sh⟩ould have turned me back.

    Some places a stop and a break together: and
scarce one of them misplaced. Nothing of all this
could she ever do before. Can I believe my e⟨yes⟩

122

To John Lind

5 October 1774 (Aet 26)

    One word, my dearest friend, in the midst of the anxiety that
my own foolish sensibilities have brought upon me, about *the Book*.
I have looked it over—I have found juster sentiments in it, that is
sentiments more correspondent to my own (for that is all that any
man in such a case can mean) than I have yet seen anywhere in
print. At the same time, I have found in some places the sentiments
expressed otherwise than I could have wished, in others the sentiments themselves different from those I saw reason to entertain. I
have remarked what seemed to me the following imperfections.
The stile too much *agitated*—running too much into interrogations
and exclamations. Too much pathos in it in some places for an
attack upon a work which in its nature is not pathetic. Not so
uniform as could be wished: vibrating too quickly between a vein
of invective which supposes commotion, and a vein of Irony
which supposes tranquility. Scarce any part of it so light, so
Voltairian as many of your papers on other subjects that I have

122. [1] B.M. I: 322–323. Autograph. Docketed (by John Lind?): 'Whitchurch
—1774. / Bene / Critique on Comments on Commentaries.'
    Addressed: 'To / John Lind Esqr. / Lamb's Conduit Street No. 65 / London.'
Stamped: 'SOUTHAMPTON'. Postmark: '7 OC'.
    On Cover: 'My brother [. . .?] not. he is well.'
    This letter is published in *The Education of Jeremy Bentham* by C. W. Everett,
p. 72, and most of it also in Everett's introduction to his 1928 edition of the *Comment
on the Commentaries*.
    Apparently Lind had begun work on a critique of William Blackstone's *Commen-
taries on the Laws of England* (1765–69). He lent his draft to Bentham, who was
inspired thereby to write his *Comment on the Commentaries* which first saw the light
in Everett's edition of 1928. The *Fragment on Government* published in 1776 was in
fact a fragment of this work.
    Bentham was evidently afraid that he had offended Lind (and perhaps Lind's
wife-to-be)—possibly by something said in the missing part of letter 121. His
anxiety may have had some connection with Mary Dunkley; but of this we have no
positive evidence.

seen. That legereté is the quality of a mind at ease. A mind to be
at ease, must feel itself master of the subject. You are not yet
exercised enough in it to be so, and you have too much discernment
to fancy yourself so when you are not. Pardon the comparison;
your manner of treating it is much like what mine was two or three
years ago. You are teaching while you are learning: you have
instruction to seek yourself, while you have correction to give him:
you have your own ideas to form, while you have his to censure: In
pushing him down the hill, you have to climb up it yourself. Were
you already up, you could take a commanding view of the field,
choose your ground beforehand and combat him with more advantage. This makes you in some places take larger compass than
perhaps is necessary. I have always found it so myself. Leading
ideas, principles, take up many more words in their first disclosure
than are sufficient to contain them afterwards. This Locke has
seen, has intimated in his preface: and his own work as he acknow-
ledges, and as itself proves, is an example of it. Without Locke I
could have known nothing. But I think I could now take Locke's
Essay and write it over again, so as to make it much more precise
and apprehensible in half the compass. The circuits you take to
matters collateral to the principal subject seem in some places too
wide and too long continued. You stick not close enough to his
words: you put a sense upon his words, and draw inferences from
that sense after you have expressed it in words of your own: in
this you are some times much too bountiful; and by such unmerited
bounty expose yourself to censure. If he had a sense, that sense
might be put into other words: but the truth is he had none; and
so departing from his words you depart from everything. If your
inferences run counter to his own words, it is your fault and will be
laid to you: if his own words run counter to his own words, it is his
fault and will be laid to him. What you should do therefore is to
rake up his words from all quarters, drag them to the light together,
and drive them bang against each other. What I write now is from
memory, and as things struck me in the general: I will not answer
for being exact; I cannot nor will you expect I should in the compass of a letter support my observations by particular examples.
Nor can I answer for it absolutely that every observation I have
seen cause to make is includable in the heads that I have mentioned. At the same time, few alterations occurred to me that could
be made in the compass of a line or two. Your wish, I am persuaded,
is sincerely for my opinion. I give it you as sincerely. For the sake
of your present satisfaction my endeavour would be to represent

it as favourable to the book as it would warrant: for the sake of your future more lasting satisfaction not a tittle more so. This then is my opinion concerning the probable success of it: supposing it finished as began without further alterations or amendments I think it is a work ~~by which something might be gained~~ to gain by, supposing it printed at your own expence: I think it is a work which deserves that it be gained by I think for example that it is much better, much more instructive, bulk for bulk, than the short treatise on Obligation for which Payne gave a hundred Pound. But I do not think it a work, take it in its present state that would fulfill the expectations that would be entertained of a man known to be the Author of the *Polish Letters* or of *Ibrahim* to the *Haje*.[2] All this while you ought to look upon me as a very incompetent representative of the public judgment from the particular circumstances in my case that tend to make the merits of it appear less to me than they are. The principal merit of the observations in it, novelty, a merit that it will have with the public, is a merit that is lost upon me: who have now been for so many years poring over the subject, and as you know, have fallen in almost every part, into the same train of thinking.

Not bearing (you know my severity to myself and my affection to you which make me treat you as I would myself) not bearing I say, to set my fiat, such as it is, upon anything in the success of which I was so much interested that fell short of the model of perfection I could make to myself, this is what I have done. The shortest way of letting you know how I would have it in any passage I thought would be to endeavour to make it as I would have it myself. I had no notion at first of going on regularly; but I was drawn in insensibly, and have now written in quantity half or two thirds for ought I know (or more) as much as yours amounts to. In short, I have fleshed myself in the game, and have taken a fancy to the sport. In consequence of this the following proposals have come in my head to make to you: you shall see what I have done, and then determine. Take what I have done, if you happen to approve of it more than of your own, go on with it upon that plan, consider the whole as your own, most heartily will you be welcome: or else 2dly let me go on with it under your inspection, and with your corrections, and let profit or loss be equally divided between us, or 3dly if you approve of neither of these, I believe I shall be tempted to go on with it on my own account keeping it back

---

[2] This work by Lind has not been traced. It may have appeared in a newspaper or magazine, but seems not to have been separately published.

half a year if you think that enough, that it may not hurt yours, its parent, to which it will have been so much indebted. Think not that if I were to execute the remainder, the half of the profit and of the reputation if there is any would be more than in strictness is your due: it would have been just as impossible for me to have done what I have done without the encouragement and assistance I have had from you, as for you to have done it. In such case, if owned to any body, it must be spoken of as our joint concern.

This I have written upon a sudden impulse, in the midst of my pushes at our common adversary, currente calamo between the hours of 12 and $\frac{1}{2}$ after 1. The subject-matter turned in my thoughts at intervals for these 4 or 5 days. In the midst of it was brought me another letter. I have not open'd it: nor will I open it till I have dispatched this. I am afraid to open it. I am afraid to find I have injured you: I am afraid to find I have not. And yet it is in itself but a small matter, worked up and magnified by my foolish sensibilities. I tremble at the thoughts of having offended you: for never mortal loved another, if I don't you. Many things I now recollect are in my last that are expressed much otherwise than I would wish them: for I had not time nor sang-froid to ponder my expressions. Cautions made to look like threats: many other things very harsh, far otherwise than I meant, because I knew not how to soften them. Believe me if there is any thing in it inconsistent with the sincerest love and esteem for you, it is no true picture of my mind.

Thanks ten thousand thanks to you, my dear Master, for the news from Barker,[3] for the news itself, and for the haste you made in communicating it to me, knowing how it would please me. For how it would please you know too well, for me to need to tell you.

Que puis-je dire a ma maitresse? rien, jusqu'a ce que les choses se soient un peu eclaircies. C'est ce que j'attends impatiemment de ce que je tiens en poche.

Wednesday Octr. 5th 1774.

I have got a Horse pro tempore; en attendant till I have one given me for good and all. You told me you would meet me on my return. This will go from Southampton tomorrow: it will reach you on Friday. By that time I shall be at Whitchurch. A letter sent by the Post would not reach me till Sunday. Appoint time and place

[3] Presumably the merchant captain whom Bentham had met at Lind's—cf. end of letter 106. Probably the news was information about East Florida (cf. letter 101, n. 3 and letter 134).

of meeting. If you appoint Sunday evening, your letter must come by a Coach that goes through Whitchurch: there is one inns behind St Clements, another at the Bel Savage Fleet Street. Ay, send it thus at all events and to make up a packet, send me the *News-papers of the whole week*. You gave me hopes of your stretching as far as *Demezey's* Hartford Bridge. (35½). If so that would suit me excellently. A good house ⟨. . .⟩ ⟨. . .⟩ ⟨. . .⟩ ⟨. . .⟩ ⟨. . .⟩[4]

I have now open'd the dreaded letter. I can say to it but two words. Forgive! Forgive! Duty to Mistress—with the handsomest apology you can make her for my silence.

123

TO JOSEPH PRIESTLEY

November (?) 1774 (Aet 26)

On Electricity

Sir

Inclosed herewith is a Theory of the Electricity of the Atmosphere. The Author's name and address you will see on the first page—An ingenious and worthy man, with whom I formed a slight acquaintance in one of the summer months. The paper I ~~unwittingly~~ unwarily engaged to trouble you with before I had read it through. I doubt you will not find it calculated to throw *much* light upon the subject. It has been shewn to Dr. Franklin, who returned it as far as I could gather, with such a compliment as was suggested only by

---

[4] Hidden by B.M. binding.

123. [1] B.M. I: 324–325. Autograph draft. Docketed by Jeremy Bentham: '1774 I.B. to Dr. Priestley.'

The paper Bentham refers to was by Dr John Simmons (see letter 129, n. 1). Letter 125, dated 14 November 1774, reports that Simmons's paper has been left for Priestley at Lord Shelburne's, presumably along with this letter.

Not much is known of Dr Simmons. In 1775 he published at Rochester *An Essay on the Cause of Lightning.* . . . A letter by him on Nitrous Air was published in the *St. James's Chronicle* in October 1775, signed simply 'J.S.—s.' and dated from Chatham (see letter 144, n. 2). He is mentioned in several letters as a visitor to the Davies household.

Joseph Priestley (1733–1804), the famous chemist and theologian, was known as 'Proteus Priestley' on account of his many interests. In 1772 he had resigned as minister of a Leeds chapel to become librarian to Lord Shelburne, with the duty of furnishing information on topics arising in Parliament. His main scientific achievement was the isolation and recognition of various gases, including oxygen (dephlogisticated air); after meeting Benjamin Franklin in 1766, he also made important experiments in electricity.

politeness. After a hasty perusal on the spot I offer'd an objection or two, which the Author seemingly acquiesced in: but was still unwilling to give up the thought he had flatter'd himself with, of having it submitted to your inspection. The relation you bear to this branch of Science, as adopted father of it, subjects you, I doubt too frequently to addresses still less calculated than this to pay you for the trouble of attending to them. You have learnt, I suppose, to familiarize yourself to this sort of homage, which is flattering in the intention, however troublesome in the /method in which it/ manner it takes to shew itself. Tis on this consideration probably more than any other that I ought to depend for your favourable acceptance of a few hints of my own on a different subject, herewith also inclosed. The studies which /gave occasion/ produced it were taken up during the moments snatched from a pursuit as heterogeneous to the subject of it, as the most distant of those you find means so happily to combine.

The paper on Electricity, when perused, you will be pleased to return to me with such answer as you think proper to give to it, unless you think to put it to any further use. It may come by the Penny Post directed to me at George's Coffee House Chancery Lane.

I leave it to your philanthropy and address to let down if necessary as gently as possible the amour-propre of a well-meaning and ingenious man: and have the honour to be with perfect respect Sr.

Your most obedient humble
Servant Jeremy Bentham

The paper on Electricity I am sorry to own, has lain by me these 3 or 4 months. The delay has been owing partly to a wish to communicate it previously to a friend or two, and partly to other causes that you may imagine.

If you think the *disposition* that has produced you this trouble worth rewarding, you will let me know what subject you are preparing to instruct us upon next.

124

T O J O S E P H P R I E S T L E Y

November (?) 1774 (Aet 26)

Apparatus for generating Airs

Sir

The following is an account of a slight alteration I contrived in the apparatus for generating Airs: I have put it in practise with success. M is the phial wherein the mixture is to be made: It serves as a magazine for the menstruum: the solvend being dropped in occasionally. I call it the Mixing-Phial. C is the Cork with two holes through it. In one of them is inserted the Neck of a Glass Bubble B blown in form of a Retort. /The neck is bent to a right angle with the body./ This serves as a Magazine for the Metal or other body in powder which is to supply the Air. I call it the *Athanor*: from it's use being analogous to that of a part which characterizes the furnace of that name.

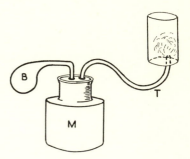

Into the other hole of the Cork is inserted the tube T for conveying the Air as in the common method to the Receiver where it is to be lodged. I call it the *Tube of Communication*.

The body of the Athanor lying horizontally may be more than *half* filled with the powder: and the filling can be performed after it's insertion into the Cork as well as before.

It would be more convenient could the neck of the Athanor be a flexible one: it would not then be limited in size: nor liable to break with it's own weight. A flexible neck may be given it, where a solid Acid is employ'd, or fluid one that, like the Vitriolic, is not volatile.

In this case it must consist of two tubes: where of one at least should be of glass. One open at both ends in the shape of the neck of a phial thus ⟨▭⟩ to fix into the cork of the mixing-phial: the other open at one end only in the shape of a whole phial. The flexible communication may be made either by leather or a piece

124. [1] B.M. I: 326–331. Autograph draft.
Evidently this was enclosed with letter 123.

of bladder, or bladder with Leather pasted over it, as may be found necessary. The rim of the piece of the phial as well as of the whole one should be as narrow as possible, for the convenience of fastening on the bladder; that is, only just broad enough to prevent the thread from slipping off: and the glass should be roughened with a file. This kind[?] of Athanor I have not made use of: I found the other answer'd very well; and in the country where I was, I could not get the leather put on so as to be Air tight.[2]

The Cork is paid on the outside with a cement to make the junctures Air-tight: and on the inside for the further purpose of guarding it against the Acid. The Cœment I have happen'd to employ is Sealing Wax: I drop it on, then smooth it and apply it to the crevices with a hot Iron.

The mixing-Phial, as far as I could judge, may be kept perfectly airtight in this way, notwithstanding the number of the Junctures. for if in making inflammable Air, for example, upon first trial I have been able to smell the Air, I have found no difficulty afterwards to put a stop to that effect.

The advantages of this Apparatus over the common one are as follows. 1. In the old method where the menstruum is applied to the solvend, it can only be applied in small quantities at a time on account of the ebullition. The application must therefore be frequently repeated; which is troublesome with regard to acids particularly the smoking ones. In this new one a large quantity of the menstruum is provided once for all: and the solvend shaken in to it as there is occasion. Acid to the Metal is, I think, the mountain to Mahomet: the Metal to the Acid, is bringing Mahomet to the mountain.

2dly. In the old method the quantity of Common Air that gets in at the times of dropping in the Acid may be considerable, if the application is frequently repeated: at any rate it is *indefinite*. In this new one the quantity may be small and that a *given* one.

In using Nitrous Air as a test of the comparative purity of the Atmosphere in different places, it is of importance to be certain of its being utterly free from all previous admixture with Common Air. If two parcels of Nitrous Air that are applied to two parcels of Common Air be unequally pure, the result of the application may be fallacious. The two parcels of Common Air for example not withstanding they are unequal in purity, may appear equally diminished. Because a greater part of the Parcel of Nitrous Air applied to *one* of them has been already decomposed (and thereby rendered

[2] These last two paragraphs are a subsequent insertion.

incapable of contributing to the diminution) than of that parcel which was applied to the *other*.

This last advantage of my method is attainable in a much superior degree, by one which I will now mention: but which on the other hand is destitute of the advantage I mentioned first. It was suggested to me t'other day by Dr. Geo. Fordyce[3] to whose excellent instructions I owe what little I know of Chymistry.[4]

Dr. Fordyce has not I believe made any experiments on this subject lately: but this is the method he used, as he tells me, to put in practice some years ago.

He provided a Trough or large pan deep enough to hold a column of water higher than the mixing-phial to be employ'd. He filled the mixing phial with the Metal and the Acid, and while the solution was going on, placed the phial in the pan or trough, so filled as that the mouth of the mixing phial was under water. He then inverted a Receiver filled with Water over the mixing phial, so as to catch the air as it was generated. In this way the Tube of communication is left out, the water underneath which the mixing fluid is plunged, answering the purpose. Consequently the Common Air that lodges in the Tube of Communication as well as that between the surface of the acid in the mixing phial and the cork, in short every particle of common Air whatsoever was effectively excluded. A small waste indeed of the materials was unavoidable: but that is no object. His way was to apply the metal to the menstruum in the phial before he plunged it under water; This is necessary where the solvend is in powder, as it must be where the Menstruum acts upon it but slowly as is the case between Iron and the Vitriolic Acid. In that case there is this inconvenience, that the rapidity of the solution, could not if there was occasion, be regulated. But it just now occurs to me, that when the Menstruum and the solvend are such as act briskly on each other, this method is free from every disadvantage. The solvend may be dropped in in pieces larger or smaller as shall be found convenient: and when the process is over, if the Menstruum is not saturated, the mixing-phial may be corked again, and the Menstruum serve for subsequent experiments. I should now expunge all that I

---

[3] For Fordyce cf. 84a, n. 6.

[4] The following passage occurs here, but is deleted: 'I have endeavoured to be short, /making it a/ thinking it my duty to be frugal of a time so pretious as Dr Priestley's is to the public.

'I will call it an Athanor: the use of it being analogous to that of the furnace of that name.

'I must leave it to your judgement and penetration to let down as gently as possible the amour propre of a well meaning and ingenious man.'

have said of my own method; were it not for one advantage over the other it has still. It is the only one of the two that is practicable in cases where heat must be applied to facilitate the solution.

One objection to his method, obvious as it is, never occurred to me. I suppose it does not hold good in practise, or he would have mentioned it. It is, that the water lying over the mixing phial might get into it, and mix with the menstruum, and dilute it to such a degree as to impede the solution. This inconvenience however if it arises, may be palliated at least by making the neck of the mixing-phial narrow. I am unable to determine à priori whether the attraction of gravity, (the acid which is at bottom being the heaviest) would prevail so as to keep them separate; or the chymical attraction so as to make them mix.

Apparatus for making Pyrmont Water[5] in the large way

For the purpose of *agitation*, a Barrel prepared upon the principles of that commonly used for churning Butter, might, I should think be employ'd. Some Precautions in the making it would be necessary, which I need not suggest to you: If you think the hint worth any thing, it were easy to enlarge upon it.

Here the apparatus I have described would be particularly convenient. Instead of the Mixing Phial a large Stone Jar to any size might be employ'd. To this might be fitted a flexible Athanor of a proportionable size. For security the Athanor and the tube of communication might be wicker'd over.

The artificial Pyrmont water, Dr. Fordyce says, tho' saturated, has not equal pungency with the natural. It may be made to have it, he says, by putting into each bottle after it is filled, a grain or two of mild Magnesia or calcareous Earth, dropping in a drop or two of Vitriolic Acid as much as or rather less than may be supposed sufficient to saturate the earth, then corking the Bottle instantly before the ebullition is over.

The pungency of the Pyrmont water he says depends partly upon a portion of the air's being upon the flight at the time of drinking it. It will be kept in a state of extraordinary compression by the small quantity of superfluous fixable Air generated in the manner above mentioned. The sudden removal of this pressure will upon that give liberty to that part of the fixable air which it is designed should be upon the escape.

This I have some notion to have seen in print.

[5] Mineral water found at Pyrmont in Germany.

NOMENCLATURE

A factitious Nomenclature when not too far fetched is of considerable use in the Sciences for the purposes of Brevity and Precision. Of Brevity, by substituting a word or two in the place of a whole sentence. Of Precision, by cutting off verbal varieties in the description of the same thing. These varieties, will be apt to cause a diversity to be apprehended where none is meant. especially by persons to whom the subject in hand is new.

Generical appellations by drawing the objects of the mind's attention to a point, simplify the course it takes in surveying them, and while they elucidate strengthen its conceptions. I need not cite instances to prove to you that the greatest improvements in science are reducible to, at least are announced and recorded by operations of Nomenclature.

The terms *Mixing phial, Athanor, Tube of Communication* I have already explained.

Stopple

To keep insulated a portion of matter in the state of vapour, and prevent it from mixing with the external common atmosphere, a fluid body was first applied, I believe, by Dr. Hales.[6] He took the hint perhaps from the Barometer.

/A fluid body/ Water was made by this means to answer the same purpose with regard to vapour as a solid body with regard to a fluid one; as a cork for instance, or other stopple with regard to the water in a bottle. The portion of a fluid that is made to answer this purpose I would therefore call a Stopple. When the fluid made use of is Water, a Water Stopple.

Mercury Stopple.

Some vapours meantime, as Fixable Air, and the Muriatic Acid were found to act upon and be taken up by the stopple when composed of water. Water therefore could not serve to confine them in the state it was meant to have them in. Quicksilver was then thought of as a substitute. This, Sir, I presume, was your invention. When Quicksilver is thus employ'd I would therefore call it Quicksilver-Stopple; when Oil, an Oil-Stopple, and so on.

Stopple-cap.

The fluid used as a stopple must have a solid vessel to contain it: This Vessel is either the general reservoir in and from which the

[6] Probably Stephen Hales, D.D., F.R.S. (1677–1761), physiologist and inventor.

Receivers are filled, or a small one in which the Air with its stopple is set by apart from the rest. I would call it a Stopple-Cap /if the term be not too uncouth/ in the first case the general stopple-cap: in the second a particular one.

In the latter case the Stopple may be said to be *limited*: in the former, it may be stated, (for the purpose, at least, of distinguishing it from the other,) *unlimited*./The distinction should have terms to express it. There is frequent occasion to bring it into notice./ You found much difference, I think, in the effect of agitation according as the stopple you employ'd was *limited* or *unlimited*.

Acid or Muriatic Air[7]

I have an objection to a term of your employing. It is that of *Acid Air*: By this you mean the Marine (or Muriatic Acid, as I have been most used to call it) in the state of vapour: the state it is always in, when pure. You mean that and no other: for you treat of no other in that Section. Now it may turn out that there are other Airs (that is bodies that can be kept in the state of vapor) that are acid likewise: That called Fixable Air for example, if the notions of some writers had been deemed well grounded—The Volatile-Vitriolic, if you could get a quantity of it in that state to make experiments upon. The Nitrous some might be disposed to rank under that name, considering it's composition of Nitrous Acid and Phlogiston. Dr. Fordyce once produced, as he says, an uncondensable vapour by distilling Alkali phlogisticated for Prussian Blue. that may turn out to be acid or as any thing else. His attention was solely bent upon condensing it: which he could not compass. To save it, in its state of vapor, did not, it seems enter into his thoughts. If then, I say, any other Air should be found out that is acid, the term acid as applied to characterize this particular kind of air would be improper. It must be alter'd. The term Muriatic (if sufficiently familiar) never could be improper and it would point to the original of the Air in question: being an Air that is produced from that peculiar kind of Acid called Marine or Muriatic Acid; or to speak more properly *is* that very Acid in it's form of vapour; the only form in which you can obtain it pure. The term Marine Air would not do so well, as it would seem to mean nothing more than *Sea-Air*, Common Air taken from over the Sea—

Judge whether there is any thing in the objection: or if there is,

---

[7] Bentham refers in what follows to Part II Section IV 'Of Acid Air' of Priestley's *Experiments and Observations on Different Kinds of Air* (cf. Priestley's reply, letter 129).

whether it may be worth while to alter the term objected to in your next edition. I need make no apologies to Dr. Priestly. It costs him no more to retract than to advance, when the interests of Science are in question.

Much more I could offer to you on the subject: /other articles of Nomenclature, other hints respecting arrangement, other species of vapor for subjects of experiment: and other methods for eliciting the properties of such as have been already practised on./ but all I have said already may be perhaps too much. I have endeavoured to be short, making it a conscience to be frugal of a time so pretious to the public as Dr. Priestly's.

I have the honour to be
with perfect respect
Sir
Your most obedient
humble Servant
Jere.^y Bentham

125

To Samuel Bentham

14 November 1774 (Aet 26)

When your letter came, I was not returned from Colchester.[2] Not but that I have been long enough returned to answer it before now—Je vous demande mille pardons, mon cher frere. Mr. Simmon's paper has been left at Lord Shelburne's[3] for Dr. Priestley. I kept it for some time to show to a friend or two of mine not then in

125. [1] B.M. I: 314–315. Autograph. Docketed: 'I.B. Novr. 14th 1774.'
Addressed: 'To / Mr. Sam: Bentham / at Mr. Gray's / Master Shipwright / of his Majesty's Dock Yard / near Rochester.' On cover occurs this list: 'Drs. Burning Lens / Franks / Welding Engine / Musick-Lamp / Writing desk / Chymical matters / French book with translating / Haunch / Mr. Giffard's case.' The list continues in pencil and is hard to make out: 'Positive . . . or repulsion / from . . . . , / Sympathetic Ink . . . / . . . ' Postmark: '14 NO'. Presumably written from Lincoln's Inn.
[2] On what was probably his second visit with Lind to Lind's sisters (cf. letter 114, n. 1).

[3] William Petty Fitzmaurice (1737–1805), eleventh Earl of Kerry, second Earl of Shelburne, first Marquess of Lansdowne. He had held office in the 1760's, but was in opposition from 1768 until 1782. He then took office under Rockingham, whom he succeeded as Prime Minister from July 1782 to February 1783. Defeated by the Fox-North coalition, he never returned to power.
Bentham first met Shelburne in 1781 and their friendship played an important part in Bentham's life.

town. Their opinion of it seems to be, that it is more ingenious than satisfactory. Dr. Priestley has been in France this Summer: and is but just returned. He is now in the Country: at Calne in Wiltshire, where his residence is, near Lord Shelburne's.

What hast thou to do with Strings for Canes? thou who hast no money to pay for them? And to blaspheme my taste, and ask me in the same breath to do thy dirty business! And what signifies my buying the obliterating substance? how art thou to have it?

As to the put-off about money—thank thyself for it. Thou knowest thou has been oft bidden to produce regularly thy accounts: thou knowest that thou oughtest to do it: for saving always and excepting the article of pocket money, thou canst have no objection, thou canst have no reason for wishing to conceal the items of necessary expences. If our father send thee not money so soon as the account shall have been produced, I will.

Again as to the stick-string. Thou wilt not trust me with the buying it: seeing that *in that one article* (I hope thou hast the grace to subjoin that limitative proposition) I am not a man of taste. Why am I not a man of taste? whence camest thou to think so? Because I shewd not myself such in the choice of that I wear. Know, rash blasphemer, that Cane string was the choice of the very Mr. Lind whose taste thou magnifiest. But why the Mr.? for I see no *S* to it—Young clown! who taught thee to resort to a man for a matter of taste and dress, and to neglect a lady?

Halloo! Halloo! at him again—Well done, Sam! there you have him! We will mash him and Blackstone to one indistinguishable Jelly.

No Doctor Mulford. How couldest thou expect the Dr.—The Doctor had no more thoughts of walking to Chatham, than I have to Jamaica.

Port Royal Grammar? How could I give thee a character of it— a particular one I mean? seeing I have not read it. A general one I have given thee more than once; partly from report; partly from dipping into it once or twice—viz: that it is a good one—I suppose the best. The Latin one I suppose thou meanest—not the Greek, for there are both. The Latin I have, (to speak for Shortness sake) in French in one close Volume 8vo Thou mayest have it if thou wilt. It is translated, I believe, (at least the Greek one is) into English by the late Dr. Nugent. In English it forms two octavos.[4]

I hope thou wert amused with thy concert.

---

[4] *A New Method of Learning with Facility the Latin Tongue. . . .* Translated [by T. Nugent] from the Monsieurs of Port Royal, London, 1758.

Monday Nov. 14 1774.

Resolutions—What is become of Resolutions? not kept, I suppose since nothing is said of them—If they had been thou wouldst have been bragging—

When thou canst honestly and truly tell me of thy having fulfilled them, then may I say to thee.

Sume superbiam

Quaesitam meritis.[5]

126

T O   S A M U E L   B E N T H A M

6 December 1774 (Aet 26)

My dear Sam, I am in no mood for writing: and yet as thou wilt have it so, and hast so many claims on me, I will write.

What need of those undervaluing speeches in thy last? Thy reflection upon Lord Chesterfield was just and pertinent: and tho' the terms of it might have been better, they might much easier have been worse. To me, tho' seemingly obvious, it was new: as such I thank thee for it. At the same time it was a natural subject of animadversion enough for thee to fall upon, his neglect of a talent which is more especially thy own. I mean *steadiness*, or that quality in a man which makes him proof against delusive impressions. His aims seemed to have been confined almost exclusively to insinuation, or that faculty which fits a man to produce such impressions as may best answer his purposes, in other people: delusive or otherwise, he cared I suppose but little. The latter may be stiled an *active*; the first, a *defensive* faculty of the mind. The latter belongs more particularly to the *imagination*: the first to the *judgment*. 'Wit' (which is the exercise of the imagination) 'is employed says Locke in striking out resemblances: Discernment (which is the exercise of the Judgment) in detecting differences.'[2] He uses the word '*wit*' in its original extensive tho' now less frequent sense: at present it is confined almost to such resemblances as are calculated to excite laughter. I might say, that

[5] Horace, *Odes*, III, xxx.

126. [1] B.M. I: 316–317. Autograph. Docketed: 'I.B. Decr. 6th 1774.'
Addressed: 'To / Mr. Bentham / at Mr. Gray's / Master Shipwright of / His Majesty's Dock Yard / Rochester.' Stamped: 'RI'. Postmark: '6 DE'.
[2] Cf. *Essay concerning Human Understanding*, Bk. ii, ch. xi, §2, *The Difference of Wit and Judgment:* Bentham gives the sense, not Locke's exact words.

218

judgment is the Ballast of the mind, and *wit* the Sails, and saying which, if I have exemplified either, thou seest it is Wit. But I see the farther I should proceed in these topics at present, the more I should be in danger of confounding thy notions, my own being no wise clear about it at present. It has been lie-abed-day with me; tho' not to a degree utterly enormous, yet to a degree sufficient to make me at once uncomfortable and stupid. It is a pain to me, and much the same sort of pain to hold a set of ideas steadily in my mind, as it is to hold a heavy body steadily in my hand. I am just now principally employd in forming and putting together a string of Definitions and Axioms to prefix to the 'Comment on the Comment[s].' and serve as a standard to which I may refer the incoherent effusions of 'our Author.'[3] Learn from me the baleful effects of (not irresolution for they mean two different things, and there is *judgment* for you) but want of resolution. A large proportion of my time (I am afraid and ashamed to think how large) is unprofitably and unpleasurably consumed for want of resolution to take that only recipe which can ensure a tolerable set of sensations for the day, the bracing influence of the morning air. 6 o'clock is the hour, after which if we continue a bed a moment, 'we have done what we ought not to have done, and there is no health in us.'

Dr. Simmon's Scheme—As to the *end* of it, you know enough of me to know I cannot do otherwise than strenuously approve of it. How far the means are calculated to attain it, I want *data* to enable me to judge. The thought, I suppose, is new, since it struck you as such. But I do not know enough of the subject, to know the difference between the management he proposes and the Common one. The Timber at present, when there is enough of it, is kept, or meant to be kept I suppose a certain time before it is worked up into the Skeleton. The Skeleton itself is purposely left in that state, for a certain time. The Timber in the mode of Houses lasts undecayed for ages but then it is protected from the weather not only at the time of building (perhaps not at all at the time of building) but ever afterwards after the house is cover'd in. It is the necessary condition of a Ship to be exposed to the weather while it is in use. and when once wetted how it can be thoroughly purged of moisture, considering how inaccessible a great part of it is to the free influence of the Sun and Air, is what I do not rightly understand. It is a misfortune attending all these projects of ⟨defence⟩ against the attacks

[3] Blackstone. See letter 122, n. 1. This seems to be the first reference to the work under this title.

of time, there is no proving them by making any expe⟨riment for the⟩ purpose. The *data* are to be obtained only by accidental ⟨. . .⟩ or such experiments as may have been made for kindred purposes ⟨in⟩ circumstances more or less similar as it may happen. ⟨These⟩ remarks you will observe conclude not to the incon⟨venience of⟩ the Scheme, but *my own* to judge of it. I am very glad to learn from you, that it begins to meet with favourable attention. A great part of this has been written in the dark, or by firelight: so that if you are able to read it you have good luck. Adieu my Dear Sam, I shall send away what I have scrawled, without waiting to take notice of any other of the particulars in your last letter. Continue Chesterfield—the stile will be of indisputable use to you, and now and then the sentiments.

Lincoln's Inn Tuesday Decr. 6 1774.

127

To Samuel Bentham

9 December 1774 (Aet 26)

Mr. Giffard's case[2] was put into Mr. Clark's hands within a very few days after you put it into mine. About a week ago I asked him whether he had looked it over, telling him you pressed for an answer. He told me he had not, but that then, term being over, he should have leisure, and would peruse it forthwith.

('Indepted') No man would spell '*indebted*' with a (p) whose thoughts were not a wool-gathering at *Deptford*. I wish you may know as little of the thing as it seems you do of the name.

An '*Immediate* Letter'? hang it, I must find out the meaning, before I can tell you how to express it. Do you mean *speedy* in point of time, or *full* and *particular* (as thus of account in Law) in point of matter? containing an *answer* to every *quaere*, an intimation of *compliance* or *denial* to every *request*? or were you hankering after a single word, that should express the meaning of *full* and *particular* both in one? There may be such a word for aught I can be certain to the contrary; but I possess it not. 'If *you was* of the common species of Lawyers'—If *you were* of the common

127. [1] B.M. I: 318–319. Autograph. Docketed (by Jeremy Bentham?): 'I.B. Decr. 9th 1774. Lincoln's Inn.'
Addressed: 'To / Mr. Sam:[1] Bentham at / Mr. Grays Master Shipwright / in His Majesty's Dock Yard / near Rochester / Single Sheet.' Postmark: '10 DE'.
[2] See also letter 125, n. 1. Giffard is unidentified.

species of Grammarians you would not have said so. My dear Sam forgive the freedom of my censures: 'I correct thee not as in anger', nor as in spleen; /but as in pleasantry. 'Ridentem dicere verum | Quid vetat?/ for thou art not to be as Blackstone is. 'Lord Chesterfeild' used to put the (*i*) before the (*e*) in spelling the last syllable of his name. Twas a whim he had, and which other people have given in to before as well as since. But if you have a mind to put the Cart before the Horse or the Rudder before the Bowsprit, don't let them be your hindrance. Say 'I am a freeborn Englishman and who's afraid?'

'Your Omers and Blueturks and Novids and stuff
'By G—d' (says a Military Gallant in a *Jeu d'esprit* of Swift's)
'By G—d, they're not worth this pinch of snuff.'

Bravo, Bravo, Signor Cimbalista—corragio—che dice? il minuetto dell'Aurelli intiero, col Basso?
Come sta il Signore *Burchetti*? non ha parlato di lui this good while.
'Graces pricked in red'—Yes, a good idea.
Harris's Hermes—I doubt thou wilt bewilder thyself in that book, as I did a long time—and that *that 'interpreter'* as it calls itself (for Ἑρμῆς is an interpreter) will not be much of an interpreter to thee.[3] The last book is Nonsense upon stilts. Indeed that's no disparagement to the two first; for it has no connection with them. In *them* there is some matter: but it is *drenched* in a multitude of words. There is some *spirit* (I speak as a Chymist to a Chymist How goes on Chymistry?) but it is drowned in a redundancy of *phlegm*. Part of it is a labyrinth—I wander'd in it a good while. Take this clew. The whole business of it is to explain the relations, the differences and resemblances of the several '*parts*' (as they are called), of speech ~~Several of them~~ being *simple* in the *expression*, he takes for granted they are so in the *idea*. But several of them are not so. Take this Example—a Preposition of those parts of speech— Good—An Adverb is given for another part of speech. *one* part of speech, and a distinct one from (amongst others) a *preposition*. But with all Adverbs certainly it is not so—Let me see—is it with *any* of them? I cannot determine that now. But with *some* I am sure it is not. Among the different divisions of them he reckons, that of 'Adverbs *of Place*' is one. '*of Time*' another. ('*Here*') is an Adverb of Place. What is ('*Here*') (1.) *In*: (2.) *this*: (3.)—*place*. ('*In*') a preposition. ('*this*') a pronominal adjective. ('*place*') a Sub-

[3] *Hermes or a philosophical enquiry concerning universal grammar* (1751), by James Harris. A strange book which greatly interested Bentham. Harris's son, also James, was Ambassador at St Petersburg when Samuel Bentham was there in the 1780's, and was a good friend to him.

stantive. I have got a rough *Tree* that I drew for Mr. Clark. It wants pruning and lopping and the branches to be drawn out clear of each other (I am speaking of the mechanical disposition of the words) But thou shalt see it when thou comest.

Am I not a good Brother? I sat down instantly upon receipt of thy letter and have been scribbling incessantly ever since: and that without leaning upon my elbow a significant expression once used to me from Pope by Mr. Lind, importing study and puzzlation suggesting an equivalent idea to, and more delicate than that of scratching heads or biting nails. And this (who would think it?) tho' I did not rise till half after 10 owing to a particular accident. Yesterday I rose before Six. But the Lord hath been tolerably gracious to me to day. And it is wonderful how the state of my health depends upon that of my mind. I believe, should the public be tolerably indulgent to me (my ever honoured Lord and Master, the Public) I should be a new creature.

Franks—thou saidst something to me in one of thy last about getting me Franks—Good Boy—Do get me a dozen if thou canst without troublesome suit and service. I mean not directed to me: but directed in these words—'Miss Lind / Queen Street / Colchester'[4]—This tho' a dozen times over will not take long to write. I am disappointed in that article: a friend whose quill I intended to set a driving lost his election.

Now I must take down thy letters from behind the Chimney-glass if I would write more. O – – – –h! the pangs of motion to a lump of indolence! No, it is not motion *quâ* motion that I am adverse to: but change of *place* with me is change of ideas: it jumbles them out of train. The length of this letter thou owest by a whimsical concatenation of things to that same indolence: I rummaged, and rummaged and could find no paper less than this but what was ruled. So I could not give you the *Curacy* (as Lord Chancellor Talbot told a poor Parson once) but the *Living* is at your service.

I don't know very well what to say about lodging you. I have got the blanket—the double blanket from the Cot and shiver still. Two only (to lay above me) had I from my Father.

The Dr. (a murrain take him) parted with his Burning lens a long time since. Servandom's[?] Scheme *referred* but not yet (I believe) *reported on.*[5]

Method of cleaning *Ivory* I will enquire about.

---

[4] The franks were for letters to Lind's sisters, and perhaps by way of them to Miss Dunkley.

[5] This reference has not been elucidated.

Lincoln's Inn Friday Decr. 9th 1774.

Priestly on Airs (the 8vo) has been out of print some time: consequently I can't get it. Bring up your's. Remember the graces, if thou wilt; but remember also, the graces of a Ship-builder, tho' a Gentleman Ship-builder, are not the graces of a Nobleman. Thou has person on thy side: the consciousness of which is one main foundation of them. Apply thyself to the girls about thee: not as matter of anxiety, but of amusement. Kiss their hands: be not sparing of their lips: and use soft violence. Whatever they take patiently do thou a little more. In general they will sooner forgive thee for doing too much than too little. Be not afraid of them: hold thy head above them: and care not what they think of thee. I had like to have forgot to tell thee, that whenever thy brother's ugliness is mentioned ⟨. . .⟩ ⟨. . .⟩ brought in contrast with it but with ⟨. . .⟩ ⟨. . .⟩ ⟨. . .⟩ ⟨. . .⟩ ⟨. . .⟩[6]

128

TO SAMUEL BENTHAM

9–14 December 1774 (Aet 26)

I said in my last (speaking of the Girls) whatsoever thou doest, and they take patiently, do thou a little more. I should have added, but do it not remarkably to one more than to another, for the reasons thou hast heard at Queen's Square place. All this tho' thou mean nothing by it, and feel nothing in it, will be putting thee in practise against thou hast occasion. At the same time be not boisterous and rampant but soft, and pliant, and gentle, and insinuating.[2] But if thou perceivest thyself to feel too much, where it is not convenient, turn aside from that object, and call off thy thoughts from it, to another: Take no thought beforehand what thou shalt say, nor what thou shalt do, nor what looks thou shalt put on. sufficient to the day is the evil thereof. Consider the coxcombs of the Town, how they manage: they toil not, neither do they study. Verily I say unto thee, a bookworm with all his learning is not received like one of these. Art not thou much better than they? O thou of little faith!

[6] Missing words hidden by B.M. binding.

128. [1] B.M. I: 320–321. Autograph. Docketed: 'I.B. Decr. 14th 1774.' Addressed: 'To / Mr. Sam. Bentham / at Mr. Gray's / Master Shipwright / of his Majesty's Dock Yard / near Rochester / Single Sheet.' Postmark: '14 DE'.

[2] About a sentence crossed out here. Two further sentences crossed out after next full stop.

Thus far I wrote in continuation of my last the same night I sent it. I should have said the same night I sealed it up: For there was nothing in it that required speed, and as no Postman was at hand I forbore sending it that night. Thou seest by the scratchings out I had not my lesson so perfect as I should have had. The more shame for me thou wilt say.

This morning I received thy answer. The Devil tempted me this day to shew my father thy four last letters I don't mean the answer to my last but those immediately before it: this I say notwithstanding thy injunctions not to communicate an article in one of them—I mean that about the accounts. I mention this that thou mayest be prepared. I thought my father seemed to have an hankering now and then to see some of thy letters: and as there was nothing particular in them that there could be any reason for concealing, and as they served in general to shew thee occupied, and that in the way of this business, I thought it would do no harm to let him see them.

'Very absurd'—that was the Epithet bestowed by the Lady upon your plan of early rising, upon it's being brought some how or other upon the carpet. 'Brought upon the carpet' did I say? Yes, but it was by herself. My Father indeed was reading your letters, in which you mention it, taking notice of the obstacles. but she did not see those letters: possibly she was mortified because she did not see them. I suppose you had mentioned something about it to him; and that it was from thence her intelligence was derived. Flatter not yourself with the vain hopes of pleasing by any plan of laudable improvement: or by any endeavours of any other kind you can use. The utmost you and I can hope for is to be tolerated. You are not on this account to look upon yourself as destitute of inducement. Your schemes will gain you no favour there—be it so—but for whose sake do you pursue them? You have yourself to profit: and you have me to please, as I have you. You have the world to please: who it is to be hoped are swayed with tolerable steadiness by their own interest. At the same time if by accident you catch a transient gale of favour, sail with it as far as it will carry you: as you did with (in the instance I mean of) the little '*Carpenter's mistake.*' Chance and caprice will now and then do something in your favour: but I cannot promise you any thing from design. I can no more conjecture what reception any thing I say or do in hopes to please will meet with, than I could what rock a cask would split upon that I were to launch in the midst of the Bay of Biscay.

I must have done—I have got a most swinging cold, which shews

itself both inside and out in all manner of shapes. Yet am I obliged
to go and dine with a man I never spoke a word to in my life. A
formal dinner visit: in consequence of a formal dinner invitation.

Adieu.

Lincoln's Inn Decr. 14 1774.

129

JOSEPH PRIESTLEY TO JEREMY BENTHAM

16 December 1774

Sir

I think myself exceedingly obliged to you for the communication of your method of generating different kinds of air, and have
no objection to it but that it appears to me that it must be rather
troublesome in practice—As to procuring nitreous air very pure, it
is not worth attending to; as its purity is continually changing if it
be kept in water; and it is easy, in comparing different parcels of
air, always to take the nitrous air from the same jar. Besides by
losing a little of the first produce of nitreous, or any other kind of
air, you may be certain of having it very pure.

It is certainly proper to distinguishing the *acid air* which I have
described by the additional epithet of *muriatic*, or *marine*, and you
will find that in one place I have done it, p. 236. But I did not
choose to make the term so complex, till the /actual/ discovery of
the other acid airs should make it necessary. Now, however, I
have produced the other acid airs, with great variations; and
accordingly, in the new edition of my treatise on air, I have, in the
titles of the sections, called the other acid air *marine*.[2]

I have made very considerable additions to my observations on

---

129. [1] B.M. Add. MS. 36524: 23–24. Autograph. Docketed by Jeremy Bentham:
'1774 Decr. 16. Dr. Priestley.' Dated: 'Calne / On Airs and Dr. Simmon's Paper on
Electricity.' Docketed in another hand: 'Priestley J. to Jeremy Bentham 1774.'

Addressed: 'To Mr. Jeremy Bentham / Lincoln's Inn Old Building No. 6 / London.'
Postmark: '19 DE'.

This is in reply to letters 123 and 124. In a further letter to Bentham on 19 March
1775 (MS. in the library of Dickinson College, Carlisle, Pennsylvania) Priestley
apologises for not yet having called on Bentham, but indicates that he will do so on
returning to London from the country about a month later. We do not know whether
the meeting took place. See also letter 142 at n. 4.

[2] On page 236 of *Experiments and Observations on Different Kinds of Air* Volume I
(1774) Priestley uses the phrase 'marine acid in the form of air' instead of simply
'acid air'. This is in Part II section IV. In the third edition (1781) and presumably
also in the second (1775?) the title of this chapter and also that of Part II Section IX
is changed from 'Of Acid Air' to 'Of Marine Acid Air.'

air, and am not determined whether to send an account of them to the Royal Society, or to make a *supplement* to my book; but I rather think I shall do the latter. I have added nothing to the second edition.

I beg you would present my compliments to the author of the paper on Electricity. I think myself honoured by the communication, and am pleased with the ingenuity which it discovers; but he will excuse me if I observe, that I find no sufficient *friction* to produce electricity in the manner that he supposes. The motion that is perceived in small clouds during a thunder storm seems to be the *effect* of preceding electricity.

I should have answered your obliging letter sooner; but I have been confined by illness ever since I received it, but tomorrow, or the next day, I hope to venture out of doors.

I expect to be in London soon after christmas, and then shall hope to have the pleasure of an interview with you, when I shall deliver to you Mr. Symond's tract; having no convenient opportunity of sending it in the mean time.

                    I am, Sir, Your obliged humble Servant
                         J. Priestley

Calne 16 Decr. 1774

130

JEREMY BENTHAM TO SAMUEL BENTHAM

8 April 1775 (Aet 27)

1 Uninteresting

That is *uninteresting*, which promises to give no pleasure, and to avert no pain or to comprehend both cases in a single expression, which promises no pleasure.

2

A discourse promises no pleasure, which giving none at present, gives none in expectation.

3 Use in a Discourse

The pleasure of expectation resulting from a set of ideas communicated in a discourse is termed *use*.

130. [1] B.M. I: 334. Autograph. Docketed: 'I.B. April 8. . . .'
    Addressed: 'To / Mr. Sam. Bentham / at the King's Dock Yard / near Rochester / Single Sheet.' Postmark: '8 AP'.

4 Dry

A discourse that is uninteresting is said, in a figurative but very usual way of speaking, to be *dry*; as it gives a kind of disappointment to him who takes it up in expectation of deriving pleasure from it, it gives him I say a sort of disappointment analogous to what a man who taking up a cup in expectation of finding liquor in it, finds /it dry/ none.

5. Definitions

Of a set of Definitions read by themselves in a suite, no use appears; the use of a definition then first appears when the word first occurs that is defined.

6. Should not be begun with

Therefore it seems that a learner in Geometry for example should not be put to get by heart a string of definitions least he find it dry: but should be made to begin with the propositions and refer to each Definition as it is wanted.

Written by way of explanation of what is said in the 2d sentence of Clairaut's Preface to his Geometry.[2]

Yes, Elmsly[3] as usual has been faithless. I will refresh his memory on Monday—and as soon as I can get the Books from him, or before, if I see no likelihood of getting them soon will send your packet.

Caveats I know nothing of by myself, but only from my Father. The notions I have about them from recollection, agree with yours.

Mr. Simmon's invention we talked of when I was at Chatham. He shewd me his cubes, and I proposed if you remember, the adding of paper dipped in Nitre of Copper to facilitate the accension. I think it a very useful and ingenious contrivance.

Falkner's Dictionary[4] promises I think to be a useful book. I did not find it in some particulars quite as full as I expected: however it contains a good deal of information and is written in a more philosophical stile than one should expect. Observe what he says of '*Pump*' with a view to your invention.

[2] *Éléments de géométrie* by Alexis Claude Clairaut (1713–65). Clairaut is better known for his expedition to Lapland with Maupertuis to estimate a degree of the meridian, and for his *Théorie de la figure de la terre*, published 1743.

[3] See letter 87, n. 5.

[4] *A universal dictionary of the marine: or, a copious explanation of the technical terms . . . employed in the construction . . . of a ship. Illustrated . . . To which is annexed, a translation of the French sea-terms, etc.* 2 parts. By William Falconer. 1769. Second edition, corrected, 1771.

Thou shammest Abraham, and knowest not what it is to sham Abraham—Thou comest within benefit of the prayer, 'Father forgive them, for they know not what they do'. For my part I do not pretend ⟨. . .⟩ ⟨. . .⟩[5]
to send a goat or a stag (or a mo⟨. . .⟩ ⟨. . .⟩[6]
undergo the operation instead of little ⟨. . .⟩ ⟨. . .⟩
Adieu—I have scribbled ⟨. . .⟩ ⟨. . .⟩
rest of your honour's commands sh⟨. . .⟩ ⟨. . .⟩
My best respects to your philosoph ⟨. . .⟩ ⟨. . .⟩
Saturday night April 8th 1775. Qu⟨.⟩ ⟨. . .⟩

131

To Samuel Bentham

10–11 April 1775 (Aet 27)

Monday April 10. 1775. Linc. Inn.
Your letter just received. My Father called on me yesterday. I read to him part of your last: the whole you know it was not to be trusted to him. We had deep consultation about it while alone; and when your female friend[2] was of the party violent disputes, I was going to say: and such the conversation would have been if the violence had been reciprocal. She will absolutely run distracted if you do not work along side: and so will *Mr. Palmer*.[3] She was cer-

[5] About five lines torn away; the first three ending respectively 'certainly the', 'pression', 'that far'.

[6] The missing parts of this and the following lines are also torn away, being the other side of the previous five lines which are lost.

131. [1] B.M. I: 335–336. Autograph. Docketed: 'I.B. April 11th 1775.'
Addressed: 'To / Mr. Sam: Bentham / at his Majesty's Dock Yard / near Rochester.' Postmark: '11 AP'.
Mr William Gray, the Master Shipwright to whom Samuel Bentham had been apprenticed in 1771 had recently died (his will was proved on 10 March 1775). Samuel 'continued in the Yard at Chatham as apprentice to his Executrix' (B.M. II: 149, unpublished), Mrs Elizabeth Whitehorn (for whom see letter 112, n. 3). This letter concerns the course his future training should take, in particular the amount of manual labour he should do. (See also Jeremiah Bentham's letter to Samuel, dated 13 May 1775, B.M. I: 341.) About this time he started lodging in Chatham with Mr Joseph Davies, who appears to have acted as his tutor. Davies was at this time one of the Clerks to the Commissioner of Chatham Dockyard.

[2] Mrs Bentham, stepmother to Jeremy and Samuel: cf. the latter part of this letter.

[3] Mr Palmer seems to have been a close friend of Jeremiah Bentham and his wife: see letter 196 for a charade upon his name. He was perhaps a member of the Navy Board, one of his name being mentioned in that capacity by Samuel in a letter to his father dated 12 June 1774 (B.M. I: 290).

tain in one breath that there will be no possibility of your having a place unless you have done the work of other apprentices: and therefore that it is the absurdest thing imaginable for you to think to exempt yourself from the work of other apprentices. She was certain in the same breath, (and especially when my Father seemed to dwell with something of complacency on your ambition of being Surveyor, and your notions of striking out improvements) she was certain, I say, that it was a very absurd notion (I don't mean that she used the word 'absurd' this time) that of your attaching yourself to the King's Yard. She was certain there was impossibility of rising in the place of Surveyor without passing through every inferior gradation. She was certain, and so my Father always is, that there is no possibility of being appointed to any one of the Offices concerned in the building part without having served out a regular Apprenticeship. You have never indeed satisfied *me* on this head: Be sure and do; furnish me with proper proofs and instances, if you know of any, to lay before my father.

In the midst of it in dropped Mr. Randal.[4] He wrote it seems very early to Pownel[5] in your favour. My Father read to him your last letter together with Davies's, who is a great favourite. Mr. R. acceded to your division of the point of knowledge in a Shipwright, and gave a name to your second branch, which (the name I mean) I have forgotten, as it did not appear to be an apposite one. 'Computing', or 'comparing' or some such word. He allowed that Pownel's notions were '*old-fashioned*' in regard to the necessity of manual labour to the understanding of theory, and in regard to the sacredness of the Mold-loft. It was a *Sanctum Sanctorum*, it seems in his time. He seemed to look upon the King's service as an unpromising track, from the slowness of promotion and the indispensability of attendance: but then he has a notion I remember on other occasions that it would be nothing to my father to advance £3 or 4000 to set you up in the business, Randal worked along side a month or six weeks himself, and whether for that or for what other reason he seems to think it will be expedient at least if not necessary for you. The *stem* or the *stern* he recommends in such case, as the part which will afford the greatest variety of instruction. He says

---

[4] Mr Randal was senior partner in a private shipyard. In 1779 when Samuel was casting around for employment, the idea was mooted that he should join Randal, perhaps as a junior partner. However Jeremiah Bentham was not prepared to advance the money and Samuel preferred to go to Russia (see B.M. II: 322, unpublished, Samuel Bentham to his father, 9 May 1779).

[5] Israel Pownall (or Pownoll), previously Master Shipwright at Plymouth, had succeeded William Gray in that office at Chatham.

that in a month or two Mr. P and you will come acquainted and then every thing will be easy. What say you? It will be more improving than copying draught, and for the sake of having it to talk of it may perhaps be worth the while. It would answer to you likewise in point of health.

My father offers to go down to talk with Pownel, or to go to Mr. Marsh,[6] or to go to Lord Sandwich,[7] but he says with respect to the latter he does not know what plea to urge to them. Certainly none, that regards the King's Service against your doing work while you are receiving pay. But these considerations seem never to enter into their heads.

To keep fair with the Navy-board, the best way I think would be, if any application for indulgence is to be made, for my Father to wait first on Mr. Marsh or Sir John Williams[8] or both: and ask them whether the Board could grant it, if not whether they would have any objection to application being made to the higher powers.

My Father is satisfied you could have every indulgence from Philips of Woolwich[9]; but then the parting from Davies strikes him as a forcible objection, and one that you would not be likely to get over.

Tuesday April 11th

Dined to day at Q.S.P. My Father told me he had written you a letter of 5 or 6 pages. I read to him all the readable part of your last to me. He hit upon an expedient which seems to me really a very good one, if practicable. It is that you should be put to work, not detached from all gangs, nor yet as one to make up the complement of a Gang, but as a *supernumerary*. The advantages are—1st The men will be pleased, as whatever little work you may chance to do will be clear gain to them—there will be no murmers from that quarter. 2d On that account they will probably be ready to lend you any little assistances that they may be wanting to put you in a method. 3dly By shifting from Gang to Gang, if that can be done, you will be in the way to engage in all the varieties of work. 4. You may make it more easy to you in this way, than if you were put to any task in which you stood alone, and where consequently the slowness of your progress would be distinguishable.

[6] George Marsh was Comptroller of the Victualling Accounts in 1772 and Clerk of the Acts from 1773 till the office was abolished in 1796, when he was appointed Commissioner without special functions.

[7] John Montagu, fourth Earl of Sandwich (1718–92) was First Lord of the Admiralty from 1771 to 1782.

[8] Sir John Williams had been Surveyor of the Navy since 1765.

[9] Nicholas Philips had succeeded William Gray as Master Shipwright at Woolwich.

My Father after dinner, Madam out of the room, Far and Charles present, was arguing very philosophically (from ideas furnished him by her the day before) against indulgences (such as that in question of your being exempted from working); amongst other topics, what curiosity they excited from persons in the same situation as the party indulged: that ⟨. . .⟩ partialities in your favour that disposed one to view the propriety of applying for them in a less favourable light than what it merited. I admitted that a natural effect of indulgence to one, was jealousy in others. But observed that this did not hinder people's pushing for indulgences when they had it in their power: and (without any appearance of jealousy but merely as an example pertinent to my purpose), I instanced the case of *Charles*. It was at that time a conversation rather than a debate: the old gentleman by no means in an ill humour. At the mention of the word Charles, I saw the inconsistency of Madam's conduct in the two cases strike him in the face. I did not press him upon it so as to incommode him by letting him see I considered it in that light. But I saw it made a deep impression; at least it struck him forcibly for the time. Soon after he happen'd to say something about the going to France: 'that is' concluded he 'if we do go: For I will *not*' (and he seemed to lay an emphasis upon the *not*) 'For I will not go without *him*' (meaning you. By this I imagine, he either saw or thought he saw an aversion in Madam to your going, and a disposition to raise obstacles.

Elmsly can't find your order; and knows not what books you order'd of him. No more do I: so you must send me word. I have order'd from him—Ainsworth and Han.'s Conic Sections[10] at a venture. They were to have come to night: but have not. On this account, write by return of post; that is if you think it worth while on your own account.

132

To Samuel Bentham

(date unknown)

all the forces he could muster, under pretence that he wanted his assistance against the Pisidae, who (he alledged) had been

[10] This work has not been traced.

132. [1] B.M. I: 339.

This is only half a sheet, stamped: 'Penny Post Paid': Its date is unknown. All that remains of the address is 'Yard' and 'ham'. It is evidently a letter addressed to Samuel at Chatham, enclosing a corrected version of a translation Samuel had made from the Greek of Xenophon, *Anabasis*, I.i.11.

troublesome to his dominions (by their incursions: as well as Socrates the Achaean and Sophaenetus the Stymphalian 2 other friends, (of whom he made the like request) under pretence of (their assisting him) in the war he was engaged in with Tissaphernes on behalf of the Milesians

And they did as he requested

Errata in your letter—'*margine*' instead of '*margin*' 'others in *it's* proper place'—instead of '*in their* proper places—'*shure*' instead of '*sure*'. '*persue*' instead of '*pursue*'

It will be a useful exercise to you, to try if you can to serve me the same sauce.

Clap down every thing upon paper about which you have any doubt or difficulty—I will give you as fast as I have opportunity every satisfaction in my power—So here ends my letter—for I have time to write no more.

You may make use if you will of my translation to retranslate—but for the future, I believe I must content myself with only polishing your *liberal* one.

As you have one of each sort, you ⟨should m⟩ake the litteral as *litteral* and the liberal as *liberal* as you can—only minding in regard to the latter never to depart from the original when you can help it.

Saty. Eveng.

Adieu.

I tore off the other half sheet to save room least the Penny post should refuse it.

133

To Samuel Bentham (not sent) and
Mary Dunkley

30 April–3 May 1775 (Aet 27)

Sunday night April 30
[My brother who is at Chatham]

My dear Sam

How shall I find words to describe to you the scenes I have within these few days been /a witness of, and/ an actor in? You

---

133. [1] B.M. I: 340. Autograph. Docketed by Jeremy Bentham: '1775 I.B. to S.B. Chatham. Not sent—sent to Miss D. with notes.'

The notes intended for Miss Dunkley (for whom see letter 114, n. 1) are in red ink. Here they have been placed within square brackets.

Bowring, as already noted (letter 114, n. 1) knew about the Miss Dunkley affair, though he did not mention it in his Memoirs. He seems never to have seen the letters

will never know how to wonder enough at some part of the story I have to tell you: but your wonder will be a most joyful one. Conceive my mother, our mother I must henceforward call her, acting the part of a most zealous disinterested friend to me, and you will conceive no more than what is most unquestionably true. The grand discovery has been made: and probably before I conclude this letter, my destiny will be definitively settled.

Monday morng. 6 o'clock

I don't know where to begin hardly, nor where to choose, among the multitude of things I could wish to tell you. I must touch upon every thing as slightly as possible.

I have not yet heard from Capt. Carleton[2] in answer to the *Volume* which I shewd you. Nor do I wonder at it, since the dispatch of that volume was retarded, by some circumstances that interven'd, till Tuesday last. Nor am I much concerned about it, as my fate will not turn upon it at all.

It was on Friday the discovery was made. /I dined at Q.S.P./ Taking a turn in the garden after dinner, my mother came up with me—'So, Mr. Jerry, I hear strange stories of you'—'Indeed, Madam? what stories?' with a look of some anxiety—'Oh no harm at all, only that you are a smitten with a prett⟨y⟩ ⟨. . .⟩ I ask you whether it is so or not?'—I could not have wished for a fairer opportunity. Her looks were kind—My Stomach was quiet, I was in a conversable humour. My Father had been just then

now contained in B.M. I. His account of the affair is given in the following manuscript note on page 77 of Volume x of his own copy of his edition, now in the British Museum:

'In the year 1775 Bentham's affections appear to have been engaged by a young Lady of Colchester named Dunkly. The attachment seems to have filled his father's mind with the greatest anxiety,—and is often referred to in his note-books. I have never heard Bentham himself mention the matter,—but I think the following memoranda in his father's handwriting worthy of being preserved.

"1775 April 28. fils Jeremy dinoit chez nous apres cela j'entendois de ma femme a *son attachement* qui me causoit beaucoup de chagrin.

29 Apres avoir passé la nuit sans dormir à cause de fils Jeremy il vient au matin chez nous and nous nous entretenons de son affaire qui me causoit de regret extreme. 30. Au matin chez M. G. W. Grove a ses Chambres, about Son Jeremy.
May 4. Au matin Miss [?] Meen[?] and fils Jeremy dejeunoient chez nous apres celà il me fait voir une lettre qu'il avait reçu de Mons. Carlton de Colchester de sa niece D—kly quand je lui fis connaitre que je ne pourrois consentir à la proposition contenu dans la lettre. M. G. W. Grove dinoit chez nous when conferred with him on Son Jeremy's affair."'

'Miss Meen' has not been identified: It seems possible that Bowring copied the name wrongly from Jeremiah Bentham's notebook, which seems not to be extant.

[2] Miss Dunkley's guardian: the last paragraph but one of n. 1 above shows that Bentham had received an answer from Captain Carleton by 4 May.

telling me of a piece of good fortune that had happen'd in the falling in of a Reversion of about £40 a year. We were all in high spirits upon the occasion and a party had been formed to go down to Pyenest as this day, to take a view (for some *legal* purposes) of the new acquisition. I am this instant setting out: and so good morning to you.

Wednesday.

[The affair ending so unhappily I had not the heart to finish my narrative: so this letter was never sent.

To be short, my Uncle who had promised me his house, retracted. He and my Father (my Uncle tho' a well-meaning man, is of a cold, misgiving apprehensive temper) set one another against my wishes: and all my Mother-in-law could say on my behalf was unavailing.]

134

TO SAMUEL BENTHAM

18 May 1775 (Aet 27)

Thursday May 23d 1775

Oh! my dear Sam, how shall I set down to write to thee? or now I have set down, how shall I know when to leave off? Yes—bad success indeed—that is the reason of my long silence. Tis impossible for me to think of giving the particulars by letter—This however thou canst not know too soon—that my Mother has been my zealous and (for any just ground that I can possibly form to myself of suspicion to the contrary) my sincere advocate. I believe if I had gone all lengths, I might have extorted my Father's consent, but it would have made him supremely wretched, and could have put an end to your Gallic expedition. I could not bear that my Mother should be so early and severe a sufferer for her

---

134. ¹B.M. I: 343–4. Autograph. Docketed: 'I.B. May 23d 1775.'

Addressed: 'Mr. Bentham / at Mr. Jos: Davies's / Chatham.' Postmark: '18 MA'. Bentham's date is clearly wrong. 23 May 1775 was a Tuesday, and the postmark suggests that the letter was written on Thursday 18 May.

The following entries for 17 and 18 May are taken from Jeremiah Bentham's journal by Bowring in the manuscript note quoted above in letter 133, n. 1:

'17. Fils Jeremy dinoit chez nous and je le menois à ses Chambres dans Lincoln's Inn dans ma Carosse and il me fait entendre qu'il avoit proposé de louer ses Chambres and demeurer chez M. Lind à propos de finir son ouvrage. 18. Je me promenais dans les Jardins de Grays Inn avec M. Lind about fils Jeremy et ses affaires interessantes.'

generosity to me. She has given me such proofs under her own hand of her encouraging me to persist, as would ruin any scheme, if she had formed one, of recommending herself by means of it, to my prejudice. My present plan is in a few words this—I believe I shall spend the next half year at Mr. Lind's. My Father, (when will miracles cease?) knows it and tolerates it. Mr. Lind will assist me in rummaging over the Statute-book for materials and heads etc. for a Digest. In the intervals of that employment which will be many I shall go on with my Comment on the Commentaries—I hope to have compleated it in 3 months or so at farthest. Tis on this rests my sole dependance now for the accomplishment of my marriage Scheme—I find that according to the course of the Market £120 may not unreasonably be expected from a Bookseller for a handsome 8vo volume. If the reception that my first volume meets with is such as entitles me to think I can have alacrity enough to produce one every year, I shall trust to that, and take the desperate leap, trusting to the chapter of accidents and my mother's good offices, for reconciling my Father—At present we are all the best friends imaginable. He certainly does love you and me next to his money I was going to say however very nearly if not altogether equal to his wife. But I must not enter into details or reflections. Mr. Lind offer'd me his house as an Asylum if I would venture immediately upon marriage but I declined (you may imagine with what gratitude) for the reason I have above intimated, and because I could not justify it to myself to be hazarding every thing upon the uncertainty of his affairs. From the Contract Scheme, I doubt nothing is to be expected. I expect to day an answer from a Gentleman who has seen my chambers, and seems to be inclined to take them. If so, I shall migrate to Mr. Lind's in a day or two and there if fortune should smile upon me, shall be in readiness to receive my Polly. I now know her age exactly—she is ⟨not⟩ 18 till December next. The affair of Browning hill is uncertain.[2] If that should not succeed my wish would be to find out some snug Parsonage or something in that stile near you at Chatham. East Florida will not do. None of our fruits will grow there—according to De Brahm.[3]

I am now hard at work with Mr. Lind revising his book.[4] It will be out of the press in about a week. As soon as it is, I hope to take a

[2] Presumably the offer of the house there to Bentham by his uncle George Woodward Grove (cf. the end of letter 133).

[3] Cf. letter 104 at n. 3.

[4] *Remarks on the Principal Acts of the 13th Parliament of Great Britain*, 1775 (see letter 99, n. 2).

run to Chatham, and spend two or three days with you. If I do, a previous condition will be, your assuring me that Mr. Davies will accept a week's board from you (propose it as from yourself) and then you and I will adjust it between ourselves. I am to pay at the rate of £40 a year to Lind for myself: by which he will be rather a gainer: and 60£ a year for ⟨myself⟩ and Wife, by which he would be rather a loser.

Adieu—that is all my dear Sam, I can give you at present.

Since the writing of this I have received your letter to Mr Lind.

[*A few lines missing except for some odd words including 'Mathematical knowledge'.*]

[*On cover:* I would fain thank you, my dear Sir, for your Letter: but having this day been honoured with assurances of a long unaltered affection from the Lord of Q.S.P. I am too proud to speak to anyone: Only I assure *you* with *more truth*, I believe of my unaltered Esteem and regard.]

135

To Samuel Bentham

27 May 1775 (Aet 27)

I hope to be with you, my dear Sam, on Tuesday or else on Wednesday—Your distress in the Article of Shirts I will take upon me to relieve. I will bring with me two ruffled and two plain from Barker's; unless you desire me not, by the return of the Post. I wish it were in my power to relieve the other: but before I saw your last I had already done something towards it. I intimated to my Father that you were disappointed about the Boat, and that you found it would come to more than you had thought for—He took it patiently. He started an idea that you might dispose of it: and that your going abroad if it did not furnish you with a reason with respect to yourself, would at least furnish you with a pretext with regard to other people. And it is much his wish: but whether practicable or no I must leave to you to judge.

If Mr. Davies is seriously hurt by my proposal, I am very sorry: settle it with him any how to make it up. But if he is reconciled to

135. ¹ B.M. I: 345–346. Autograph. Docketed: 'I.B. May 27th 1775.'

Addressed: 'Mr. Sam: Bentham / at his Majesty's Dock Yard / near Rochester.' Postmark: '27 MA'. On cover (autograph): 'Locke on Education Character of? Any preferable?' There are also some pencil jottings, perhaps by Samuel, starting 'Poor Ned'.

it, I shall be so much the better pleased, and would have you say nothing about the matter.

My Father is out of Town to day: but will return I believe to-morrow. I don't know that it signifies any thing asking him yet: as he told me but yesterday he had no money. However he told me he expected some soon, and then will be the time for both of us: for I have not received a farthing from him yet. In three weeks at farthest I take it you may expect some. Has Peake[2] paid his? If you want any thing brought now is your time to mention it. I shall send down a Cloakbag. I have some Shirts that want ruffling and collaring—if that sort of work is done cheap and neat with you perhaps I may bring them down.

The French scheme seems to be pursued in earnest.

Adieu—It will answer no purpose my saying any thing more to you at present—My sincere respects to Mr. D. and Dr. S.[3] ask whether either of them have any commands that I can execute. I should have room enough for a small parcel or two.

Satday. 27 May 1775.
Linc. Inn.

136

To Samuel Bentham

8 June 1775 (Aet 27)

Half a dozen lines, or thereabouts, my dear Sam, are all I shall be able to give you by this Post. I dined at Q.S.P. to day. You go to France for certain: and probably even before Midsummer-day. Caen, capital of lower Normandy, about as far as Paris is, is the place of your destination. Letters of recommendn. are procured. Three houses have been heard of where you can be accommodated. In one it is proposed my F. and M. and Far shall take up their quarters; Charles and you, one in each of the other two. I think there can be no time for taking lessons of a French Master. But I can not see why Mr. Davies, for the short time you have, can

---

[2] Henry Peake had been Master Shipwright's Assistant and Master Caulker at Sheerness from 1768 to 1771. He was at this time Master Shipwright's Assistant at Chatham, a post he held from 1774 to 1779. In 1778 he was aboard the *Victory*, Keppel's flagship (see letter 261, n. 2). In 1780 Samuel Bentham tried to entice him out to Russia (see letter 356, §11).

[3] Joseph Davies and (probably) Dr John Simmons (see letter 123).

136. [1] B.M. I: 347–348. Autograph. Docketed: 'I.B. June 8th 1775.'
Addressed: 'Mr. Sam. Bentham / at His Majesty's Dock Yard / Rochester.' On cover: 'Boat price / House where young ladies / Gallicisms.' Postmark: '8 IV'.

not, if he will submitt to the trouble, answer every purpose. The grammatical part, I believe you do not want: or if you do, books will give it you. For conversation, learn to put the necessary questions (such as you will have most occasion to put in a strange Family) to Mr. Davies; then notice, and endeavour to understand his answers. Enquire at your circulatg. library whether there are any books giving an account of Caen or of any places in the route to it. At least read what concerns Normandy in Guthrie's Geogr[1]: Grammar.[2] Don't give way to indolence. It will be a trouble to you to learn how to express yourself upon the ordinary occasions by means of Mr. Davies: But it will be beyond comparison greater to do it by means of persons still less conversant in your language than you in their's.

My things are all come safe. I forgot I believe to pay you for the Barber. Do the needful on that behalf and I will repay you when we meet.

Dispatch the letter for leave to the Navy Board out of hand, that *that* may not be to be waited for. You have I understand, the felicity of a letter from my father.

Many thanks to your honour and Mr. Davies for your remarks I cannot say anything more to them at present.—

My best Compliments to our kind Host and Hostess. Remember me also to the Dr. etc.[3]

Thursday June 8th 1775.

Lincoln's Inn.

It is uncertain whether you will take a sweep to Paris at your return. My Father shrinks at the expence. But my Mother is for it. At *Caën* the *exercises* are to be learnt.

137

To Samuel Bentham

17 June 1775 (Aet 27)

There is a possibility of your seeing Paris at your return: tho' my Father's intentions, I understand are otherwise at present. My

[2] *A new geographical, historical and commercial Grammar* ... 2 vols., 1771 (1st edition 1770, *New System of Modern Geography, or A Geographical* ... *Grammar* ...) by William Guthrie of Brechin (1708–70).
[3] Probably Dr Simmons.

137. [1] B.M. I: 349. Autograph. Docketed: 'I.B. June 17 1775.'
Addressed: 'To / Mr. Sam. Bentham / at his Majesty's Dock Yard / near Rochester.' Postmark: '17 IV'. On cover various pencil jottings, starting: 'About eighty a year.'

Mother is for it. I hope you have made those advantages of Mr. Davies's assistance that I recommended to you. Be not ashamed to speak French before Q.S.P. Speak it ever so bad, you cannot speak it worse than they do.

I wish you could try the comparative respirability of Comm. and Red Lead before you come away, by means of Mice: or if there is no getting Mice, by means of Birds.

My father you know I suppose from himself was to go on Monday to Northampton Shire. He returns next Monday. Nothing consequently could be done about payment for your boat till your coming up.

Adieu—In great haste having but this instant thought to write to you. I am still at Chambers, and there I believe shall continue.

June 17th Saty. night 11 o'clock 1775 Linc. Inn.

My best Compliments to Mr. and Mrs. D.

Nothing have I said to my Father about your matrl. schemes.[2] I can continue to do it though you are here.

138

To Jeremiah Bentham

27 August–5 September 1775 (Aet 27)

Honoured Sir

I am now at last in a situation to thank you for your letter, dated so long ago as the 27th of last month, but written and sent (I cannot but suppose) several days earlier, for the day I received it to the best of my recollection was the 29th, but I am certain not later than the 30th.[2] On the Sunday after I think it was the first of

---

[2] Possibly Samuel, aged 18, was enamoured of the Miss Ousnam mentioned in letters 140 and 234.

138. [1] B.M. I: 351–352. Autograph. Docketed by Jeremiah Bentham: 'Fils Jeremy, Letter to me at Paris datd. Sepr. 5, 1775.'

Addressed: 'Monsr. / Monsr. Bentham / chez Monsr. / Monsr. Blanchard / au (. . .) St Germain en Laye / France.' This address has been deleted, and the letter forwarded to Jeremiah 'Chez M'patté / gentilhomme anglois / place Royalle / pres Les minimes / a Paris.' Stamped: 'D'ANGLETERRE'.

Jeremiah Bentham and his wife had moved on to Paris when this letter arrived, having left their children in Caen (cf. B.M. I: 353, Jeremiah Bentham to G. W. Grove, 10 September 1775).

[2] Part of this letter is in B. M. I: 350. It is dated from Caen, 27 July 1775, and describes the arrival of Jeremiah, his wife, Samuel, and Charles and Farr Abbot in Caen, Normandy, on 2 July. The parents lodged in one house and the young people in another.

this month, I called upon Mrs. Far,[3] to communicate to her such of the contents as were communicable, and to pick up the freshest of such intelligence as I thought would be interesting to you or to my mother, before I wrote, that you might not be troubled with repetitions. I intended in the same view to have called upon Mr. Browne,[4] and Mr. Barret[5] your other correspondents. I was then a good deal indisposed; I had some slight symptoms of a fever: and by that, and some troublesome but neither very painful nor at all alarming eruptions the consequences of it, I have ever since been confined to the house till within these 4 or 5 days. I was at that time attending a course of Dr. Fordyce's lectures on the practise of Physic, to which I had a right by a former subscription. I reconciled that well enough to my other studies, as it diversified them, and took me up but an hour before breakfast, which scarce ever is my time for writing. I had already picked up a little instruction relative to the management of fevers, of which I availed myself very happily: the remedy I took having precisely the effect I was taught from theory to expect from it. It consisted in nothing but a vomit. Still there remained the eruptions: these I found myself unable to master without medical advice. I preferred a Physician to a Surgeon. A Surgeon must have dressed me every time: and I remember'd Mr. Grindal.[6] One visit from Dr. Fordyce enabled me to compleat the cure. Appearing very trifling at first I had disregarded them: and from the exercise I had occasion to take about that time they turned to sores. They were seated on the inside of my right thigh, and on the scrotum on both sides. As they were so critically seated, though I was very soon freed from pain, I durst not stir out of doors till they were completely healed. Though I could very soon have written, I could not therefore *go my rounds* till 3 or 4 days ago, and you had told me, that at that distance you did not desire a frequent correspondence.

All this while, Sir, where do you think I have been? alone at Mr. Lind's. Mr. Lind's health began to require a little fresh air and exercise: Mrs. Lind was wild to get into the country: The house wanted some repairs. At this juncture ⟨their⟩ cousin Gillies[7] made

[3] See letter 92, n. 2.

[4] See letter 45, n. 3.

[5] Probably one of Jeremiah Bentham's tenants (see B.M. I: 350, unpublished, and later references in this volume).

[6] Richard Grindall, f.r.s. (d. 1797), of 2, Austin Friars, for many years surgeon to the London Hospital: Bentham no doubt remembered him because in 1773 he had treated Farr Abbot for a prolonged period (cf. B.M. I: 256, Jeremiah Bentham to Samuel Bentham, 15 May 1773).

[7] Unidentified.

them an offer of a little Box of his near Stanmore for two or three months, being the time he proposed to be absent on a trip to Flanders. The temptation was not to be resisted. They would have taken me with them; but my medical lectures, and the difficulty of getting my books and papers about me, kept me fixed to London.

In spite of chagrin, my 'Comment on the Commentaries' hastens to a conclusion. My 'plan for a Digest' is considerably advanced. One or other of them, if not both, I hope to have to present to you at your arrival, if your stay is as long as you proposed. I live here in perfect ease and tranquillity, as far as exterior circumstances can give it. A reputable old gentlewoman, who has seen better days, left in charge of the house by Mr. Lind, gives me her services and her company. While my indisposition continued, I was necessitated, in the oeconomical sense of the phrase, *to keep house:* and I have lived in luxury at a less expence than at the eating-houses I live in nastiness. My luxuries indeed are soon provided. A spatious and airy bed-chamber, a hair-mattress over the feather-bed, and the use of the bark (which I take now in substance) have remedied to a considerable degree that relaxation, by which my health of late years has been so much affected.

My horse I have parted with to Mr. Clark a very few days after you left England, for the price he offer'd me, which was 4 guineas. Whenever I receive it, my intention is, to give it to Mr. Lind towards the purchase of another, if he should be about buying one, if not to keep it. Mr. Clark by letting the breeding time slip away, has made it a bad bargain to him. But Mr. Martin (the Painter) whom I had told as well as Mr. Clark that she was good for nothing else, when I mentioned it to him told me if I could get her again, he would be glad to give me more for her. You need not have doubted, Sir, but that your pleasure once signified to me, I would not keep her an instant longer than I could help. So much, at least for the present, as to myself. I will now give you as full, and at the same time as brief, an account of the state of your affairs as I can so far as they have come to my knowledge.

Of the disagreable business of the Malt house you could not wish, I suppose to hear much.[8] It will be a satisfaction however to you to know that with respect to the *Extent*, the Assignees have got

---

[8] This was a property at Barking which Jeremiah Bentham had conveyed to Jeremy in 1766, the rent forming a substantial part of Jeremy's income of £103 a year (see letter 67). Later references show that there was considerable difficulty in letting it, and a tenant was not found until 1780 (see letters 346, and B.M. III: 106). Meanwhile Jeremiah made up Bentham's missing income by an allowance (see letter 355, n. 2). This still leaves some obscurity in the present passage.

the better of the thing. This makes a difference of about £250 in favour of the Creditors. One Low a Publican, who keeps the Brown Bear in Leman Street Goodman's fields has been with me about taking it. But as he would offer no more than £30 a year I told him I could give him no encouragement to expect that you would close with his proposal. The manner and appearance of the man I liked much; but as I have very little faith in physiognomy, and never think it a sufficient ground for judgement when better can be had, I put a number of questions to him to serve as a ground for the enquiries I intend to make concerning his character and circumstances. All the rest I have to say to you on this subject, Sir, may wait till your return.

Pope's affair, Mr. Browne desires me to tell you, rests in *statu quo* till your return. Alas! Dear Sir, I am sorry that you are now for the first time to learn by bitter experience, what I have long since understood from frequent observation, that the so much boasted maxim 'wherever the Law gives a right, it gives a remedy,' is no more or less than a Conundrum. The key to it is, that if it does not give a remedy, it gives no right.—Where there is no legal right, there can be no legal wrong.[9]

Now for better news—Mr. Browne has received the rent of the houses in Petty France up to Midsummer. I took a view of them last Thursday. The Beams and Joists of the 1st floor are laid, and the side walls carried up almost to the 2d. There seemed to be a good many men at work. You have heard from Mrs. Far of Mrs. Leech's death.[10] To this I may add that before the old lady was carried out of the house, two persons Chamber Milliners who lived next door to Mrs. Delap[?],[11] came to look at the Apartment, as I understand, in the view of taking it. But persons so circumstanced I suppose you would hardly wish to have for Tenants. If you can fix upon your plan at that distance, and should think proper to communicate it to me, or any body else, it might save some as to the letting it. It might at least be advertised.—I forget whether Mr. Browne had told that the assignment of your Lease of the Houses in Petty France has been executed by all parties.

Your Coachman Daniel is hired to a Mr. Jeakes's in James

---

[9] In his letter of 27 July, Jeremiah Bentham expresses mortification at his inability to obtain satisfaction for damage done to his property by a deceased Mrs Farmer: this was Mrs Ann Farmer, widow, of Tottenham, whose will was proved on 6 April 1775, John Pope of Lombard Street being her executor.

[10] Elizabeth Leech, widow of Jeremiah Bentham's former landlord, John Leech (see letter 59): her will was proved on 1 September 1775.

[11] A resident in or in the neighbourhood of Queen's Square mentioned several times in the correspondence at this period.

Street[12]; but would not engage himself for longer than till your return, till he knew whether you might not be willing to take him again into your service. Such a testimony of attachment in a servant, cannot I should think but be pleasing.

At the same time (Thursday 24th) that I went to look at the houses, I called upon Mrs. Far, and at Mr. Barret's. Mr. Barret I was told was out of town; and had been so, I understood from Mrs. Far, ever since a week after he had written to you. The old lady looked purely well, and had been hard at work she told me in the garden. Weeding, I think it was, and gathering of the onions. She was kind enough to show me the last letter she had received from my Mother, by which I learnt how to direct to you at your new quarters.

It gave me a sincere pleasure to learn from your letter that your situation was so agreable, and that your time had passed till then so much to your satisfaction: and from my mother's, that for the single inconvenience you found in your original quarters you found so pleasant a remedy in exchanging them for better. Indeed I had set you down in my own mind at Paris, before, though not so long before, the end of your excursion. My mother's inclinations seemed to point pretty steadily that way, your's seemed wavering: and I thought, you may tell her, you would not resist the most irresistible of all persuasions.

Among persons whom I know to be of your acquaintance there are dead since you left London, Mrs. Payne the Bookseller's wife,[13] and Mrs. Thomas Dyer.[14] Mrs. Dyer (by the newspapers) died Wednesday the 16th at Kensington. Mrs. Payne a fortnight or three weeks before.

It is possible you may see at Paris Mr. Corsellis of Wivenhoe.[15] To re-establish his finances which are a little deranged, and shake off a set of acquaintance whose society he finds as prejudicial to his health as to his fortune, he has raised his rents, and is going over with his whole family at Michaelmas to live for a time somewhere

---

[12] Unidentified.

[13] Wife (née Elizabeth Taylor) of Thomas Payne (1719–99), the bookseller, whose shop at Castle Street near the Mewsgate was a favourite place of resort for the literati. Bentham was evidently a frequent customer there. See later references and cf. letter 7, n. 1. Payne was the publisher in 1789 of Bentham's *Introduction to the Principles of Morals and Legislation.*

[14] Mary, daughter of Richard Smith, a London merchant, first wife of Thomas Dyer (d. 1800) of the Treasury, second son of Sir Thomas Dyer, 5th bart., and father of Sir Thomas Swinnerton Dyer, 8th bart.

[15] Nicholas Corsellis (1744–1826); matric. Lincoln College, Oxford 1762, M.A. 1766; later rector of Wivenhoe.

in France. His brother Cæsar[16] quits his house in Red lion Street to live wholly in the country: I think it is at General Gansill's[17] that he has purchased.

So much for private news—As to the political, that you have now in sufficient plenty, I suppose from the foreign papers.

I am obliged to my Mother for giving me an opportunity of testifying the pleasure I shall always take in obeying her commands. The fate of Mrs. Rudd and the Perreau's[18] still continues in suspense. They stand respited till after her trial; and her trial has been put off upon her and her Attorney's affidavit of the absence of a witness. In the mean time she has given a fresh specimen of her villainy. A woman who had lived with her as a servant, from motives of gratitude and compassion, went to see her old mistress in her distress, and to make a tender of her services and her little purse. Mrs. Rudd thanked her, told her she was in no want of money, on the contrary she was in a condition to reward her liberally for one very essential piece of service it was in her power to do for her. When this service came to be explained, it was, to get a lesson Mrs. R. had invented, and swear the forgery upon Sr. Thos. Frankland[19] and Mrs. R. Perrau. For this service 900£ was offer'd or even £1000. And to quiet her conscience—the fact was true, only there unfortunately wanted evidence. The poor woman astonished, and not knowing what to make of it, gave no definitive answer, but went and told her husband. Her husband is a Carpenter, who works every now and then for Mr. Gillies, and who told Mr. G. this story. This happen'd about 6 weeks ago. I have not seen it yet in print. However I have seen it in the papers that a Bill has been found against Mrs. Rudd for subornation.

Two other passages of domestic life have since that engaged the attention of the public. One is, the death of Mr. Scawen of Woodcote in Surrey, Uncle to the member.[20] The other is, a paper war between the Dutchess of Kingston and Foote.

[16] Nicholas Cæsar Corsellis (1746–1806) of Woodford and later of Wivenhoe.

[17] Lieutenant-General William Gansell, Colonel of the 55th Foot, had died on 28 July 1774 in the Fleet Prison, where he had been imprisoned for debt.

[18] Daniel and Robert Perrau were executed for forgery on 17 January 1776. For Margaret Caroline Rudd see *Facts, or a . . . narrative of the case of Mrs. Rudd. Published from her own manuscript . . .* , London, 1775. The Rudd-Perrau cases produced an extensive pamphlet literature—including also *Observations on the Trial of Mr. R. Perrau. With . . . remarks on Mrs Rudd's narrative . . .*, London, 1775.

[19] Admiral Sir Thomas Frankland, Bart., M.P. for Thirsk (c. 1717–84), had lent substantial sums to Robert Perrau, who had been his apothecary.

[20] Jane Butterfield was acquitted of the murder of William Scawen after a trial which produced a number of pamphlets. The victim's nephew was James Scawen (1734–1801), then M.P. for Surrey.

Mr. Scawen had kept in the house with him for 5 or 6 years past a young girl of the name of Butterfield, whose chastity he had bought it is said of her father at the age of 14, and whom for some years past he had permitted to take his name. He had taken great care of her education, and was known to have made a will in her favour to the amount ⟨. . .⟩ ⟨. . .⟩. For this year or two last past, he had ⟨. . .⟩ ⟨. . .⟩ very declining, scorbutic, state of health. ⟨There⟩ was a young Officer, who for some time past had been intimate at Mr. Scawen's. Him and Miss B. Mr. S. it is said had encouraged to think of making a match as soon as Mr. S. should die. Mr. S. had for a long time been accustomed, contrary to the persuasions of all his friends to tamper with quack medicines. He would take nothing but from Miss B.'s hands. At last being very ill, and in a state of salivation, he called in *Sanxay*[21] the Surgeon, an old practitioner, who lives I think in Norfolk Street. Sanxay when he saw him, and heard his story, took up a suspicion that he had been poisoned by Miss B. with a mercurial poison. Mr. Schawen gave in to the suspicion, and he suffer'd himself to be taken to a house of Sanxay's, where he continued 3 weeks, and then died. On Sanxay's evidence Miss B. was indicted last Surry assizes, but acquitted. Notwithstanding the circumstances I have mentioned, Miss B. is almost universally believed innocent. Sanxay has hurt himself very much in the affair. I should have mentioned, that while at Sanxay's house, Mr. S. cancelled the legacy he had given to Miss B. Sanxay's known opulence acquits him of any criminal design, but his profession charge him with great ignorance and rashness. What is remarkable is, that all the time Mr. S. was at his house, neither did he (Sanxay) call in any Physician or Surgeon of note to warrant his proceedings, nor on the other hand did Miss B. send any person of the faculty to inspect them, though she knew she was suspected. On the other hand, though she might easily have absconded, she did not. She is said to be very handsome, to have served Mr. S. with great appearance of tenderness and fidelity, and to have been in all respects a most irreproachable character. If innocent, her situation is truly lamentable. The revocation of the legacy, it is said is likely to be contested, upon the ground of the verdict, and the evidence at the trial.

The war between the Dutchess and F. has served as a farce to alleviate the horror of this tragedy.[22] F. had taken off her Grace in

[21] Edmund Sanxay, surgeon: Sanxay and Bradly, druggists, opposite Craven Street, Strand.

[22] A war of words between Samuel Foote, the playwright, and the self-styled Duchess of Kingston (see letter 160, n. 6, also letter 248, n. 1).

a new piece he had designed for this summer's entertainment, to have been entitled 'The Trip to Calais.' The Lord Chamberlain refused to license it. This produced an expostulatory letter from Foote to his Lordship in the papers. Soon after appeared a l⟨etter from⟩ F. to the Duchess, with her answer, both published by ⟨. . .⟩ ⟨. . .⟩ offers to forbear publication of the piece, out of tenderness ⟨for⟩ her Grace upon condition of her putting an end to the attacks which at her instigation, he says, have been made upon him in the papers; intimating that she had made pecuniary offers to him which had been rejected. The Dutchess's answer betrays violent indignation with an attempt a very awkward attempt at pleasantry. Foote was not long before he put in a reply, to the last degree humourous and severe. The affair concluded with an affidavit of the Revd. Mr. Foster, Chaplain to her Grace (our Mr. Foster)[23] purporting that upon his calling on Mr. Foote to talk with him upon the subject by her Grace's order, Foote had offer'd to suppress the copy for £2000. These four letters when you see England again will afford you much diversion. It is astonishing how the Dutchess could think of descending to a personal altercation in the Newspapers with the veteran Buffoon.

Mr. Burgh,[24] Mr. Darling's acquaintance, Master of the Academy at Newington, Author of the 'Political Disquisitions', a well meant but superficial performance, of which he had just lived to publish the 3d and last Volume, is dead.

By means of Sam's zealous and attentive friend Mr. Davies, I have lately negotiated for Mr. Clark the purchase of a lot of the King's Timber. I was at Chertsey t'other day. He is very busy clearing, cleaning, embanking and planting his two acres. But if I was in his place I should be afraid of draining my purse of money, before I had drained my estate of water. I think what I am going to mention was not done before you went—He has taken Mrs. Evance's house till Christmas, and now lives in it. She has taken Mr. Wynt's, who is gone to live in the family house upon his Mother's death.[25]

My old friend *Gwatkin*,[26] I understand, is arrived somewhere in Great Britain, but I have not seen him. He has been employd for

[23] The Rev. John Forster: cf. letter 248, n. 1.

[24] James Burgh (1714–75), political writer, had died on 26 August.

[25] Richard Clark had purchased in 1774 the Porch House (later known as Cowley House from its association with Abraham Cowley) at Chertsey; but he did not live in it until 1798 (Brayley, *History of Surrey*, ii, 217). The other Chertsey residents mentioned here have not been identified.

[26] The Rev. Thomas Gwatkin: cf. letter 75, n. 1.

some time by Ld. Dunmore, Govr. of Virginia[27] as tutor to some of his children. The spot grows too hot to hold him, as well as his patron. I have several times been in company with a brother professor of his, lately arrived from America on the same account; one whom just before his departure he had introduced to my acquaintance.[28] With regard to *Mrs. Rudd*, I should have told you, that a few days after you left England, she published her narrative under the title of '*Facts*', which has gained no more credit than *Perrau's* did.

Sam will probably have new and perhaps better quarters to come upon his return. Mr. Davies's Wife's Father in law[29] is dead. The Widow is to live half of her time with Mr. D. and on that account he tells me he is about taking a larger house.

Tuesday evening. Sept. 5.

I am sincerely sorry, Sir, that the dispatching this letter has been so long delay'd. As far as a good way in the 6th column was written so long ago as Sunday sen'night. I was prevented by different accidents dispatching it the two last post days. On Friday detained at a distance from it (at Mr. L's country house) by stress of weather; Being by that means obliged to defer sending it till this day, I thought I would take advantage of the delay to send you the freshest intelligence concerning Q.Sq.Pl. I am this moment come from thence. Mrs. F. purely well. Nothing had happen'd particular since I called last. Mrs. Leech's goods were sold by Auction on Saturday last. They applied to Mrs. F. and she gave them leave. It was over in two or three hours. The buildings in Petty France seem to go on very well. The Brick work is now carried up in front higher than the tops of the windows of the first floor. They are very busy in paving Queen Square, and new laying the steps down to the Park. Mrs. Far was kind enough to give me 4 or 5 bunches of black grapes; They are not very large this year but perfect, not a wasp nor a fly about them. She has bagged up about 50 bunches, and I recommended it to her to bag up more, being so perfect this year, and so capable of preservation.

I am now once more got back again to my chambers. Bugs are got

[27] John Murray, 4th Earl of Dunmore (1732–1809), Governor of New York 1770, of Virginia 1771. In June 1775 his differences with the colonists had reached such a pitch that he withdrew with his family aboard a warship. He returned to England in 1776 and was Governor of the Bahamas from 1787 to 1796. Bentham evidently made his acquaintance some time after his return to England and they 'made trifling chemical experiments together' (Bowring, x, 124).

[28] This was Samuel Henley: cf. letter 143, n. 12.

[29] Edward Acworth of Chatham, stepfather of Mrs Elizabeth Davies.

into several rooms at Mr. Lind's: and as some of the rooms were a painting, he in a panic, order'd the house to be painted all over. Now I perceive again the inconvenience of a soft featherbed and confined bed-chamber of which I cannot change the Air. I do believe I must get a Mattress.

I have got a new neighbour in the Chambers opposite me, who I hope will prove an agreable one. His name is Fitzherbert[30]: Son of the Lord of Trade who made a voluntary exit. He is of some College in Cambridge, where he is at present: has lately I find been at the Duke of Devonshire's at Chatsworth. Till now he occupied an apartment at Somerset House. He has travelled a good deal, seems an agreable man, but not very knowing, yet disposed to knowledge. I have a slight acquaintance with him, having met him once at Mr. Lind's. I hear he has spoken of me in terms of respect.

My affectionate respects wait upon my Mother—My love to the young folks when you see or hear from them. I have had a letter from Sam directly besides two by way of Mr. Davies: but have been so wicked as never to have written to him yet. I shall soon, perhaps next Post. I dined on Sunday at Mr. Browne's. All well. I hope the *length* of this epistle if not the *speed* of it, will serve in some measure to prove with what sincerity I am Hon'd. Sir

Your dutiful and affectionate Son Jeremy Bentham

139

To John Lind

11 September 1775 (Aet 27)

The first thing I perceive, upon opening your letter, is that the meaning of mine has been mistaken. The first thing I have to do, is, as far as it is in my power, to rectify the consequences. Inclosed you

[30] William Fitzherbert (1748–91) had been at school with Bentham, who had forgotten this. (Bowring, x, 184). He was at a later date Recorder of Derby, but never, as Bentham says (probably confusing father and son) member for Derbyshire. (Bowring, x, 238). In 1784 he was created a baronet. His father, William Fitzherbert, had been member for Derby, commissioner of the Board of Trade. He had committed suicide in 1772. Bentham's later correspondent, Lord St Helens, was his brother, Alleyne (see letter 189, n. 2). In 1779 William Fitzherbert showed himself very ready to use his influence on behalf of Samuel (see letters 307 and 309).

139. [1] B.M. I: 355. Autograph. Docketed by Lind[?]: 'Lincoln's Inn 1775. / Bentham Sepr. 11 / Ansd.'

Bentham had spent much of the summer lodging at the Linds' house in Lamb's Conduit Street (cf., letters 134 and 138). It seems that he had also lodged for a time with Lind's sisters in Colchester. Probably Miss Dunkley had been there for many

will receive back again what I suppose to be two Bank notes of £20 each: for I have not looked at them. Along with them you will receive your note of hand, agreable to your desire. I am very sorry it has so happen'd: it may have put you to inconvenience. It may even have distressed you: and I know not, even with all your kind assistance, how long it will be before I shall have brought myself to that convenient frame of mind as to be insensible to the thoughts of your being distressed. I did indeed express myself ambiguously; or rather perhaps improperly. I said '*settle*'—I ought to have said '*state*': The whole view I had in my letter was to *know* what was due from me to you; not to receive what might be due from you to me. Must I offend your ears with the sound of the odious word board? I know no remedy for it. Time was when you could mention it without any of those violent marks of aversion. Somthing then I owe you for my board from Midsummer day to the day of your going into the country both inclusive. Calculate it upon what footing you please: either that at which Mr. Clark[2] pays you, or your Sister Letty pays at Mr. Crowther's[3]: or my Brother pays at his Hosts. The first I have known but have forgotten: the second I never knew. The third I know. But that I be suffer'd to pay for my board I insist on as *a right*: because such was our agreement. I also insist upon it as a right that the sum you fix upon be such as you can vouch upon your honour to be not less than what you believe yourself to be out of pocket: making due allowance for my enormous appetite. This I say I insist upon as a right: because that the Sum should be adequate to what we should compute you might be out of pocket was our agreement: and I am not now in an humour to give up my rights. Compliment is out of the question. That I remember was the period I proposed, and you acquiesced in. For a considerable time before that period I dieted a great part of the week at your house. With respect to that do as you please: you will please me either way. I did so, because you expressed

[2] Cf. letter 189 (22 November 1776), referring to 'Mr. Lind's Mr. Clark'.
[3] Not identified.

meals, and Bentham wished to reimburse the sisters for these as well as his own expenses.

He seems to have worked in close collaboration with Lind for much of this year. In May he was helping Lind with his *Remarks on the Principal Acts of the Thirteenth Parliament* and intending to work with Lind on a Digest of the Statute Book (see letter 134). Throughout this period he was working on his *Comment on the Commentaries* which had originated in a project of Lind's.

We do not know exactly how matters stood between Bentham and Miss Dunkley at the moment, but the strained relations here manifested between Bentham and Lind may have arisen from Lind's not liking the part Bentham was playing in the affair.

yourself two or three times displeased, as it seemed to me, when I went away to dine at a time that I was at work for you.

The Desk is paid for according to agreement by Thurloe's state papers[4] which I negligently enough have suffer'd to remain here all this time: though they have been taken down and dusted for the purpose of sending away for a considerable time: and orders actually given about the carrying them before I saw your letter.

The two Guineas is not nor ever was your's unless you choose to make it so. /your right to do which certainly is what nobody can dispute/ I gave it you; as you may remember upon trust: thinking the point of delicacy provided for by transmitting it through your hands. Even had I paid it with my own . . your Sisters surely were not above taking boarders. /Your concerns and their's were at that time separate./ You I did not consider in it, as I told you. I considered only the expense incurred on my account and Miss Dunkly's. I considered only strict justice—my means gave me no pretensions to be generous—/I went there you may remember *uninvited*. I invited myself: I did not mean to obtrude myself as a burthen. Nor ought I to have been suffered thus long to appear in their eyes as if I had meant so./All these matters /taken together/ I should conceive might have been better settled vivâ voce: if the thoughts of meeting had not been full as irksome to me as they can be to you.

What I have to answer to the remainder of your letter I will defer to another time. I could not trust myself to write upon some of the topics contained in it in the frame of mind I am now in. I know not what extravagances I might run into—nor what imprudences I might be guilty of—nor what weaknesses I might betray—Nor what injustice I might do to the memory of my departed Friend.

Monday eveng. Sept. 11th 1775.
Lincoln's Inn.

My wish is not to hear from you untill you have heard from me again: unless it be simply to tell me that this letter has come safe.

[4] *A collection of the State Papers of John Thurloe Esq., secretary, first to the Council of State, and afterwards to the two Protectors, Oliver and Richard Cromwell; in seven volumes, containing authentic memorials of the English affairs from the year 1638 to the Restoration of King Charles II,* edited by Thomas Birch, M.A., F.R.S., 1742.

140

TO SAMUEL BENTHAM

12 September 1775 (Aet 27)

Could I have thought, my dear Sam, that it would ever prove disagreeable to me to write to *you*? And yet, to confess the truth, it is so. Having thought of what I should say to you so much, it has for some time been disagreeable to me to think of it any longer. For even the thoughts that give me the greatest pleasure at the instance of their production, as appearing new and of importance to my darling projects, grow insipid to me and even nauseous after having been brooded upon for a certain time. And the sense of being so much in arrears to you has made the time of payment more and more formidable. But now the Ice is broke I hope I shall sail on with tolerable celerity. As to my love affairs what shall I say to you? To tell you all, I must say an immense deal to very little purpose; I will therefore (I mean as to particulars) tell you nothing. Suffice it for the present, that my mind is perfectly calm upon the subject: and that nothing will be concluded upon till I see you. You may banish therefore all anxiety on that head from your mind.

Thank you for your grammatical communications. I see you catch in every thing my systematical strain. I hope you will not want courage to persevere. I hope you have resolution enough to fly the alluring company of your countrymen, and to profit to the utmost by your foreign residence. As to the rest you have told me a good deal of what I did not wish to hear (your reverse, I mean, considering that it might very well have kept) not a little of what I wished not to hear (your conversation with my Father) and very little about what I wished much to hear, your manner of spending your time, your pleasures and your chagrins in the novel situation in which you have found yourself. Had you done that, I might possibly have suggested to you the means of availing yourself of it to the best advantage. Am I not got into a very tutorly, fatherly kind of ⟨. . .⟩ ⟨. . .⟩

As to the dissatisfaction he expressed to you respecting me, you should have considered that no fresh occasion for it could possibly have intervened since we parted. And whether I told you or no but so it is, at that time there was all the appearance of amity on

140. [1] B.M. I: 357–358. Autograph. Docketed: 'I.B. Septr. 12 1775.'
Addressed: 'A Monsr. / Monsr. Bentham (le fils) / chez Monsr. / Monsr. Le Hardi / Rue St. Jean / a Cäen / France.' Stamped: '21'.

his side imaginable. You *must* know by this time that nothing that
I can do, or you can do or any body can do, in short nothing that
can happen, can make him easy for two days together: to what purpose then distress me with the picture of his discontents? The talk
then was, he was to *disinherit* me for not 'opening' to him; now he
had never talked about disinheriting me before, even when I was
quite *shut*: and you know I have *open'd* to him of late about my
work, which for the moment gave him great satisfaction. I *rather*
think he will *not* disinherit me; nor would even were I to marry: but
if he does it is what I have again and again thought of, and what
I am thoroughly prepared for. My Mother's Marriage settlement will
keep me from starving. What I have at present, was, I have reason
to think, comprized in it. I am entirely convinced that there is
nothing whatever I could do that would secure me against such
occasional expressions of his disfavour: If I was to *open* to him to
the utmost tell him every word, deed and every thought: that
would not do. He could not know but there might be more behind
unopen'd. This also I would have you know, that were I certain
inherison or disinherison depended upon it, I would not be bound
to be constantly with him, and give up my time to the round of
company he keeps. Your offers, my dear Sam, are what I might
expect from a Brother at the period of life you are at, and not insensible to the zeal with which in every way I have been able to
devise I have for such a course of years endeavoured to deserve
well of him. Of the sincerity with which they were made, I can make
no doubt: but it is not on them that I can place any dependence.
At present every thing almost that you value yourself for, or felici-
tate yourself on, you seem to think you owe to me. All your
pleasures almost you either ascribe to, or look for from or expect
to share with me. As you advance in life, I shall become less
necessary to you. You will derive your pleasure more from yourself,
or from other sources. Your judgements you will have learnt to
form for yourself. Your affection for me at present serves as a
screen to hide from you my failings: hereafter they will rise up to
your view. Affection for an object depends upon the capacity of
that object to afford pleasure. At present you love me: in time you
will feel that you *ought* to love me rather than you will love me.
Disgusts more or less will unavoidably arise in every connection:
occasions will arise, on which for the time being I may appear to
deserve ill of you: what is present seizes on us with a force not to
be resisted. I was going on with tracing the progress of that disposition of things by which according to the common course of

nature you would be led to repent of having made any such offers, and to think yourself dispensed with from fulfilling them,—but the subject I doubt not gives you pain, and would take up too much time and paper to discuss fully. Suffice it for me as the result of all to say that though I can trust entirely to what you *are now*, I can not trust to what you *may be hereafter*.

When my Father held that discourse to you, either he had no views in it, and meant only to give present vent to a present fit of spleen, or else his views if he had any, were, either 1st to bribe you to desert me, and come over to his party or 2dly to make you a vehicle for his threats. He had been cautioned by Mr. Lind against threatening me directly, least by irritating, it should confirm me.

I have received a letter from him which I have answer'd; and before my answer reached him, another. In the first he compares my *crime* to *Suicide*, but concludes affectionately, and promises to write no more to me on the subject. The 2d. is only to inform me of his change of quarters: very mild, considering my apparent neglect of him. Mine to him was chuck full in this hand.[2] It consisted of news, such as you would not give a rush to hear.

I suppose you will go to Paris, before your return. If so, that, I take it, would be the best place to make purchases. Certainly it would be for Books. The ruffles (Women's) I would wish to have are Muslin worked in the manner of Dresden. Mr. Clark got a pair for his Mother at a Convent of Calais I think it was, for no more than 12s.—or I am much mistaken. /Put my Mother in mind of this./ At that price or a few shillings more I would have two pairs. At Boulogne perhaps they might be cheaper, being not so directly contiguous to England. The money you have of mine is £2. 1s. Take advice of my Mother telling her that Mr. D. gave you a general loose commision to lay out from £1.1s. to £2. 2s., if you saw it worth while in wearables or trinkets for Mrs. Davies. No earrings, they are nasty things. Nor Necklace unless very pretty and very cheap. I don't know whether they are worn without earrings. If you can get nothing useful so as to be worth while, get if you can some trifling toy at the prison of the *Bicêtre* in Paris; a sort of *Bridewell*. This for the *History's* sake: or any thing else that is particular, and whereby 'hangs a tale.' Mr. L. brought a toilet of coloured Straw at the Bicêtre, very curious for 2 Guineas, and gave it to Princess Poniatowski. Books, considering the bulk, I question

---

[2] This part of the letter is written in a very small hand. The letter here called 'the first' would seem to be B.M. I: 350, dated 27 July 1775 (see letter 138, n. 2). But all that part of it concerned with poor Bentham's marital project was, apparently, destroyed. The second letter is not extant.

whether it will be worth while: especially as you can only get them news[?].

Let me thank thee, my dear Sam, while I think of it, and tell thee, thou art as candid an advice-giver, as my imagination itself can paint. There is as much vanity after all as gratitude in this acknowledgement, for my dear Sam, thou art my Son.

Ask my Mother about a piece of Silk with a sprig of embroidery on it, for women's shoes. If you get nothing else buy enough for two or three pair. Mr. Wilson[3] brought over a piece and gave to Mrs. Lind. I am persuaded embroidery is cheaper there than here.

Beg the favour of my Mother to buy for me a Lyons Wastecoat somewhat in the manner of that I had before at from $1\frac{1}{2}$ Guinea to 2 Guinea's price; the piece unmade. Termath, a German Taylor, a very honest fellow, has my measure. He did live Fauxbourg St. Germain, *Rue de Seine*, almost opposite *Rue de Colombier*: on the opposite side of the way. He will hardly recollect my name, but mention my being with Mr. Smith, the last time Mr. Martin was there. Madame *Godin* who keeps a lodging-house in the same street (it was with her I lodged) knows him. As she (if she is alive) keeps a *whole house*, she will be easier found than he. Call on her if you can, talk to her about me and Martin, and give her a kiss for me and another for Martin. tell her *Smith* (you must call it *Shmeet*) is at Edinburgh in Scotland, goes on very well, and has good business.[4]

Faites a votre respectable hôte les compliments d'un *compagnon de metier*, et marquez lui a quel point je suis sensible aux egards qu'il vous temoigne, et aux bontés dont il ne se lasse pas de vous honorer. Pour faire matiere de conversation vous pourrez par fois lui faire connôitre quel espece d'animal je suis: vous pourrez lui expliquer mon caractere et mes desseins: comment et par quelle raison je suis un espece d'Avocat *in partibus* Avocat sans cause par choix. Voici une chose que serois curieux de savoir de sa part. Je veux dire, si le barbare *droit d'Aubane* subsiste encore (c'est a dire envers les nations qui n'en sont pas expressément exemptés) en toute rigeur. S'il n'y a pas quelque pratique par lequel il est d'usage de l'evader. Par exemple, donation fait par le moribond a quelque parent ou ami; par devant Notaire, ou autres

---

[3] Probably George Wilson (see letter 149, n. 12).
[4] It has not been possible to identify Smith.

temoin ou autrement avec forme, ou sans forme. Ou bien par rapport aux effets mobiliers, en le reputant marchand, conformément a l'Arret du 27 Juin 1579. Demandez lui aussi au profit de *qui* (je ne veux pas dire nommément car c'est a celui du Roi) mais effectivement ce droit est exercée. Chez nous ce droit ne s'etend qu'aux biens immeubles, ni même tout a fait a ceux la. Aussi peut-être pourroit un etranger en jouir sa vie durant et disposer des profits de la vente d'iceux par testament par voye de *fideicommis* sans beaucoup danger d'en être empêché. Marquez lui aussi, a ⟨quel⟩ point je serois charmé de lui temoigner ma reconnoissance en satisfaisant quelque curiosite qu'il puisse avoir au sujet de nos loix, ou de toute autre façon.

The above you may shew him if you will, as from yourself—and if he should mention letters of naturalization (de naturalité) ask him whether they are easily obtained or no, by what means and so forth, and what they cost. I have reason for all this, more than simple curiosity: but that, you know, you are not to let him see. Therefore, don't let him see more than just what is in French: For there are words in the English which he would see to be relative to the subject.

I will now copy a scrap I had written to thee, immediately upon the receipt of your first to Mr. Davies. I left off, fearing the paper might be too thick.

Dix mille graces, mon cher Sam, (car mille ne suffisent pas) pour la lettre que j'ay reçue ce moment par l'entremise de Mr. Davies. J'y vois toute la bonhommie de mon cher frere, avec toute la legereté Françoise. Vous avez meme attrapés quelques mots characterisques de la langue, que vous avez sçu pour la plupart mettre assez bien a leur place. Courage! mon petit bijou, (aussi petit par rapport a moi qui vous ecrit cela qu'un hanneton (hornet) vis-a-vis d'un guêpe) si je ne suis pas plus mauvais prophete que tous les douze ensemble, vous ne manquerez pas de tourner votre sejour bien a profit. Accrochez vous sur-tout a cette belle dame qui a eue la bonté de vous prêter son dictionaire—Tellement quellement, d'un facon ou d'autre, faites vous en entendre.

Write to me once more, to tell me of your destination (if you know it,) till your return. I hope you will go to Paris, if it be but for a day or two. Make a hard push for it.

Is any thing settled between you and the Davies's about meeting at Battle? If Q.S.P. were to return by way of Brightelmstone, it would not be, I believe, a great deal out of your way. They might then set you down, in the equipage etc. If you think there is any thing feasible in this, I would open the matter to my Father by letter: and, if requisite, to Mr. Davies. He might be desired to mention it as a scheme of his own, to Mrs. Davies. You know I suppose, of old Acworth's[5] death; and that the Widow is to be with her two daughters by turns, and that D. is looking out for a larger house.

I have a scheme in my head, which I will mention to you, that you may have somewhat to look forward to perhaps with a little pleasure. It is this. Davies wrote to me to ask me to go down to Chatham in your absence. This, for many reasons, I declined. Hindrance to my studies, Fordyce's lectures, you not there. Now my book hastens to a completion. I shall want an *amanuensis* to transcribe it for the press and I should like to read it over to you and Mr. D. You scrutinize more closely a vast deal than Mr. Lind: and you would take more interest in a work of mine, than he does in his own. And Mr. Davies would certainly now and then be of some use. I wonder whether Chatham could furnish a correct and *fluent* amanuensis: or in short any amanuensis—My *Tom* is drawling he won't do at all.[6] There would be somewhat sociable in our Triple Junto: our *Trinity* if you please. And by that time Miss Ousnam[7] perhaps may be returned; and we might have some Music.

As D. will have a larger house (with some little encrease I suppose of assets to support it,) who knows but it might be possible to get the fair incognita[8] there, some time or an other. If my health were to hold especially, we could court her together to perfection. Lincoln's Inn Tuesday 12 Sept. 1775.

This is Baskerville's Paper. Is it not beautiful? Poor Bask: is dead and we shall have perhaps no more.[9] Adieu.

[5] See letter 138, n. 29.

[6] Tom was Bentham's amanuensis: cf. letter 115, n. 3.

[7] Cf. letter 137, n. 2.

[8] It is not clear to whom this refers: possibly Miss Dunkley, but perhaps more probably some friend of Samuel's.

[9] John Baskerville, the celebrated printer (b. 1706), had died on 8 January 1775. He had introduced the making of 'wove' paper in 1750.

141

TO JEREMIAH BENTHAM

22 September 1775 (Aet 27)

Hond. Sir

I have but just time to thank you for your very kind letter, before I proceed to what must be the subject of this.

A Tenant has offer'd for the apartment that was Mrs. Leach's: and as I thought her likely to prove an acceptable one, I thought no time was to be lost in taking your commands upon the subject. You had given Mrs. Delap[2] the preference in the recommendation of a Tenant: but a lady she had in view, and has proposed it to, declined it on account of the height of the rent, at the sum you had first fixed. The lady I am about to mention made no objection to that rent (£30)[?] when mentioned to her by Mrs. Far and Mrs. Delap: for *she* also though not before acquainted has been to Mrs. Delap about it. but when I mentioned to her the new terms you seemed to have resolved upon, she would not hear of any advance. Her name is *Sarney*[3]: she is I believe a Widow, seems between 50 and 60, and has I think a good deal of the gentlewoman in her appearance. She has lately lost a Son, I understand, who died in the East Indies; and for whom she is now in mourning. A daughter of her's is married to Mr. Harcourt, a Gentleman nearly related (as I understand from Mr. Clark) to Lord Harcourt.[4] He occupies, (or rather his wife, for he is a Lunatic) *Little Foster House* near Egham; a house which you may remember belongs to old Counsellor *Vernon* who succeeded to it on the death of his Nephew *James*.[5] Mrs. Sarney's chief residence has been and will be at this daughter's; but she has occupied an apartment in Somerset House as a home

---

141. [1] B.M. I: 359. Autograph. Docketed by Jeremiah Bentham: 'Letter from Fils Jeremy to me at Paris. Septr. 22d 1775.'

Addressed: ' / Monsr. Bentham / chez Monsr. / Monsr. Pattle / Gentilhomme Anglois / A la Place Royale / au Coin des Minimes / a Paris / France'. Stamped: 'D'ANGLETERRE'.

A large part of this letter is concerned with the letting of the apartment in Queen's Square previously occupied by Mrs Elizabeth Leech: cf. letter 138 at nn. 10 and 11.

[2] See letter 138, n. 11.

[3] Unidentified.

[4] Simon Harcourt (1714–77), second Viscount Harcourt of Stanton Harcourt, had been created Earl Harcourt in 1749. The other members of the Harcourt family mentioned in this letter have not been identified.

[5] James Vernon of Egham died in 1769 (*Gentleman's Magazine*, xxxix, 415). Counsellor Vernon has not been identified; but cf. letters 67 at n. 2 and 71 at n. 4.

of her own to resort to upon occasion: All the occupants of apartments in that building are suddenly warned out[6]; which is the reason of her removal: and she is pressed for time; so that if your answer is not favourable to her in the first instance, she will be obliged to provide herself elsewhere. It is either a Brother of that Mr. Harcourt's or he himself that occupies occasionally an apartment in a House in Queen's Square kept by a person of the name of *Wells*[7] It is the second house on the right hand going from Queen's Square Place. Her connection with the Harcourt family has often brought her to that house: and the other Mr. Harcourt who occupies that apartment not being in Town, she was in case of necessity to have made use of it as a temporary repository for her furniture. It was there I suppose she heard of your *apartment*. A Miss *Elliot*, Sister to Admiral Elliot, who lives at Colchester, and whom together with his wife and this Sister I was in company once at Mr. Gray's,[8] this Miss Elliot, it seems, who lodges in the same house (Wills's) accompanied Mrs. Sarney to Mrs. Delap's; to make enquiries concerning the terms, and to bespeak her recommendation. Mrs. Sarney told Mrs. Delap that she once had a house in *Baker* Street which it seems is in the neighbourhood: and gave her to understand that she then lived in a stile much superior to that which she is induced to appear in at present. I suppose that was in the lifetime of her Husband. She told Mrs. Delap that she was well-acquainted in the neighbourhood; that she *knew* (not that she had any intercourse with) my Mother: but that she had used to visit Mrs. Buckle.[9] and when I saw her this afternoon, she told me she had been to visit Mrs. Buckle within this day or two upon the occasion. I have not been (indeed there has been no time for my going) to Mrs. Buckle's, to learn particulars of Mrs. S. from the first hand: very likely I may between this and the time of my receiving your answer: though I think there seems ground enough already to conclude she would be a desirable Tenant. When I waited upon her at Somerset House this afternoon she happen'd to be walking in the court with a lady who has apartments there,

---

[6] This was because old Somerset House was about to be demolished to make way for the present building, which was erected between 1776 and 1786.

[7] Richard Wills occupied 5 Queen's Square in the late 1770's (L.C.C. *Survey of London;* St Margaret's Westminster, i, 114).

[8] George Elliott (d. 1795) had held various naval commands in the 1740's and in 1762 retired with the rank and half-pay of a rear-admiral to his estate at Copford near Colchester (Charnock, *Biographia Navalis*, v, 298–299). His will shows that the sister here mentioned had, between 1775 and 1790, married and been widowed.

[9] Presumably the mother of the Miss Buckle who seems at one time to have been considered as a possible wife for Bentham (cf. letters 150 and 151).

whose name I had occasion to learn was Townsend. It is my
opinion that Mrs. Sarney would not give more than the £20 a year:
especially as that was the Sum mentioned to her (agreably to
your instructions) both by Mrs. Far and Mrs. Delap: at the same
time it seems as if she were desirous to have it by the pains she
took about it. She not only called upon Mrs. Delap in the manner I
mentioned, and upon Mrs. Far twice to see it, but called at my
chambers, and as I was not at home left a note mentioning herself
under the description of 'a person recommended by Mrs. Delap.'
That was going rather too far, as her acquaintance with Mrs.
Delap was no other than that I have mentioned: neither could
Mrs. Delap therefore recommend her from her own personal knowledge. Upon my mentioning to her the resolution you seemed to
have taken up not ⟨to⟩ let the apartment but from quarter to quarter, she seemed startled; and said that it would not be worth her
while to remove her goods for so short a time: and therefore should
not think it advisable to engage for less than a year in the first
instance, though after that time she should be satisfied with a
quarter's warning. She took notice that the apartment wanted
painting (as indeed it does very ⟨. . .⟩) and some other little repairs
of that sort; but that she did not seem to lay any *great* stress upon.
I told her when I expected you home; and I suppose she might be
induced to wait till then, for your determination on that article.
The paint is so dingy, that for the sake of the apartment itself, I
should think you would have no objection to give it that repair.
I have now given you as full a representation of the case as lies in
my power; and now submitt it to you Sir to form your judgement;
and to determine whether it is better to close with this lady, or to
take your chance for getting £5 a year more from another Tenant.
As to the probability of that, my opinion is not worth troubling you
with; but as to the lady herself, if you can put up with her terms,
she promises I think to be the most eligible tenant you will have
had yet upon that spot.

I write this at Mr. Clarke's chambers with whom I have been
drinking Tea; and who has left me in possession. His intention was
to have answer'd your letter this post: but finding that I was to
write, he postponed writing till the next. I saw Mrs. Far to day:
she was purely well. She hoped that you were now thinking of your
return; but I was silent on that subject, as you enjoined me. The
new buildings in Petty France now make a figure to the garden:
but I think can hardly be tiled in by Michaelmas day as you were
given to expect: however they seem not to want much of being

finished on the out side. If I am not very much mistaken, Mr. Browne when he told me that he had received the rent, added that he had paid it at the Banker's: if so, you can have no reason I should think, for wishing it in Pope's hands sooner than is necessary: I will enquire, and if I find it was not paid in, will communicate to Mr. B. your directions as soon as he comes to Town which will be on Wednesday: for he has been for some time past in the country—[10] I am glad to learn by Mrs. Far that you design to treat the young folks with a view of Paris before their return: I hope you will at least give them a week; and that as your situation is in every respect so happy, you will prolong their enjoyment of the advantage ⟨you⟩ have been at so much pains to give them, to the utmost verge (as you propose) of your convenience.

Fortune seems to smile upon you, my dear Father, that she may continue to do so these many, many years is one of the first wishes of your dutiful and affectionate Son. In return, I have but one favour to sue for to you in addition to what I am indebted to you for already, and that is Peace.

My sincere and affectionate respects wait upon my mother. Remember me also to my Brothers when you write. I have written to Sam. I hope you will enable me to give an answer to Mrs. S. by the return of the Post. My time and my paper are both spent, and I must conclude.

Septr. 22d 1775

142

To Samuel Bentham

25–26 September 1775 (Aet 27)

Je viens ce moment de recevoir un de tes lettres de la date du sixieme de ce mois. J'en suis redevable a notre bon ami Mr. Davies. Depuis votre depart, plusieurs lettres se sont passées entre lui et moi principalement sur le sujet de quelque bois de charpente qu'il a eu la bonté d'acheter pour le compte de Mr. Clark. Je lui ai prié il y a quelques jours, s'il avoit quelque chose de votre part /qu'on pût detacher/ qui pouvoit etre separé de tout ce qui pourroit

---

[10] Cf. letter 138, n. 9.

142. [1] B.M. I: 361–362. Autograph. Docketed: 'I.B. Septr. 26. 1775.'
Addressed: 'A Monsr. / Monsr. Bentham le fils / chez Monsr. / Monsr. Hardi / Rue St Jean / a Caën / France / Feuille simple / Single Sheet.' Postmark: '26 SE'. Stamped: 'D'ANGLETERRE'.

toucher ses affaires particulieres, qu'il voudroit bien me faire le plaisir de me le communiquer. En même tems je lui ai envoyée la premiere feuille de la lettre que je tiens de vous directement. Vous y aviez entamés l'affaire de mon ouvrage, mais cela ne m'empeche pas de la lui envoyer, vu la confiance que que [*sic*] savois pouvoir mettre en lui.

En verité, mon enfant, je suis tout-a-fait charmé a voir le progrés que vous avez fait. Je compare ma lettre avec la sienne, et c'est avec un veritable plaisir que je souscris a l'observation qu'il a faite, que vous avancez a grands pas. Que vous vous trouverez heureux de posseder bientôt une langue qui vous payera si bien de votre travail! Oui vous lirez avec lui, (et pourquoi non avec moi?) le divin Helvetius. Demandez si ce bienfaiteur de l'humanité est enterrè quelque part a Paris: si cela est, allez-y en pelerinage, et baisez son tombeau.[2]

Je sçais maintenant que j'ecris aussi pesamment que pourroit un Docteur en theologie; en voici la cause. Peu de tems aprés celle de Mr. Davies on m'a apporte une lettre de votre part. Je ne l'ai pas ouverte: je crains de l'ouvrir. Elle est courte comme une billet de *penny-post*. Je le tourne ça et là, avant que d'en rompre le cachet, je mets un doigt entre les plis, et j'y epis dedans: j'en use comme un chien avant que d'entamer son os. Parbleu! il y a si peu de cet os, il doit y avoir force moelle.—Enfin dont—craquons le, et suçons. En attendant, souffrez que je vous dise, que je vous ai donné, moi, de quoi charger un portefaix en y repondant.

Oh, mon frere! vous n'aviez dont pas encore reçu la mienne quand vous avez ecrit celle-ci. Que votre chagrin me touche! mais a l'heure que j'ecris ⟨. . .⟩ ⟨. . .⟩ ⟨. . .⟩ at an end this good while. ⟨. . .⟩ ⟨. . .⟩ de long temps.

Que je me console de cette pensée. Diable! c'est maintenant le 25. et la votre est daté le 16! Neuf jours entiers a passer ici de Cäen.

Eh bien donc! vous avez fait connoissance avec un Chanoine, Professeur, Physicien, pedant, et Moliniste. Fort bien. j'en suis charmé,—connoissance utile a bien des egards. Quel diable d'espece de scholastique est-ce qu'un Moliniste? savez vous? C'est un Anti-Janseniste: et les Jesuites sont anti-jansenistes: il doit être donc en quelque sorte ami du parti des Jesuites. Les Jansenistes, un espece de Schismatiques, sont par rapport au Molinistes (lesquels je crois s'accordent pour la plupart avec les orthodoxes, s'ils ne sont

---

[2] Claude Adrien Helvétius, whose *De L'esprit* was such an important influence on Bentham's own thought, had died in December 1771 at the age of 56.

pas les orthodoxes mêmes) a peu pres ce que sont nos Methodistes par rapport aux Orthodoxes de notre Eglise: sinon[?] ils penchent contre la liberté de l'homme dans ce dispute galimatia⟨s⟩-theologique de la predestination. Toutesfois les Jansenistes ont ils beaucoup plus de sçavoir que nos Methodistes—la philologie leur a du plus qu'a personne dans le siecle passé. Les grammairiens de Port-Royal etoient de ce secte. C'est parmi eux seuls (en exceptant les philosophes) que s'est entretenue cette foible ombre de liberté politique qui subsiste encore en France. C'est le Jansenisme qui a eu beaucoup de part en disposant les Parlemens a ⟨. . .⟩ chasser les Jesuites de la France. Lisez, si vous pouvez les attraper, le 6 ou 7 tome de l'Histoire general de Mr. Voltaire et l'essai sur la destruction des Jesuites par Mr. D'Alembert. Mais je doute si on puisse les trouver là ou vous êtes. Ce sont des livres suspects au moins s'ils ne sont pas defendus.

A ça—je vais vous donner de quoi vous entretenir avec votre Professeur. J'ai reçu un lettre de Mr. *Priestly*, quand il m'a rendu mes *Hints* dont je lui ai fait part, au sujet des Airs. La voici. je vous donnerai un copie de l'original avec une traduction a coté. Ce sera une exercise pour vous que de couvrir ma traduction, d'en faire une de vous-meme, et ensuite les comparer, la votre et la mienne. C'est a ce dessein que vous en avertis: ils se trouvent au commencement de la 2de. feuille. Voila ce qui vous donnera une espece de *relief* auprès de votre Chanoine que d'avoir un frere a qui un sçavant aussi celebre que Priestly ecrit de cette façon. Mandez moi s'il est possible de trouver moyen d'envoyer une livre a Cäen pendant que vous y êtes, parce que, cela etant, je pourrois vous envoyer sa nouvelle volume dont il me parle. Ce sera un bel exercise que de tâcher de la faire entendre a votre Chanoine. L'interêt qu'il doit avoir de posseder un ouvrage *vierge* dont il n'y a personne que vous qui puisse le faire jouir, lui fera prendre toute la peine du monde à vous aider à vous exprimer.

Oui—c'est Belidor[3] qui est l'auteur de ce livre que vous avez vu chez M. Villion. Mais je crois que le sien est ⟨en⟩ 4 vols. en 4to., au lieu de deux dont vous parlez. Les 4 ont paru a plusieurs reprises: je veux dire qu'ils n'ont pas été publiées tous a la fois.

Il y a un Pere Adam ex-Jesuite que Voltaire a entretenu chez lui depuis quelques années, en qualité de bouffon, et de joueur aux echecs. Voici la façon dont il avoit coutume de le presenter a ceux

---

[3] Bernard Forest de Bélidor (*c.* 1693–1761), a French engineer. His works include *Architecture hydraulique* (1737–51) and *Traité des Fortifications* (1735). It is the first of these which is in question here (cf. letter 143).

qui venoient le voir: 'Monsieur un tel, voici le Pere Adam, mais non pas le *premier des hommes.*'

Ah! que je serois charmé de me trouver a coté de vous et du bon Pere lors que vous faites vos experiences!

Mr. Davies dit qu'il vous a envoyés 4 lettres: et vous me paroissez n'en reconnoitre pas autant: Mon Dieu, est ce dont que quelqu'unes en sont manquées? Il se pourroit donc que la mienne aura eu le même sort. Voici encore une chose qui m'a donné a penser. Vous et lui avez ecrit tous les semaines; il vous a deja ecrit quatre fois: pendant qu'entre vous et moi il n'y a en eu encore que trois? c'est ma faute, ⟨. . .⟩ j'en conviens: Cependant tous les semaines une; cela lui doit être avec votre depart un object de 24 francs au moins. Et une seule des siennes vous a couté a peu près 6 schelings.

A propos de vos experiences. Il se propose, le bon Pere de faire revivre des lapins par le moyen de la secousse Electrique. S'ily y reussit, donnez-en moi un recit detaillé: peut-être que je m'aviserai de le communiquer a la societé qui s'est formée ici pour le ~~retablissement~~ de gens (apparemment) noyés /en apparence/.

De ce que vous voyez chez ce Professeur, entretenez vous avec Mr. Hardi: vous voila encore un sujet de conversation.

Mr. Davies vous a ecrit 4 lettres: mais dites-moi franchement, valent ils ces 4 lettres, en fait de quantité, celle-ci et cet autre que autre que vous avez de moi?

Tout, jusqu'ici, sans Dictionaire et sans Grammaire. Ne voila t'il pas que je suis bon François? Quand j'ai temps de reflechir un peu, je fais assez bien.

Voila donc cet apres-diner depuis 7 heures que je vous ai donné. Il est maintenant onze, ou peu s'en faut.

Bon soir.

Lundi 25 Sept. 1775.

Mardi 26. Sept.

Votre nouvelle touchant le retablissement de l'Edit de Nantes, me paroit trop bonne pour être vrai. D'ailleurs si cela etoit en veritè sur le tapis dans le cabinet, d'ou est ce qu'ils pourroient le savoir ces gens qui vous en parlent? A coup sûr l'Edit même l'Edit en sa teneur actuelle ne sera gueres retabli. Il ne convient pas a l'etat present des choses. Tout ce qui est dans le chapitre des possibilités c'est que quelques provisions en pourroient être retablies en substance, a cet effet, qu'on leur accordera l'exercice de leur religion, et peut-étre, (mais c'est un très foible *peut-être*) qu'on les mettra sur le même pied que les Catholiques quant a l'admissibilite aux charges. *Facile credimus, id quod volumus.* Il y a long temps qu'on a parlé par fois de ce même evénement.

N'en parlez pas a votre Chanoine, que faute d'autres sujets de conversation. Un entretien Theologique pourroit lui echauffer la bile, et faire ensorte qu'il vous regardera d'un oeil moins favorable; et qu'il se communiquera avec vous moins librement sur des sujets ou vous pourrez en tirer quelque instruction.

Ce papier n'est il pas charmant? Je me le procur⟨e⟩ exprès pour vous ecrire la-dessus. C'est du papier de la manufacture de *Baskerville*. Le pauvre homme vient de mourir; et je crains qu'il n'y en aura plus manufacturé.

Mais qu'il fourmille de fautes! je veux dire corrigèes a ne pas parler de ceux qui ne le sont pas. Cependant ç'ont ètè pour la plupart des fautes d'inattention plutôt que de pure ignorance et corrigèes sur le champ.

Il faut cultiver votre Chanoine—payez-le avec du respect, et des petits soins, attendu que vous n'avez pas autre chose a lui donner. Peut etre que vous pourrez lier correspondance avec lui, ce qui pourroit vous être avantageux a plus d'un egard. Tachez de vous informer par son moyen quels autres savants il y peut avoir la ou vous êtes. S'il fait ou s'il dit des sottises en fait de physique (ce qui est plus que probable attendu qu'il n'est pas philosophe, ne lui faites pas sentir que vous en appercevez; a moins que vous ne pourez lui corriger sauf son amour propre.

Vous avez mal a la tête; et vous vous plaignez de relachement. Pourquoi ne pourriez vous prendre du Quinquina (Bark) la ou vous êtes? On pourroit le prendre en forme de Bolus, a la quantitè d'environ un $\frac{1}{2}$ once par jour, a trois reprises: Après le lever, avant le diner, et avant le coucher. Les Bolus en seroient plus ou moins grande selon qu vous pouvez les avaler. Pour leur donner la forme de Bolus vous pouvez vous servir de solution de Gomme Arabique en y melant un peu de Syrope de Capillaire si vous voulez ou de quelque autre Syrope qui n'aye pas des qualitès medicinales particulieres. Après qu'ils sont formès pour les tenir separès et les empecher de se coller les uns aux autres, on les saupoudre de *farine* de *froment.* Tout cela vous pouvez faire de vous même—Le Quinquina ne doit pas être plus cher là. Il faut qu'il ait été reduite en poudre tres fine. De cette facon je ne le goute pas le moins de tout. S'il arrive qu'il vous purge, mais non autrement mêlez-y de la Tinctura Thebaïca ⟨en⟩ raison de 8 ou 10 gouttes par once de Quinquina ⟨. . .⟩ ⟨. . .⟩ ⟨. . .⟩ grossissez le dose de *Tinctura,* si celle-là n' ⟨. . .⟩ prevenir cet effet.

[*The letter from Dr. Priestley*] [4]

'Dear Sir
    'I return your paper of *hints* after perusing it with much
pleasure. I have no doubt but that if you were to go to work in
good earnest you would do something considerable. Some of your
queries you will find are solved in my printed volume, and others in
the volume that is in the press. But a few I have taken hints of,
and if I should pursue them, I shall with pleasure make a proper
acknowledgment. But when the ⟨volume⟩ which is in the press is
printed, I think to ⟨let⟩ myself rest for some time, and attend to
other things in which I find more satisfaction.
    'I shall be very glad to hear from you when you begin to do any
thing, and am with much respect

Dear Sir
Your very humble servant
J. Priestly'

'Calne 23 Aug. 1775'.
    N.B. It is a town in Wiltshire near Ld. Shelburne's. Ld. S. puts
in Members.
    [*Bentham's French translation stands alongside it, but is omitted
here.*]

Informez v⟨ous⟩ si votre Chanoine, en fait de Physique, est
Cartesien. Si'l est, a coup sûr ses idées sont en brouillard.
    If you find a difficulty to make out a word any where in my letter,
consider what letters are most apt to be confounded. These are i
with e; n with u; m with $n\,i$; a with u; and so forth.
    Sur les endroits qui ont la mine d'etre *communicables*, vous
pourrez consulter les gens parmi lesquels vous vous trouvez, tant
pour vous assurer des mots, que pour savoir si l'expression est juste.
    N'y a t'il point de voiture publique qui va periodiquement de
Caën an Roüen; et ensuite le meme ou bien quelque autre de la
à Dieppe? Par un tel moyen on pourroit vous remettre ce qui
falloit.
    Je suis persuadè que, quoique les regles de la Grammaire n'y
soient pas violés, il n'y a pas la moitiè de mes phrases dont la
tournure soit /tout-a-fait/ a la françoise.
    J'ai ecrit pour la seconde fois a mon Pere vendredi dernier.

---

[4] Priestley was apparently returning letter 124 (see also letter 129). Priestley's
original letter is in the possession of C. W. Everett.

Mardi 26th Septr. 1775 Linc. Inn.

I shall follow your example in cropping the paper to save postage.

Je suis ravi d'apprendre que vous verrez Paris; et que vous y ferez un si long sejour. J'aurai soin de vous y envoyer un lettre pour ce Mr. Godefroi[5] dont je vous ai parlé dans ma derniere. Elle vous sera addressée chez Mr. Pattle etc.

Martin[6] vous fait ses Complimens—Nous avons dinè ensemble aujourd'hui. Il m'a priè de vous ⟨. . .⟩ un nouveau projet de mechanique a vous communiquer. La poste me presse: je n'ai pas le temps de ⟨. . .⟩ ecrit. A letter is so long a coming, and I suppose ⟨you⟩ would not lose this post, to wait for an answer ⟨. . .⟩ I sent this.

143

To Samuel Bentham

1–3 October 1775 (Aet 27)

Dimanche 31 Septre. 1775[2] Linc. Inn

Vous avez priè Mr. Davies de se servir en vous ecrivant de la langue française; pour raison, vous lui avez dit que l'interêt que vous prendriez aux idees qui feroient le corps de ses lettres, pourroit bien s'etendre en quelque sorte au language, qui en fait l'habillement: qu'ainsi, a la faveur de cet intèrêt, l'un et l'autre pourroient bien se fixer dans votre memoire. *Me* croyant aussi compris dans *la raison* de la loi que vous avez donnèe *lui* (ah! que la langue française est inferieure en fait d(e l) *'energie* a l'anglaise! Thinking *myself* (comprized) within the *reason* of the law you gave to *him*) je me suis servi dans ma derniere de la même langue: c'est aussi pourquoi je continue de m'en servir. J'ai fait passè a ce bon ami la dernière qu j'ai recu de vous: Vendredi quand il me l'a renvoyèe, il m'a mandè que—il m'a mandè enfin une nouvelle que je vous

---

[5] There is no such reference in letter 140. Bentham had met M. Godefroi on his visit to Paris in 1770. According to Bowring (x, 66) Godefroi 'gave him several books, because he had heard that he was a "philosopher," a title which greeted him then for the first time'. Cf. letter 144a.   [6] See letter 90, n. 2.

143. [1] B.M. I: 363–364. Autograph.

Addressed: 'A Monsr. / Monsr. Bentham le fils / chez Monsr. / Monsr. Hardi / Rue St. Jean / a Cäen / France / Single Sheet / Feuille Simple.' Address scored out with comment: 'A present chez Mr. Pattle Gentilhomme Anglois Place Royale au coin des Minimes / a Paris.' Postmark: '3 OC'. Stamped: 'D'ANGLETERRE'.

[2] Sunday 1 October 1775 was presumably the date Bentham meant by 'Dimanche 31 Septre'. Subsequent dates in the letter are consistently erroneous.

traduirai mot pour mot—'Notre ingenieux ami le Docteur (je veux dire Simmons) a rencontrè depuis peu une methode prompte de procurer *l'Air nitreux*, a titre de quoi, il ne s'en glorifie pas peu. Peut-être, qu'il en pourroit remplir un Tonneau (a Hogshead) en cinq minutes. L'Air se procure par la deflagration du nitre, a l'aide du Charbon, *sous* l'eau.'

Voici ce que je lui a repondu—

Ce que vous m'avez mandé touchant la decouverte fait par Mr. le Doctr. me plait beaucoup. Si peut la constater, l'idèe m'en paroit en veritè heureuse. Ce n'est pas sans cause qu'il en est fier . . . . Ce qui me paroit un peu difficile, c'est de persuader a l'Air Nitreux, d'abord qu'il est mis au jour, d'attendre avec patience la disposition que pourroit avoir l'eau de lui faire place. Je suppose qu'il n'est fait deflagrer que de petites /masses/ portions a la fois. Car s'il entreprendroit de lâcher contre un tonneau d'eau autant d'air nitreux qu'il falloit pour remplir le Tonneau, je suis garant, qu'il n'y auroit pas petit tapage entre ces deux elements. Que le Nitre (melè avec du charbon) puisse au moyen d'un verre a bruler se deflagre dans un recipient ⟨au dessus⟩ sur l'eau, c'est ce qui est aise a concevoir: mais, comment cela peut se faire /au dessous/ *sous* l'eau, c'est vraiment plus que je peux deviner a present. A toute force, il ne se peut pas, que l'eau et le nitre se touchent: quand on y met feu. C'est pourquoi, il faut qu'il y ait de *l'Air commun* entre deux; cela etant, Air nitreux, en raison de la quantitè de l'air commun qu'il y a par rapport a celle de ce dernier, doit etre impur. Il n'est gueres besoin, je crois, de lui faire remarquer, qu'avec l'air nitreux qui vient de l'acide nitreux qu'il y a dans le nitre, joint ⟨. . .⟩ phlogistique du charbon, il y aura aussi apparement de l'air fixable provenant de ce dernier; peut être aussi une certaine quantitè *d'air commun* qui pourroit bien avoir etre combinè avec les autres éléments dans le charbon comme nous avons trouvez qu'il est avec le chaux de plomb dans le *minium*. Pour l'air fixable on peut l'en debarasser en l'agitant / le mixte/ dans de l'eau: cela fait il fera bien de constater la puritè de ce qui reste en le comparant avec l'air Nitreux qu'on aura obtenu par les moyens ordinaires. . . .

Lundi 1. Oct. 1775. Linc. Inn.

Ta lettre du 26. dernier (ou environ comme vous dites—vous— mais je vous dis, moi, qui connoit mieux que vous, que c'etoit le 25.) me parvient ce moment. Je ne sçaurai vous exprimer a quel point j'ai été mortifié d'abord de cette nouvelle, que vous avez supportè avec tant de sangfroid a ce que vous me dites. Mais heureusement la même poste qui m'a portè avertissement de votre (warrant of execution) me l'a portè aussi de votre (reprieve). C'est ce dont m'a informè notre cher Pere, dans une lettre, laquelle à d'autre egards, est une aussi maudite lettre qu'on pourroit desirer. Envoye-moi. je te prie, mon enfant, quelques grains de ton *impassibilitè* pour en avaler une dose suffisante, toutes les fois que j'aurois une lettre a ouvrir de ce quartier là. /(Ce n'est pas qu'il y ait des menaces, ou choses comme ça, mais ⟨. . .⟩ *galimatias*./ J'aurais donc le bonheur de vous voir tous le 4me. ou 5me. du mois suivant; au lieu du 9 ou 10, comme on avoit fait croire. Ah! que je voudrois, que ce ne fut que le meme jour de Decre.! 'Le meilleur souhait que je puisse former a votre egard' dit Louis 14 a notre Jacques 2d a qui il donnoit du secours pour le ramener en Irlande lors de la revolution) 'c'est que nous ne nous reverrons jamais.' Voila le compliment que fit un Roi a son *frere Roi* qu'il aimait comme dût un Roi en aimer un autre: moi qui vous aime (quoique nous ne sommes que freres et non pas Rois) d'un façon que vous ne sçaverez douter, je vous dis, que le meilleur souhait que je pourrois former a votre egard, c'est non pas que je ne vous reverrai jamais (Dieu me defend d'un tel misere) mais cependant que je ne vous reverrai que le plus tard qu'il sera possible. Là—bon soir—je ne peux pas davantage—Ah! que vous êtes un Coquin, avec votre Archange, de m'envoyer un *echantillon* de lettre comme celle-ci!

Mardi au matin 2. 8re.

Pour les commissions, je les revoque toutes, si ce n'est quelque petit bijou a très peu de prix de la [. . . . ?] que je vous ai indiquè dans ma derniere.

Les Loix que nous t'avons donnè sur ce qu'il faut faire pour ce qui regarde notre auguste personne, restent de la même teneur qu'auparavant. N'omettez pas de vous pourvoir d'une epée. La mienne qui auroit coutè dix guineas ici ne m'a coutè que 5½ louis. C'est comme vous savez d'acier incrustè en or. Voila ce qui sera un peu trop fort pour vous. Toutesfois vous pourrez en avoir une pour 1½ Louis d'acier dorée, qui fera aussi bonne apparence que la mienne, mais qui ne seroit pas si durable. Mais cela n'importe gueres, attendu que vous aurez si peu d'occasions de vous en habiller. Si je la trouve, l'adresse de mon coutelier, je vous la donnerai. Pour le foureau qu'il soit non pas de cuir, mais d'une apparence *ecailleuse* ⟨scaly⟩ comme la mienne. On a des foureaux de cette sorte a Paris pour moins de la moitiè de la prix qu'il en faut donner ici.

C'est de même q⟨u⟩ant à the Belt or Hasp or whatever appurtenances you use with it. Conseillez mon Pere de se pourvoir aussi d'un
foureau de cette espece pour les galas.

Vous me reprochez de ne vous avoir donnè point de conseils sur le
sujet de votre mèthode apprendre le François: et c'est un reproche
dont je ne me suis pas lavè dans ma seconde. Pour les conseils, il
faut vous faire ressouvenir, que vous ne m'en avez point demandez;
vous m'avez exposè ce que vous aviez fait, et je n'y ai rien trouvè
a redire. Pour les regles, ne s'etre fiè a ceux qu'on aura trouvees, et
s'en avoir faites de nouvelles, c'est ce que j'attendois de votre
esprit d'independance, ou si vous voulez, de votre independance
d'esprit, de votre penetration, et de votre sçavoir faire. Vous savez
bien, qu'un homme quelconque, est tout-a-fait aussi bien en droit
de faire des regles de grammaire (ou même de quelque autre
science que ce soit, dans laquelle il aura porté son attention)
qu'aucun autre. Que ces regles ne sont que l'enonciation qu'on
fait de quelques rapports de convenance ou de disconvenance qu'on
aura observè entre les objets de la science dont il s'agit. Et pour
qu'on y aura observè quelque part de tels rapports on n'a que se le
dire. Tout ce a quoi il faut prendre garde, c'est de se tenir pret
(surtout dans le commencement d'un etude lors que la masse des
observations particulieres qu'on aura faites n'est encore que
petite) a corriger celles qui ont precèdè par celles qui leur succedent.
Moi, je possede tout cela (au degre auquel je le possede) méchan-
iquement comme je fais par rapport a ma propre langue: pour les
regles touchant les inflections et la syntaxe, je ne m'en souviens pas
de tout, ni ne m'en suis fait: c'est a dire en forme: je consulte
comme on dit mon oreille: c'est a dire me memoire, pour savoir
si l'expression dont il s'agit soit d'usage ou non. Ainsi je ne puis pas
vous en donner. Mais tout ce qui concerne la Grammaire, qui est
quasi la partie morte de la langue, vous importe peu par rapport a
celle qu'on en peut nommer la vivante: je veux dire la prononci-
ation, et ces tours de phrase dont on ne trouve des exemples que
dans la conversation familiere, et point de tout dans les livres.
C'est pourquoi, parlez; n'importe bien ou mal: parlez toujours.
Remarquez ce qu'on se dit sur telle ou telle occasion de la vie
familiere; ce qu'on se dit, quand on demande, qu'on repond, quand
on prie, quand on refuse, quand on loue, quand on blame, quand on
se rencontre, quand on se separe, quand on donne, quand on recoit
etc. caeterorum. Quand quelqu'un parle a quelqu'un, ou bien a quelque *une* par exemple a une Arcange, demandez vous s'il est probable
que vous serez dans le cas de vouloir parler a même effet; si cela est

(et il est difficile que cela ne soit pas) prononcez a vous meme les phrases Anglaises qui y repondent, et fourrez les deux ensemble (je veux dire portion de discours Anglais et portion de disc. Français) dans le même petit sac de votre memoire. Aussi *è converso*, si vous voudriez parler a tel ou tel effet, et ne savez pas comment dans l'instant, mettez en la phrase Anglaise dans un sac toutes seules; cela fait, *guettez* toutes les phrases Françoises que vous entendez prononcer, et lorsque vous en epiez une qui convienne le moins de tout a la pauvre solitaire, ouvrez le sac, et mettez les ensemble. Voila comme il faut aller a la chasse des paroles. Vous vous plaignez de manquer de conversation—Diable, comment est ce que cela peut être. Est qu'on va nud dans ce pays-là? qu'on ne mange rien? qu'on n'a point de meubles dans ses apartemens? point de livres dans son cabinet? point de maisons dans ses rues? point de vegetaux dans ses campagnes? que les femmes n'ont point de vanitè ni de babillardise? qu'on n'a point de voisins? qu'il n'y a point de distinction de rang ni d'etat? qu'il n'y a point de Religion? que ce qu'on achete ne soit ni bon ni mauvais; ni beau ni *ugly*: ni cher ni a bon marchè? qu'il n'y a point d'amusement ou d'occupations serieuses? Vous me direz, que faire des questions sur quelques uns de ces sujets-là, ce sera impertinence—Rassurez-vous, mon enfant: il n'y a point d'impertinence en France. En Angleterre même ou on est si serrè est si soupçonneux, il n'y a point d'impertinence dans un etranger. Vous me direz que ce sont des bagatelles, sur quoi vous n'avez aucun motif de vous informer: . . passe pour cela, mais la langue, elle n'est pas bagatelle. Si on vous repondroit en Anglois, d'accord.

Pour *Belidor*[3] je ne puis pas vous mander encore rien de positif: Mr. Villion est a la campagne je ne sais pas depuis quand: je tache de faire ce que vous souhaitez la-dessus avant que vous devez quitter Paris.

Je ne pouvois pas m'imaginer, lors de votre premiere lettre, ce que c'etoit que vous voudriez avec the *Steam-Engine* la ou vous êtes: je vous ai cru bien bizarre: j'ai cru que vous me faisiez cette demande par voye de '*prolepsis*' (ou '*anticipation*' comme on dit dans le *White Bull*.) en attendant que vous retournâtes en ce pays-ci pour mettre a profit mon repose. A ce moment le mystere s'eclaircit: c'etait apparement pour le pere Adam: mais, soit-ce le *pourquoi*, ou non, peste, pourquoi ne me l'as tu pas dit? Je ne

---

[3] Cf. letter 142, n. 3.

scais pas si je pourrai être en état de vous satisfaire la-dessus ou non.
[*Four lines torn away.*][4]
pas alors tout-a fait.

Au Soir

J'ai été cet avant diner chez Payne: et voici le resultat de mes enquêtes. J'y ai vu le livre de Belidor. Il s'intitule Architecture Hydraulique. Il est en 4 tomes in 4to. gros, *gras* in 4to. des dates respectifs de 1737, 1739, 1750, 1753. Les Tomes ne sont pas numerotés 1, 2, 3, 4; mais il y a soi-disants deux parties, de deux tomes chacun. Le prix de cette copie que j'ai vue laquelle etait *neuve*, est de 4½ Guis. J'y ai vu aussi in 4to. les livres suivants aux prix suivants, (c'est a dire mentionnès sur le Catalogue, car pour les livres mêmes, ils été vendus) 1. Bouger Traité de la Marine 1753 9s.[5] D'Alembert Traité de Dynamique (à δυναμις potentia Mechanical powers) 1743. 2s. 6. | Machines and inventions approuvées par l'Academie des Sciences 6 tom. tres bien reliées 5 Guis.[6] Souvenez vous qu'il y a encore Du Hamel sur la construction des vaisseaux (ou quelque titre pareil)[7] et je ne sçai pas si ce livre la est le seul qui est de Bouger sur la suject. J'ai vu quelque part dans un Catalogue Bouguer Traité de la Navire.[8] Il y a aussi un livre Espagnol intitule 'Examen theorico-pratico—' and so forth upon the building of ships. J'ose gager que dès a-present on l'a traduit en francois. Il est tout herissè de Mathematique. L'auteur en est Don Antonio de Ulloa[9] Je pourrois bien vous donner d'autres renseignements touchant les prix des livres avant que vous devez quitter Paris. A present voila tout ce que ⟨j'en⟩ ai a vous dire. Remarquez que les livres François sont ordinairement a bon marché chez Payne: a meilleur de beaucoup qu'ils ne sont chez ⟨Elms⟩ly ou tout autre libraire *neufs*.

[4] These phrases remain: 'assez lent...' 'et le Dr.,' 'les esp', '...pliquer, quoique pour vrai'.

[5] Pierre Bouguer (1698–1758), *Nouveau traité de navigation* (1753).

[6] These volumes cover the period from 1734 to 1747; a seventh volume appeared in 1777.

[7] Henri Louis Duhamel du Monceau (1700–82), *Eléments de l'Architecture Navale ..* 2nd edn., Paris, 1758. An abridged translation, *The elements of naval Architecture ..* appeared as part II of Mungo Murray's *Treatise on Ship-Building and Navigation* in 1754.

[8] Pierre Bouguer (cf. n. 5), *Traité du Navire, de sa construction, et de ses mouvements* (1764).

[9] Bentham's memory had played him false here: Antonio de Ulloa (1716–95) was not the author of the book in question, which was by Jorge Juan (cf. references in later letters), with whom, however, Ulloa had collaborated in certain other publications (cf. letter 248).

J'aurai peut être a vous presenter lors de ⟨votre⟩ arivée un *Professeur de Mathematique* au College de *Williamsburgh* en *Virginie.* Il s'app⟨elle⟩ Maddison.[10] Il m'est venu chercher ce matin, avec une lettre de recommendation de la part de *Gwatkin.* Ce dernier est actuellement en Angleterre mais je ne l'ai pas encore vu. Il est malade a ce que me dit Maddison, chez son Oncle en Herefordshire. Il s'est retournè dans ce pays-ci avec Miladi Dunmore (Ex!-) Gouvernante de la Colonie, dont /je veux dire de la Comtesse,/ il a quelques enfants sous sa tutelle.[11] Maddison a en juger par le peu j'en ai vu

⟨. . .⟩⟨. . .⟩⟨. . .⟩ homme doux and debonn⟨aire⟩
⟨. . .⟩⟨. . .⟩⟨. . .⟩⟨. . .⟩ des ta⟨ches⟩
[*About two lines torn away*]

faire un cours de Chymie avec le Dr. Fordyce, a qui je dois le presenter. Ce n'est pas le premier Professeur de ce même College que j'ai eu chez moi depuis votre depart, et qui m'a été adressé par le meme quartier. Il y a eu, un nommè Henley, Professeur de Philosophie Morale, que j'ai connu un peu avant son depart par le moyen de Gwatkin:[12] mais Maddison me paroit valoir bien le Professeur de Phil. Morale. Maddison est originaire de l'Amerique: il a été élevé de Gwatkin: c'est le premier homme que j'ai vu de ce pays là qui ne m'a pas paru avoir quelque chose de rebutant: quelque chose de unsocial et designing. Il a été en Ecosse; ou il a fait connoissance avec le fameux Chymiste le Doctr. Black[13]: dont il se loue beaucoup. Il a lu Priestly sur les Airs.

Encore un fois ne voilà t'il pas que je suis bon garçon. En verité, mon cher frere, ami de mon coeur, vous ne scaurez vous imaginer a quel point j'ai été touchez de vos reproches. C'est pourquoi je voudrois faire tout ce qui dependoit de moi de vous faire reparation. Toutes fois il y a eu des causes de mon silence que vous ne scaurez que lors de votre retour. D'ailleurs, votre premier il faut l'avouer, a été assez tardif; et dans votre second vous avez parlé de vous inquietudes d'une air de légerité, qui m'avoit fait croire qu'elles

---

[10] James Madison (1749–1812), later president of William and Mary College and first Bishop of Virginia in the Episcopalian Church.

[11] Cf. letter 138, nn. 26 and 27.

[12] Samuel Henley (1740–1815); Queens' College, Cambridge, 1770. After his return to England he became a master at Harrow and held various benefices. In 1784 he published an English translation of William Beckford's *Vathek.* From 1805 till his death he was the first principal of the East India College at Hertford.

[13] Joseph Black (1728–99), Scottish chemist, author of *Experiments upon magnesia, quicklime and some other alkaline substances.* He was the discoverer of 'fixed air' (carbonic acid). In 1756 he succeeded his teacher William Cullen as lecturer in Glasgow, where he also became Professor of Medicine.

n'avoient pas été bien fortes, ou bien qu'elles s'etoient calmer. Un autre fois s'il y a quelque chose qui touche votre repos tres particulierement, je veux dire *très-particulierement,* en avertissez moi par quelque signe, dont nous nous conviendrons; par exemple la figure d'un Coeur; de cette, façon-ci ♡. A vue d'un tel signe, je mettrai apart toutes autres affaires, et ferai ce que vous me voulez.

Ah! que je voudrois bien que vous puissiez lors de votre retour scavoir mieux le Francois que Charles qui a eu auparavant, et toujours ce fois ci, un Maitre! Que cela ⟨. . .⟩ ⟨. . .⟩[14]

Ne souffrez pas que mon Pere scache que vous m'avez une lettre (celle-ci) de la meme date que celle que je vais au lui ecrire.

Je ne le promets pas: mais il se *peut* faire que vous ecrive encore un fois a Cäen: par exemple si la reponse de Mr. Davies contienne quelque chose d'interessant sur la sujet de la decouverte de Simmons. Si vous n'avez rien de tres particulier de me dire, vous pourrez ne pas repondre/je veux dire envoyer un reponse[?]/qu'après que vous êtes arrivè a Paris. Mais alors rendez-moi mot pour mot, petit gueux! ou bien je ne sçai pas ce que je te ferai. Mettez tout sur le papier: donnez moi surtout un journal de votre voyage. Que votre stile (mais c'est Anglois dont je parle à present) que votre stile se perfectionne! Vous finirez même par devenir eloquent. Je n'ai pas le temps de relire tout ce galimatias: aussi vous y trouverez mille fautes. Encore une fois Adieu. Faites mes amitiés a Far et Charles. D'ou est que je hear nothing from them, nor so much as of them, at least for any thing that you have in charge from them.

144

To Samuel Bentham

5–6 October 1775 (Aet 27)

Dans ma derniere je vous **ai** recommandè de faire attention aux formules dont on se sert pour exprimer les diverses *volontès* ou sentiments qu'on peut avoir á exprimer touchant les diverses occasions de la vie commune /familiere/ /ordinaire/. Par exemple quand on a occasion de prier quelqu'un de faire de telle ou telle

[14] Several lines torn away. A few words can be read, including one which looks like 'Paris'. What follows is written between the previous lines in red ink.

144. [1] B.M. I: 365–366. Autograph. Docketed: 'I.B. Octr. 1775.'
Addressed: 'A Monsr. / Monsr. Bentham le fils / chez Monsr. / Monsr. Hardi / Rue St. Jean / Caën / France.' Forwarded: 'De present chez Mr. Pattle Gentilhomme Anglois / Place Royale au Coin des Minimes / Paris.' Postmark: '6 OC'. Stamped: 'D'ANGLETERRE'.

sorte. Les formules dont on se sert a /en/ telle occasion sont diff-erentes selon la degrè plus ou moins haute de superioritè ou d'infer-iorité qu'on se suppose, ou bien qu'on veut parôitre se supposer par rapport a celui a qui on parle. En voilà un petit *échelle*, un *climax*, ou plutot un anti-climax.

1. Fais, (ou fais-tu) cela.
2. Faites, ou faites-vous cela.
3. Veux-tu faire cela?
4. Voulez-vous faire cela?
       I drop the singular.
5. Voulez-vous bien faire cela?
      Ayez la bontè de faire cela?
      Voulez-vous avoir la bontè etc.
      Voulez-vous bien avoir la bontè etc.
      Faites-moi le plaisir etc.
      Voulez-vous etc. me faire etc.
      Qu'il vous plaise de vouloir bien etc.
      Qu'il plaise a votre Excellence de vouloir bien etc.

Plus il y a des paroles, plus il y a de gêne; plus des marques de la contrainte qu'on epreuve en exprimant sa volontè: volontè qui doit mettre celui qui doit agir en consequence a une certaine degrè de *peine*: contrainte qu'inspire la crainte ou on est sa superioritè: c'est a dire de son pouvoir de *nuire* ou de profiter: c'est a dire encore de causer de la douleur ou de ne pas causer du plaisir.

J'ai dit (voyez ci-devant) 'la degrè de superioritè ou d'infer-iorité . . car s'il n'y a ni l'une ni l'autre, s'il y a ègalite entre les deux personnes, il y a *equilibrium* entre les deux volontès: l'une ne peut pas faire ensorte que l'autre se meuve[?]: l'un n'a point de determinatif a presenter a la volontè de l'autre. L'action de la 2de. personne laquelle est l'objet de la 1re. (c'est a dire du requéreur) ne se fera pas. Il faut bien en tout cas qu'il y ait superioritè et cela de la part du requereur.

Comment donc, dites vous, *en tout cas*? A quoi bon donc toute cette echelle? . . . Je m'explique.

Je ne dis pas (qu'il doive etre superioritè) *constante* et *ordinaire*: mais au moins actuelle et momentanée, dans l'occasion dont il s'agit. 'Et encore, comment est-ce que peut être?' Qu'un *gueux* par exemple, soit superieur /ou se croye superieur,/ même pour le moment, au *Roi* dont il demande l'aumône? Je vous dirai. Cette superioritè qu'il n'a pas par ses propres forces, il emprunte ou espere l'emprunter si non de la *Sanction* (si non politique, au moins de la) *morale*. Vous savez qu'est ce que la *Sanction* morale; je vous en ai souvent parlè. Il y en a trois par rapport aux trois sources vraies ou supposées du plaisir et de la douleur. La Religieuse en est la trois-ieme. Or ce que dit le gueux au roi qu'est ce que c'est? C'est . . 'Donne-moi ce sou que je vous demande, ou bien vous ne serez pas humain (entendu toutefois que je te l'aurois demandè d'une façon aussi humble et aussi propre a marquer mon inferioritè *ordinaire* que cela se pourra faire, et c'est pourquoi c'est de cette façon que je te l'ai demandè) Cela etant, les autres hommes des quels tu depends en quelque sorte (tout Roi que tu és) pour les plaisirs et les secours contre la douleur que vous en attendez; ces autres hommes vous puniront de votre defaut ⟨. . .⟩ humanitè, par une certaine portion de leur haine[?] ⟨et⟩ de leur mauvaise volontè qui en depend, et en consequence (quelque moment quand l'occasion arrive) par le refus de quelque plaisir ou de quelque secours contre la douleur qui pourroit être a leur grè de fournir ou de ne pas fournir.

Ah ha!—ha! me voila dont ici, cher Sam. Sorti du quartier de la Grammaire ou je me promenois pour le cueillir quelques fleurs, me voila donc assis dans le sentier èpineux de la metaphisico-morale, ou mon penchant et le grand oeuvre qui en est l'objet m'entrain toujours. Est ce que tu m'as entendu? dis-moi.

Pour retourner a la Grammaire d'ou je suis parti ou plutôt l'art de la politesse, la science des petites moeurs—I was going to tell you, how commodious a phrase, I had lately found 'kind enough' to be. It is a sort of new acquisition to me. Be so kind as: Be so good as is tedious and hissing—but I have not time to say any thing more on this subject—therefore *be kind enough* to excuse me.

An Account of an easy and expeditious Method of obtaining Nitrous Air[2]

Take Saltpetre One Pound, Charcoal three ounces reduce them by grinding them together in a Mortar into a very fine Powder. Let

[2] This is in Dr Simmons's writing, and it is his method which is described. As Bentham mentions rather scornfully below, Simmons sent an account of his discovery to the *St James's Chronicle or British Evening-Post* where it appeared in the issue for 3–5 October 1775 (No. 2184). It opens, 'Sir, If the St. James's Chronicle is a proper Channel for the Communication of the following easy and expeditious Method of obtaining a new-discovered Air, I apprehend you will by inserting it, oblige many of your ingenious Readers. I am, Sir, your's etc. J S——s. Chatham. Sept. 29, 1775.'

The bulk of what follows is as given above, but he explains that his interest in obtaining Nitrous Air in large quantities arises from his 'daily experiencing the great antiseptick Power of that Air on animal substances'. He has 'put some Animal Substances into this Air, which I intend for Food some Months hence'.

this composition be gently rammed into Tubes made of white Paper the diameter of whose Bores should be near 4 Tenths of an Inch and their lengths between 3 and 4 Inches which will be found to be the most convenient size. Perhaps it would be worth while to try Touchwood instead of Charcoal. [*Insertion in Bentham's hand:* 'perhaps a less quantity would serve'.]

The Composition in the Tubes being set on fire and then put into water, and held under the Jar, the Deflagration of the Nitre will continue and the Jar will be presently filled with Air.

When the Air is first separated some smoke will be among it, but that will soon subside, and then by transferring the Air, it will be perfectly clean.

The above Quantity of the Composition will produce about 20 Gallons of Air.

By this method I can obtain nearly as much Air in a few Minutes as could be done by the usual means in as many days, and from a variety of Experiments it appears to be the true Nitrous Air.

I find it most convenient to hold a Receiver with one hand in a pool of water, and put the Tube under it with the other.

[*Bentham gives his own translation of the above into French along-side. Here it is omitted.*]

Vous voyez bien que quelle que soit la composition du physicien, la composition de l'ecrivain est a peu pres la meme que jamais; mais n'importe: tenons nous-en a ce qu'il y en a de bon.

Et pour vrai dire, ne vous voila t'il pas une jolie decouverte? Ma foi, on peut donc maintenant faire de l'air nitreux a très bon marche.

Remarquez par parenthese, par rapport a ma traduction; que 1mo. Le memoire ne peut gueres se traduire litteralement c'est a dire en conservant a chaque phrase sa forme. 2do. Que j'ai tachè de la traduire aussi litteralement que cela pourroit se faire: c'est pourquoi 3o. Je ne l'ai traduit ni aussi literalement qu'elle pourroit l'être ni aussi bien, a en negliger pour ainsi dire la *literalitè*.

Vous ressouvenez vous de votre idée de servir de l'Air Nitreux en qualitè d'anti-putrescent, en saturant par son moyen l'air commun de phlogistique? Voila une belle occasion de la verifier avec le Pere Adam.[3] Prenez quelques fruits, (et comme le temps vous

---

[3] The canon Samuel had met in Cäen (see letter 142).

presse qu'ils soient des plus *tendres*, des plus prompts a *s'alterer*) et operez.

A—ça—Ne pourriez vous pas par le moyen de ce saint pere vous procurer des lettres de recommendation a quelques savants ou soi-disants tels a Paris? C'est a dire s'il en a de connoissance. Le moyen de lui en donner l'occasion, sans se compromettre, c'est de lui demander, if he has any commands for Paris? et pour presenter la chose d'une facon plus particuliere a son esprit (c'est villaine-ment exprimè) you may bid him think whether he has any thing to send in the philosophical way or any other dont vous pourrez vous charger.

C'etoit ~~Mardi~~ (non pas—) Mercredi (c'est a dire hier,) que Mr. Davies m'a envoyè ce memoire /je veux dire que j'en ai reçu./ ecrit de la main du Docteur.[4] Peu après vient un Porte-faix du Blossoms Inn avec un petit paquet de ces tuyaux que le dit Docteur avoit bien voulu prendre la peine de m'envoyer. Cet après diner j'attends Mr. le Professeur Maddison. Je lui proposerai de faire experience du contenu du paquet.

Cependant pourquoi est-ce que vous penchez si fort contre le pauvre Docteur? Si sa vanitè philosophique n'a pas tout le titre qu'on pourroit espérer, et qu'elle se montre un peu trop a de-couvert, qu'est ce que cela vous fait? Mais, lui voila a present un titre. Cette vanitè n'est elle pas un des motifs les plus nobles et les moins interessèes que puisse avoir un homme pour lui faire agir. Cherissons toujours une disposition si necessaire au progrès des sciences et ne soyons pas trop difficiles sur les façons un peu bizarres dont elle peut se manifester. Si a l'amour de la considera-tion qui fait qu'on se livre aux travaux /utiles/ de l'esprit se joint la delicatesse de l'esprit qui fait qu'on est difficile sur la façon dont on la mette en oeuvre, tant mieux pour la personne même: mais qu'il se livre a ces travaux, /tellement quellement/ tant mieux toujours pour le public.

Avez vous peur que de la ridicule que ses manieres lui attire, quelque portion ⟨n⟩e tombe sur vous qui êtes de ses amis? Cet inconvenient est aisè a eviter. Donnez lui dans vos discours tout le mérite qui lui appartient, et même prenez soin de la presenter sur l'aspect le plus favorable, mais faites sentir doucement que vous vous appercevez de ses ridicules tout aussi bien que les autres. /C'etoit en badinant que j'ai dit la plupart de ce que j'ai dit touch-ant le Dr. dans ce que vous avez dit, pour moi je crois que vous avez raison j'y consens./

[4] Dr Simmons (see n. 2 above).

Vendredi 6. 8re.

Ah! Monsr. le Doctr! Il y a bien quelque chose a rabattre sur le compte de votre dècouverte—Je l'ai essayé deux fois: hier au soir avec Mr. le Profr. Maddison a la lueur de chandelle; aujourd'hui au matin en plein jour avec Mr. le Doctr. Fordyce. Voici ce qui en est. La composition brûle sous l'eau a merveille. Un de ces tuyaux a donnè un peu plus d'une pinte (quart English measure) d'air. /Cet air/ On l'a decantè pour le debarrasser de la fumèe. Outre la decantation on l'a secouè dans le second recipient pour le debarasser de ce qu'il pourroit y avoir d'Air fixable. On y a fait entrer par degrés plusieurs bulles d'air commun. /La-dessus/ Il y ⟨a⟩ eu rougeur, et diminution, en veritè *incontestable*, mais *très-foible*. L'odeur d'acide nitreux s'y est trouvè assez forte. Voici ce qui est mon idèe la-dessus.

Vous savez d'après le rapport du Doctr. Priestly, qu'après que tout l'air respirable ⟨qui⟩ se trouve combinè avec le /du/ *minium*, en ait ete chassè par le moyen du feu, le /ce/ minium etant mouillèe d'eau forte /et distillè de nouveau/ donne du nouvel air de la même sorte qu'auparavant. Il se peut etre donc que le produit entier de la deflagration soit composè des principes suivants—savoir

1mo. Une certaine quantitè /assez petite/ *d'air fixable*, provenant du charbon. C'est ce qu'on negligera, attendu qu'il n'y a point de doute la-dessus.

2mo. Une certaine quantité d'air respirable, de l'espece *très-respirable*, qu'on a obtenu, comme vous vous ressouvenez du minium (4 fois ou davantage plus pur que l'air commun de l'atmosphere).

Cependant quand on y ajoute de l'air commun il y a encore rougeur etc. c'est a dire decomposition d'air nitreux, quoique foible.

Donc je conclus, que la proportion qu'il y a d'air nitreux a l'air respirable, est un peu plus qu'il ne faut du premier pour saturer la quantitè du dernier qui est produit au même instant et qui est au plus haut degrè de puritè qu'il puisse etre.

D'après ces principes en ajoutant ce qu'il faut d'air de l'atmosphere ou bien de l'espèce tres respirable, vous pouvez calculer exactement le rapport des quantitès respectifs qu'il y a de ces deux elemens dans une portion donnèe du produit total de la deflagration. Voyez dans le Dict. du Chymie l'a⟨rticle⟩ '*Clyssus de Nitre*'. C'est le nom qu'on y don⟨ne⟩ ⟨au⟩ produit d'une deflagration du nitre fait sous l'eau. Savez-vous ce qu'a fait ce pauvre sot Simmons? la même memoire qu'il m'a envoyèe au lieu de la garder pour la communiquer a la Societè Royale /ou en faire une brochure/ il l'a fait publier dans le *St James's Chronicle* d'hier mot pour mot, a ce que m'a dit Fordyce. Qu'il possede peu cet art si important, l'art de se faire valoir! Il y a des gens, qui avec une telle decouverte, auroient fait fortune en fait de reputation. He has given it to the world in a crude state without staying to establish and improve upon it /turn it to account/ by proper experiments. And this in a manner which will just have the effect of making it stale, without procuring him a grain of reputation. Most people of the very few readers of a newspaper that trouble themselves about such matters will neglect it, from seeing it where it is: And it is ten to one but that most if not all the still fewer that may think of trying it, pronounce it false, for want of attending to the considerations above mentioned.

Du Steam-Engine,[5] ce n'est qu'une idee tres generale et très-imparfaite que je peux vous donner. L'idèe qu'en a le Dr. même n'est que très imparfaite; et la façon dont il me l'a decrit l'a été

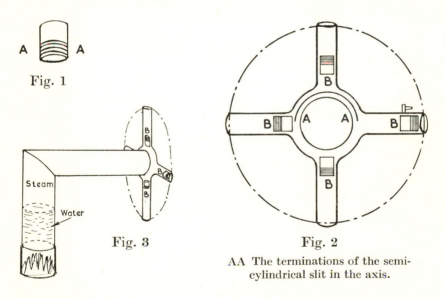

Fig. 1

Steam

Water

Fig. 3   Fig. 2

AA The terminations of the semi-cylindrical slit in the axis.

encore plus; la moitiè (j'en ai été force) il m'a falu en tirer a force de questions.

L'inconvenient de la machine ordinaire a quoi on pretend remedier par celle-ci est comme ensuit. Pendant que la piston monte, voila du mouvement produit: mais pendant qu'il descend, voila

[5] In a letter to Jeremy (not extant) Samuel asked for information about a steam engine (see letter 143).

autant de temps perdu. Here several pistons playing in so many trunks disposed around the main one, communicating with it, and playing round it as the spokes of a wheel round the fixed axis, while one is descending, another is ascending.

Conceive a Coach-wheel without the Fellies (Circumference) the spokes we will say 4 in number: cylindrical and hollow. The axle-tree hollow and communicating as in Fig.3 with the upright hollow Cylinder in which the water is boiling. In each one of the fellies plays a Piston B which is prevented[?] by being pushed out by a ring which contracts the diameter of the felly at the circumferential end of it where the Pistons by means of bars or chains etc. are connected with the wheel work that is to be set in motion. At the centrical end, each felly opens into the *nave*, ⟨which you know is⟩ a concentric cylinder embracing the axis and turning round it. In the upper half of the axis is a semicylindrical slit of the breadth of the nave: forming a communication therefore with, in short opening in to the nave, and by that means into the fellies, when in turning round they pass over that upper half of the axis. Conceive a felly setting out from its perpendicular situation it then opens fully into the axis by the slit: the steam issuing out at the slit begins to force up the piston in the felly: by the time the felly is got down to an horizontal situation the piston is got to the *circumferential* end of it and has done it's duty. The *momentum* it acquires by being forced to such a distance from the center of the machine makes it turn round and carry the other fellies round with it. At the time that it is exactly horizontal, half of it opens into the slit; the lower half is below the slit, and falls in with that part of the axis that is closed. When the whole is below the slit, then the /cold/ water is let in by some contrivance to condense the steam: this done the piston that is on the felly in question meeting with no resistance from within, is pressed up to the centrical end of the felly, by the pressure of the external atmosphere. In the mean time the opposite felly has got to where the slit in the axle-tree begins; and so the wheel goes round, two of the pistons out of the four being constantly /ascending/ at work. How the refrigerating water is let in I know not. I suppose in the same manner as in the common engine, whatever that is. Dr. Nooth[6] the inventor, who was a pupil

---

[6] John Mervin Nooth, M.D., F.R.S., author of several works on medicine. He graduated from Edinburgh in 1766. In the *Philosophical Transactions* for 1775 (Volume LXV) he published a paper entitled *The Description of an Apparatus for impregnating Water with fixed Air; and of the Manner of conducting that Process* (see also letter 279, n. 5).

of Fordyce's, has one a making; which is to be set up somewhere in or about London.

There, my dear Sam, I have done what I could for you, and now must bid you good night. I was prevented by an accident sending the letter that I had written to my father for last post: and now I must say something more. Don't wonder if some time or other he should be the death of me. But don't be alarmed, as I should keep myself were it only for your sake, till your return. How happy it is for man, that tyranny extends not beyond the grave!

Fordyce is not particularly acquainted with Belidor's Architecture Hydraulique: mais en general il dit, que tout ce qui est de Belidor est bon: which is a great deal for Fordyce to say.

A friend of Fordyce's has got the Commission for victualling the forces at Boston. He sends amongst other things *Sauer Crout*: Cabbages which are made to undergo to a certain degree the acetous fermentation: a great dish in Germany. They are stow'd in $\frac{1}{2}$ Ton Casks. As the fermentation will continue while they are on ship board, Fordyce has contrived a method to give vent to the vapour that will be discharged. In the middle of each Bung, which is of cork he introduces a flat circular brass valve which opens by the force of the vapour and shuts itself again by a spring. Each Bung thus prepared costs half a Crown.

144a

To — Godefroi

Early October 1775 (Aet 27)

Au bord de 5 ans, Monsr., je ressens encore trop vivement les /marques de/ politesses dont je suis redevable a vous et votre famille, pour ne pas embrasser avec joie une occasion qui se presente de vous en remercier. Je garde encore soigneusement le |

| /en qualité de temoignages/ ces deux marques de l'amitié dont il vous a plu me temoigner pendant mon sejour a Paris. Celui qui aura l'honneur de vous presenter ceci est mon frere,

144a. [1] B.M. X: 564–565. Autograph draft.

This is a draft, headed 'Letter to Godefroi, Paris', of the letter promised in letter 142. It is undated, and we do not know for certain that a corresponding letter was actually sent; but it seems likely that it was, and if so, the date must have been early in October 1775.

For the recipient cf. letter 142, n. 5. It has not been possible to identify him further, though it is tempting to suppose that he was a member of the distinguished legal family of Godefroy.

puisque il est né de meme pere et mere, autrement je l'aurois pu
nommer l'enfant de mes soins. Je doute s'il pourra mieux se faire
entendre que son ainé: d'ailleurs vous le trouveriez en /quand a l'/
esprit /aux manieres et a l'esprit/ plus Anglois que François, mais
aussie bon garçon, s'il m'est permis de le dire, qu'on peut etre. [*In
margin:* A l'age de 18 ans quoique sage comme un devot il est deja
philosophe d'apres soi et non pas sur parole.] Il est à present etabli
a Chatham dans un des chantiers Royaux pour y etudier l'architecture navale. Il vous instruira a son mieux de tout ce dont vous
pourrez souhaiter savoir de moi. Moi je me bornerai a dire, que
Possedant un somme qui suffit a mes petits besoins /Ayant juste-
ment ce qu'il faut pour me subsister/ j'ai [*in margin:* congedie, bien
au regret de mon pere comme vous pourrez vous imaginer, et]
laissé la profession pour travailler a la reforme de la science: etude
/emploi/ penible[?] laquelle /lequel/ si elle /s'il/ me (dont si je serois
assez heureux pour remporter) a moi tant soi peu d'honneur, et a
ma patrie de profit, c'est tout ce que j'en attends.[2] D'ailleurs, vous
savez que chez nous on peut en tout genre proposer impunement
/en toute sureté/ des projets de reforme, et que pour ceux qu'on
trouve mauvais, il n'y a d'autre punition que le mepris. Notre
Jurisprudence, comme la votre, et comme toute Jurisprudence,
presente une bien abondante moisson d'abus et de sottises, pour
qui y veut mettre son faux. Votre divine Helvetius, le saint tute-
laire que [*in margin:* j'adore, est mon sentier[?] et mon guide]
Comment en sont /se portent/ les Arts? Ils se retablissent /On peut
esperer et se raniment sous les auspices d'un regne actif et benin/
roi jeune et aimé.

Mon frere connoit notre ancien ami Monsr. Martin: mais non pas
Mr. Smith.[3] /De ce dernier/ Tout ce que je sais, c'est qu'il est etabli
a Edingburgh, ou a ce que m'en dit Mr. Martin, il fait assez bien ses
affaires. Je ne l'ai pas vu depuis que suis a Paris. A peine Mr. Martin
l'a t il vu pour quelques moments, chemin faisant de Paris a
Edingburgh.

Le pauvre Mr. Martin a perdue il y a trois mois sa femme, laquelle
il aimoit on ne peut pas mieux. Cela l'a plongé dans une tristesse
dont il ne sortira pas apparemment de long temps. /Cependant/ Si
on pourroit se trouver a son aise après un tel coup, il le seroit. Sa
bonhomie et son talent lui ont procuré la protection de Milord
Mansfield d'un [. . .?] distingué. Ce Seigneur qui est comme vous

---

[2] Bentham's marginal and interlinear insertions make it almost impossible to
construct a coherent text for this sentence. The sense, however, is fairly clear.
[3] For David Martin cf. letter 90, n. 2. For Smith cf. letter 140 at n. 4.

savez un des premiers du royaume /hommes de la Nation/ se comporte envers lui plutot en ami, ou en pere, qu'en protecteur. Pour faire diversion a son chagrin, Mylord l'a pris dans sa maison de campagne, ou il a eté il y a un mois ou d'avantage comme un de la famille.

Mme. Martin n'a pas laisse enfans a son mari, ceux qu'elle a eus sont morts, avant leur mere: mais elle lui a laissé en proprieté un bien de 4 a 5000 francs de rentes, ce qui vaut bien une petite litière d'orphelins, dont la mere vient[?] a mourir pendant qu'ils sont encore [. . .?]. l'amitié entre (lui et moi) /nous deux/ qu'a commencé notre rencontre en France, subsiste toujours. La vie sedentaire /et laborieuse/ que je mene ne me permet pas de le voir bien souvent: mais quand nous nous rencontrons c'est toujours avec plaisir: et il me consulte en guise d'ami sur tous ses affaires (juridiques). Je peux vous assurer qu'il ne vous oublie pas: et vous aurez bientot /dans peu de temps/ des marques de son ressouvenir. Il m'a parlé il y a peu de jours de quelques vases, qu'il a commandés, et qu'il vous destine pour present. Peut etre qu'ils sont deja en chemin. Il sont d'une pierre singuliere et precieuse qui ne se trouve qu'en Angleterre et qu'on n'a decouvert que depuis quelques ans. [*In margin:* C'est, je crois, une terre de [. . .?] qu'on appelle chrystallum[?] qui ne se travaille que tres difficilement. Les naturalistes l'appellent Radix amethystina. Les gens du commun Spath ou Petrificatum de Derbyshire, Province d'ou il est tiré.][4] Je serois veritablement charmé de scavoir que vous continuez de | | le bonheur parfait dont vous m'avez paru jouir avec une epouse des plus aimables et des enfans /une petite/ qui lui ressemblent: mandez moi, je vous prie, en quoi maintenant elle[?] consiste. Je baise respecteusement les mains de Madame et de Mademoiselle sa soeur, de laquelle je serois bien aise de savoir, que pour le bonheur de quelque homme de merite, elle n'est plus demoiselle. Le jeune Chevalier comment s'occupe t'il? Est il pour les arts?

Si vu l'espace qui nous separe, il y avoit /se trouvoit/ quelque chose en quoi je pourrois vous etre utile, permettez moi de vous assurer, que rien ne feroit plus de plaisir a celui qui avec le respect et la reconnoissance les plus parfaits a l'honneur etre

Monsr. Votre tres obeissant serviteur et ami

J.B.

[4] Bentham is evidently referring to Derbyshire-spar (he uses the spelling 'spath', described in the *N.E.D.* as 'now rare') or Derbyshire-drop—i.e. fluor spar, native calcium fluoride.

145

To Jeremiah Bentham

6 October 1775 (Aet 27)

Hond. Sir

Your commands dated on Wednesday came to hand last night. This morning I waited on Mrs. Sarney to give her your *ultimatum*. I am sorry to have to tell you, she did not chose to engage upon those terms. When I mentioned them to her, she herself ascribed the shortness of the time you were willing to engage for to an intention she attributed to you of letting the whole in the manner you propose: saying it was what people expected you would do: in which she was joined by her friend Mrs. Townsend[2]; and that as, besides the expence, at her time of life the trouble of moving and shifting the scene was irksome, she could not justify to herself to run the risk of being obliged to it in so short a time. At the same time I placed your wish and my Mother's to have her for a tenant and a neighbour and your willingness to make the abatement you mentioned on her account in the light I thought you wished it should appear to her; a mark of respect of which she seemed duly sensible, and made many polite acknowledgements. In answer to her apprehension all that I could say, was that I rather thought, in my own opinion, you would not adopt that plan; as indeed I am disposed to think: not imagining that you will be able to get for the mere ground and the few materials any thing approaching to the £90 a year you make (including the new apartment but) exclusive of the warehouse which is and probably will remain unoccupied.

When at Mrs. Sarney's, I found myself in *pays de connoissance*. As Mrs. Sarney herself was not yet stirring when I called, I was introduced to her Landlady Mrs. Townsend; whom, as I said in my last, I had seen her with before. This Mrs. Townsend turns out to be own Sister to Mrs. Hills of Colchester, Micay Hills is absolutely turned Hermit. He shuts himself up (I understand from that and other quarters) among his well-bound books and Cockle shells, and

---

145. [1] B.M. I: 367–368. Autograph. Docketed by Jeremiah Bentham: 'Fils Jere^y Bentham Letter to me at Paris. Octr. 3d. 1775.'

Addressed: 'A Monsr. / Mr. Bentham / chez Monsr. / Monsr. Pattle / Gentilhomme Anglais / au Coin des Minimes / a la Place Royale / Paris / France. / Single Sheet / feuille.' Postmark: '6 OC'. Stamped: 'D'ANGLETERRE'.

[2] A resident in Somerset House: see letter 141, and cf. below for her connection with the Hills family of Colchester.

exercises the most 'strenua inertia.' His house must certainly be a magnificent one; the old gentleman, I understand from Mrs. Townsend gave him *Carte Blanche*, with regard to the expence; and it is to be absolutely his own, with the estate around it. Yet I have all along that this son was not at all in favour with the father; but that the younger who is in the business was the favourite. Every body supposes the young man will marry, when the house is finished, but nobody pretends to know the person. All this while the Old Gentleman himself, dresses plain, sees nobody, goes no where, but confines himself wholly to the business.[3]

I am very sorry that I should have disappointed you, Sir, by not answering your question respecting the Bookseller. Your commands on that head were by no means 'unattended' to or forgotten. But the manner in which you mentioned the matter at first gave me not the least reason imaginable to think you were in any hurry about it, or had any reason to be so. You talked of making purchases in the book way, and it was in view to *that* that you seemed to have put the question; and I could not suppose that you would make any purchases of that sort for the young folks till they were with you to choose. The Payne's have been both out of Town when I have called, and the foreman who was left could only tell me the name of the Bookseller you enquired after. He was present when you spoke about it to young Payne: The name he says is Cressonier: The address he could not recollect nor hit upon any method of finding out. But this can not be at ⟨all⟩ material, since as Cressonier is a Bookseller of note, you have but to bid Francque call in at the first Bookseller's shop he happens to pass when he goes for the 'Rolls and Butter', and he may, I think, be pretty sure to know. At the worst, in the *Rue St. Jacques* I think it is which is the Paternoster-Row of Paris, there can be no doubt of hearing of him. You did not express any wish to have any thing more than the man's name and address—You do not desire, I see, to have another letter to him in lieu of that you left behind.

The affair of the money was really as you suppose. It has *not* been paid in at Gines's.(?) I thought it better to go there to make the enquiry than to put the question of Mr. Browne. I know not how

[3] Micay Hills was Michael Robert Hills (*c.* 1743–89), admitted to Trinity College Cambridge in 1762 (B.A. 1767) and to Lincoln's Inn 1766. He travelled abroad for some years before settling, as Bentham here describes, at Colne Park, Earl's Colne, not far from Colchester (cf. obituary in *Gentleman's Magazine*, lix, 957–958). His father, Michael Hills, seems to have been a man of some substance in Colchester, though we have little detailed information about him. For a further reference to the Hills family, cf. letter 149, n. 6.

I came to take it into my head; but I was strongly possessed with the notion of his having told me it was paid in there. It certainly however must have been my mistake, as it could have answer'd no end for him to tell me it was, when the fact was otherwise and must be known to be so. I will take care to see him tomorrow, and do all in my power to ensure his compliance with your directions. Since the time I mentioned for Mr. Browne's return, he has been out of town a second time; being called suddenly to Winslow to see his Brother's Wife, who at the time he was sent for was expected to die every hour. She is now I understand somewhat better and Mr. Browne is come to town again.[4]

I could have wished to have said more to you, Sir, upon various subjects; but really the contents of the latter part of your letter have pressed and do continue to press so hard upon my mind, that I find myself unable to say more. I could wish for fear you should think I neglect your commands, to dispatch my letter this post. If so I must put it up this moment or not at all.
Tuesday Oct. 3d 1775

Friday Octr. 6 1775
While I was running with my Letter to overtake the Bellman, a very stout ill looking fellow threw himself into my way, and thrust an elbow into my stomach: at the same time making a plunge for my handkerchief, which succeeded no farther than to open the button of my pocket. The pain this put me to for the moment, put all thoughts of what I was about out of my head; and for some time I thought of nothing but getting home. However I felt nothing of it the next day, nor do I now. Since the above I have seen Mr. Browne, and made him promise to settle the affair before your return. He would have staid till he could see you, grounding himself upon your first letter to him: and on an over-charge which he thinks there is on the Plff.'s Bill to the amount of about a Guinea. He says he received the rent for the houses as of course, upon the compromise of the suit, as your Attorney in that matter. That Mr. Barrett was not present; and that had he been, the people would not have paid the money he thinks to any other person than your Attorney in the cause. If you had given directions to him to pay the overplus to your Banker, he would have done it he says: but that without such directions, he could not have been safe in paying in that manner, supposing for instance your ⟨. . .⟩

---

[4] The nature of the property transactions mentioned here and below is not clear, nor have William Browne's brother and sister-in-law been further identified.

should have failed. That I know not how to join with him in. It may be so, but I can't help doubting it. However all this is now to little purpose. He offers now upon your order to pay in the residue. But can now hardly be worthwhile.

One thing I will take the liberty of mentioning, Sir, while I think of it, and while I am able. Sam has not had the advantage of a master that Charles has. He has been left entirely to himself: in which state had he not a steadiness and a disposition to attend to every laudable means of promoting his own interest, that is not to be found in one in a hundred at his age, scarce any thing could have been expected from him in so short a stay. Could not you find means to indulge him with a month or if it were only a fortnight longer? Could not you drop him at Montreuil, or Abbeville, or Boulogne or Lisle or Dunkirk etc. according to the road you take: or possibly at Paris. Caën is by your account of it a very dear place indeed. But in some places in France Boulogne for instance I am very well informed that every thing is at least as cheap again as in England. Lisle I myself found very cheap. He might therefore board I should think as cheap in some one or other of those places, as he does in ordinary at Mr. Davies: and his journey home by Diligences and the Sea together might be render'd not much more expensive I should hope than his returning with you would be.

Shall I make any answer, Sir, to the latter part of your letter? Prudence whispers, no—Could I but swallow my affliction, sunshine might possibly succeed this last storm, as it did the first. Shall I? Yes I must speak: Prudence will not always be listen'd to by an ulcer'd mind. No. I will forbear: I will take another chance; since my congratulations on the happiness of your situations, and (God knows they were sincere!) and my filial wishes have been so unfortunate. Let me acquaint you then, Sir, that I have not the least thought of present marriage: not the least thought of marriage at all without a full assurance, of what in my own judgement shall be a comfortable subsistence. Whether my own judgement and your's may agree upon what is a comfortable subsistence, I know not: if not I see no help for it. Let me assure you of this also, that in point of appetite, I am as cool as any anchorite would wish to be: but which does not in the least alter however my way of thinking. I am Sir, and will be, as long as you will permit me to be

Your dutiful and truly affectionate
Son
Jere:^y Bentham

As to purchases, it is not my wish to give you any further trouble than by what I have mentioned already to Sam. Unless it be for a pair of lace ruffles if my mother thinks it will answer. I have not any such thing as a pair of what can be properly called lace-ruffles. But this as well as the wastecoat mentioned to Sam I beg leave to commit to his and your discretion. French books I want none. My sincere and affectionate respects attend her.

146

To Samuel Bentham

14 November 1775 (Aet 27)

I thought to have gone down to you tomorrow by the Coach: but the fates have decreed otherwise. The Coach is full. Nevertheless I believe my baggage will go on that day, and by that conveyance. I shall follow probably the next day; or possibly I may go down by hook or by crook even tomorrow.

The reason of my dispatching the luggage at all events is, that part of it is of a nature not to keep: I mean a Turkey which was sent me by my Tenant Boozey [2] yesterday evening—You will send for him at a proper time (if he should not come of his own accord) and introduce him to the acquaintance of Mrs. Davies—Don't let them wait the dressing till my coming, as that you see is uncertain —The most probable mode then of my arrival is by the Coach on Thursday.

---

146. [1] B.M. I: 369. Autograph. Docketed: 'I.B. Novr. 14 1775.'

Addressed: 'To / Mr. Bentham / at his Majesty's Dock Yard / near Rochester.' Postmark: ' . .NO'.

Samuel Bentham was now back from France, and again domiciled with his tutor, Mr Davies.

[2] This was William Boozey, a letter from whom to Bentham is in U.C. cxxxiv: 92 (6 April 1774). According to Bentham's statement to Bowring, Boozey was tenant of 'a little estate' at Rochford in Essex. 'Boosey', Bentham adds, 'was a Dissenter. We went one day and dined with him. After dinner, he took us to his meeting. I went with him a short way up the gallery; and the minister was making his prayer, and saying, as it appeared to me, "O Lord! that *alterest* all events." "O", said I, "that is ultra-omnipotence;" and I broke out into a most violent but irresistible burst of laughter. I was near the door, and I made my escape without disturbing the congregation. It was a paroxysm; but it disturbed me greatly. At that time, Boosey was overseer of the poor; who lived in clover. He told me there had been a meeting among them, because he gave them sheep's heads, which they called *offal*. Not long after, dining with Adam, (the father of all the Adams who had got places), there was a sheep's head (*Scotticè*) with the hair singed. I thought it a strange coincidence that the poor of a parish should rise in rebellion against a dish which was the favourite dish at the table of an aristocrat' (Bowring, x, 55). Cf. also letter 67

I have received your Letter of yesterday as well as that from Battle. Adieu—Compliments to our friends. The Dr's. message shall be attended to.[3]

Tuesday 14th Novr. 1775.
 No work this time.

147

TO SAMUEL BENTHAM

17 November 1775 (Aet 27)

Mon Portmanteau vous avez apparement deja reçu: pour mon auguste personne vous ne la verrez pas, je crois, avant Lundi. Toutes les places pour le lendemain son preoccupées; ainsi qu'elles ont été pour touts les jours depuis mercredi inclusivement.

J'ai été in very bad spirits toute cette semaine: j'ai langui dans un assoupissement inconcevable: c'est un violence que je me fais maintenant pour vous ecrire ce peu des mots.

Friday Nov. 17 1775.

148

TO JOHN LIND

9 December 1775 (Aet 27)

There was a time when I doubted whether, so long as you were alive, I could live without you. It became necessary for me to try: I have tried and I have succeeded. I cannot write. I could not say any thing without saying a great deal: and the subject is become stale and wearies me to think of. However I fancy now and then that I should like to see you; and in that intent I called about 3 weeks

---

[3] Probably Dr Simmons.

147. [1] B.M. I: 370. Autograph. Docketed: 'I.B. Nov. 17 1775.'
 Addressed: 'To / Mr. Bentham / at his Majesty's Dock Yard / near Rochester.' Postmark: '. . NO'.

148. [1] B.M. I: 371–372. Autograph. Docketed by Lind[?]: 'Bentham Decr. 9 1775.' Docketed by Bentham: 'to Lind'.
 Addressed: 'To / John Lind Esqr. / Lamb's Conduit Street / No. 65 / By the Penny Post.' Stamped: 'PENNY POST PAID'.
 For Bentham's quarrel with Lind see letter 139 and n. 1. The quarrel was patched up by 8 February 1776 (see letter 149, at n. 9).

ago, as probably you heard. Since then I have passed ten days at Chatham: on my return yesterday sen'night I found your name upon my table. I have from that time been intending, and intending still to call upon you; waiting, as it were, for an impulse which perhaps may never come. Least it should not, I have made an effort and written thus much to you. You often come close /almost/ to my door: you know my hours: If you should happen to think it worth your while to call again, I shall at any time be glad to see you.—My compliments to Mrs. Lind.

Saty. Decr. 9th 1775.
    Lincoln's Inn

149

To Samuel Bentham

8–9 February 1776 (Aet 27)

Linc. Inn Thursday Feb. 8. 1776.

Ah! you young scape-grace you, what a world have[*sic*] plague hast thou put me to, by running away with the key of that sacred mansion! Besides bestowing on thee a whole peal of 'Rakas',[2] I should have called thee 'fool' a hundred times for it, had not I consider'd that like as the puissant Amasis saw no reason why he should be damned himself for the *love* of his fair daughter the tender Amasida,[3] no more was there why I should damn myself to satiate my wrath, howsoever merited, against thee: ainsi with equal prudence and piety je me suis contentè de te maudir. Pour la clef, graces a dieu, j'en suis maitre encore une fois, par la politeesse de Mr. Nairne,[4] qui a eu la bontè de me l'envoyer par un de ses gens.

149. [1] B.M. II: 1–2. Autograph.
    Addressed: 'To / Mr. Bentham / at the King's Dock Yard / near Rochester.' Postmark: '9 FE'.
    [2] Cf. Matthew 5: 22.
    [3] Characters in Voltaire's *Le Taureau Blanc*.
    [4] Edward Nairne (1726–1806) had a shop at 20 Cornhill as an 'optical, mathematical and philosophical instrument maker'. 'In 1771 he began to contribute papers on scientific subjects to the *Philosophical Transactions*, and possibly about this time made the acquaintance of Joseph Priestley.' In 1774 he 'constructed, on plans supplied by Priestley, the first considerable electrical machine made in England' (*D.N.B.*). He was elected F.R.S. in 1776 (cf. letter 169 etc.). Mrs Davies and her sister Mrs Wise (cf. letter 151, n. 4) were the daughters of Richard Nairne of Chatham (cf. B.M. XVII: 57). It seems likely that they were relatives of Edward Nairne.

Pour la vieille, il ne faut pas la laisser aller avant que l'Arcange[5] soit de retour: c'est une occasion que ne faut pas laisser echapper. No—no. Il faut positively lay an embargo on her.

No—I cannot say I am violently struck with Miss S.[6] She has indeed a most enchanting set of teeth—seems well made; and is of a very good size. But her features viz: nose and mouth are too large for her face: eyes I do not recollect much about. Indeed I could not get a full view of her face: she was dressed very unbecomingly which could not but be a great disadvantage to her. However I should like very well to have an opportunity of being better acquainted with her: but do not see that probability of her suiting me to warrant me to ask for it of myself. I will tell you what you might do: you might mention it as a scheme of your own merely of your own to the Doctor, thought of and proposed without my privity. In this case, if he should come into it, and would invite his Sister to his house for the purpose, I would go down to meet her. But you must make sure about the Assets first—see what grounds he has to grow upon—for Mr. D. says he never understood it to be more than £3000, and that the Dr. knows nothing of his father's affairs. In the article of person as far as I can judge by what I have seen hitherto, I think I give the preference to Miss Clark[7]: what pleases me in Miss S. is her little acquaintance with London and the vanities of the Queen's-Square-Place-ish world.

I have little hope of decomposing Respirable Air unless it be by *Compound* Elective Attraction.

[5] This is the first of a number of references during 1776 to a young lady—the 'Archangel'—to whom Samuel was apparently paying his addresses. See below letters 165, 177 (where 'Miss H.' is presumably the same person) and 193 (referring to a letter received by Samuel). U.C. cxxxiv: 1 bears a number of scribbles by Samuel in which he appears to be trying out phrases for a love-letter to someone called 'Daphne'. See also letters 137, n. 2 and 140, n. 8.

[6] The state of Bentham's relations with Miss Dunkley at this period is rather obscure. After a visit to Colchester a month before the date of this letter he told his father that the affair was ended. Cf. the following entry from his father's journal quoted by Bowring (see letter 133, n. 1): '1776 Jan. 17. wrote a letter to mon fils Jeremy on the subject of his sudden Journey to Colchester last Monday was se'nnight the 8 instant. A midi fils Jeremy called on me on his return from Colchester, and to my great joy and surprise brought me the happy tidings that his courtship with Miss Dunkly was entirely broke off and at an end. il dinoit chez nous.

'Au Soir went to Mrs.[?] Hill's Chambers in the Temple and acquainted her[?] with the account reçu de mon fils Jeremy to prevent Mr. Hills from mentioning the affair to Mr. Carlton at Colchester l'oncle de Miss D—ly'. (For the Hills family see letter 145, n. 3.) Nevertheless, as later letters will show, Bentham was at least occasionally until the end of the year in touch with Miss Dunkley. At the same time with a desperate cynicism he seems to have fallen in with his father's plan that he should find a rich wife. The Miss S. here mentioned seems to have been the sister of Dr Simmons (see letter 123, n. 1), and not the Miss Stratton of subsequent letters.

[7] Perhaps a sister of Richard Clark.

Many thanks to the Dr. for the account of his thermometrical observations—I like it much—It seems very well drawn up, both in point of arrangement and diction. Mr. Nairne and his family I like wonderfully: they were all exceedingly civil to me—and Mrs. Nairne gave me a general Sunday-dinner. You, I find, are quite upon terms of intimacy there: she spoke of you by the name of *Sam*. I never that I remember felt myself so soon at my ease in any family as there. One of the girls plays I find upon the *Piano forte*: that will be a coementing principle. Tomorrow I go to Mr. Anderson's.[8]

Whether Mr. D. is commenced 'simple' or no, is more than I can tell. I have not been to Qu S.P. since he was.

I dined yesterday at Mr. Lind's to meet Mr. Mazeres,[9] quondam Attorney-General of Quebec, now Cursitor Baron of the Exchequer: a kind of sine-cure given him by the Ministry for his meritorious industry in projecting plans of legislation for that province.

I have bespoke a Coat of the colour of Far's with breeches of the same—the lining marone-coloured silk: buttons of the fashion reprobated by Buckmaster, save that mine have eight rays to the star; instead of six only which that you saw had.

As to the Preface[10] I shall never have done it. The Printing has gone on but heavily. The Frost put a stop for some time to that as well as so many other operations. They are now about the 7th Sheet. The 6th returned last night corrected.

What surprises me is, I have not heard yet from Miss D.[11] I wrote to her last when you were with me.

[8] Probably James Anderson (1739–1808) the writer on agricultural and economic matters who figures later in the correspondence and whom, apparently, Bentham met through George Wilson (cf. letter 304). His contributions to agriculture included the introduction of 'the Scotch Plough'. He farmed in Aberdeenshire. Several letters between Anderson and Bentham were published in Bowring's *Memoirs*, in one of which Bentham with tactless frankness urges him not to publish a pamphlet on the Western Fisheries (Bowring, x, 127). The Bentham brothers came to know him quite well, and Samuel later helped him keep in touch with agricultural experiments in Russia (see letter 350 etc. below).

[9] Francis Maseres (1731–1824), mathematician, historian and reformer. He was attorney-general of Quebec from 1766 to 1769, and cursitor baron of the exchequer from 1773 until his death.

The aged Bentham said: 'Baron Maseres was an honest fellow, who resisted Lord Mansfield's projects for establishing despotism in Canada. He occupied himself in mathematical calculations to pay the national debt, and a good deal about Canadian affairs. There was a sort of simplicity about him, which I once quizzed and then repented. I had not studied the Deontological principle as I have studied it since' (Bowring, x, 183; see also x, 59).

[10] Preface to *A Fragment on Government*. This was in fact the only part of the *Comment on the Commentaries*, on which he had been working since the autumn of 1774, which Bentham ever published.

[11] Miss Dunkley: cf. n. 6 above.

Poore is in Town—I will see him on your affair on a day or two. Wilson[12] desires to be remember'd to you in the most magnificent manner imaginable.

Friday Feb. 9.

Tes boutons te seront renvoyès quand je t'envoye un exemplaire de mon livre—Ah, pardon, Monsr. mon cher et trés honore frère avoir oublier de les envoyer par le moyen de Monsr. Davies— C'est aussi alors que je ferai ce que je pourrai pour vous envoyer le livre de Euler sur la construction des vaisseaux.[13]

150

TO SAMUEL BENTHAM

15 February 1776 (Aet 28)

Pardon me, my dear Sam—in truth I had forgotten all the articles thou hast mentioned—I am glad I have them now in writing—We both of us are apt to talk over a number of projects which we do not execute. When I send thee my pamphlet thou shalt have all, not forgetting the buttons—I have found mine.

To come to what is more material—Inclosed in this you will receive either a 10£ note or the half of one I am not determined which—I have taken the Number etc., No. B. 53. Payable to Henry

[12] George Wilson (d. 11 June 1816) was a young and very tall barrister of Lincoln's Inn with whom Bentham became acquainted about this time. His father had been a collector of the Customs in Aberdeen, and Wilson had studied at Edinburgh University. He was related by marriage to Dr George Fordyce, through whom he met Bentham.

According to Sir Samuel Romilly, who met him in 1784, and became a close friend, Wilson was an excellent barrister, and well fitted to be a judge. He supposes that it was his liberal politics which stood in the way of this. Wilson took silk late in life, and was leader of the Norfolk circuit. In 1810 an attack of palsy compelled him to quit the Bar, and he retired to Edinburgh. The friendship between him and Bentham seems to have cooled long before this. Bentham probably found Wilson too moderate. For instance, in 1808 Wilson dissuaded Romilly from bringing in a Bill for criminal law reform—though his grounds were simply that its inevitable failure would prejudice later chances of reform. (See Bowring, x, 133–4, and several passages in the *Memoirs of Sir Samuel Romilly*.)

[13] *A compleat theory of the construction and proportion of vessels* . . . London, 1776, translated by H. Watson from *Scientia navalis, seu tractatus de construendis ac dirigendibus navibus*. St Petersburg, 1749 (French version, St Petersburg, 1773) by Leonhard Euler (1707–83) the great Swiss mathematician.

150. [1] B.M. II: 3–4. Autograph.

Addressed: 'To / Mr. Bentham / at the King's Dock Yard / Rochester.' Postmark: '15 FE'.

Green Esq. dated 20. Jan. 1776. signed W. Gardner—Enterd S. Blomer. Marked at top by some holder 1569. Unluckily your letter did not come to hand till near 12 last night, or you would have had this a day sooner. I this morning dispatched to the Printer's the last sheet of my Pamphlet[2] (but alas! I don't mean of the Preface) I thought I should never have done that plaguy 4th chapter. Would you think it? it is swelled to 54 pages. The whole will be little short of 200 besides Contents and Preface.

Q.S.P. has just left me—he has had a cold these ten days but is got about again. He asks me to do him the favour or some such expression to drink tea with him on Monday next. There is to be a young lady, he tells me, who plays on the Harpsichord and guittar, and who told him 'tother day to his surprise of her having heard of my playing very well on the fiddle—He will not tell me who she is— I suppose it to be Miss Buckle.[3]

I was at Mr. Anderson's t'other day staid till 2 in the morning but saw no niece—however I shall probably have other opportunities.

What thinkest thou I have done about thy golden-feathered Archangel? I have commissioned *Gwatkin* to make enquiries after her—Gwatkin is a sure man—He was to go to Bath last Monday.

Thursday 15th Feb.

1776

God's-daddikins! it is my birthday—say something pretty to me on the occasion.

What are you about?

Send me word who *Arnold's single lesson for the Harpischord* is printed for—I have been enquiring after it, and have been told there is no such thing.

151

To Samuel Bentham

22–23 February 1776 (Aet 27)

Ce ne fut pas Madlle. Buckle, mais Madlle. *Stretton* fille de Made. *Brickendon,* dont le mari le Dr. Brickendon est mort il y a

---

[2] *A Fragment on Government.*

[3] Unidentified; but cf. letter 141 at n. 9.

151. [1] B.M. II: 5–7. Autograph.

Addressed: 'To / Mr. Bentham / at the King's Dock Yard / near Rochester.' Postmark: '23 FE'.

This letter concerns the young lady, Miss Stratton, to catch whom for Bentham father and son schemed throughout the greater part of 1776. Sarah Stratton was the

environ une année. Je l'ai vue il y a deux ans chez Q.S.P. avec Mad. sa mere et Monsr. Son (beau pere) selon ce que je crois vous avoir dit.—Peste! je ne puis pas ecrire Francois maintenant—cela me gene trop—et le tems me manque. I did not like her much the first time—I like her much better now: so well that I know not whether I may not give into the Q.S.P. projects: provided always that the fortune be a large one. less than £30,000 in possession or expectancy it must not be. Her features are not pretty—Teeth regular, but not close set—complexion far from blooming—Her shape is elegant. She appears good-natured affable and unaffected: and upon the whole her countenance, especially when she smiles is far from being unpleasing—c'est a dire by candle-light: reste a voir ce qu'elle paroitra by daylight. I thought and so my Father remarked, that she seemed to look sociably enough at me—there was with her besides her Mother a Miss Brickenden, a girl much about her own age, daughter of Dr. B. by a former wife. She (Miss S.) plays upon the Harpsichord and Guittar, and sings. Upon the Harpsichord I should suppose pretty well as she plays Abel's musick, which is far enough from easy[2]—Voila a caementing principle—She does not play thorough-base: if she will learn I will teach her I know nothing of it at present myself: but that you know makes no difference. What is best of all she loves retirement: and lives in the country 9 months in the year by her own choice rather than her mother's.

daughter of Edward Stratton (d. 1768) who had lived near Jeremiah Bentham in Westminster. His widow, Mrs Sarah Dorothy Stratton (d. 1801), married as her second husband John Brickenden, a Westminster physician who died in the summer of 1775. From her second husband she inherited the estate at Ripley, where Bentham's courtship of her daughter was largely to take place; her first husband had left substantial property in the Isle of Thanet.

Bentham in later life referred to the episode in the following terms, recorded by Bowring in the manuscript note in his own copy of the *Memoirs* already quoted in letter 133, n. 1 and letter 149, n. 6:

'Dr. Brickenden an acquaintance of my father married a lady who had a daughter whose name was Storer. There was a scheme for me to court the lady who had a handsome portion. They had a country house at Ripley in Surry. I visited them and was well received. She played on the harpsichord and I played on the fiddle. When George Wilson and I went to Fetcham I asked the ladies to dine with us—but I found they were going to Chatham, and I offered my services to escort them, they in their carriage I on horseback. I introduced my brother to them. There was a young apothecary of the party as well, a young Scotchman, Forbes of Culloden, who lived in the neighbourhood under the care of a parson of the name of Rose. This Mr. Forbes married Miss Storer but it was not a happy marriage.'

Bentham has evidently forgotten the young lady's name: it is variously spelt, in his letters and elsewhere, 'Strutton', and 'Stretton', but Stratton appears to be the authentic form.

[2] Karl Friedrich Abel (1725–87), the German composer and instrumentalist, had lived in England since 1759.

The misfortune is the acquaintance between **Q.S.P.** and them is like all the other acquaintances of **Q.S.P.** very distant: **Q.S.P.** made while I was there several overtures for parties etc. which were received but coldly: Possibly the old lady smelt a rat: If I could once get access upon my own bottom I have a sort of presentiment that, if I found myself in the mind I might succeed. But how to do that is the question. They stay but a few days longer in town: and will not see town again these 8 or 9 months. Their house is at Ripley in Surry—not a vast way from Chertsey: but where precisely I know not. What think you is in the wind? For **Q.S.P.** to take a house in the Summer as near to Ripley as they can find one. They see little company—there is little in the neighbourhood for them to see—Miss rides out sometimes—The old Lady I suppose hardly. Voila des occasions. Et cependant if the old lady smells a rat and has no stomach to the alliance—all this will not do. I am not the man for a coup de main—I must have access, and be intimate before I can do any thing. If it should appear worth while, I have a scheme of my own to graft upon that. **Q.S.P.** for such a purpose would do any thing: kick J.C. out of doors and hug the Devil in his arms. I will make him caement anew his 'unalterable friendship' with Mr. L.[3] and I will then make Mr. L. take a house in the neighbourhood too. Parents *trumpetings* especially those of such a parent signify nothing. Mr. L. would trumpet me to the purpose: and *disassociate* dans l'esprit des dames the idea of your humble servant from that of **Q.S.P.** As to Assets they consist in 1. A landed estate in the Isle of Thanet—The value and the exact place as yet unknown—In the Will, mention is made of Manors— *Mr. Wise*[4] probably knows or could learn—Mr. Stretton died in 1768. The Land is left to Mrs. Stretton (now Brickenden) for life— afterwards to Miss: but in a plaguey strict kind of settlement as I am apprehensive, that will make it but a sort of apron string tenure. 2dly. Money in the funds: left immediately and absolutely to Miss. The amount as yet unknown—It can be known to a certainty by searching the books. This **Q.S.P.** you may take for granted will not fail in. When he knows I shall know and when I know, you shall know. I wish you would set Mr. Wise about it, saying you have a particular reason for desiring to know, but begging as a particular favour that it may be kept a secret. Mention

---

[3] Presumably John Lind.

[4] Robert Wise, the husband of Mrs Davies's sister, Sarah Nairne, Mrs Davies being wife of Samuel's landlord at Chatham. Wise's subsequent bankruptcy and desertion of his wife involved many labours for the Davies family and the Bentham brothers (cf. letters 194 ff).

seems to be made in the will (according to an extract hastily taken by my father) of a brother of Mr. Stretton's as then living. The Exors and Trustees Emerson Maseres of some parish about London I fancy I know something of his history—and Sam. Frimoult or Frimault (pronounced Frimò) a parson—Rector of Wootton in I know not what county.[5] This is not much to the purpose—As the Isle of Thanet (in Kent) is no very large district. It is probable that if Mr. Stretton's estate was a large one there will be no great difficulty in getting tidings of it. If the money in the Stocks amount to 12000£ or thereabouts, or the old Lady could and would give up Land enough to make up the interest of that sum reserving to herself a residue = 30,000–12,000. and alors, au pis aller when either of the old folks dies I come into Parliament, a coup sur. Here is speculation enough for you: to which I leave your worship for the present. All this, Dieu merci, sits as easy on me as an old glove.

The sooner thou doest thy part in the business the better. You may if you think proper communicate it to Mr. D. but sub sigillo profundissimi silentii. Any intimation of the project coming round to Ripley could blast every thing. Ay true—the best way would be for him to write to Mr. W. as on his account. Parishes, Number of Farms, Tenants' names Rent of each farm, Number of Acres on each farm—all this is too much to expect—but as much of it as one *could,* one would wish to know.

You must tell me in writing how many Ink Glasses you would wish to have: item how many spouts what do you call them to each—1 for you and 1 for Mr. D. that's two—Well and good—but would you not have a third to hold a pen with a broader nib than ordinary—viz: for printing?

Thursday Feb. 22. 1776.

    Linc. Inn.

Let me know if any thing is done in the affair of the Secretary-ship?[6] I interest myself in it greatly—Bestir yourself—conquer our friend's backwardness, and your own. As I do not know Mr. Wise, I cannot consent to his being trusted with the motive to the enquiry—Q.S.P. has just been with me—I intimated to him my design of getting intelligence through your means—He pursed up his mouth and made a piece of work about it, thinking it would be

---

[5] The trustees under Miss Stratton's father's will were Emerson Massarede of the parish of St Martin-in-the-Fields, and Samuel Fremoult (d. 1779), rector since 1739 of Wootton, about nine miles from Canterbury.

[6] Probably a reference to Joseph Davies's prospect of being appointed secretary to Lord Howe (cf. letter 153, n. 2).

a means of the project's getting air—You see therefore what caution is required. Remember the Estate is now Mrs. Brickenden's, and known probably by her name. Think what will be my situation perhaps in a month or two courting sous les yeux d'un pere—et d'un tel pere!

He told me the scheme of taking a house near Ripley was my mother's—it is possible—as she and I have been sociable of late. He recommends it to me to make up to her.

Ripley is 6 miles on this side Guildford.

Old Jones your music master and mine used to go now and then to Mrs. Brs. to teach Miss S. the guittar: and it is from that quarter that Miss had heard of my playing on the fiddle. The poor old man has now access there no longer. He has been desired to forbear his visits (so said Mrs. B. without assigning any particular reason—But I suppose he was troublesome—grown perhaps by this time childish, and uncleanly as people of a certain age are apt to do.)[7]

Notre cher Pere me faire l'honneur toujours comme vous savez de me croire depourvu de sens commun—Upon my mentioning my communicating the affair to you, he cautioned me against opening the affair to poor old Jones; asking him particulars of the fortune etc.

Friday—a diner

Je t'ecris dans ce moment parce que je n'ai point d'autre chose a faire—je comptai mettre dans ma poche une lettre que j'avais commencée pour Miss Dunkley: mais au lieu de ce papier-la j'y ai mis par meprise une autre.

J'ai été deja une deux fois chercher Poore sans fruit—cependant il est en ville.

152

To Samuel Bentham

24 February 1776 (Aet 28)

A Diner chez les 3 Tons.

J'ai été parler avec Poore ce matin: et j'en ai tirè des avis tres utiles. Je l'ai trouvè parfaitement instruit de tout ce qui regarde

---

[7] Cf. Bowring, x, 8–9, where Bentham describes his last visit to Jones, dating it 1775.

152. [1] B.M. II: 8. Autograph.

This letter concerns a project of Samuel's for solving the problem of accurate time-keeping and hence navigation on sea voyages (cf. letter 156). He hoped to gain one

L'Horologerie. Pour te faire plaisir (pour ne pas dire davantage) en deux Mots—(mais ne va pas me chicaner sur le nombre)—Votre projet est nouveau: je l'en ai trouvè bien persuadè. Mais aussi vous fait il des objections bien instructifs et bien dignes de votre attention. Je ne sais pas si il y en a contre lesquelles vous n'êtes pas en garde. A Pendulum clock it cannot be. To keep such an one on board ship is found absolutely impracticable even with all contrivances of Gymbols etc. etc. It must be a *Watch* that is a Time piece that goes by a Spring—there are it seems no other *primum mobilia* in use.   A watch must be wound up not seldomer than every 15 or 18 hours: how will you wind it up so often? It must not be taken out. that sudden change from hot to cold you know would derange the whole œconomy of the Spring. This I believe you are aware of. 2. There is no knowing a priori how metal may perform in a degree of heat so much superior to that of the atmosphere. This however is to be apprehended. The teeth and pinions etc. etc. which fitted on the heat of the atmosphere will fit now no longer. It is not certain that they will expand in proportion—the *female* parts of the work may no longer admitt the male: at least to play with equal freedom as before. Metals specifically the same are composed of strata of unequal densities and degrees of expansibility. The rate of expansibility between two strata may in different degrees of heat be different.

Courage mon ami. It was in obviating the inequalities of expansion that Harrison's[2] time-pieces were principally deficient. He could temper by long practise a piece of metal I should say combination of metals so as to make it answer the purpose: but then he could not give any *principles*—any rules whereby apparatus's could be made. Your plan is unembarassed by these difficulties. You must now go to watch boiling. Take your old watch (I believe I have got it here) observe how it goes during a given time in the heat of the atmosphere. Then afterwards in one of your contrivances. I can now no more—Poore is perfectly communicative and perfectly ready as far as seemeth to assist you in everything in his power. He promised secresy: which I hope he will keep.

24 Feby. 1776.

I expect your Shirts by Tuesday.

of the rewards offered by the Board of Longitude for improved methods of determining the longitude at sea. Jeremy consulted his friend Poore about it, as he had in the case of Samuel's chain pump scheme (see letter 96, n. 5), and himself prepared the Memorial on the scheme which was to be put before the Board of Longitude.

[2] See letter 72, n. 3.

Let me hear from you soon—you received one I suppose from me 4 days or two ago.

I need scarce tell you that Poore commended the invention.

153

TO SAMUEL BENTHAM

27–28 February 1776 (Aet 28)

Feb. 27. 1776 Linc. Inn

Ce n'est que ce matin que cette maudite engeance du Caffé m'ont portè votre lettre. O my dear Sam, never think of meddling with Æther: it is by an enormous deal too expensive—so is alcohol. Perhaps it may be necessary, or at least useful, in order to obviate the irregularity in the pressure of the external air, which would make a variation in the boiling point, to have a loaded valve: if so the fluid must escape and be lost—No—upon second thoughts, not necessarily. Nor by the bye will the loaded valve obviate the irregularity. for the pressure which the vapour of the water will have to overcome will always be the pressure of the weight put upon the valve, *plus* the pressure of the external atmosphere: which last will still be a variable quantity.

Qu. however whether Æther is easily condensible as well as easily convertible into vapour? If so, *avec beaucoup de menagemens*, it may possibly be made to do after all. The objection you make touching elasticity seem very pertinent and very worthy of attention.

Oh, my dear Sam—I am quite charmed at the happy prospects of our friend—the instant they are realized let me know.[2]

I mean rather to prefer 'we.' I mean that we should lessen or rather take off altogether the burden of reproach, from the persons in question, by sharing it ourselves. The 'on' the 'one' the 'man' is a remedy of the same kind, but *not so strong.*

153. [1] B.M. II: 9–10. Autograph.
Addressed: 'To / Mr. Bentham / at his Majesty's Dock Yard / near Rochester.' Postmark: '28 FE'.

[2] By March Mr Davies had obtained an 'advantageous appointment' under Lord Howe (as we learn from the unpublished portion of letter 154): it was presumably the secretaryship mentioned in letter 151 (cf. n. 6).

Richard Howe (1726–99), 4th (Irish) Viscount Howe, was Treasurer of the Navy 1765–70, became Rear-Admiral in 1770 and 1st Lord of the Admiralty in 1783. He was created Earl Howe in 1788. In 1775 he had been appointed commander of the British naval forces against the Americans. He resigned his command in 1778 in protest against the government's war policy.

Je suis charmè de la finesse et de la circonspection de votre politique touchant the enquiry—Bien des remercimens a notre ami —Qu'il soit fait au plutôt ce que vous avez proposè.

Joy to Mrs. Davies—What *one* only? I expected a whole litter.

The stockings are come from Aberdeen. The biggest are scarce too big for me—they will not be at all too big for you—I shall pack you off 3 pair out of the 6. Not that there is any great catch in them: for they are somewhat dearer than I was in hopes they would—9s.[?] a pair—about the price I take it of yours.

Come up on Friday bringing your French Coat worked[?] ruffles etc. to go to Wilson's on Saturday—unless you hear any thing to the contrary on Thursday which possibly you may.—You would be tired If you were not to come before Saturday—otherwise there would be time enough. Q.S.P. must not know any thing of the matter.

Wednesday.

I was last night at Wilson's: and staid with him giving him his physic till the Bell-men were gone by. What to do about going to Wilson's, of Kensington Lane[3] I know not. I am in 150 minds about it. I should like very well to *have* been but the thoughts of going are irksome to me beyond measure. There must be the trouble and expence of your cloathes coming and returning. A Coach thither if not back again—altogether between us it would not come to much less than a guinea.

'Tis done—I won't go.

Unless you have a mind for it.

If you have the least mind for it, let me know by return of post— Write at any rate by the Return of the Post.

I have been to hear 'Omnipotence'[4] and have been shot through and through by a Charming pair of black eyes.

11 o'clock.

[3] Unidentified.
[4] This was an oratorio set to Handel's music with words selected from Scripture by Samuel Arnold and Edward Toms, first performed at the Haymarket in February 1774. The performance Bentham attended was at Covent Garden.

154
JEREMIAH BENTHAM TO SAMUEL BENTHAM
2 March 1776

Dear Sam

*　　　　*　　　　*

Your Reflection upon the account your Brother has given you of his fresh pursuit, is a very just one—I shod. be happy, if it shod. succeed—and if it shod. not, it however proves as you observe, that his mind is no longer shaggled to its former object—I have a notion he mention'd it to you, for the purpose of making some Enquiry on the Isle of Thanet—but I cod. wish you wod. make no such Enquiry for I am satisfied there needs none—and the less said about it the better—the Fortune is unquestionable the Object is full young enough—and some time is requisite to bring matters about—as the Summer advances an opportunity may offer or be endeavoured at—In the mean time, it wod. be of great Consequence to your Brother to be able to make somebody of himself—his work is printed off, all but the preface—which I hope is nearly if not quite finish'd—and when his Book comes out, he will be able to Judge how far a litterary pursuit of that Sort may answer—and in case he shod. find them not to answer in the Track he has struck out, It is not too late, and it is to be hoped—he will act the same part he has happily done upon another occasion of changing his pursuit, in one case, as he has done his Object in another—in the latter, he is sure of losing nothing—tho' his gains may be great in case he succeeds—Have you as yet heard any thing of our friend Clark's[2] Marriage, I forget whether it was in hand when you was in Town— He has been Benedic the married man, now, this fortnight—but I can't help saying (entre nous) that the Fetters are not sufficiently gilt—⟨. . .⟩ *all things*—she is said to have £10,000, ⟨. . .⟩ she shod. at

154. [1] B.M. II: 11–12. Autograph. Docketed by Samuel Bentham[?]: 'Q.S.P. March 2d. 1776.'

Addressed: 'Mr. Bentham / at his Majesty's Dock Yard / near Rochester / Kent.' Postmark: '2 MR'.

About half this letter is omitted, including his invitation of Mr Davies to dinner and congratulation on that gentleman's new position.

[2] Richard Clark (for whom see letter 62, n. 1). The so harshly described lady was Margaret, daughter of John Pistor, a woollendraper in Aldersgate. She bore Clark two sons, and a daughter.

least have had £30,000—If you have never seen her—she is of the Dwarf Size—is not young, and looks still much older than she is—and for my own Part—I cannot see any thing in her mind or manner to make up for Person—He has taken a large House in new Bond Street, mentioning the House calls to my mind, yt. you was over it when you was in Town consequently know some thing of his being about to change his condition—but tho' Fortune is absolutely necessary to the Comfort of Life in any Station, more especially in that of marriage which, as to wants, is a kind of Multiplication Table, yet I shod. be sorry you or your Brother shod. engage in it, under the Circumstances of making so great a Sacrifice as I fear our Friend has done—where there is nothing in the least agreeable in the Person, there shod. be something engaging as well as agreeable in the mind and manner—but when every thing of that kind is wanting, a man must be a Stoic even with Fortune to be able to make a good Husband—when ever your Brother and you are of that Number, that you may be happy as such is ye. hearty wish of your affecte. Father.

Jh—B—m

*   *   *

155

Jeremy Bentham to Samuel Bentham

5 March 1776 (Aet 28)

Thursday morning—no—Wednesday my Father tells me it is.

It was not till just now that I took notice of that passage in your last where you tell me you shall not come up till you hear from me. The word '*not*' was broken off with the wafer—That passage out of the question, I expected you of course. It is worth half-a Crown a word to write to you—I have cursed Tooth-ach Ear-Ach etc. that has plagued me more or less for near a week. Your Shirts did not come to town till Saturday. I had them not till yesterday. I have not yet opened the box. As you are to be in town yourself it were as well you should be yourself at the buying of the purse. Your glasses I believe were done on Friday—but as yet I have got hence but two of them. When I recd. your last it was in a hurry, and

155. ¹ B.M. II: 13–14. Autograph.
    Addressed: 'To / Mr. Bentham / at the King's Dock Yard / near Rochester / Single Sheet.' Postmark: '5 MR'.

catching up the circumstances of your being to come to town so soon I thought nothing of sending to you any of your things— Indeed part of that passage was almost illegibile, and part covered by the wafer. I am a miserable sleeveless being just now, waiting for determination. I am vibrating between two tooth-drawers: and between tooth-drawing and no tooth-drawing. Not that the pain frightens me: for it would be a pleasant sensation at the first to have the offender griped: and the pain that succeeded it would be over in an instant—But my gum is swelled a little: and I am in doubt whether in that case extraction is proper or would indeed effect a cure. It is the last tooth in my left upper jaw. So the loss of it will be no disfigurement. I lay abed this morning till 10 to see whether that would do me good but it has done me none. I wish thou wert here —not that I could take any pleasure in thy company—However I am rather sleeveless than miserable.

But what signifies writing all this trash—This does not help on my Preface. It is almost done though not quite. It will be, as usual, longer than I expected. The Book itself is all printed. Mr. Davies called on me on Saturday—I have not seen him since.

Poor Wilson is still close prisoner—He and I sing psalms together —and bless the giver of all good gifts as Tooth-achs and swelled Testicles. *Omnipotence* is an Oratorio.

I had almost forgot to tell you that I like your contrivance (as far as I know of it) much: but I have not yet talked to Poore about it. When I have called he has not been at home.[2]

Qu. Whether it would not be proper to include a Thermometer in the machine.

As I shall be every day in expectation of seeing you, I shall not pack off your things, I believe, till you come. You will then see to the packing them up yourself—which will be rather a ticklish operation. The box they came in will do, and as there will be eleven shirts of mine taken out of it, there will be room in abundance for the glasses.

Higgins, I hear, is about answering Priestley.[3]

---

[2] Cf. letter 152, n. 1.

[3] Bryan Higgins (1737?–1820) physician and chemist, who opened a school of practical chemistry in Greek Street, Soho, for which he published a syllabus in 1775. He claimed that Priestley had published as his own experiments due to him, and gained some support from Dr Richard Brocklesby F.R.S. Priestley published letters between himself and Brocklesby and Higgins in which he unsuccessfully demanded that the accusation be retracted, with a commentary upon them, in a pamphlet entitled *Philosophical Empiricism* (1775). It is not known whether Higgins in fact published a reply to this.

There is just now come out by a Mr. Gibbons M.P. a history of the Roman Empire from Trojan to Constantine which is to be continued. I have a great account of it––He is quite one[4] of us and attacks ⟨. . .⟩ ⟨. . .⟩ ⟨. . .⟩ ⟨. . .⟩ ⟨. . .⟩ ⟨. . .⟩ when you have read it. It is a 4to Volume price 1£.1s. Qu. Could you get it at your library.

No it is Tuesday—my Father was mistaken. March 5th 1776.

156

To Samuel Bentham

8 March 1776 (Aet 28)

Friday March 8th. I believe it is. 1776. Linc. Inn

Tout doucement, mon cher ami: n'allons pas si vite. A great deal depends you know, on the unbulkiness and manageability (add these words to your dictionary) of the apparatus. In this view therefore, the one thing needful to be known, and that *d'abord*, avant toutes choses, is what length of tube, what diameter of the cylinder, inscribing the spiral worm, what distance between the *threads*, in short what proportions in the volume (solid content) of the refrigerating fluid it will require to that of the *refrigerand* (supposing the *refrigerand* to be æther) in order to condense the latter; and this in that (degree of the) heat of the atmosphere which can be depended upon as being the greatest which the ship can ever be in.

The Sea itself can hardly be made to do for a refrigeratory. Since for this purpose it must be in every part of it higher than the place where the condensed fluid is to re-enter the *magazine*: else if it should be condensed in the low part (which it may be in cold weather, and not in hot) there it will stay, and so much of it will never come into circulation. It is for you to determine whether it (the Machine) can be conveniently observed if kept in the hold for instance, below the surface of the water. You must moreover make allowances for the changes of position the ship is liable to undergo in storms: though these you will say, will never be of long continuance.

[4] From 'of us' to 'read it' inclusive has been carefully crossed out, possibly by someone other than Bentham.

156. [1] B.M. II: 15–16. Autograph.

Addressed: 'To / Mr. Bentham / at his Majesty's Dock Yard / near Rochester / Single Sheet.' Postmark: '8 MR'.

For the subject of this letter see letter 152, n. 1.

Another thing. The timepiece itself I take it for granted must be hung upon *gimbols* or somewhat of that sort. The refrigerating apparatus being connected with the timepiece must therefore rest upon the same gymbols. This makes it necessary to bring the latter in as small a compass as possible.

If the Sea itself is not to be the refrigeratory, you must then have a cistern for that purpose: which must be supplied by a pump from the Sea.

Qu. whether instead of having the cistern to enclose the worm as in the common distilling apparatus, it might not be better to have it placed above the worm, and not connected with it: but contrived so as to let the water drop upon the worm? In this case the worm might be cooled externally with (woollen) rags, to retain the dropping water, and the refrigeration would be formed not by the application of a body of fluid, so much as by the act of evaporation.

What you have to do then, seems to be to set about experimenting which you may do without the timepiece as well as with, in order to determine this problem.

The heat of the atmosphere (which must be any degree from the lowest to the highest that has ever been known) the degree of heat of the *focus*. The area of that surface (of the fluid) to which the heat is first applied (i.e. the lower surface of the fluid from whence the bubbles begin to rise) and the area of the upper surface, being given, to find that bulk and shape of the refrigerating apparatus, that shall be least *cumbersome* (most compact) so as to answer the purpose: that is, that shall acquire least *momentum* by the agitation of the ship, so as to bear upon the common fulcrum of the whole machine that is kept suspended.

N.B. In this view that apparatus (time piece refrigeratory etc. and all together) seems to be in point of form the most compact (least cumbersome) in short most commodious that can be inscribed within the smallest globe (sphere) (that will admitt the smallest sphere to circumscribe it.

In many of these things ' I speak as a child' (as St Paul sayeth)— therefore thou must make allowances. What thou hast to do therefore seemeth, to be, to get one of your including cubes (which may be of tin to save expence) fit to it a worm of tin (which let be composed of many pieces, viz to make it longer or shorter also an inner cube with pieces of nails and brass etc. to represent the time piece, and go to work. Put into it one of the Drs. Thermometers if he will give you leave.[2] Tin canisters I think can not be very dear.

[3] Doubtless Dr Simmons.

You must keep the room in 100 degrees of heat at least—better if 110.

Aether is but 20d. an oz. and an oz. is almost 2 oz. measures of water. I have bought an oz. at that rate at Corbyn's in Holborn almost opposite to Lyon Street.

Written between 7 in the morning and ½ after 8.

Q.S.P. has not yet heard about the money in the Stocks. Mr. D has taken instructions from me to write. Q.S.P. is satisfied yes but it is without /sort of/ reason. He loves to go hand over hand in every thing. Vague report mentioned 70,000. This he has reduced by random conjecture to 30,000, and these are his grounds.

Qu. How could your boiling a naked watch-spring determine any thing about its elasticity? nobody suspected it would lose all its elasticity and become like a bit of cheese did they? besides did you try the elasticity of it while boiling? It might lose the requisite degree of elasticity (whatever that is) while in that degree of heat and recover it in that of the atmosphere. Remember I speak as a child.

A raw hint, unripened will never be looked ⟨on⟩ as a discovery— Something must have been done in the way of experiment, I should conceive; or at least it were better it should, (to stand as a foundation for) a claim to discovery. The mere idea, you may find many to contest with you. The business is to do something to demonstrate its practicability. You *then* make it your own.

Mem. If the machine is never to be opened during the whole voyage, the variation in the pressure of the atmosphere will not signify a rush with respect to heat of the cooling fluid, because the air will be always of the density the atmosphere was of when the vessels were filled[?]—I should have said *closed*.

Ten 000. Devils take—what (shall I say) my negligence or my ill-fortune? a piece of one and a piece of t'other. Poore is out of town—no wonder I have not been able to find him—He went on Monday, and probably will not be back these three weeks. However he knows nothing about refrigeration: and concerning clock-making I think we have got information enough from him for the present. Did I ever tell you what Poore told me that nice [?] Astronomers observed that the Sun shining upon their Quadrants played the deuce with the divisions? However our time [?] keeper itself will bid defiance to the Sun—but then the refrigeratory water must be kept shaded from it. For in the Sunshine the heat is sometimes as high as 120 which is I believe about the heat of boiling Æther.

Ay, do come to town—there's a good boy, and let us talk these matters over. You might walk, or come by a Gravesend boat—My cursed book will not be out the soonest these 10 days—Come and read over with me the preface. If you let me know you will come to town, then I will send you your things forthwith.

Did you ever hear of the Balancier? it is a contrivance I think to remedy the loss of force which the spring undergoes as it unwinds itself. This the Balancier does I think by winding the spring up somehow or other every minute, which it does in an imperceptible instant of time—i.e. practically speaking without loss of time. In this and the gridiron contrivance to correct the effects of unequal expansion, consists as I understand from Poore every thing material that has been done by Harrison etc. But a-propos. Comyns on Watchmaking[3]—a very modern book—he a very ingenious and well known man—in 4to this will tell us every thing.

11 o'clock. Maddison has this moment sent a message to me which makes it necessary I should have his notes of Blacks lectures within '3 or 4 days.' my word stands engaged—my word I say stands engaged—let me have them therefore *without fail.* voila un additional motive to you to come up now rather than a few days hence; since it will save the expence of carriage, postage, etc. on the notes.

My tooth-ach is in a manner gone.

157

To Samuel Bentham

25 March 1776 (Aet 28)

How it mortifies me my dear Sam, that I can not make one in your happy circle!—and what is more, how it shames me to think of my having neglected thus long to answer Mrs. Davies's obliging invitation! That I must forego too the only opportunity I may have till I don't know when of 'throwing myself at' my adorable Mrs. Wise's 'feet'[2]! Well—I must bear the mortification as well as I can, and like Sr. Anthony Branville in the Discovery[3] 'defer that happi-

[3] This is Alexander *Cumming* (1733–1814), an Edinburgh man who became a celebrated watchmaker in Bond Street and a Fellow of the Royal Society. He published *The Elements of Clock and Watch Work* in 1766.

157. [1] B.M. II: 17–18. Autograph.
Addressed: 'To / Mr. Sam. Bentham / at the King's Dock Yard / near Rochester.' Postmark: '25 MR'.
Doubtless written at Lincoln's Inn.
[2] Mrs Sarah Wise was Mrs Davies's sister.
[3] This play by Mrs Frances Sheridan was first produced at Drury Lane in 1763, with Garrick in the part of Sir Anthony Branville.

ness to another opportunity.' However I have got her name, written in her own fair hand: that is something. I shall not fail to consult those who are learned in these matters, and to imprint on it as many kisses as shall be deemed suitable to the occasion. But this 'desperate fellow of a husband'? I shudder at the very thoughts of him: you know we pretty fellows have a mortal antipathy to those desperate fellows. You have heard by this time of my having got a glympse of him: I have been quaking like an aspen leaf ever since. You heard I suppose how he surprized me in my shirt. Here is an end to my scribbling—I have met with two or three chagrins which incapacitate me utterly from scribbling—make my excuses as well as you can to the Ladies: Moreover I am under the Surgeons hands for my face; and am likely to have a tedious job of it.

The last of my Book went to the Press on Saturday.[4]

I have looked into the last Longitude Act (14 G. 3) and find such powers given by it as answer our wishes powers to give rewards for improvements and inventions tending only to the *discovery*: with a view to defraying the expences of the more costly and tedious experiments. Only the moneys received on this account are to be counted into the money received for the compleat discovery.[5]

Adieu—tell me how you go on experimenting—Thanks for the verses—I can say no more.

Monday 25 March 1776.

158

TO JOHN LIND

27–28 March–1 April 1776 (Aet 28)

A word or two I must trouble you with on the subject of the 3d. and 4th. Letters of Attilius. I would have called on you: but I

---

[4] *A Fragment on Government.*
[5] See letter 152, n. 1.

158. [1] B.M. II: 79–80. Autograph. Docketed by Lind[?]: 'London | | 1776. Bentham. On his right to the Definitions of Liberty and Right. With one from Mr. Wilson to him enclosed.'

This letter concerns the use Lind made of certain definitions of Bentham's in some letters he published in *The Gazetteer* signed 'Attilius'. They began to appear there on 2 March 1776. The fourth letter appeared on Wednesday 27 March and the fifth on Friday 29 March. The eighth and last appeared on 9 April. They were shortly afterwards published (anonymously) as *Three Letters to Dr. Price, containing Remarks on his Observations on the Nature of Civil Liberty, the Principles of Government, and the Justice and Policy of the War with America. By a Member of Lincoln's Inn, F.R.S., F.S.A.*

am detained at home, expecting a Surgeon whom I have appointed to consult with about my face.

In these 3d. and 4th. letters you give a definition of the word *Liberty*: in those that are to follow you mean to give a definition of the word *Right*. For the latter you meant to quote my book; had it been out time enough: which it would have been, if you had waited to publish your attack on the Dr. all together in form of a pamphlet, as you first intended. With respect to the former you did not that I recollect express any such intention.

My title to the one of them is much the same as to the other. It may have been half a year or a year or more. I do not precisely recollect the time, since I communicated to you a kind of discovery I thought I had made, that the idea of Liberty, imported nothing in it that was positive: that it was merely a negative one: and that accordingly I defined it *'the absence of restraint'*: I do not believe I then added *'and constraint'*: that has been an addition of your own. You mentioned it to me t'other day with this addition.

Bentham says that this book has just come out in letter 173 dated 5 July 1776. The main part of this letter then was presumably written on 27 or 28 March, and the last paragraph on Monday 1 April.

The letters were an attack upon *Observations on the Nature of Civil Liberty, the Principles of Government, and the Justice and Policy of the War with America* (1776), by the economist and moral philosopher Dr Richard Price (1723–91), a nonconformist minister. This work which reached nine editions that same year is regarded as one of the inspirers of the Declaration of Independence. It was out early in the year, for it is reviewed in the *Gentleman's Magazine* for February. On page 42 of this work Price criticizes Lind's *Remarks on the Principal Acts of the 13th Parliament of Great Britain etc.* for claiming (re taxation of the Americans) that a people has no rights other than those allowed by its civil governors. Bentham complains at Lind's using the definitions of *Liberty* and *Right* which Bentham presents in his *Fragment on Government* before its publication, thus seeming to be their originator. The *Fragment* appears to have come out towards the end of April (cf. letter 160). When Lind's letters appeared in book form he made a number of complimentary references to the *Fragment*, and met Bentham's request for an acknowledgement as follows:

'That liberty is nothing positive, that it means only the absence of *restraint*, was an idea first suggested to me by a very worthy and ingenious friend, whose name I am not now permitted to mention. In turning this idea over in my mind, I thought the definition imperfect; a man may be compelled to *do* as well as to *forbear* an act; liberty therefore I thought meant the absence of *constraint*, as well as of *restraint*. I mentioned this some time after to my friend from whom I received the original idea; he had already perceived the defect, and had substituted the general term of *coercion* to the partial one of restraint. It was on many accounts necessary to make this acknowledgement; on one more especially, that this notion of liberty will make a leading principle in a work which this gentleman means, and I hope soon, to give the world. In that work, whenever it appears, Dr. Price may learn, what he already professes to teach, without having learned—to give "correct ideas", "distinct and accurate views"' (pp. 16–17, footnote).

Bentham himself prepared a note on Richard Hey's *Observations on Civil Liberty* (another rejoinder to Price) for possible inclusion in Lind's pamphlet (cf. U.C. LXIX: 57–68).

In the mean time I had discovered the defect: and had changed in my papers, the word *restraint* into *coercion*, as that which would include both *restraint* and *constraint*. This new term I then communicated to you, and you have adopted it in preference to the other two.

Whither you will say does all this lead? To this, that you should find some means of exculpating me from a charge of plagiarism I may otherwise stand exposed to. The Definition of Liberty is one of the corner stones of my system: and one that I know not how to do without. I must make use of it; and perhaps at no long time hence. When I do, my enemies (of whom I shall not fail to have abundance) will be objecting to me that what I have said is stolen from a man who wrote in a newspaper. The disproof of that charge is what will come with a much better grace from you than from myself. What I expect from you in that view then is simply this: not that you should make any acknowledgement about the matter in a newspaper—that would be preposterous: but only that when you publish the letters together in form of a pamphlet you should insert a note to this effect. viz. that the idea you found occasion to give of liberty you took from a person who has not permitted you to give his name.

Time was when I knew no distinction of property where you were concerned: that time you have chosen should be at an end. I have still the same opinion of your honour that I ever had: and to that honour I trust for your doing what is necessary, to save mine.

As to any hints that it may be within my capacity to afford you without prejudice to myself, you have more convincing proofs, I hope, than mere assurances of my readiness ⟨to give⟩ ⟨. . .⟩ ⟨. . .⟩ ⟨. . .⟩⟨. . .⟩[2] such as they are to make you master of them.

Forgive my plainness—having once banished the language of reserve and ceremony, I find it impossible to resume it.

Linc. Inn. Monday Morng.

What I can tell you without ceremony and without compliment is that I admire your letters much, and am impatient for their continuance.

[2] These words have been scored out.

159

To Samuel Bentham

before 17 April 1776 (Aet 28)

Take an account of the number of the Shirts and Stocks.

Let the Stocks that are worth it be new taped.

If any Shirts should be found to want new wristbanding or collaring let it be done with rather purer cloth than that of the shirt itself—especially wristbanding.

Collaring they certainly will want several of them.

Your glasses (pox on the man) are not yet done he says he has orders by him that he has not been able to execute these three weeks—He says they will be done by Thursday. Mr. D perhaps may take them.

There is a Pound of Aether it came to £1-4-3d. Bottle excluded. The man told me Aether condensed more readily than water.

160

To Samuel Bentham

17 April 1776 (Aet 28)

Let me have my stockings as soon as you can. I have none to wear that are decent.

Wilson is ambitious of the honour of your correspondence. He would be very happy to receive a letter from you though it were only a blank piece of paper: to speak the truth that is all I believe he wishes for. To explain the mystery, you are to know he wishes to try whether a letter would reach here that should be directed simply to 'G. Wilson Esqr. Cook's Court London' in order to diminish as much as may the trouble of writing Franks.—You may bestow on him therefore the value of half a sheet of paper full of nothing by the return of post—at least do not say any thing to him

159. [1] B.M. II: 22. Autograph. Docketed: 'I.B. April 1776 Capitulation.' The last word is upside down.

That this letter is earlier than that which follows (dated 17 April) seems to be indicated by the various references to Samuel's 'glasses'. (These were presumably the 'Ink Glasses' mentioned in letter 151, dated 22–23 February.)

160. [1] B.M. II: 19–20. Autograph. Docketed: 'I.B. April 17th 1776.'

Addressed: 'To / Mr. S. Bentham / at the King's Dock Yard / near Rochester.' Postmark: '17 AP'.

or me that is of any consequence for fear the experiment should not succeed.

I have been hard at work for your honour upon the Memorial[2]: but I must have Comyns ere I can go on. In short I must learn Watchmaking I see: in order to understand the manner in which your apparatus can be adapted to the other work: and in order to see how much of Harrison's[3] work it may supersede. This I doubt will not be much: no more than that part which is calculated to obviate the effects of heat and cold, and which he calls the *Thermometer-kirb*: which makes but a small part of the whole Machinery. I have got an account of the Principles of Hs's Timekeeper published by the B. of Longitude: as likewise an account of the going of it published by Maskelyne under ye. direction of the Board[4]: But the first I cannot possibly understand by the Plates that accompany it.

You tell me nothing of your having learnt the Mechanism of a Watch by the Dictionaries: nor of your having consulted your friend the Watchmaker. I see nothing in your papers but what we have talked over together. I was in hopes you would have particularised matters a little more. I find the labouring oar is to rest almost wholly upon me.

Those I mentioned are all the publications of the Board of Longitude, except Tables of Astronomical Observations.

Dr. Mulford is in Town—I have a notion he understands the mechanism of a Watch. If so, I will make him teach it me.

I saw Mr. Davies this morning (Apr. 17th) Wednesday, he tells me Mrs. D. talks of coming to Town: if so send me *Comyns* by her: together with my Stockings: and any Shirts and Stocks if any of them are done.

When she returns I can take that opportunity to send you your glasses and the Fragment: as her stay will probably not be long.

As for your coming up, I see no immediate occasion for it. I find I must work up the whole by myself as far as I can, and if I should be at a stand it will then be time enough to consult you, by Letter or in person.

My Fragment is advertised for Tomorrow—price 3s. 6d. I expect a few copies of it to day.

[2] On Samuel's horological experiments (see letter 152, n. 1).

[3] See letter 72, n. 3.

[4] The first of these 'Accounts' was *The principles of Mr. Harrison's time-keeper, with plates of the same.* Published by order of the Commissioners of Longitude, 1767. Nevil Maskelyne (1732–1811), Astronomer-Royal since 1765, had published in 1767 *An Account of the going of Mr. John Harrison's Watch at the Royal Observatory.* . . .

It is possible I may send a Copy of it or two abroad—1 to D'Alembert, and one perhaps to Morellet whom you do not know. In this view I am scribbling some French Letters.[5]

Q.S.P. knows of the Longitude Scheme: and is very well satisfied about it. He even offer'd to go himself and get for me the Books I mentioned. Madam was yesterday at the Dutchess's Trial.[6] Sir called upon me and we dined together at a Tavern.

161

To Samuel Bentham

26–30 April 1776 (Aet 28)

Friday April 26. 1776

As ill luck would have it, Dr. Mulford went out of town on the sudden yesterday sennight, a fortnight or more before, as he told me, he had proposed. I was told however at his lodgings that he talked of returning again in a short time. I wrote to him last night to know when. I know of some business he has, that will probably bring him to town within these three weeks.

Mr. Wise was in town a few days ago, and brought me a Letter from Mrs. Wise.

Your letter to Wilson came to hand.

As to keeping accounts, for your own satisfaction the measure would by no means be a bad one. At present perhaps it might be of no great use. But if your money concerns should ever come to be a little more complicated, it might be absolutely necessary. As to shewing them to him, that is quite another thing. C'est une servitude a quoi si j'etois vous je ne voudrois guere me soumettre. Cependant, le meilleur parti peut-être ne seroit pas de s'en excuser

---

[5] Bentham did not send any such letters to D'Alembert and Morellet at this time. But in 1778 he did send each of them a copy of the *Fragment* along with his pamphlet, *A View of the Hard Labour Bill* (see letters 249, 250, 252).

[6] This was the trial for bigamy of Elizabeth Chudleigh, Countess of Bristol, and self-styled Duchess of Kingston (1720–88), which had begun on 15 April. She was found guilty on the 22nd.

161. [1] B.M. II: 21 and U.C. cxxxiv: 2. Autograph. Docketed: 'I.B. April 26th 1776.'

Addressed: 'To Mr. Bentham / at his Majesty's Dock Yard / near / Rochester'. Postmark: '30 AP'.

This letter has survived in two parts, that which is now in the University College collection having apparently been separately filed by Samuel Bentham because of its mainly mathematical and scientific content.

formellement: mais de n'en dire rien: et s'il jamais lui vienne en l'esprit de demander qu'on les lui fasse voir les comptes, ce que je ne crois pas, alors et pas avant de s'en excuser. D'apres l'experience que vous en avez eu, vous devez savoir combien il ecrit d'apres l'humeur, et combien peu d'apres reflection. Il s'etoit enrhume about that time: and was very low spirited: and he told me he was dissatisfied with every thing and every body. Il lui manquoit un objet to vent his spleen upon: (et le hazard fit qu'il (vous rencontroit) se prit a vous.) Il en trouva un: et le hazard fit que cet objet, c'etoit vous.

Saturday

Poore est en Ville—je l'ai recontre hier: he told me he came to town the day before.

Q.S.P. is mad. He is going not only to take a Country-House, of which my concern is perhaps rather the pretext than the cause; but also to make an addition to that in town. The front of the old part is going to be pulled down for the sake of making an addition of a few feet by means of a Bow: And this at a time when Madam charges and he owns that he has not got a coat to his back fit to be seen, and when his miserable guests are obliged to go away with half a dinner for want of greens to the Salt Beef.

This I had from the Alderman[2] yesterday with whom I spent the day and part of the beginning of this. His wife was fetched away by her Father into the country: and he and I sung old Rose—and burnt the Bellow[3] till past midnight.

Monday.

I shall send you a copy of the Fragment, together with your Glasses if they are done, by Thursday's Coach. I stay till Thursday in order to hear if you want any thing else, that I may send it by the same conveyance.

Mr. D. tells me you are about an improvement to your Boat. I should be glad to hear some thing about it.

[4]La mathematique (tout *utile* et tout *vraie* qu'elle est) n'est (cependant) d'aucun *usage* ni d'aucune *verité* qu'autant qu'elle est applicable aux corps particuliers. L'objet de cette science c'est la

---

[2] Richard Clark, for whom see letter 62, n. 1.

[3] Wright, *English Dialect Dictionary*, cites a Northamptonshire glossary for the phrase, as Bentham uses it, meaning rejoicing at the end of a long and tedious task. Cf. letter 219.

[4] The remainder of the letter is in U.C. cxxxiv: 2.

quantitè [. . .?] C'est d'eux seuls que l'idèe de la quantitè est tiré
venue. C'est *dans* /en/ eux seuls, ou dans leurs modes (c'est à dire
encore en eux) que la quantitè même existe. 'Dire que' . . . etc. (a
proposition it was his purpose to represent as being false) dit
Montesquieu, 'c'est dire qu'avant qu'on eu tracé de cercle, tous ses
rayons n'etaient pas egaux.[5] Paradoxe malheureuse! comme s'il y
avait une chose appellé cercle, qui eut rayons *egaux* avant qu⟨il y⟩
eut des *rayons*.

Chemistry [6]

Think of what follows—It is a new consideration but one that I
am apt to think it will ⟨be⟩ necessary to attend to.

In regard to the business of trans[. . .?] heat and cold, it seems
that with respect to any given body not only its *conducting* power
is to be considered, but its retaining power. Silver, for example,
however it be with regard to conducting sooner or not so soon, is
found to retain heat longer than China.

To come to particulars. Take a Silver Tea Pot, and a China one
of the same dimensions and standing on the same table. Pour into
them at the same time boiling water. The masses of water in each
Tea Pot, and the Tea pots themselves will, I suppose be thereupon
/at first of/ at an equal degree of heat. If not, let them be made so. Let
them stand on the same Board. The China Pot and the water in it
will cool I suppose three or four times as fast as the Silver one.

I made this observation from a Silver Tea Pot of my neighbour
Fitzherberts. Suppose we were to make the experiment with
Simmon's Thermometers. It would not be difficult I suppose to
meet with a metal Tea Pot. You will say that one can hardly expect
to meet with a China one of the same dimensions. But take *two*
China ones, one of dimensions which you suppose more favourable
to cooling than those of the tea-pot, the other of dimensions less
favourable, and if the result is nearly alike in both, that will establish the fact as well. If Simmons's thermometers won't do it we
might get it tried[?] at Nairne's.

Perhaps Silver may retain heat longer than China on account of
the former's being denser: it is specifically heavier, containing a
greater quantity of matter in the same space. If that be so, the
Rule is that the time during which bodies retain heat is as their
specific gravity.

[5] *De l'esprit des Lois*, i, i.
[6] This sub-heading is a later addition.

Tuesday

By forgetfulness I have let a day slip. I shall therefore for reasons above given stay till Friday before I send your things. Mr. Davis called on me this morning to take leave. He tells me my Father complains heavily of your silence. The Glasses are done. I called at the house just now and saw them.

162

To Samuel Bentham

1–2 May 1776 (Aet 28)

Mathematics. Pure. Use of[2]

Wedny. 1st May

As there is nothing strictly speaking but bodies *that exists* mathematical propositions, if true of any thing, must be true of bodies. For this same reason they cannot be true of any thing else but bodies. They may be true, it will be said of motions. Right[?]— but what are motions? If any thing, they are motions of some bodies. To be true of motions therefore, they must still be true of bodies: true of some bodies (to wit) that are in motion. N.B. When I mentioned bodies I should have added portions of space. Propositions in Trigonometry which are of use in the measurement of distant bodies are exemplified in great measure in portions of space to wit determined by reference to Bodies.[3]

Of consequence there is no single proposition in Mathematics but what if true at all is true of some particular (sort of) body. If then it be, mention (point out) that sort of body, and if motion be concerned that sort of motion of that sort of body. Point out the use it may be of to know that it is true of that sort of motion or that sort of body; that is point out the use that one may be enabled to put that sort of body to (either by giving it position or by putting it in motion) from knowing the proposition in question to be true. In doing this you will have exemplified the proposition and shown its use. Tis by this means and this alone that you can have given

162. [1] U.C. cxxxv: 1 and B.M. II: 23. Autograph.
  Addressed: 'To / Mr. Bentham / at his Majesty's Dock Yard / near Rochester.' Over the address is written: 'sing loud / sing loud.'
  This letter like letter 161 (cf. n. 1) has survived in two parts.
  [2] This subheading is a later addition.
  [3] The last seven words have been added in the margin.

/assigned/ the specific motive /inducement/ that a man may have for submitting to the fatigue that is necessary to enable him to apprehend it.

[4]Thursday May 2d

I sympathize with you, my dear Sam, most cordially.

I cannot say I am in a very comfortable state of mind myself: and that is the reason why you will not have received the Longitude Memorial as you have desired and I could wish. I have need of thy presence to animate me; as thou hast of mine to comfort thee. I am at present in a state of great inertia, and *abbassement*: however I am not wholly idle.

You had as good not send your Letter to Q.S.P. till I talk to him —that shall be tomorrow. I shall tell him the effect his letter had on you: and that will do more good than any thing you can say yourself.

163

To Samuel Bentham

3 May 1776 (Aet 28)

Linc. Inn Friday May 3 1776

My dear Sam

The Watchman has just called Ten, and Wilson is with me: so that whether I shall be able to say to thee all that I would say to thee, which however is not much, I know not. I saw my Father this morning he was coming down Southn. Buildings from Staples Inn. As I wanted you know to have a few words with him alone, I thought that would be as good an opportunity as any, and I might take the occasion to make him the compliment of inviting him up. So I open'd the window, bow'd and beckoned to him.

When I mentioned to him the state of mind into which his letter had thrown you, he said what might be expected and what was *proper* on the occasion, that he could not be happy, if he knew of your being otherwise, and so forth: when I mentioned these words which you took amiss, he said he did not remember any such words and seemed inclined if it had been possible to deny them. I said he could not suppose it could answer any purpose to invent such words

[4] The remainder of the letter is in B.M. II: 23.

163. [1] B.M. II: 24–25. Autograph.

Addressed: 'To / Mr. Bentham / at the King's Dock Yard / near Rochester / Single Sheet.' Postmark: '3 MA'.

to impute if they were not really in the letter. I added that he neither surely could be surprized, nor ought he to be displeased that what he said to you in the way of disapprobation should make a deep impression: on the contrary it would be a much more reasonable ground of concern if you were to treat it lightly and hear it with indifference. I likewise took occasion to introduce (with a little variation in the words) what you had said in your last but one, that it was a cruel stroke upon you to receive such language as you mentioned from a quarter from whence you would naturally expect encouragement. I told him withal, that I imagined his letter was written at a time when he was out of order—This he seemed to admitt: and talked in half-serious half-ironical way, of writing to you to beg your pardon.

We then enter'd upon the subject of the accounts—I told him, that supposing the measure to be right, there was no occasion to force it upon you in this manner, and that a simple recommendation would answer the purpose much better. To that he replied that he had been talking to you about it at different times for these two or three years and had not been able to prevail with you to oblige him in that particular.

Really, entre nous, my dear Sam, I don't see the extreme hardship and difficulty in it that you do, nor do I see, considering what a point he makes of it how you can avoid complying with his desires, without subjecting yourself to the reproach of obstinacy.

I could not say any thing against the utility of the practise, nor could I possibly say any thing that could have any chance of persuading him (or indeed any body else) of that extreme difficulty which you say you had in it. There are not many ways in which you can have it in your power to oblige him: and when what he wishes you to do, and that so strenuously, is what is *apparently* at least to your advantage, I really see not what you can have to say that will appear plausible against it. He always has been and always shall be he says ready to do every thing in his power to contribute to your happiness, etc., etc., etc., and in one of the very few occasions that you can have of doing any thing to oblige him, will you peremptorily refuse it? If you ever have any thing to ask him for he will be flinging this in your teeth—'no—you will do nothing for me —I won't do any thing for you'—And what can you have to say in your defence.

Wilson to whom I shewed your letter thinks you ought to comply: he smiles at your objections, and without pronouncing them groundless thinks them however rather refined than satisfactory.

I can see I must own the extreme hardship of taking out your pocket book at some certain time, either immediately before you go to bed for example, or immediately after you get up or immediately after dinner etc., and if you have happened to lay out any money since the last of these times, to set it down, if you have had no intermediate opportunity of doing it. If it should happen you have laid out nothing within that period, why then the trouble is saved. Adieu—here I must make an end.

N.B. I do not understand that he expects to see your accounts, but only that you should keep them for your own satisfaction—I will keep mine—if you will your's.

164

To Samuel Bentham

7 May 1776 (Aet 28)

I wrote to thee on Friday—why hast thou not answer'd me?

Inclosed I send thee a letter I intend to send to Miss D.[2] I received one from her on Thursday.

There are some slips of the pen in it. These I find upon looking it over in a place where I had no opportunity to correct it.

Take a copy—but let me have it if possible by return of the Post. It has been delay'd a day already by accident: and I should be sorry to delay it longer if I could avoid it.

Dr. Mulford comes to town some day this week: and I shall take the opportunity to make him teach me Watchmaking.

Least it should have miscarried my last letter was to persuade you to keep accounts. I am now in haste, I cannot write more particularly.

Tuesday May 7. 1776. Linc. Inn.

164. [1] B.M. II: 26. Autograph.
Addressed: 'To / Mr. Bentham / at the Kings Dock Yard / near Rochester / Two Sheets.' Postmark: '7 MA'.
[2] Doubtless Miss Dunkley.

165

To Samuel Bentham

9 May 1776 (Aet 28)

Go now to Battle? Why yes I think you ought for the reasons that you mention—When you go with Mrs. D. I shall go too—You may remember it was agreed between us of old that you should get the first peep of the Archangel[2] by yourself.

As to expence G. Guy[3] has two legs, has not he? and you have as many—I should humbly conceive those four legs might serve to carry you two without the assistance of any others.

As for coming to town from Battle I see no use for that—You would in that case I suppose come by the Post Coach. But if you walked back to Battle you might in the course of a few days or a week afterwards walk up to town by your own dear self. G.G. would be only an incumbrance.

Dr. M.[4] is in town: and will teach me watchmaking. Poore would do the same: but I choose rather to have it from the Dr.

I received yesterday a doz. of Burgundy as a present from Mr. and Mrs. Wise. I was sorry for it—I can't say but it gave me pain to think they should have put themselves to the expence. I have sent a letter of thanks to night of which you may possibly hear from them.

I am grown stupid—Adieu—I have 150 things to talk to you about, but there is no doing it upon paper. One thing I should have told you of before—Wise had been telling me of something that he had tried to do or wished to do—I don't very well remember what— but I believe it was with a Mrs. Worge[?][5] that is a neighbour of his—while Mrs. Wise was in the straw—Oh, say I, I find you are a man of gallantry—No, says he, it's your Brother that is a man of gallantry. How so, says I—He then mentioned your being pretty frequently in Mrs. D's[6] Bedchamber—That should not *be*:—you must take care of those appearances—or it will raise a talk to her prejudice.

---

165. [1] B.M. II: 28–29. Autograph.

Addressed: 'To / Mr. Bentham / at the King's Dock Yard / near Rochester.' Postmark: '9 M'.

At Battle was the home of Robert Wise and his wife Sarah Nairne (sister to Mrs Davies). See the address in letter 175, n. 1.

[2] See letter 149, n. 5.   [3] See letter 196, n. 10.
[4] John Mulford.   [5] Unidentified.
[6] Elizabeth Davies.

Thursday May 9th 1776

There are some who praise my Fragment most extravagantly—
I am to be in the H. of Lords tomorrow to hear a debate on American affairs.[7]

Q.S.P. went yesterday to see after my Archangel[8] and were to return to day—But I have good reason to think that it will end in smoke.

166

To Samuel Bentham

15 May 1776 (Aet 28)

Ay, do my dear Sam, come up—on Friday as thou sayest—I shall be glad to see thee—A very good opportunity of learning Watchmaking has presented itself to me—and I shall probably have availed myself of it before you come. R. King at G. Coffee House is a Watchmaker by Trade, and has some Watch '*motions*' by him which he has engaged to take to pieces for my instruction— the Dr. referred me to him—He himself (viz. the Dr.) could not undertake the job—And when you come up we may very likely take a lecture together.

Shall I tell thee? Yes verily I will—There is to be a Board of Longitude, I understand, on Saturday and I hope to be at it with my memoir—I *hope* I say if possible—I am working double tides for that purpose—I am not absolutely determined whether it would be better for you to be there or not. However, in case it should be determined for you being there—you had better be provided with a decent suit of cloaths to appear in viz: your best—I don't mean the French ones. Q.S.P. will be in the country Friday and Saturday, so that you have nothing to fear from him.

I shall have to two or three of the Board a recommendation

---

[7] This debate was opened by the Duke of Manchester on the occasion of the evacuation of Boston by the British forces under General Howe. Among the speakers whom Bentham may have heard were the Marquess of Rockingham and Lord Shelburne (*Parliamentary History*, xviii, 1345 ff).

[8] Presumably Sarah Stratton (see letter 151, n. 1).

166. [1] B.M. II: 27. Autograph.

Addressed: 'To / Mr. Bentham / at his Majesty's Dock Yard / near Rochester.'
Postmark: '15 MA'.

from Forster[2] of Colchester—a much more strenuous one than I should get from Poore. Poore however is in Town and I shall make what use I can of him.

Wednesday May 15. 1776.

My love to Mrs D.

Make an exact drawing (a neat one, fit to show) of the apparatus for winding up and regulating without admitting the Air; and bring it with you. The Commissioners are most of them stupid fellows, I understand, and will suppose nothing. Get if possible the proper names for the several parts of it. Call at Nairne's if you can and get the name of his new ⟨. . .⟩ hinge—borrow one of them too if you can to produce—You might even say what it was for.

167

To Samuel Bentham

22 May 1776 (Aet 28)

No letter from Dr. Smith[2]—This is rather unfortunate—however Mr. Foster promises to let me know by letter as soon as ever he does hear from him—Mr. Foster leaves Town to-morrow—He has asked him to go and see him at Colchester this summer.

The news your note contained gave me much concern as doubtless it ⟨did you.⟩ However no concern of ours can mend the matter—

[2] Nathaniel Forster (1726–90), a distinguished writer on economic matters, who had published in 1767 *An Enquiry into the present high Price of Provisions.* He was a fellow of Balliol College and rector of All Saints', Colchester, the living previously held by the Rev. Dr John Abbot, first husband of Bentham's stepmother. It was Forster who introduced Bentham to Mrs Abbot at Oxford before she had met Jeremiah Bentham (cf. Bowring, x, 61–62). The acquaintanceship with Forster had recently been renewed through John Lind. Forster had for some years been working on an index to the House of Commons Journals. He was a warm but not uncritical admirer of the *Fragment on Government,* as we learn from two letters to his cousin the Rev. Peter Forster, dated June 1777 (B.M. Add. Ms. 11277: 49–50). Bentham visited Forster at Colchester in August 1778, when Forster offered to work under Bentham as a disciple (cf. letter 269). For further information see Bentham's letter to Bowring of 30 January 1827 (Bowring, x, 55–65).

167. [1] B.M. II: 30. Autograph. Docketed by Jeremy Bentham: 'I.B. May 22 1776.'
Addressed: 'To / Mr. Bentham / at his Majesty's Dock Yard / near Rochester.' Postmark: '22 MA'.
It seems from this letter that Bentham did not finish the Memorial for the Board of Longitude meeting on Saturday 18 May (cf. letter 166).

[2] Probably one of the members of the Board of Longitude whom Nathaniel Forster was approaching on behalf of Samuel's longitude scheme (cf. letter 166). Perhaps John Smith (see letter 40, n. 5) who had been Savilian Professor of Geometry at Oxford since 1766, and whom Forster would probably have known at Balliol.

therefore let's away with it. I did not rise till after 12 today. however I have made some advances in the Memorial: and hope to make further ere night is over.

Mr. Foster fore warned me that Dr. Smith was a 'shatter brained fellow'—I hope not so shatter-brained as utterly to neglect an application of this sort—I should think he would not were it only on Foster's account with whom I understand he has been for a great many years in perfect intimacy.

Wednesday May . . . 1776.
Linc. Inn.

168

To Jeremiah Bentham

23 May 1776 (Aet 28)

Linc. Inn Thursday 23d. May 1776
Hond. Sir

I am sorry the not seeing me yesterday was a disappointment to you—had I understood that you made a point of it I would certainly have waited on you. Whether it was that I mistook you when I was with you, or that you have since alter'd your intentions, I laid my account on finding you at Q.S.P. to day; where it was my intention to have waited on you, had not your letter informed me of your having left it. I will wait on you without fail on Saturday; and probably go down with you to Kingston.

Russel[2] does not intend parting with his Horse. I have looked with Mr. Lind at the Horse which Burton the Stable-keeper near Lincoln's Inn has to sell at 25 Guineas. The Horse seemed by no means a bad one, but Mr. Lind thought not so good an one as might probably be had elsewhere for the money, and Burton did not seem disposed to take a farthing less.

Another string which I thought I had to my Bow has also failed

---

168. [1] B.M. I: 31–32. Autograph. Docketed by Jeremiah Bentham: 'Fils Jeremy Lr. datd. 23d. May 1776.' Postmark: '23 MA'.

Jeremiah Bentham was looking for lodgings near the home of Miss Stratton in Ripley (Surrey), whence Jeremy could pay court to her. Doubtless Miss Stratton and her mother, Mrs Brickenden, were supposed to believe the proximity coincidental (see letter 151). George Wilson entered the scheme now or later, and rooms were eventually found for the two of them in Fetcham near Leatherhead (see letter 173). The horse Bentham was anxious to obtain was intended for service in the courtship.

[2] Unidentified. Possibly Russel of Battle, mentioned in letter 230 (19 January 1778).

me. I heard from Sam of a very pretty mare Mr. Wise had, which
there was reason to think he would be inclined to sell. Sam and I
had accordingly concerted a Scheme on the sudden for him to go to
Battle, and fetch the Mare upon trial; to which there was no doubt
of Mr. Wise's consenting: but before he left London, he heard by
accident that the Mare has but very lately had a Foal which must
render her unfit for service for some time. As things stand I know
of no other method than that of taking one's chance at an Auction;
in which Mr. Lind will be kind enough to give me his Judgement
and assistance. Russel was telling us that he bought a Mare not
long ago at Tattersal's for £7—1s.—0—which he sold afterwards for
25 Guineas. You seem desirous to leave the matter to me: this
therefore is the course I propose to take if I hear nothing from you
to the contrary. I will as soon as it suits Mr. Lind visit the stables a
day or two before the Auction day and if I pitch upon one or two
that I think will do and will be likely to sell for a moderate price,
will endeavour to take the benefit of Mr. *Barret's* Judgement.

I fear I shall hardly be able to go to Ripley quite so soon as
Monday or Tuesday: a day or two I suppose will make no great
difference. I have no coat at present that I can ride in. My Casimeer
coat I intend to have washed and new-furbished up for that purpose. It is a kind of cloth that I know by experience will wash like
a stocking. I would not have it washed before it was wanted that it
might not grow dirty: and I did not think of its being washed so
soon. The last time I was with you, or the time before, I asked you
about going to Ripley, or contriving some plan of meeting. You took
me up rather short, saying 'it was time enough to think of that
when you were settled: that you should not be settled yet a while:'
as if importuned by what you looked upon as impatience. I therefore thought it best not to say any thing more to you on that head:
but to wait till it were your pleasure to mention it to me yourself:
which from what passed then I did not think would have been so
soon. Now I know your pleasure on that behalf I will make all
diligence to conform to it—

[Signature etc. torn away]

My respects wait upon my Mother. Sam returned to Chatham
yesterday morning.

169

To John Lind ?

12 June 1776 (Aet 28)

Chatham Wednesday 12 June 1776

When I was with you this morning I did but half my errands: I am therefore reduced to the necessity of setting down in this place to supply the omission in the midst of half a dozen people men women and children; who distract my feeble brain to such a degree that I cannot help doubting whether I shall be able to make myself intelligible.

Part of my business with you was to have begged the favour of a vote which it is in your power to give as F.R.S. It is in behalf of Mr. Nairne, an eminent Mathematical-Instrument-maker; I believe the most eminent Mathematical-Instrument-maker we have; who is to be ballotted for *tomorrow* (that is *Thursday*) sennight. I sounded Fordyce, and found than an opposition was to be made, in which he (Fordyce) seems to be engaged. The ground that Fordyce mentioned for it was a notion that some of them have taken up that it is not right any artist in that branch should be a Fellow of the R.S.: that if he were might procure an undue advantage to himself in the way of his trade by stamping his title of F.R.S. upon his instruments.

This was the *only* reason Fordyce assigned—I must own I do not see any great force in it. Nor in point of fact has any such rule been pursued. *Short* who died a few years ago F.R.S. was an Optician—Watchmakers there have been several. There was a Frenchman however excluded a week or two ago; and if I may depend on

---

169. ¹ B.M. II: 33–34. Autograph. Docketed (by Mary Bentham?): '1776 J.B. to [. . .] / June 12.'

We do not know whether this letter was in fact sent (though it seems probable that it was), nor with certainty to whom it is addressed. It seeks the support of an F.R.S. for the election to a fellowship of Edward Nairne (see letter 149, n. 4). Bentham had connections with several Fellows of the Royal Society, besides those mentioned in the letter. The reference to Dr Dargent may suggest that this letter was addressed to John Lind; for James Dargent, a London surgeon, was, as we learn from Lind's will, both his doctor and a close friend. Another possible recipient is Francis Maseres (see letter 149, n. 9).

Besides those annotated at greater length here or elsewhere, Bentham refers in this letter to the following Fellows of the Royal Society: James Short (1710–68), optician; the Hon. Charles Greville (1749–1809); Kenneth Mackenzie (1744–81), created Earl of Seaforth 1771 (Irish Peerage); Robert Mylne (1737–1811), architect, designer of the first Blackfriars Bridge, opened 1768. Irwin the water-distiller, does not appear in the list of Fellows, unless he is to be identified with Joshua Iremonger.

Fordyce, on a similar ground. His name is *D'Antic*[2]; and the objection against him was that he was a maker of glass of the sort that is used for Telescopes. Whether there was any other objection to him I have not heard.

On the other hand Nairne is known to advantage in the Society by several papers of his that have been published in the Transactions. He has more names to his Certificate than ever were known to have been annexed to a Certificate before; among the rest those of some people (Dr. Solanders[3] for one) who I understand intend ballotting against their own recommendation. I never heard of any personal objection against Nairne: but he apprehends himself to have incurred the displeasure of Banks[4] (whose irascible and vindictive temper stands upon record in the Preface to Parkinson's publication, in the affair of Cooke's last expedition with Forster[5] in which Banks you know, had it not been for a pique of his was to have been engaged, and in other instances) of Banks, I say (take breath) by not making a Marine Barometer for him so soon as was expected. If there is any thing personal in it, Nairne supposes it to originate from him. You may if you please, talk with Poore about it, but let me beg of you not to let either him or any one know that you have been applied to on the occasion by me. I would wish to keep fair with Fordyce, and some other people; which I should not do were they to know of the part I take in it. Poore esteems Nairne highly, and got Cyril Jackson[6] t'other day to introduce him to N. in order to sign his certificate. Poore heard of

---

[2] Paul Bose D'Antic (1726–84), a French physician who became an expert manufacturer of and writer on glass.

[3] Daniel Charles Solander (1736–82), a Swedish botanist, favourite pupil of the great Linnaeus, settled in England in 1760. He catalogued the natural history collection in the British Museum and in 1763 was appointed assistant librarian. He was elected F.R.S. in 1764. In 1768 he was engaged by Banks to accompany him on Cook's expedition, and later he became his secretary and librarian.

[4] Joseph Banks (1743–1820), a rich and well-known naturalist, who had accompanied Cook on his 1768 expedition to Australia in the *Endeavour*. He was elected F.R.S. in 1766. In 1778 he succeeded Sir John Pringle as President and was created a baronet in 1781.

[5] *A Journal of a Voyage to the South Seas in H.M.S. Endeavour*, by Sydney Parkinson (1773). Banks did not accompany Cook on this expedition, as had been arranged, out of dissatisfaction with the accommodation offered. Dr Johann Reinhold Forster took his place.

[6] Cyril Jackson (1746–1819) owed much of his success in life to the patronage of Dr Markham, having been at Westminster under his headmastership shortly after Bentham. From 1771–76 he was sub-preceptor to the elder sons of George III, while Markham was preceptor. Later he took holy orders and was preacher at Lincoln's Inn from 1779 to 1783, in which year he became dean of Christ Church, Oxford. He was a close friend of Charles Abbot, Bentham's stepbrother.

Nairne's being to be with me yesterday to shew me some experiments, and on that account appointed without saying any thing to me, to meet him at my Chambers: as on many accounts I did not choose to be troubled with him, as soon as N. was in, I shut my door. Poore pounded but in vain.

As for my motives for interesting myself in the affair, I must acknowledge them to be personal. I see not that the interests of science are concerned one way or another. If it appears to you that they are likely to suffer by his admission, I would by no means be understood to persist in my request. Otherwise I should be extremely glad to have contributed to his success. He has for some time past been very civil to me and my Brother: to both of us he is very attentive: and to my Brother he may be and seems disposed to be particularly useful. He is now making an Instrument that is to be subservient to my Brother's Longitude Scheme.

You might probably be able to press several into the service. Dr. Dargent, I should imagine, without difficulty. Adieu—excuse the trouble I have been giving you.

The chief if not the whole of the opposition lies in a club[7] of which Fordyce, Banks, Solander. Ld. Mulgrave,[8] Ld. Seaforth, one of the Greville's, Comyns the Watch-maker, Ramsden the Math-Instrumt. maker, Mylne the Architect, Irwin the Water-Distiller, John Hunter[9] the Surgeon cum multis aliis are members. I am also a member but have never frequented it since I have known you. Fordyce spoke of Nairne's rejection as a thing that was certain since the club had resolved it.

Nairne in consequence of my intelligence intends to get some friend to undertake for him, that he never will put F.R.S. upon any of his Instruments. Thus the great and only ostensible objection will be obviated—

You are at liberty to make what you please of the inclosed letter.

[7] Fordyce (see 84a, n. 6) introduced Bentham into this club. However, he failed (so Bentham felt) to let the others know his high opinion of Bentham, who, being less distinguished than the other members, was ill-at-ease in it (cf. Bowring, x, 133, 183).

[8] Constantine John Phipps (1744–92), second Baron Mulgrave (Irish Peerage), Captain in the Navy and politician. 1768: M.P. for Lincoln, counting as one of the 'King's friends'. 1773: Commander of the *Racehorse* in Arctic expedition. 1777: M.P. for Huntingdon and appointed one of the lords of the Admiralty. 1778: Commanded the *Courageux* in Admiral Lord Keppel's fleet—as a witness at Keppel's court-martial he supported Sir Hugh Palliser's account of the Battle of Ushant. 1784: Appointed joint paymaster general, also commissioner for Indian affairs. 1790: Created a Baron in peerage of the United Kingdom.

Samuel sought his patronage in 1778 and met him several times (see letter 248 etc).

[9] John Hunter (1728–93), the celebrated anatomist and surgeon, F.R.S. 1767,

¹⁰I shall herewith enclose you an original letter, which from the subject of it I thought you might be glad to see. It came to Mr. Davies's, this very day. The writer of it went out Master of the Isis[?], and is now as he says Lieutenant.

170

TO SAMUEL BENTHAM

22 June 1776 (Aet 28)

Q.S.P. Saturday June 22d 1776

A disappointment my dear Sam—a disappointment—I dined here on Tuesday and while we were at dinner came a letter from Mrs. ———— and Miss| |² informing us, I should say my F. and M. for I was not mentioned that they were detained by unexpected visitors, and appointing tomorrow sennight instead of last Thursday. I received your letter at Linc. Inn before I came out. How many words more I shall be able to say to you I know not. We are here all in confusion—a temporary Coachman who was hired in the room of poor Daniel who is very ill has given us the slip—We were to have set out for Richmond at 6, and now it is seven and no Coachman to be found.

I am exceedingly sorry Mr. Wise thinks of giving himself the trouble to send his Servant with the Horse to London. I had not the least idea of any such thing—I thought it would have been sent by the Carrier.

You surprize me much by your account of this second expedition that is projected—I like not the thoughts of it at all: it can not possibly be executed without an expence very unsuitable to the circumstances of all parties. Mrs. D. is by no means in a condition to bear it herself—and you are as little in a condition to treat her. Mr. W's circumstances make the best of them must be far from affluent.³ I can not comprehend why it should be necessary for him

---

¹⁰ What follows is written vertically at the edge of the first page.

170. ¹ B.M. II: 35–36. Autograph.
Addressed: 'To / Mr. Bentham / at the King's Dock Yard / near Rochester.' Postmark: '22 IV'. Stamped: 's.o.'
The meeting with Miss Stratton here mentioned as postponed, did take place on Sunday 30 June and is referred to in letter 171.
² Mrs Brickenden and her daughter Miss Stratton, whom Jeremiah Bentham hoped to catch for his son, Jeremy. The letter ends with a reference to her assets (see letter 151).
³ Mrs Davies, wife of Sam's tutor, and Mr Wise, her sister's husband.

to travel in a Post Chaise; certainly it cannot be necessary for him to saddle himself with the expence of two women all the time he stays.

Nairne's election came on yesterday—he succeeded.[4] There were 18 Black balls, and 72 white. Scarce ever was there known so great a number present and I got him 4 votes.

I will call on him on Monday about the Pelican.[5]

I must have done . . . I am called off.

Mr. Clark has enquired about the assets—They turn out to be considerably more than £25,000—how much exactly I cannot tell you.

171

To Samuel Bentham

2 July 1776 (Aet 28)

Tuesday July 2d. 1776

The Hog I understand from Nairne sets out on Thursday—By that Hog you will receive your Pelican. I am afraid the Valve has too little play though it has full as much as it should have according to your draught. Caustic Alkali will not do—It will combine with the Alcohol—I must send you some mild. Glass Tubes I could get now of any bore intermediate between those which you will see—I hope however one or other size will do—If not Nairne may possibly assist us.

I am now in great haste—I hope to write fuller tomorrow or at least the next day—Tomorrow! O ye Gods! be propitious but tomorrow! Tomorrow is to determine whether Lodgings shall be 'findable' no more than $\frac{3}{4}$ of a mile distance from Miss | |.[2] I have bought a Horse at E. Shene—a small thing too small I fear to do for a Continuance but very pretty—The price no more than 12 Guineas.

Instead of a Horse which was to have come from W. on Wednesday, came a letter of excuse on Friday in Mrs. W's hand, alledging that the Horse had got the distemper—[3]

[4] See letter 169.
[5] A vessel used for distilling liquor by fermentation.
171. [1] B.M. II: 37–38. Autograph.
Addressed: 'To / Mr. Bentham / at the King's Dock Yard / near Rochester / Single Sheet.' Postmark: '2 IY'.
[2] See letter 168, n. 1.
[3] There follows a heavily scored out line.

I wrote to Mrs. W. on Saturday excusing myself from postponing my engagement which she had asked me to do: she seemed to take for granted that the time of it would clash with that of her proposed excursion hitherwards, and I did not undeceive her.

Tomorrow I expect an answer from the Parson at whose House Wilson and I hope to be quartered—He is to breakfast with me.

Nothing very material happen'd at Sunday's meeting. I could not get to be 5 minutes alone with her. Yet some little progress I think was made—We all go to dine at Ripley Friday sennight—and I alone am asked to come early in order to have some music.

I am actually under the hands of a leader of two-paw'd bears—His name Abingdon—recommended by Mr. (Aldm.) Clark. Terms 2 guineas entrance and 2 do. 12 lessons—twas in Beaufort buildings a little beyond Exeter Change.

You can certainly make the tube as well as Nairne. I have not yet been able to get a Boerhaave[4] to find out the Receipt.

172

TO SAMUEL BENTHAM

3 July 1776 (Aet 28)

Alas my dear Sam! the scheme I mention'd in my last has failed—I mean however only the *individual* scheme: for something of that sort I have still strong hopes of. *Rose* the Parson[2] who we were in hopes would have taken us in, (at least one of us) could not. however he was very civil and communicative—and told us of another place, which if the good gods should have kept it vacant, will suit us I cannot say quite but almost as well—a place about 6 miles distant—an apartment in a farm house that once was occupied by *Rousseau*: and has room in it for *two*. The name of the village *Abinger*—[3] 2 miles from Dorking—The country (I

[4] Hermann Boerhaave (1668–1738) was a Dutch physician, botanist and chemist. His *Elementa Chemica* translated into English in 1735 as *Elements of Chemistry* was a standard textbook and is probably referred to here.

172. [1] B.M. II: 39–40. Autograph.
    Addressed: 'For / Mr. Sam. Bentham.'
    [2] Unidentified; but apparently parson at or near Ripley (cf. letter 180 at n. 4).
    [3] While Rousseau was at Chiswick in February and March 1766, Daniel Malthus at his request sought accommodation for him near Dorking; but this had apparently come to nothing before Rousseau left for Derbyshire (cf. *Correspondence Générale de Rousseau*, ed. T. Dufour, xv, Paris, 1931, 73–7, 94–5, 122–4, 140–142.) But according to the *Victoria County History of Surrey* (iii, 130 and n. 12) Rousseau stayed with John Spencer at Parkhurst, Abinger.

understand) delightful—Rose thinks it is not now occupied—he knows it was not in April.

Tomorrow we set out in quest of it.

I have sent thee a Pound of Fixt veg. Alkali bought under the denomination of Salt of Tartar—It cost 2s.

The Leather is for my shoes   The two skins cost 6s. 9d. each The man told me they would make about 3 pair each—They were brought at Sterry's Snow-hill.

Ask the Shoemaker how many pair they will make; before you tell him how many the Leather seller said they would. Ask him too how much he will abate on the pair for my finding my own leather. He ought so to charge me and so to husband the leather that at least they should not be dearer this way than the other—Let him make the two pair immediately which bring or send by the first opportunity with the pumps. The shoes he made me fitted me exceedingly well till I changed them and then I found them gape incorrigibly in the exterior quarter ⟍⟍ comme ça. Let him know this—If you come to town within a week don't send them—otherwise do—direct them to be left till call for and give me notice beside the common enveloppe, put them up in separate papers, that I may put them in different pockets.

Satum sapientiae in my next: which will probably be on Friday.

In a paper you will find some *Zaffre* (see Chym. Dict.)

I want to make some sympathetic Ink for Miss| |. What I want is to get it as concentrated as possible for what I have been able to make hitherto has been too faint—it would not shew much of a colour without the paper's being heated almost to scorching, or at least to such a heat as renders it ineffaçable. The misfortune is Zaffre is apt to contain Bismuth and the Salt of Bismuth has not the property desired. Thence the solution is *diluted quoad hoc*, while it is concentrated quoad corroding and discolouring the paper. If I can get a piece of Reg. of Cobalt to send, I will. we can then dissolve it at once in Mur. Acid—and have the Symp. Ink pure—In that case try by your Thermometer at what degree of heat it changes colour and so forth. See Reg. of Cobalt. Chym. Dict.

Thermometer I have got one made for you by Nairne—suited to the Pelican.

Get a twopenny print of Winter: i.e.: that has trees in it without leaves—put Sympathetic Ink to it and dry it, and so *toties* quoties, and see whether you can make it into a tolerable summer Land-scape—Burkit would assist you.

Stockings of yours I can find none—describe them to me.

Wednesday—July 3d. 1776.

173

TO SAMUEL BENTHAM

5 July 1776 (Aet 28)

from Riply. After a variety of toil and dissappointment we have at last fixed upon a place which promises to answer our res-pective purposes very well. It is a neat house enough at a place called Fetcham, a mile and a half from Leatherhead, where you and I slept in our vehiculo-pedestrian return from Portsmouth to London. It is about 6 miles from Ripley—about 19 or 20 from London. We go there on Monday or Tuesday. I shall go to Ripley on Monday to shew my horses and so on between Monday and Friday as often as I can get licence or pretence. The country at Fetcham is pleasing; a mile or two from Fetcham, enchanting. The apartment we are to occupy is at a neatish house enough kept by one Wells and his wife. Wells is Gardener to Sr. G. Warren whose house is close by.[2]

Concerning Q.S.P.'s disposition towards you, *data* at present I can give you none: no incident has happened of late to occasion your being mentioned: our conversation has been engrossed by my affair. I shall go to Richmd. Park on Sunday, where I shall meet Aldm. Clark and Mrs.— At Richd. I shall probably sleep that night and go to Ripley the next morning.

Wilson lies grunting and groaning by my side, without a morsel of skin upon his backside. The utmost we have ridden in the two days is 50 miles, and yet such is the condition he is in, we are almost apprehensive of a fever.

Lind's affairs begin to wear a very favourable aspect. His book against Price is out.[3] Ld. North and Mansfield approve of it highly

---

173. [1] B.M. II: 41. Autograph.

Addressed: 'To / Mr. S. Bentham / at the King's Dock Yard / near Rochester.' Postmark unclear, apparently: '5 IY'.

Cook's Court, Lincoln's Inn, made way for Waterhouse's New Court built about 1874. Probably Bentham was writing from Wilson's chambers.

[2] George Warren of Poynton, Cheshire, K.B. 1761, had acquired Fetcham Park by marrying, in 1758, the only daughter of Thomas Revell (d. 1752), M.P. for Dover 1734–52. She died on 9 December 1761 (*Gentleman's Magazine*, xxxi, 603).

[3] *Three Letters to Dr. Price* etc. (see letter 158 and n. 1).

—Ld. M. has reproached Ld. North for not having yet done anything for him. This day sennight he received a letter from the K. of P. giving him hopes of a favourable diet in August, and promising him in that case money for a seat.[4]

You understand sufficiently why I could not write by return of Post.

Friday July 5th 1776. Cook's Court.

174

To Samuel Bentham

c. 17 July 1776 (Aet 28)

Why has thou not sent me some Tea?

Not receiving the parcel till ½ after 5 I have postponed going into the Country till tomorrow.

I shall go directly to Fetcham if I find my Father in Town by breakfast time as I expect to do.

My Uncle is in Town—and has given me a sort of half promise to dine with us at Fetcham on Sunday—He goes through Leatherhead on business tomorrow—

Nairne à reparè les torts que j'ai cru a avoir avec lui—Hier en passant par le Caffè, on m'a donnè un paquet—En l'ouvrant j'y ai trouvè un de ces appareils electriques qu'il m'avoit promis—Ce matin je me suis entretenir avec lui.

Lind s'est expliquè avec Mylord N. On lui a dit que dès la Saint Michel, on trouveroit une '*niche*' pour lui (c'est a dire dans quelque partie de l'administration) faute de quoi, on lui satisfera en attendant par un autre voye—Il me l'a indiquè cet autre voye: mais il m'a fait promettre d'en garder le secret envers tous des hommes: selon qu'il s'est dit etre rèsolu de le garder, lui, meme envers toutes les femmes—a commencer par la sienne.

I have looked, and can find no stockings here that answer to the description you have given me. If anywhere they are at Fetcham.

---

[4] The King of Poland was promising Lind money for a seat in Parliament.

174. [1] B.M. II: 44–45. Autograph. Docketed: 'I.B. July 1776.'
Addressed: 'Mr. Bentham'.

The reference to his uncle's half promise to dine with him and Wilson at Fetcham next Sunday, taken together with letter 175 shows that this letter was written in the week before Sunday 21 July 1776.

[*On cover:*] I like Marmontel's Contes Moraux[2] much—fail not to bring with you the other volume.

175

TO SAMUEL BENTHAM

21 July 1776 (Aet 28)

If you should find an opportunity I should be glad to have a little Frontenac. That wine is to be had at Battle sometimes very cheap. cheaper (Mr. W. told me an instance when bought by the pipe) than Port wine in the proportion of £18 to 40. I would be glad to have it even at Port Price. The quantity if there should be opportunity from 1 doz. even to 12. Any surplus not exceeding that amount I could make sure of getting rid of. Miss S. loves Frontenac.

See if you can the Horse that Mr. W. talked of for me. If Burgundy or Claret but rather the former could be got as low as 36s. I would be glad to have a dozen if no Frontenac could be got: but rather Burgundy than Claret. You have money enough to pay something by way of earnest; and the rest shall be paid when deliver'd: of which should the negotiation succeed fail not to give me notice.

My Uncle was to have dined with us here to day: but did not come.

Q.S.P. come bag and baggage on Tuesday: they come to breakfast and stay dinner—happy day!

Wilson's posteriors salute you: and thank you for the concern you express on their behalf.

I told you in my last, I think, of Lind's prospects Payne told him tother day that the Fragment begins to sell very well: better even than Lind's last piece. A man has written against him in the papers. I hear no more of the antagonist I told you of—tant pis. Lind has undertaken to give him a flogging for what he has done already[2]—and he has begged of me to answer his man; which I

---

[2] Jean François Marmontel (1723–99) began publishing his *Contes Moraux* in the periodical *Le Mercure*, of which he became editor in 1758. The first of many collected editions was published in 1761: an English translation appeared in 1764, with a second edition in 1766. Bentham later undertook for Elmsley the bookseller a translation of Marmontel's *Les Incas* (cf. letter 194).

175. [1] B.M. II: 42–43. Autograph. Docketed (by Bentham?): 'I.B. July 26 1776.' Addressed: 'Mr. Bentham / at Mr. Wise's / Battle / Sussex.' Postmark: '. . I Y'. Stamped: 'LEATHERHEAD'.

[2] The *Morning Chronicle* had published two letters over the signature 'D.' attacking Bentham's *Fragment* on 6 and 13 July 1776. Lind's 'flogging' of the author took place

have just been doing.[3] His man speaks civilly and was to be spoken to accordingly. Lind who has been told that he is good at flogging will whip to the bone, I fear, a poor devil, who if he would but have gone on would have done me service, and against whom I have no malice.

Fetcham Sunday 21. July, 1776.

Wilson directs this, that [they] may not know that I have written to you and take no notice of them. What you mention they will suppose came from what I might have said to you when I was at Chatham.

Send Lind's book by all means to Davies—tell him Ld. Mansfield read it through without stopping.—And Ld. North took particular notice of it to Lord Mansfield—with the recommendation, he might put it into Lord Howe's hands.

176

TO SAMUEL BENTHAM

July 1776 (Aet 28)

Je serai demain chez vous—je viens en compagnie de Madame— et Mlle. . . . . . Je vous les ferez voir pour cet effet tenez vous bien

in the *Morning Chronicle* for 26 July. He signed himself 'A.B.'. The three letters are reproduced in Bowring, I, 256–259, at the end of Bentham's *Historical Preface* to the *Fragment*. (The note on page 256 of this illustrates the fallibility of the old Bentham's memory, for he says that Lind's intention of replying on his behalf was not known to him till executed.) The content of the correspondence is very slight, much of it concerning the author's failure to advertise the *Fragment* properly.

[3] Bentham was to answer an attack upon Lind's *Three Letters to Dr. Price* (i.e. the pamphlet version of the letters of Attilius—see letter 158, n. 1) which had appeared in *The Gazetteer* for 13 July, over the signature '*Ignoramus.*' It was directed mainly against the Bentham-Lind definition of liberty and Bentham—as 'Hermes'— defended this in two letters published on 26 July and 1 August. A further letter from 'Ignoramus' appeared on 31 July, but neither Bentham nor Lind replied to this.

Lind's original Attilius letters in *The Gazetteer* had drawn several earlier rejoinders: letters from 'Seneca' appeared on 2, 10 and 26 April; letters from 'Regulus' on 23, 25 April, 2, 7, 9 May. The latter is the attack mentioned by Lind in the pamphlet edition (its author also published about this time his own *Letter to Dr Price*, having previously published a reply to Dr Johnson's *Taxation no Tyranny*).

176. [1] B.M. II: 46–47. Autograph. Docketed: 'I.B. Dartford 1776 about July.'

Addressed: 'To / Mr. Bentham / at Mr. Jos; Davies's / near the Market Place / Chatham.'

Apparently Bentham found that Mrs Brickenden and her daughter, Miss Stratton, were going on a visit to Chatham. Since his brother was at Chatham, he had an excellent excuse for offering to accompany them. Bentham went on horseback, they in their carriage (cf. letter 151, n. 1).

habillé des 9 heures du matin—elles ne scavent pas que je vous ecris
ceci. Vous viendrez chez nous a l'auberge je vous viendrai chercher
je resterai avcc vous—Adieu mon cher

Dartford 6 ou 7 heures du soir chez le George.

177

To Samuel Bentham

14–17 August 1776 (Aet 28)

Let me see—ay, that's very true: so I had—I had once upon a
time an animal belonging to me they called a Brother. It used to go
upon two legs, and now and then write letters—Is it alive, I wonder,
or dead? I should like methinks, for the joke's sake to know what
is become of it. Alas! my dear Sam—for all this nonsense, I am by
no means in a joking humour. I am as melancholy as ten church
mice. Here have I for more than this week past been dancing
attendance upon a little . . . . . . (what shall I call her?) my hopes
growing every day less and less. On Monday sennight I came to
town to write her a letter: and a letter I did write her on Tuesday
and Wednesday an enormous long one. The English of it was in the
first place to desire her not to stay long: in the next place to appoint
time and place for me to meet her. It is now Wednesday and in all
this time not a syllable have I heard from the little vixen. On
Monday last I wrote her another by way of reinforcement to the
first. In the first I had forgot to desire her in case she should not be
able speedily to fix the time, to write to me. however *en attendant*
to tell me that she had received my letter and would or would not
fix it. The purport of the second was to supply this omission, and to
tell her how uneasy I was at not having heard from her, and that I
did not know whether to impute it to the cause above mentioned or
to her having taken something amiss in my first. This latter apprehension I begged her to relieve me from as soon as possible; telling
her that if I did not hear from her by Thursday (tomorrow) which
is the soonest I could have an answer to this 2d letter, I should
believe the worst: I should conclude I had offended past forgiveness.
Gods and Goddesses! What a miserable animal shall I be if no letter
comes tomorrow!

177. [1] B.M. II: 48–49. Autograph. Docketed (by Bentham?): 'I.B. Augst. 17th
1776.'

   Addressed: 'To / Mr. Bentham / at His Majesty's Dock Yard / near Rochester /
Single Sheet.' Postmark: '17 AV'.

Saturday 2 o'clock.

I am just setting out for Fetcham.

I have just received a letter of which the following is a Copy.

Birchington[2] Aug. 15th 1776

Sir

Having been absent from Birchington some time, your obliging favours did not come to hand so soon as they otherwise wou'd. Many circumstances render it quite uncertain when we shall leave this place, and as we are engaged to make a visit, or two to friends very distant from hence, can no way determine as to the time of our return to Ripley. My Mother joins with me in Compliments to you and I remain

Sir

Your humble Servant

Sarah Stratton

P.S. I hope the Melon Buzley[3] gave you proved good.

You see the situation I am in—My hopes very much diminished, but however not absolutely extinguished. We shall see what may be the result of a vivâ voce explanation. How I long for their return!

A few words about your affairs.

I was at Q.S.P. as I said on Wednesday. We talked a little about you. My Father asked me if I had heard from you. I told him no—not since I saw you at Chatham—forgetting the letter you wrote since. He asked me whether he was ever to hear from you. I told him I supposed he would, but mentioned as a reason for your not having written the discouragement you were under in account of your not receiving any answer to a letter you wrote previous to your seeing him at Kingston. I understood after all that he expected to hear from you again, therefore you must write. All the account that I could get from him of the reason of his not having answer'd those of your's was your '*bolting in upon him in that manner.*' This was repeated over and over again—when I pressed for an explanation I at last got from him that he was displeased because the shortness of your visit gave him no opportunity of talking with you in private and the old story of want of confidence: He would wish to have known I suppose about the Longitude scheme directly

---

[2] In the Isle of Thanet, where part of the estate of Miss Stratton's father was situated.

[3] Not identified: perhaps the gardener at Ripley.

from yourself: and to know every time of your coming up to town beforehand: in short that you should ask his leave to come up to town: to go every where you go: and in short to do every thing you do. Upon the whole however he was in a very good humour: and I did not say much in opposition to this because I did not care to anger him. The result of all is that you must write. You may mention as an inducement that you heard from him he wished it, and that if you wrote, (which indeed he said) he would answer you. Not that anything you are likely to say is likely to satisfy him. He expects, I suppose, or at least would be glad to have a penitential letter: or at least a letter full of expressions ⟨. . .⟩ ⟨. .⟩tion to which his behaviour never will give him any title.

It is a long time since I have heard from you—you have told me nothing about your Battle expedition—nothing about Miss H.[4] Nothing about the wine though that as matters stand I am very indifferent about. When am I to have this £10.

178

To Samuel Bentham

18–19 August 1776 (Aet 28)

Monday 19th.   Fetcham Sunday Aug. 18th. 1776

You have received I suppose a Letter I wrote you yesterday as I was setting out from London. Upon my arrival here I was surprized with one from you. Yes come by all means my dear Sam, as soon as you can make it convenient. You say nothing about the subject upon which you wish to consult me and 'the calm Wilson'. I suppose it is the affair between Q.S.P. and you. On that head I hope what I said to you in my last will afford you some satisfaction. Let me know if you can before you come: unless you should come so soon as to leave no time for it. I am tolerably composed, thanks to Wilson's nursing I may call it, to whom I have been lending a

[4] Perhaps Samuel's 'Archangel': see letter 149, n. 5.

178. [1] B.M. II: 50. Autograph. Docketed (by Bentham?): 'I.B. Augst. 18th. 1776.'
Addressed: 'To / Mr. Bentham / at his Majesty's Dock Yard / near Rochester'. Postmark: '20 AV'.
Shortly after this, Bentham received a letter (B.M. II: 51) from his uncle, G. W. Grove, dated 'Whitchurch 18th. Augt. 1776' explaining that the best venison will soon be gone. He understands that Mrs Brickenden and her daughter are soon to return. If Bentham wants the venison for them he should write immediately. He wishes Jeremy success in his present pursuit. Mrs Grove is recovering from her illness. Both she and his daughter present their compliments.

willing ear while he has been endeavouring to persuade me that the complection of the affair is not so bad as I at first apprehended. To be sure I did write 5 sheets and a piece brim full of a sort of stuff which if not downright love (since the word 'love' was not mentioned in it) was to my understanding scarcely to Wilson's not at all distinguishable from it. To have this and the other letter called 'obliging favours' and not to be forbidden the house, and to have an answer in pursuance of my entreaties, and to have hopes that the Melon proved good was something: it certainly might have been worse. Last night I scarce closed my eyes. To night however I hope to sleep as usual. My endeavour will be to plunge into Metaphysics as deep as possible. Wilson has been the best man alive to me. As I could not bear to stay any longer in town he tore himself away from one of the oldest and dearest friends he has whom he had not seen nor will see again for years to come, and bear me company. I forget whether I told you that he went to town at the same time with me. To see that friend was his errand.

As to Pownall's prejudices you know my sentiments already[2]: if you persevere in disregarding them, I can not say a syllable to Q.S.P. or any body else in your justification.

179

TO SAMUEL BENTHAM

21 August 1776 (Aet 28)

Fetcham Wedny. Aug. 21 1776

Alas, poor Sam. Why mopest thou? I for my part have done moping. Q.S.P. is perfectly well satisfied with the letter I transcribed for you: and they both join in telling me that considering what mine was to her, it is full as much as I had reason to hope for.

Yes, thou must come down /hither/. I will tell you how we have settled it. *Wilson* is very desirous of taking another farewell of his friend *Mercer*.[2] I am now fit to wean: I want no more nursing. He was half resolved therefore at any rate to have gone to London in a few days for about a week. When I was in town last Mrs. L. was pulling me to

---

[2] Cf. letter 131 and n. 5.

179. [1] B.M. II: 53. Autograph.
Addressed: 'To / Mr. Bentham / at his Majesty's Dock Yard / near Rochester.'
Postmark: '22 AV'.
[2] Cf. letter 178.

pieces to go down to them at Mill Hill on Saturday to help keep Mr. L.'s birthday.[3] Go therefore I will: and for that purpose I will be in town on Friday. Wilson will go to town the same day. I shall /be back/ return from Mill Hill on Sunday morning. Do thou meet me in town: and on Monday you will come together to this place. You will then occupy Wilson's bed. We will upon that consideration give him leave to stay in town for a few days. It would certainly be better if we could be all three together all the time. However, part of the time you are here we will: and for that part we must make shift for lodging some how or some how.

Q.S.P. will be here on Friday morning to breakfast and fetch home a Hawk I have got for them. When they set off on their return I shall set off for Town. I was over at Richmd. Park on Monday. My Father drank your health by the name of 'poor Sam.' This I knew not how to account for: He did not tell me of his having heard from you.

Write to me in London by the return of the post. I shall by that means have your Letter on Saturday. Oh but then I shall be at Mill Hill so I should not receive it till the time you might come yourself. However if a letter would come sooner than you, write.

[4]The spirit of Metaphysics hath come strong upon Wilson. His words are like the words of the wise man: full of grace and truth. When my kingdom cometh lo! even then shall he sit upon my right hand. Thou mayest think thyself well off to sit in his lap. Unless thou preferest to snuggle in Abraham's bosom.

179a

To John Lind

2 (?) September 1776 (Aet 28)

ANSW. TO DECLAR. PREAMBLE

'hold to be inalienable'. This they 'hold to be' a (among truths) 'truth self-evident'. At the same time ~~they are~~ to secure these

---

[3] John Lind, was born on 13/24 August 1737.

[4] The following paragraph is a minutely written postscript placed upside down at the top of the page.

179a. [1] B.M. XV: 359–360. Autograph, Docketed: 'Ans. to Declaration / Hints B. Addressed: 'To / John Lind Esqr. / Lincoln's Inn / London / Two sheets.' Postmark: '2[?] SE'.

Only the second sheet of this letter—comprising, apart from the address, three pages numbered 5–7—seems to have survived. The letter was apparently Bentham's contribution to Lind's pamphlet, published later in the autumn, *An Answer to the Declaration of the American Congress.* The heading and sub-heading here given at the

rights they are satisfied (content) that Governments should be instituted. They see not, or will not seem to see that nothing that was ever called government ever was or ever could be in any instance exercised save at the expence of one or other of those rights. that (consequently) in ~~so far~~ as many instances as Government is ever exercised, some one or other of these pretended inalienable rights is alienated. [*In margin:* It is thus they endeavour by a cloud of words to cover (veil) the ~~atrocity~~ enormity of their (crimes) (misdeeds) enterprizes.]² If ~~life is one~~ the right of enjoying life be the unalien-

---

head of the text are repeated on each page: 'Preamble' refers of course to the Preamble to the Declaration of Independence. Most of Bentham's 'hints', as given here, were substantially incorporated in the 'Short Review of the Declaration' which fills the last fourteen pages of Lind's pamphlet: cf. pp. 120–122. It has not seemed necessary to indicate the many points of detail where the printed text departs from Bentham's draft: major omissions are indicated in subsequent notes and one passage is cited to illustrate the kind of change that was made before publication.

The missing sheet of Bentham's letter may be supposed to have contained the basis for the opening paragraphs of the 'Short Review'. These read as follows (pp. 119–20):

'In examining this singular Declaration, I have hitherto confined myself to what are given as *facts*, and alleged against his Majesty and his Parliament, in support of the charge of tyranny and usurpation. Of the preamble I have taken little or no notice. The truth is, little or none does it deserve. The opinions of the modern Americans on Government, like those of their good ancestors on witchcraft, would be too ridiculous to deserve any notice, if like them too, contemptible and extravagant as they be, they had not led to the most serious evils.

'In this preamble however it is, that they attempt to establish a *theory of Government*; a theory, as absurd and visionary, as the system of conduct in defence of which it is established, is nefarious. Here it is, that reasons are advanced in justification of their enterprises against the British Government. To these maxims, adduced for *this purpose*, it would be sufficient to say, that they are *repugnant to the British Constitution*. But beyond this they are subversive of every actual or imaginable kind of Government.

'They are about "*to assume*," as they tell us, "*among the powers of the earth, that equal and separate station to which*"—they have lately discovered—"*the laws of Nature, and of Nature's God entitle them*." What difference these acute legislators suppose between the laws of *Nature* and of *Nature's God*, is more than I can take upon me to determine, or even to guess. If to what they now demand they were entitled by any law of God, they had only to produce that law, and all controversy was at an end. Instead of this, what do they produce? What they call self-evident truths. "*All men*," they tell us, "*are created equal*." This surely is a new discovery; now, for the first time, we learn, that a child, at the moment of his birth, has the same quantity of *natural* power as the parent, the same quantity of *political* power as the magistrate.

'The rights of "*life, liberty,* and *the pursuit of happiness*"—by which, if they mean any thing, they must mean the right to *enjoy* life, to *enjoy* liberty, and to *pursue* happiness—they "*hold to be unalienable*" . . .'

Some brief extracts from the present letter are printed in M. P. Mack's *Jeremy Bentham: An Odyssey of Ideas* 1758–1792, New York and London, 1963, p. 186. But the source is not precisely indicated (cf. n. 96 on p. 203) and the extracts seem to be linked with Lind's *Remarks on the Principal Acts of the Thirteenth Parliament of Great Britain*, not with his *Answer*.

² This sentence was not included in the printed text.

able right of all men, whence came their invasion of his Majesty's
province of Canada, and the unprovoked destruction of so many
lives of the ~~Canadians~~ inhabitants of that province? If the right of
enjoying Liberty be an unalienable right whence came so many of his
Majesty's peaceable subjects among them (without any offence or
so much as any pretended offences), (merely for being suspected
not to wish well to their enormities) to be held by them in durance?
If the right of pursuit of happiness is a right unalienable (why (how)
are thieves restrained from pursuing it by theft, murderers by
murder, and rebels by rebellion)[3] how is it with so many others of
their fellow citizens whom with the same injustice and violence
they have made miserable by ruining their fortunes, banishing
their persons and driving them from their friends and families?[4]
[*In margin:* before any exertion of his Majesty's chastising power,][5]
or would they have it believed that there is /in themselves/ that
peculiar (virtue) (sanctity) (privilege) that makes those things lawful to them which are unlawful to all the world besides? Or is it
(that coercion only is unlawful which is imposed by regular accustomed government?) among acts of coercion those only (whereby
life or liberty are taken away and the pursuit of happiness restrained those only are unlawful which their delinquency has
brought upon them, and which are exercised by regular, long-
established accustomed Government?

   [6]In these tenets they have out done the utmost extravagance of
/all former/ fanatics. [*In margin:* (The extravagance of these tenets
has never yet been equalled by) the wildest fanatics have never yet
equalled etc,] The German Anabaptists indeed went further went
so far as to speak of the right of enjoying life as a right unalienable:
~~but they went no further~~ (Mortal punishment tho' inflicted by the
Magistrates they held unlawful) To take away life even in the
Magistrate they held unlawful. But they went no further. It was
(a discovery) reserved for the American rebels to add (the right of
liberty, and the right to pursue happiness to the number) [*In*

---

   [3] The phrase in brackets does not occur in this form or at this point in the pamphlet;
but a similar phrase is there inserted at the end of the next paragraph of the text.
   [4] The concluding part of this sentence may serve to illustrate how Bentham's
'hints' were modified in the final text. In the pamphlet it reads: 'how is it that so
many others of their fellow-citizens are by the same injustice and violence made
miserable, their fortunes ruined, their persons banished and driven from their friends
and families?'
   [5] This phrase was not inserted in the printed text nor is it at all clear where Bentham meant it to go.
   [6] Above the opening of this paragraph Bentham has written and then deleted the
following: 'What mean they when they say that all men are created'. Cf. the beginning of the next paragraph.

margin: to the number of unalienable rights, that of enjoying liberty, and that of pursuing happiness] that is if they mean any thing of pursuing happiness wherever a man thinks he sees it. It was a discovery reserved for them that for the Magistrate to do any thing in any case to take away Liberty, or to restrain from the pursuit of happiness is unlawful.

What (mean they) is it they mean when they say that all men are created equal. (What is it /(that)/ they mean?) Do they know of any other way in which men are created Do they know of any other way in which they themselves were *created*, than by being *born*? Do they mean that every man is born equal to every other? Is the child born equal to his Parents, born equal to the Magistrates of his country? In what sense is he their equal? If in any, what inference would they draw from this equality?[7]

[8]'Governments long established', they do vouchsafe to admitt, 'should not be changed for light and transient causes'—Can any cause be so light, as that which wherever Government has subsisted or can subsist has always and must continue to subsist. What was their original their only original grievance. That they were taxed more than they could bear? No, but that they were liable to be (so:) more than they could bear. Is there any where, can there be imagined any where that Government whose subjects are not /so/ liable to be so taxed more than they can bear?

180

JEREMY AND SAMUEL BENTHAM TO JEREMIAH BENTHAM

6 September 1776 (Aet 28)

Fetcham Friday 6th. Septr. 1776

Hond. Sir

Not having it in my power to wait on you in person, I must content myself with writing. My Mare is not at present in a con-

[7] This paragraph does not occur in this form in the pamphlet; but the point about equality is made towards the end of the third of the opening paragraphs quoted above in n. 1.

[8] The first two sentences of this paragraph do not occur in quite this form in the printed text; but the points are made in an expanded form in two short paragraphs on p. 122.

180. [1] B.M. II: 54–57. Docketed by Jeremiah Bentham: 'Son Jeremy Lr. datd. Fetcham 6th. Septr. 1776.'

Addressed: 'Jeremiah Bentham Esqr. / Queen Square Place / Westminster.' Postmark: '7 SE'. Stamped: 'LEATHERHEAD'.

dition by any means to be ridden: it was with the utmost difficulty I got her to and from Ripley yesterday. Her disorder, whatever it is, does not shew itself by any external symptoms except extreme sluggishness and failure of appetite. The master of the Talbot recommended it to me to get her bled yesterday and I did so: he told me that horses would every now and then get those symptoms from a redundance of blood occasioned by high feeding. To day she is rather better than she was yesterday: should she grow worse I intend to apply to a man I have heard of in this neighbourhood who looks after Sir George's horses.[2]

It was about $\frac{1}{2}$ after 10 yesterday when I reached Ripley. The Ladies had been returned ever since Sunday. In all that time they had not seen a single creature of their neighbours. They had sent word to nobody: and I happen'd to be first visitor. The Footman open'd the gates to me, and left me to dispose of myself at my discretion. I went into the fore-parlour and sat down to the Harpsichord. I staid half-an-hour I believe before anybody came in. Mrs. B. was the first; but by that time there had come two Ladies, a Mrs. Draper an elderly widow Lady, and her daughter also a widow, and not very young. They live in the village, and called in their way to Mrs. Barbot's, whom they mentioned I believe as being a relation to them: I think the daughter spoke of her under the name of Aunt.[3] They were already in the room when Mrs. B came in; so that I had no opportunity of reading her disposition in her first looks. On account of the presence of these ladies I did not think it proper to make any advances to salute her. In some respects fortune was rather unfavourable to me. The weather being changeable, the old women staid fiddle-faddling a long while. Their errand was to compare a pattern of their's for ruffles with a pattern of Miss Stratton's; and no Miss Stratton appeared. They had staid I suppose an hour when I thought I might take the liberty of taking a turn by myself in the garden. Just as I was going out at the Garden door, whom should I meet coming in but Miss S. The sight of her made me start a little; however I went up to her, 'hoped she would permit me to welcome her back again to that country', and summoned up courage enough to take a transient salute. After Miss S. went in to them, the Ladies staid a matter of half an hour longer. When they were gone, after a little chit-chat in which no mention was made of my letters, the topic of Music came upon the

[2] Sir George Warren. Cf. letter 173 and n. 2.
[3] Mrs Barbut of Ripley Green died 16 May 1793, aged 90 (*Gentleman's Magazine*, lxiii, 484). Mrs Draper and her daughter have not been identified.

carpet. I then took occasion to observe that a note or two in the Harpsichord was out of tune, and asked for a key to tune it with: Miss S. went out to make enquiries, and presently in came the man with a key and the fiddle into the bargain: That I thought looked well: but whether it was Miss S's orders to bring the fiddle, or whether it was only his own thought I could not be quite certain. However that might be I then thought myself sufficiently authorized to propose a tune. We had been playing about 20 minutes when Mrs. B went out as we were in the middle of her tune, to try on a new gown as I found afterwards: telling her daughter she should not be long. She did stay however, I suppose an hour: but unluckily she had not been five minutes gone, (and we were still in our tune) when in came Mr. Rose.[4] He staid an unconscionable long time: till past two, owing partly to a mistake of the servants who desired him as on the part of Mrs. B. to stay till she came down which otherwise he would not have done, having as he said another place to call at. Late as it was I did not think myself bound to make a motion to go while Miss S. only was in the room, before Mrs. B. returned. If I had I must have lost my chance of being asked to stay dinner, as Miss S., I thought, of herself would hardly ask me. At the same time I resolved not to offer to go at the same time with Mr. R. as then they could not well have invited me without inviting him. I saw him out, and then that it might not seem as if I staid merely for that purpose, I proposed finishing the tune which upon his coming had been broken off. It was already past their dinner time, but no preparations for laying the cloth had as yet been made. When I offer'd at last to go I was asked by Mrs. B. to stay dinner: as I was debating myself whether to accept the invitation or no, she determined me by mentioning what she had for dinner and making apologies. To be short I drank Tea, and staid till near seven. They will not have the Hawk: they had had one once which they killed on account of it's flying at the Pidgeons. They thanked me for the cuttings of Geraniums, etc.; we went into the garden to look at them: but just as we had got to the hot-bed where they were, we were driven in again by the rain. I had got a copy of a little book that has lately had a great run called the Father's Legacy to his daughters; written by the late Dr. Gregory a Physician at Edingburgh.[5] This I folded up in a sheet of white paper sealed it, directed in a small hand to Miss Stratton, and

---

[4] Cf. letter 172, n. 2.

[5] John Gregory, *A Father's Legacy to his Daughters*, first published in 1774; it went through 24 editions in the following 103 years.

locked it up in the Harpsichord; so that nobody could see it till she saw it, and the first thing she saw when she opened the Harpsichord, would be that. They took notice of it, thanked me, said they had already read part of it, and commended it. Miss Stratton upon that occasion mentioned 'The unfortunate Ladys advice to her daughters' and asked me if I had read it. that introduced a conversation about the authoress. I got out of them, though they seemed rather backward to own it, that the Lady they had been to see in Buckingham Shire, as they had said they should was no other than Lady Pennington.[6] They staid three days with her; and during that time did not see a soul besides. So you see they are not at variance as was imagined. They were at Mr. Mawl's[7] but one day. They reached London on Sunday; and sat out for Lady P's on the Wednesday. Further particulars about her Ladyship I must defer to another opportunity.

When I asked them to come to Fetcham, Mrs. B. at first seemed to decline it in a manner that made me afraid I should not have been able to prevail on them: however before I took my leave I returned to the charge, and did obtain what I looked upon as a promise. I would have fixed on Monday: but as they had not paid any visits in the neighourhood, they would [not] then fix a day. Mrs. B. proposed drinking Tea: that you may imagine I would not accept. As an inducement I mentioned your having dined with us several times, and said I made no doubt but you would be very glad to meet them. If they stipulate for it so it must be: but it would be very confidential in them, and would be a great point gained if they would come by themselves. I said as you had bid me that I understood from my Mother, Mrs. B. had been kind enough to say that she would let her know when they were come back: she replied 'true: she had like to have forgot it; and begged me to let my Mother and you know, and that she should be very glad to see you.'

If my Mare should not get well, or even if she should (so sluggish is she at best) I don't know what I shall do. My only chance for any thing of a tête-à-tête is a ride; and time grows pretious. It is not above 6 weeks longer that I can stay with any decency in the country: and they do not come to town till after Christmas.—They were not once at the rooms at Margate: but they spent a week at Canterbury, which they like much. It was the race week and there were balls etc. Miss S. danced but with whom I did not learn. I

    [6] Sarah, Lady Pennington, *An Unfortunate Mother's Advice to her Absent Daughters*, first published in 1761. A fifth edition had appeared in 1770 and another, entitled *Instructions for a Young Lady*, in 1773.
    [7] Unidentified.

must now leave off. I am pressed to finish: I am afraid I shan't be able to get rid of Sam till the beginning of the week. He talks of sending his things to town on Tuesday, to be ready to be carried down in the Coach to Richmond the next day. He wants to speak for himself. but you see there is but half a page left for him.

[*The remainder is in Samuel Bentham's hand*][8]

It was not till a day or two ago that your poor younger Son has recovered his Senses. he is now making great progress in his occupation, he begs you will excuse his absence till Monday or Tuesday next. We are your

Dutifull Sons
Sam[l] /and Jere:[y] /Bentham.

If you should find a letter from Mr. Pownell, Pray be so kind as to open it, and according to what he may say therein, if you approve of it, I should be obliged to you if you would consult Mr. Bromley[9] how you may obtain leave of absence for me for a Month, it will be best to get leave enough if it be necessary to apply to the Navy Board.

181

To John Lind

12 September 1776 (Aet 28)

My dear Lind
how go you on? What is it you have been about? How comes it I have not heard from you? Oh I believe you had reason from somewhat I said in a former letter to wait till you had heard from me.

Sam has been here and is gone. Wilson goes to town on Wednesday. He stays till Saturday. Then is your time for coming: and not yours only but if it please God and the parties concerned, another's.

[8] Except 'and Jere[y].'
[9] Mr Bromley of the Navy Board is mentioned in a letter from Jeremiah Bentham to Samuel dated 15 May 1775 (B.M. I: 341). He is presumably R. Bromley, who was Chief Clerk to the Surveyor of the Navy.
181. [1] B.M. II: 58–59. Autograph.
Addressed: 'John Lind Esqr. / Lamb's Conduit Street No. 65 / London.' Postmark: '3.E'. Stamped: 'LEATHERHEAD'.
Partly printed in Everett, *Education*, 106–107.

There is a two-legged creature I have heard you speak of as belonging to you. Were it to come here, could you answer for it's being quiet? If you could, I should like of all things to see it. You must consider and it must consider it could not see a creature of its own sex here all the while above the degree of my Landlord's wife who was Sir George's laundry maid; so that what it has to consider is whether it would prefer its Master's arid company and mine and nobody else's for four days to such as it might have were it to stay at home. Toilette furniture and all its other rattle traps it must bring of course: moreover it must engage to go up stairs and sit in its own room or let us sit in mine if ever we should find it in the way, when you and I in our profound wisdoms are sitting in council over the affairs of state. A servant, if your indolent, proud ostentatious humour should think it necessary, you must bring: though I will be c—d if I can see any occasion you can have for him, and there is not the least crack nor corner I can put him in the house by night or day: so that if he exists at all, he must exist at Leatherhead which is one mile off. This is the black side of the picture—au reste le place ne laisse pas que d'avoir ses agremens. There is a large paddock park with a pleasant garden to range about in unquestioned, unstared at, and unmolested—unstared at? quotha—tant pis says the animal I have been speaking of. The kitchen-garden thereunto belonging has produced us for some time ten or a dozen peaches and nectarines upon an average while there have been two of us—a dozen or 14 while there have been three of us—together with now and then an odd dish of green gages—Nuts the country affords in tolerable plenty; with the pleasure of gathering them into the bargain. Pies and garden stuff of all kinds (inter alia stew'd cucumbers) we abound in. A bottle of Burgundy I have reserved to moisten your fat guts with. Come by all means, I beg of *you* speaking always in the plural number—if it were only to keep me from the blue devils. I write this in a spirit of etourderie which comes now and then to enliven that dejection which (I shall never have done with this sentence) characterizes at present by much the greater part of my time. I trudge (or if you please drudge) on in the pursuit you mention, not absolutely without hopes, but alas! with very faint ones.

After all this I am desired to inform you that it is not absolutely certain that the occasion will subsist that is to call Wilson to town but it is more than probable. Should it subsist I will give you timely notice; and if you hear nothing from me you may conclude that the coast is clear.

Let me hear from you as soon as you can—If you come bring with you Kenricks Review[2]—and bring with you the news of your being made Secretary of State, or something of that sort.—Bring likewise the news of the taking of New York. My most respectful Compliments wait upon your Lady.

Fetcham near Leatherhead
    Thursday Sept. 12th. 1776.

In Lloyd's Evening there has been a suite of six letters on American affairs signed Philanthrop, which you ought to see. There is likewise one in yesterday's signed Britannicus that may be worth looking at.[3]

[2] *The London Review of English and Foreign Literature*, 1775–80, conducted with others, till his death in 1779, by William Kenrick (b. 1725?), a copious and scurrilous writer. It carried a review in instalments, with long extracts, of the *Fragment* in its July, August, and September numbers. Lind's *Three Letters* was also favourably noticed there in July.

[3] The first of the letters signed 'Philanthrop' appeared in *Lloyd's Evening Post* for 14–16 August 1776; the sixth in the issue for 2–4 September 1776. This last, like the others, is marked 'To be continued' but it does not seem to have been so. The letters discuss the complaints of the American Congress against the British Government, in particular their charge that the year 1763 saw the commencement of a plan for enslaving the colonies. 'Philanthrop' insists with some heat that the principles concerning taxation, jury-trial etc. in America implied in the legislation since that date all have precedents in much earlier acts, and that the complaints are just so many excuses for their unreasonable demand for independence. One passage which must have pleased Bentham may be quoted:

'Thus the complaint of a *new trial*, like those against the *Revenue Laws*, and the *Courts of Admiralty* is without foundation, and falls to the ground; and to call an *Act of Parliament illegal*, is a contradiction in terms; it may be *unreasonable*, but illegal it cannot be, because an Act of Parliament is certainly a *Law*: and to talk of an *illegal Law* is a glaring absurdity, and self repugnant.' (From Letter III in the issue for 23–26 August 1776.)

The letter from 'Britannicus' appeared in the issue for 9–11 September 1776. It is in reply to a letter signed 'Amicus' (in the issue for 30 August—2 September 1776) which charged *Lloyd's Evening Post* with being a Ministerial paper in that it published such unreasonable attacks on the Americans as those of 'Philanthrop.' The 'Britannicus' letter is a vigorously written, though not very substantial, defence of British policy.

182

TO JEREMIAH BENTHAM

12 September 1776 (Aet 28)

Fetcham Thursday Septr. 12th. 1776

Hond. Sir

Yesterday I was again at Ripley, and fortune was again perverse. To anticipate any company that might come in, and to give time to Miss S. to get ready for riding, should she be disposed to it, I got thither with my poor forlorn beast a little before 9. It was plain it was not Miss S's original intention to ride out that day, as she came down to breakfast in a gown: but upon my proposing it first to her Mama, and afterwards as soon as Miss came into the room to herself, she came into it, at first word: gave orders to the Coachman to get up the horse, and as soon as breakfast was over went up to put on her habit. The dressing of her hair took up an uncommon length of time. Mrs. B. apologized for it, and assigned as a reason that as they were going out to make a visit in the afternoon, Miss was dressing her hair in such a manner as that it might serve once for all. It was about 12 when Mrs. B. who had been above stairs for a few minutes, came down and told me that Miss had been taken with the complaint she is subject to in her stomach, that she had taken some of the Medicine she kept by her for the purpose, but that she was afraid she would not be able to ride out that day. Soon after Miss herself came into the room, mentioned her indisposition, and said that under the circumstances she was afraid to venture upon riding, as the motion of the horse was apt to make her worse. I then thought it was time to take my leave: but first my business was to endeavour to get them to appoint a time for coming over to Fetcham. From what had passed when I was there before I had really thought they meant it; and indeed Mrs. B. for it was she alone who spoke, acknowledged that I had reason: but when it came to a trial I had the misfortune to find all I could say would not prevail. She assigned first the length of the way, shortness of the days, and so forth, their expecting a Lady who was to come and spend a fortnight with them soon, and who might come so

182. [1] B.M. II: 60–61. Autograph. Docketed by Jeremiah Bentham: 'Son Jeremy Letter datd. Fetcham 12 Septr. 1776.'

Addressed: 'To / Jeremiah Bentham Esqr. / Queen's Square Place / Westminster.' Postmark: '13 SE'. Stamped: 'LEATHERHEAD'.

soon as Monday or Tuesday. When answers were given to all these objections at last she owned to me purely that she could not think of paying a visit to a single gentleman: that indeed it was not her custom to dine with any body, and that her dining with my Mother was a particular exception to the rule. I said that I was persuaded my Mother and you would meet them at Fetcham with great pleasure, and that I could not expect them but upon that condition: and when that would not do, pleading the disappointment it would be to me if they retracted, I added that upon the strength of the hopes they had given me, and which I looked upon as tantamount to a promise, I had gone so far as to propose it to my Mother and you, and that you had declared your readiness to come whenever it should suit them. All however would not do, and I was obliged at last to give up the expectation I had so long been feasting upon. All however passed in perfect good humour and without any signs of pique or displeasure at my importunities. When that conversation was over, I took my leave. Mrs. B asked me to stay dinner; but I had determined with myself before-hand not to stay this time until I was pressed, that I might call with the more freedom another time: besides I thought that as Miss S. was not well there would be no playing on the Harpsichord, and that the greatest part of time betwixt that and dinner would be taken up in her dressing for her visit.

Their behaviour I thought seemed much more free and unreserved this time than the preceding; so that till the last fatal denial came I was all along in high spirits. When Mrs. B. asked me after your health and my mother's, she added she was in hopes she should have seen you before now. When Mrs. B. told me of the Lady she expected to stay a fortnight I asked (Miss S. in the room) whether she expected Mr. Mussarede[2] this autumn. Miss S. smiled; as much as to say, this is not a question of mere chit-chat curiosity. Mrs. B. said she did not know. She had asked him. but she did not know whether he would come. He would come if he pleased: as 'she had given him a general invitation.' This did not look, I thought, like any very particular intimacy.—Talking with Mrs. B. about her netting, she said she had thoughts of taking to net large nets for the Garden. She had seen Lady Lyttelton[3] do that kind of netting work; /The instruments for it are called a pen and a

[2] Cf. letter 151, n. 5.

[3] Apphia Peach (1743–1840), daughter of Broome Witts of Chipping Norton and widow of Joseph Peach, former governor of Calcutta; wife of Thomas, 2nd Baron Lyttelton (1744–79), whom she married in 1772 but soon deserted. She had a house at Ripley.

needle/ and Lady Lyttelton had promised to put her pen and needle into the hands of her carpenter, to make a pair by them for Mrs. B. This was before they went to Birchington: since then they have been to Lady L's: but her Ladyship did not say anything about it. This, I think, seems to be a favourable opportunity for me to make her a present of a pair of these instruments. If you approve of it, Sir, I will beg leave to trouble you with the commission. They are to be had I should suppose in ivory: or some other neater material than the Carpenter would make them of. If it should suit you, they might be got when you come to town on Saturday; and Sam might be despatched express with them on Sunday; or soon after as convenient. Whenever I present them, Mrs. B. need not know but what I may have been myself in town, and taken the opportunity of getting them.—I think to go again tomorrow if the weather should suit: and if not tomorrow, on Saturday. If it should suit and you think it not improper, I should be glad to think that you and my Mother would pay a visit there on Monday: you two only, without either of my Brother's. If not Monday, Tuesday perhaps might do. Wednesday for a *pis-aller*: But the sooner the better, that you might be there before the visitor comes. I am in hopes you see, by that time that I may have had a tête-à-tête with Miss. At any rate such a visit may be of use in strengthening the intimacy; and possibly some little incident may occur, or some little hint drop in conversation, to assist us in forming our conjectures of their dispositions. Returning yesterday from Ripley I met Mr. Rose: he had before promised to come and see us and I took that opportunity to fix the time. He and Mr. Forbes[4] are to dine with us on Tuesday. I thought the acquaintance of a person who is upon such a footing with the Ladies, and who lives so near them, might for a variety of purposes, be of use. I long much to hold a council, with my Mother and you: but I think it will be a great assistance to your deliberations your having paid your visit.

I have just now received a letter from my Uncle wherein he tells me that he sent a haunch over to Winchester on Tuesday. It either reached Ripley then I suppose yesterday, or will reach it today; according as the Carriages go. My Uncle says he would have sent you a side; but as he apprehends you make frequent excursions round the country was fearful it might not reach you while it was sweet.

[4] Arthur Forbes of Culloden (who died between 1801 and 1806) was the young Scotch apothecary who married Sarah Stratton in April 1779. He was lodging with Mr Rose.

I had like to have forgot thanking you for your letter: it came safe to me on Sunday morning.

My Mare eats better than she did: but is grown amazingly thin with her late abstinence. It is impossible for me at present to get with her as far as Richmd. Park. I nurse her as much as possible to make her serve for carrying me to Ripley. The road thither across the Common is now intolerably bad. I am, Dear Sir,

Yours most dutifully and affectionately
Jere:^y Bentham

P.S. In my long letter to Miss, something was said that was intended to have the effect you hint at. If she believes a bit more about the matter merely from being told as much in plain terms, she has more faith in professions, than I can bring myself to suppose a person of ordinary discernment to possess. If the whole success of the affair depended upon it, I could not bring myself to tell her that concerning my own dispositions [5] which I did not feel was true. This I feel to be true, that I prefer her at this moment to any woman that I know: and that could I gain her consent upon the terms of leaving everything that is hers together with what by your bounty may be mine, to her absolute disposal, I should think myself the happiest of mankind. If this will warrant me in 'assuring her that fortune is not the object', I can most truly say it: but I can go no further.

I hope, Sir, you will not be displeased, nor much surprized, if in the course of a week or thereabouts, you should receive a state of my receipts from you and of my expectations. I have staid thus long in hopes that my moderation of which, I believe, you are satisfied, and my patience of which you are a witness might at length have render'd it unnecessary to remind you of those wants which you could not but imagine must subsist. I should conceive that you are not much the better, and I know very well that I am much the worse, for my being always obliged to speak in the stile of a beggar before I am relieved. Your forecast and exactness in your accounts will not allow me to suppose that you could have engaged in a plan of new expence without having made allowance for the regular fulfilling those standing engagements which you had been pleased voluntarily to enter into with your Son for his support. As to any thing beyond, I think I need not tell you whatever may have been the subsequent accessions to your income I have never sollicited a farthing. You cannot I think but remember

---

[5] 'My own dispositions' has been substituted for 'myself'.

instances where I have declined accepting even what you yourself have been kind enough to offer, till I knew whether I should find it necessary.

183

To Jeremiah Bentham

13 September 1776 (Aet 28)

Ripley Septr. 13th. 1776

Hond. Sir

The few lines you will now receive I write from Ripley. Breakfast is just over, and we have been inspecting the Venison. The general opinion is that it cannot possibly keep till Tuesday: at least that it will not be safe to venture. The Ladies desire me to mention this to you: they told me they had given you the option of Monday or Tuesday: for the reason above given they can only propose Monday to you. If I had not happen'd to call in this morning, they would themselves have written. I offer'd to save them the trouble. This afternoon they were to have sent the man over to Fetcham if I had not come.

It is proper I think that you should know, that in my long letter I said enough to Miss S. for her to conclude that that part of Mrs. B's conversation with my mother that concerned the fortune had come round to me.

My affectionate respects wait upon my Mother—love to all the boys—at the same time with this or before you will have received I suppose a letter which I sent yesterday—

I am

Dear Sir

Yours most dutifully and affectionately

Jere:ʸ Bentham

The Ladies desire their Compliments.

183. ¹ B.M. II: 62–63. Autograph. Docketed by Jeremiah Bentham: 'Son Jeremy Lr. dated Fetcham 13th Septr. 1776.'

Addressed: 'Jeremiah Bentham Esqr. / Queen Square Place / Westminster.' Postmark: '14 SE'. Stamped: 'RIPLY'.

184

To John Lind

18 September 1776 (Aet 28)

Thanks to you my dear Lind for your caution: which however, as I am circumstanced, is altogether needless. Females, or no females here makes no sort of difference with regard to my present pursuit. Between Fetcham and Ripley there is no sort of communication save what I make when I pay my visit to the Latter. They are 6 miles distant. I met my Father and Brother at dinner there on Monday last: whether you are here or not, I shall not go again this week. I can't help thinking my Mrs. would like to come and see her Servant—She need not be more forlorn here though the weather should prove bad then she is at Heywood Hill, now Mr. and Mrs. Anderson are not there. Taking this for granted if you come single in a vehicle that would carry double I am not at home.

You might apprehend that Mrs. might get intelligence of my pursuit from my Landlady: but no incident has happen'd that carried any likelyhood with it of having given the latter any suspicions. Besides she is a reserved modest woman without any thing of the prate apace.

If you come alone, you must leave your Horse at Leatherhead: and walk on; it is but $\frac{3}{4}$ of a mile. There is no place that will hold him at Fetcham: nor would it be easy to get any body to take him back to Leatherhead.

Wilson will be back on Saturday Evening—not before 6. I had forgot to tell you that his being in the way will be no obstacle at all to your sleeping here though you should come double. One room I suppose will hold you and your appurtenances—One room held me and Wilson, all the time my Brother was with us which was a fortnight. He occupied my bed, and I slept upon an extemporary bed of my own contrivance in Wilson's room.

Thank you heartily for your Polish news[2]—It gives me the most pleasing prospects—I long to talk it over with you—

I don't believe it signifies any thing my sending duty to my Mistress—I would venture a small wager you have not dared to

184. [1] B.M. II: 65–66. Autograph.
    Addressed: 'To / John Lind Esqr. / Lamb's Conduit Street / London.' Postmark: '19 SE.' On inside of cover (by Lind?): 'Sepr. 17–2 months—Bukati to William.' On cover (by Lind?): 'Fetcham 1776 Bene—no date.' For Bukati see letter 342, n. 13.
    [2] See end of letter 185.

shew her either of my former letters, for fear she should teaze you to let her come.

Fetcham Wedny. 18th 1776 or rather Leatherhead—where I have been breakfasting with Wilson on his way to Town. I write from the Swan, which ought to afford a man a better quill than this miserable stick.

Come or not come write at all events on Thursday. I shall have your letter on Friday morning between 7 and 8.

185

To Samuel Bentham

18 September 1776 (Aet 28)

Leatherhead Tuesdy. Sept. 18 1776

Wilson is come to town, my dear Sam, and I, poor I, am left alone. He does not return till Saturday. I must have thee or somebody to keep me from hanging myself. I did expect Lind, but he does not come. Thou must therefore play truant from Q.S.P. Richmd. Park at least for to morrow and next day and part of Saturday. Shirt and Stockings thou needest not trouble thyself about. Thou shalt have mine. Thou might'st be with me at Breakfast if thou beest good for any thing. He that can walk 20 miles, a fortiori can walk 13.

There is no such thing as my getting to Richmd. Park. Thither and back again in a day is too far to walk while the roads are in such condition. My Mare is under the Doctr's. hands—stuffed with Rowel and fed with pissing-balls—excuse me, so the Dr. is pleased to call them. The Farrier tells me I may use her again on Friday. But Monday is as soon as I can want her.

It is possible Lind may come on Friday—if so, off you pack. Indeed in case of very bad weather we might manage your staying, so as not to turn you out to drown.

Duty to my Father. I have nothing particular to say to him at present—Oh yes—I have—Yesterday I was again unfortunate. Rose and Forbes did not come—the extreme bad weather indeed sufficiently accounts for it. We scarce expected them.

'In Poland every thing seems to favour the King. They talk of

185. [1] B.M. II: 64. Autograph. Docketed: 'I.B.: Septr. 18th. 1776.'
Addressed: 'Mr. Sam: Bentham / Queen's Square Place / Westminster.'
18 September 1776 was a Wednesday.

the Throne being declared hereditary. Diets abolished, and giving him an Arch Dutchess to Wife.' Thus saith Lind in a letter I have just this instant received. I write now by Wilson's means. We are at Breakfast at the Swan.

186

TO JEREMIAH BENTHAM

1 October 1776 (Aet 28)

Hond. Sir

Inclosed you will receive my account—You will observe it does not include among my receipts the Sum you favoured me with by draught on the Schoolmaster I think it was the latter end of June. It amounted I think to £36-9s.-0d. A few days afterwards you took back £5-5s.-0. (I gave it you in the summer-house at Q.S.P.) This reduced it to £31.4s.0d. The Sadler's bill comes to £5.1s.0d.—that will reduce it to £26.3.0d. The expence of the Mare and the other extra expences of the campaign I forbear giving you an account of till the whole is closed which it will now be in about a fortnight. I doubt I must beg of you not to expect much to be coming to you on the ballance. I must look at some memorandum I have in town before I can deliver it to you compleat with dates etc.

Many thanks to you, Sir for your kind letter. To find my conduct so fully approved by you is the greatest comfort that could happen to me. What little incidents have occurred since I saw you, I will beg leave to refer you to Sam for an account of. I can now give you the satisfaction of knowing that my mind is at ease, I may almost say at perfect ease; and I am going on briskly with my work. The worst was over before they returned from Margate: since then my hopes have been let down gradually and gently. I doubt not of your pardon for having kept my Brother. Mr. Wilson's stay proved unexpectedly long: so that had it not been for my Brother, I should have been quite alone.

I am now at work upon my capital work: I mean the Critical Elements of Jurisprudence.[2] I am not now as heretofore barely

186. [1] B.M. II: 67–68. Autograph. Docketed by Jeremiah Bentham: 'Fils Jeremy Lr. datd. Fetcham Surry 1st. Octr. 1776 giving some Accnt of his Plan, for a work proposed to be Entitled Critical Elements of Jurisprudence.'

Addressed: 'To / Jere:ʰ Bentham Esqr. Written on cover in pencil: 'Hawk'.

Part of this letter is published in Bowring, x, 77.

[2] This work was never published as such, though the Mss. were used by Dumont in preparing *Traités de Législation* (1802) and *Théorie des Peines et des Récompenses* (1811).

collecting materials but putting it into the form in which I propose that it should stand. I am working upon a plan which will enable me to detach a part and publish it separate from the rest. The part that I am now upon is the Law of personal Injuries: from thence I shall proceed to the Law relative to such acts as are Injuries to Property and Reputation. This will include the whole of the Criminal Law relative to such offences as have determinate individuals for their objects. This part may be characterized by the name of the Law relative to Private Wrongs. The remainder in that case will come under that of the Law relative to Public Wrongs. But a much clearer and more natural line will be drawn between the offences that respectively come under those divisions than the technical mode of considering the subject would admitt of Blackstone's drawing. Previous to these details will come that part of the work which contains the general principles by which the execution of these details is governed. Of this preliminary part the plan is pretty well settled and the materials in good measure collected.

By what I have seen and learnt concerning Sam's work, I doubt not his doing great things in Geometry. The rogue is pressing me— so I must have done.

I have sent him upon the Mare thinking this would be a good opportunity of his having a couple of rides.

I am
Dear Sir
Your's most dutifully and
affectionately
Jere:^y Bentham

Fetcham
  1st. Octr. 1776

187

To Samuel Bentham

9 October 1776 (Aet 28)

Your two letters came to hand—Q.S.P. goes to Northampton Shire you say on Friday—You I suppose do not go with them— What should hinder you walking down and taking another last farewell of Fetcham?

187. [1] B.M. II: 69. Autograph. Docketed: 'I.B. Octr. 9th. 1776.'
Addressed: 'To / Mr. Sam:[1] Bentham / Lincoln's Inn Old Buildgs. / No. 6 / London.' Postmark illegible. Stamped: 'LEATHERHEAD'.

Wearables you need bring none—but bring ¼£b of 10s. Bohea from Norths etc. the corner of Chancery Lane and Fleet Street— you may then take back with you Lind's reviews—which I hope will be soon enough—You might be down with us to dinner—Send us a line to tell us whether you will come or no—We shall receive it, you know, before breakfast. Tell Lind we all return positively on Monday sennight—Ask him whether that would not be time enough for the Reviews.

Wedny. Oct. 9th. 1776.

188

To Samuel Bentham

14 November 1776 (Aet 28)

My Father called on me yesterday and shew'd me the letter he had received from you relative to Pownal. It answer'd every purpose you could wish—the old gentleman seemed wonderfully pleased with it—you may imagine I did not labour very hard to weaken the impression I saw it made on him. He talked of transferring you to Portsmouth if Pownal should prove troublesome to you. This I mention only to let you see that you have got him over to your side in regard to working alongside.

While I was writing as above, in came Alderman Clark: and soon after in came your letter for which by the bye I paid a groat: not thinking to quarrell with the Postman about it for the pleasure it gave me—Ald. C. being in the way I thought it would do you no harm to shew it him.

I reproached myself as soon as it was too late for not sending you a line by Mrs. Davies. I don't know how it happen'd but it did not so much as come into my head at the time that such a thing was feasible. I believe the case was that I expected to have had a letter to answer from you in answer to one of mine before Mrs. Davies went, and not receiving any such letter, thought there was nothing for me to say. You were a very good boy for sending me those extracts, and I a very bad one for not telling you so before.

Forbes, Culloden Forbes an admirer of Fanny Nairne's?[2] you

188. [1] B.M. II: 72–73. Autograph. Docketed: 'I.B. Novr. 14th. 1776.'
Addressed: 'To / Mr. Bentham / at his Majesty's Dock Yard / near Rochester / Single Sheet.' Postmark: '14 NO'.
[2] Presumably a daughter of Edward Nairne (cf. letter 149, n. 4). Bentham was quite at home at the Nairnes' and evidently liked the daughters. Mrs Davies's hints

surprize me. How should the acquaintance come? tell me all you do
or can know about it.

The Mare is not sold—She was put up at Tattersal's—nobody bid
for her—But Q.S.P. was told by Clark (his old Landlord Leech's
Executor) (who had been in partnership with Beaver the Horse-
Auctioneer) that if kept till the spring she might probably fetch 18
or 20 guineas; and was advised not to take under 12. So she is sent
to Pyenest to grass where she will stay the winter at 40s. or 50s.
expence. Q.S.P. not being in cash to buy new Coach-horses—has a
half-job—a pr. of Horses better than any he ever had, 3 times a
week—a lady who lives in Q. Square has them other 3 times.[3]

Sr. J. Hawkins is this day to present his History of Music in 5
vols 4to to the King—He has advertised it 'dedicated by permission' to his Majesty.

The poor Fragment is every body's but mine. Dr. Johnson
(Dictionary Johnson) has read it and commends it much. He has
found out that it is Dunning's[4] by the stile—No it is not Dunning's
—it is Ld. Camden's.[5] So somebody has discover'd that has told it
to Alderman Clark. After all it is neither Dunning's alone, nor Ld.
Camden's alone, but the joint production of them both. My old
friend D. I understand is at it again in a third letter: I have not
seen it: it must be curious if it is like 'the former two.'[6]

---

referred to in letter 189 may have concerned Arthur Forbes's interest either in
Fanny Nairne or in Sarah Stratton (cf. letter 182, n. 4). If the former, it indicates
that Mrs Davies thought that Bentham was interested in Miss Nairne.

[3] The Clark mentioned in this paragraph is evidently not Richard Clark and remains unidentified. Pyenest was a farm owned by Jeremiah Bentham in the parish
of Waltham Holy Cross, Essex.

[4] John Dunning (1731–83), later first Baron Ashburton, a prominent barrister and
politician. From 1768 to 1770 he was solicitor-general. He was one of the Calne
M.P.'s returned under Lord Shelburne's aegis, and spoke against Lord North's American policy. He was a powerful orator, and in April 1780 he moved and carried the
famous resolution that 'the influence of the crown has increased, is increasing, and
ought to be diminished'. He was a member of the cabinet, as Chancellor of the Duchy
of Lancaster, from 1782 till Shelburne's resignation in 1783. In 1781 Bentham met him
at Lord Shelburne's country seat, Bowood.

[5] Charles Pratt (1714–94), created Baron Camden in 1765 and Earl Camden in
1786, had been Lord Chancellor from 1766 to 1770. In the early 1760's Pratt had
become a popular hero for his ruling (as chief justice of the court of common pleas)
with reference to the arrest of Wilkes, that general warrants issued by Secretaries of
State were illegal. As Lord Chancellor he was opposed to the American policy of his
colleagues, as also to the expulsion of Wilkes from the House, and was eventually
forced out of office. In 1782 he became Lord President of the Council, which position,
with one short interruption, he held till his death. Bentham met him at Bowood in
1781.

[6] Cf. letter 175, n. 2.

I had more to say—but that I may not make you wait a day longer I will put up my letter now—
past 11 o'clock Good night
Thursday Novr. 14th. Linc. Inn

189

To Samuel Bentham

22–23 November 1776 (Aet 28)

Friday Novr. 22d. 1776

Publick News I have none to tell you but what is or will be in the News-papers. The News of the day is that a Quebec Gazette is come over of the 24th or 26th last—I forget which. It brings advice of the demolition of the Rebel Fleet upon the Lakes. It consisted of 15 Vessels 12 were destroyed or taken; the remaining three for the present escaped—particulars are promised in the next Gazette. Mr. Lind's Mr. Clark got this intelligence from the Post Office this afternoon; at which place a paper was handed about to the effect above mention'd, a copy of which he shew'd me.

There is said to be a terrible crash among the W. India Merchants. One failed for 700,000£. Another for nearly that Sum, who will not pay 10s. in the £.

Fitzherbert's Macaroni Brother,[2] who was in his Brother's

189. [1] B.M. II: 74–75. Autograph. Docketed: 'I.B. Novr. 22d. 1776.'
Addressed: 'To / Mr. Bentham / at his Majesty's Dock Yard / near Rochester / Single Sheet.' Postmark: '23 NO'.
[2] The macaroni brother of William Fitzherbert (see letter 138, n. 30) was almost certainly Alleyne Fitzherbert (1753–1839), later 1st Baron St. Helens. Educated at Derby, Eton, and St John's College Cambridge, where he received his B.A. 1774. After going on the grand tour through France and Italy he was appointed Minister at Brussels (February 1777–August 1782). He then went to Paris to negotiate the peace with the European powers. 1783–87: envoy extraordinary to Catherine II of Russia. 1787: Chief Secretary to Lord-Lieutenant of Ireland. 1789: envoy extraordinary to the Hague. 1791: ambassador extraordinary to Madrid, to negotiate a trade agreement; became 1st Baron St. Helens (Irish Peerage). 1794: ambassador to the Hague. 1801: on mission to the newly acceded Alexander I of Russia; created Baron St Helens in the United Kingdom Peerage. 1803: retired from diplomacy with pension. 1804: Lord of the Bedchamber to George III.
No reference to him as sub-preceptor to the Prince of Wales has been found. In 1776 Dr Markham handed over as preceptor to Dr Hurd (later Bishop of Worcester), and Dr Cyril Jackson handed over as sub-preceptor to Mr Arnold, tutor of St John's Cambridge. This was Alleyne's college, and he may possibly have assisted Arnold for a short time.
Bowring publishes a number of letters between Bentham and Lord St Helens, falling between 1790 and 1810. Bentham treasured Fitzherbert's (evidently Alleyne)

Chambers when my Brother was in mine is made one of the Sub-preceptors to the Prince of Wales. He is said to be a man of sense and knowledge—He is lately come from France Italy Germany etc. and has the appearance of a great Fribble (I believe you saw him) but seemed very obliging and well-bred.

Wilson and I dine chez moi every day. We manage matters very comfortably. He is studying the doctrine of conveyances and every day at dinner—except when he goes to Westm. Hall, brings me a sheet or two of his writing, which we talk over in the evening. I am by that means making advances in that *most* intricate branch of the Law quite at my ease. He treats the subject with metaphysical exactness and altogether upon my plan. Sometimes when a thought occurs to me, I myself contribute a page or two to the common stock. I have brought him even to set up a mint of his own for coining words.

Since my last I have heard of the Fragment's being Ld. Camden's from another quarter.

Yesterday I went to Boulter's and bespoke 6 boxes for my papers. Length 13—breadth $8\frac{1}{4}$—depth 6. He promises I shall have the latter end of next week.

How fares it with contra-ordinate proportion? Has Pownell's nonsense put it entirely to a stand?

I congratulate you on your change of habitation—tell me when it is to take place. I am obliged to Mrs. D. for her invitation: but I see no great probability of my visiting Chatham very soon. I must confess I do not feel any violent propensity to go to a place where there seems to be a determination to force a conversation upon a subject in which I alone am, if any person is, interested, and on which it is thought I choose not to converse. My silence and your silence after her repeated importunities might I should have thought have satisfied her that either I had no such plan on foot, or that if I had I did not choose to communicate with her on the subject. I suppose you have told her ere this, what you know to be the case, that so far from being jealous of young Forbes, I can have no objection to his marrying any person that he and I are acquainted with. But though this is now the case with respect to him, it may not always

description of him as 'the Newton of legislation'—to a group of diplomats at the Hague. (See the inordinately long letter to Lord Lansdowne (Shelburne) in which Bentham complains of Lansdowne's not bringing him into Parliament. Bowring, x, 238.)

   William Fitzherbert had three other brothers according to the *D.N.B.*, which credits William Fitzherbert senior with five sons. The two mentioned in *Burke's Defunct and Extinct Peerage* are certainly not those here intended, and though one remains unidentified, it is more likely that this reference is to Alleyne than to him.

be so with respect to every body: and if a stop is not put to these sort of interrogatories in the first instance, I can never engage in any plan of that sort, without giving an account of myself to her: and furnishing a topic of conversation to the whole circle of her acquaintance. It is probable enough that if there had been any thing of that sort upon the carpet, and I had been *left at liberty* I might of my own accord have talked with her on the subject, but I think it is somewhat singular if I am not to choose whether I will or no. As to any thing more about Forbes, you may imagine I do not wish you to fill up your paper with it: and I suppose your curiosity respecting a person so little known to us both is not strong enough to induce you to give her much trouble on the subject. As to the subject you tell me ⟨she⟩ hints at, *to* me she may talk on that as well as on ⟨any⟩ other subject when she sees me; but *with* me she certainly will not talk.

It is a strange notion she has got that an apology is due to her for every thing written by either of us to the other which she does not see. When I called upon her after receiving your letter I put it with me in my pocket to show her the extract from that to G. Guy. You know there was nothing in that letter of your's but what might be seen by anybody. Upon my just casting my eye over it before I put it in her hands, she took notice of it as if it were something extraordinary and which should not have been done, my looking at it, to see whether there was any thing in it that was not to be shewn. The consequence was I was very near putting it up in my pocket again. Mrs. Nairne was in the room. This did ⟨not⟩ hinder her from telling me that she had seen a Gentleman who ⟨had⟩ seen me at Ripley: which was done in a m⟨anner⟩ and with a look that, when compared with what she ⟨has⟩ said to you at different times, sufficiently shewed she had ⟨a⟩ particular meaning in the observation. I saw the drift of ⟨it⟩ and therefore not a syllable about the gentleman did I say to her.

It is wonderful that upon matters of a nature so delicate (at least according to my notions so delicate I don't know what it may be according to hers) as that which she supposed to be concerned, a man should not be at liberty to choose whether he will or will not communicate: and that not only with persons with whom he is on an intimate footing, but with people who in comparison are strangers. I told you I believe. that Mrs. N. was in the room. It is not thus I deal with Mrs. D. I suppose I have as good a right to expect to hear of her concerns from you as she of mine. Yet I dare say, you must remember that if at any time you have received a letter from her, and have expressed the least degree of backwardness to tell me the contents, I have said not a syllable about it. Adieu, my dear Sam, my paper is out, and there is an end of it.

[3]Vous pouvez si vous voulez montrer a la personne ce qui la regarde. C'est a vous a juger.

Saturday 2[3]

I began working very late last night, and got wet through hunting the Bellman to no purpose—so you will receive it a day the later.

190

TO PETER ELMSLEY

27 November 1776 (Aet 28)

To Elmsly in answer to a letter received from him.

Novr. 17 1776

Dear Sir

I am much obliged to you for the trouble you have so kindly taken on my account. I am also obliged to the Gentleman you mention for his intended favour. I am flatter'd by his good opinion: *but I take no Briefs.* To be plain with you, it is some years since I

---

[3] This passage in French is added in at the top of the first page. The English passage which follows it is squashed into a space on that page, and stands out by being in red ink.

In the margin of the first page there are some crossed out sentences, which evidently do not belong to the letter but to some of Bentham's work. They read thus:

'and to say nothing of the corrective measures the wealth of the aggressor the /circumstances/ rank in life as well as wealth of the aggreived and the ⟨...⟩ of the offender: which comes in question without any particular provision—quantum of it, therefore, to be /expedient/ just should be governed not by one or two of these considerations but by all of them together.'

190. [1] U.C. CLXIX: 13. Autograph draft.

Said to have been in folder marked by Bentham: 'Legislaturientes epistolae, Brouillons Unsent 1774? to 1784?.' It cannot be safely concluded from this that it was not sent. It is on the same sheet as the letters to Catherine the Great and to Voltaire which follow.

Peter Elmsley was one of the foremost booksellers of the day (cf. letter 87, n. 5). An admirer of the *Fragment on Government* had hoped to engage the anonymous author's legal services. Letter 248 identifies this admirer as William Pulteney (d. 1805), M.P. for Cromarty (1768–74) and for Shrewsbury (1775–1802) and author of various pamphlets on current affairs. He was brother of 'Governor' Johnstone (see letter 243) and had changed his name from Johnstone when he inherited, by marriage, the estate of William Pulteney, 1st Earl of Bath (1684–1764). Bentham wrote to him in 1802 asking him to support an enquiry into Pitt's conduct regarding the Panopticon (see Bowring, x, 384–386).

gave up practise. As the Gentleman seems disposed to take a man's writings for a specimen of his abilities as an Advocate, suppose you were to mention to him Mr. Lind? He is called to the Bar and practises.

I have heard from several quarters of the Fragment's being attributed to various persons of distinction—once to Ld. Mansfield: several times to Ld. Camden and Mr. Dunning. I would wish for the present not to dissipate so favourable an illusion. I could wish therefore that your answer to the Gentleman might be to the effect above mentioned without entering into any explanation by which it would appear manifest to him that the Fragment belongs not to any of those great names.

191

To Catherine the Great

November 1776 (?) (Aet 28)

Madame,

J'ai l'honneur d'envoyer a votre Majestè un ouvrage que des Magistrats (eclairès et patriotiques) commissionès par elle, ont paru chercher. J'ai vu dans la Gazette² un article date Moscow . .

On demande des eclaircissemens (entre autres) sur le sujet des peines. Voici ce que j'ai fournir (la-dessus).

Citoyen d'un etat libre et exercant de cette libertè dans toute son etendue, il n'y a que deux puissances [*originally*: Souverains] sur la terre auxquelles j'ai eu quelque esperance de plaire. Celle qui se voit contenue au dedans par des bornes /un frein/ manifestement immuables: et celle a la quelle /pour la bonheur du peuple/ il n'en faut pas.

J'envoye une copie pour votre Majestè; j'envoye un autre pour le Roi de Pologne.

191. ¹ U.C. clxix: 13. Autograph draft.

Said to have been in folder marked by Bentham: 'Legislaturientes epistolae, Brouillons unsent. 1774? to 1784?'. Page headed: 'To Vol and C.' Letter 192 to Voltaire which is on the same sheet seems to have been written late in 1776, and this presumably belongs to the same period.

Both letters represent castle-building as Bentham had at that time published no thick volume on the Theory of Punishment. In or about 1780, Bentham composed various further letters to Catherine, as well as to other sovereigns and statesmen, intended to accompany presentation copies of his *Introduction to a Penal Code* (the work subsequently published as *Introduction to the Principles of Morals and Legislation*). See letter 351.

² I.e. the *Gazette de Leyde:* cf. letter 248.

Si les ideès que j'ai hazardeès, sont telles que je desire | |
| |, il faut des lumieres pour les gouter: il faut du pouvoir
pour s'en servir. Il n'y a qu'un seul endroit ou j'ai esperer trouver
l'un et l'autre en dose suffisante /tous les deux/. Je suis Madame
avec le plus profond respect qu'a jamais ressenti un coeur libre
De votre Majeste le très humble serviteur

Il y en a sous presse une traduction françoise. On dit que Votre
Majeste n'en a pas besoin.

Voici une lettre que je viens d'envoyer a M. Voltaire.

192

To François Marie Arouet de Voltaire

November 1776 (?) (Aet 28)

Sr.

By the first conveyance that offers itself you will receive a
thick volume which very probably you will never read. It is entitled.
Theory of Punishment. It is part of a work to which if ever it
should be compleated I intend to give some such title as Principles
of Legal Policy; the object of it is to trace out a new model for the
Laws: of my own country you may imagine, in the first place: but
keeping those of other countries all along in view. To ascertain what
the Laws ought to be, in form and tenor as well as in matter: and
that elsewhere as well as here. All that I shall say to recommend it
to you is that I have taken counsel of you much oftener than of our
own Ld. Coke and Hale and Blackstone. The repose of Grotius and
Puffendorf and Barbeyrac and Burlamaqui I would never wish to
see disturbed. I have built solely on the foundation of utility, laid as
it is by Helvetius. Becarria has been *lucerna pedibus*, or if you
please *manibus, meis*. Perhaps what I have done may be found but
cobweb-work. Such as it is however it is spun out of my own brain.
As such I send it you. It is neither borrow'd nor pilfer'd. I have

---

192. [1] U.C. clxix: 13. Autograph draft.

Said to have been in folder marked by Bentham: 'Legislaturientes epistolae,
Brouillons unsent. 1774? to 1784?' Page headed: 'To Voltaire etc.' On the same
sheet as the letter to Catherine the Great.

Several circumstances point to late 1776 as the date of this letter. First, it is on
the same sheet as the brouillon of the letter to Elmsley dated 27 November 1776.
Secondly, Voltaire's 82nd birthday was on 21 November 1776. Bentham was twenty-
eight at the time, that is, as he says, just a little over a third of Voltaire's age.
Admittedly Bentham did not have the thick volume ready to send at this date, but
that only shows that the letter is a piece of castle building, and was never sent.

spent upon it in the whole already about 7 years. I mean to bestow upon it the rest of my days, which at present are somewhat more than a third of your's.

One of the rewards I have been proposing to myself has been your good opinion. Perhaps I am come too soon to attain it: perhaps too late. I have seen with regret the following billet: said to have been sent to an intruder perhaps not more impertinent than myself. *Octoginta duo annos octoginta duo morbes, veniam peto si non sum visendus sed obliviscendus.* My labours have been so tedious that before they are come to an end my best rewards may I fear be lost. Helvetius is gone—years ago my eyes paid a tribute to his memory: and you and D'Alembert are leaving us.

If you should ever find any thing to say to me I need scarce tell you that it will be acceptable. Any thing directed to Elmsly's the Booksellers (successor to Vaillant) will reach me. I am a Lawyer by profession; and might have been so by practise. My name is precisely as well known to you as that of the meanest inhabitant of Siberia. It is − − − − −

193

To Samuel Bentham

24 December 1776 (Aet 28)

To Sam

Four patriotic Aldermen have taken upon them to committ 3 Lieutenants and a Midshipman who commanded a Press Gang serving in the City—This happen'd a week ago—The officers were bailed, and the Aldermen are to be prosecuted. Lee the American was one of them.[2]

Envoyez moi je vous prie un transcrit du Billet que vous avez recu de Mlle. Je voudrai le montrer a Wilson. Je lui en ai deja

193. [1] B.M. II: 77. Autograph. Docketed (by Bentham?): 'I.B. Decr. 24 1776. Rien.'

Addressed: 'To / Mr. Davies / Commissioner's Office / near Rochester / Single Sheet.' Postmark: '24 DE'.

This appears to be a postscript, addressed to Samuel, added to a letter to Joseph Davies. If so the main part of the letter is not extant.

[2] Bentham's version of this affair, which took place on 16 December, differs from the account given in the *Gentleman's Magazine* (xlvi, 576). According to this account, the officers refused all offers of bail and were committed to the Wood Street Compter. Two aldermen, not four, are mentioned and 'Lee the American' is not one of them. William Lee (1739–95) of Virginia was a merchant who had become much involved in London politics and a strong adherent of Wilkes. He is the only American to have held the offices of Sheriff (1773) and Alderman (1774–80) of London.

racontè a peu pres le contenu comme un article assez curieux—Nous le brulerons apres que nous l'aurions lu.[3]

Je viens de trouver une lettre pour moi de la part de Mlle. D. de Ipswich—Je ne l'ai pas encore ouvert.[4]

194

TO SAMUEL BENTHAM

31 December 1776 (Aet 28)

Your letter came to hand so late and the weather is so very bad, that I doubt I shall not have time to send you the things you mention. Wilson will not let you have silk garters to your velvet breeches—He says it betrays their being Manchester and not Genoa—Besides Buckmaster says nobody wears them.

Wilson shew'd me just now a letter from his Father acquiescing in his not going to Scotland as he had intended—He talked at the same time of going into the country about June—I asked him where? His answer was any where, where I would. I shew him pieces of Mrs. D's letters, and she is growing more and more into favour with him. He admires her greatly. As to your Battle scheme[2] I am still almost afraid to mention it to him myself. I'll tell you what—I wish you would write a letter to me about it proposing it to me as it were for the first time (of your mentioning it)

It is you likewise must open the matter to the Ws. It were best done I think in a letter to Mrs. W. You must mention it as proceeding entirely from yourself: you must also tell a lie, and say you mention it entirely without my participation. This I make a point of; because if they thought it was by my desire, it would lay them under difficulties: They might embrace the proposal although they did not like it, thinking themselves under obligation to me and not knowing how to refuse it. You must tell them that you shall not say

---

[3] This was perhaps a letter from Samuel's 'Archangel' (cf. letter 149, n. 5).

[4] If, as seems likely, this was a letter from Miss Dunkley, it shows that Bentham was still in touch with her nearly a year after telling his father that the affair was broken off (cf. letter 149, n. 6). This appears, however, to be the last reference to her.

194. [1] B.M. II: 78. Autograph. Docketed by Bentham (?): 'I.B. Decr. 31st 1776. Battle Scheme. Incas.'

[2] At Battle in Sussex lived Mr and Mrs Wise, with whom, apparently, the Benthams hoped to lodge, probably for a working holiday. The plan was designed to help the Wises in their deepening financial difficulties. Bentham and George Wilson stayed at Battle from late June until late October 1777. Bentham apparently had stayed there before (cf. letter 165). See also letter 196, n. 9.

a syllable to me about it till you hear what they say to it; you must
make a doubt about my being brought into it. You must tell them
that you are persuaded I should not easily enter into such a scheme,
(indeed not at all) without Wilson, on account of his having already
given up his intended journey to Scotland on my account. You must
hold up to them the opportunity they have of speaking freely as
you avoided purposely the saying any thing to me about it till you
could know their real sentiments.

On Saturday I received the following note from Elmsley

Sir,

I should be much obliged to you would you be kind enough to
ask the Translators of the White Bull if they will amuse themselves
with turning a very pretty French *Roman Historique* of Marmontel's into a very pretty English Historical Novel—Mr. Murphy
having done Belisaire, I should like the *Incas* to be done as well
and would pay accordingly.

I am Sir
Your most humble Servt.
Peter Elmsly

Decr. 29 1776

Thus far Elmsly.—N.B. The Incas were the ancient Savages of
Peru.

Arthur Murphy is a Barrister of Lincoln's Inn—Author of Several Plays and farces much esteemed.[3]

I can find no purple checked handkerchieves—not I.

Decr. 31.

I open'd to tell you that instead of your cloaths this morning I
received an apology.

[3] Marmontel's *Les Incas* was to be published in Paris in 1777. For further references
to Bentham's translation cf. letters 196, 200, 201, 202, 203, and 205. Marmontel's
earlier novel *Bélisaire* was published in 1767, and the English translation published
in the same year by P. Vaillant (whom Elmsley had succeeded, according to letter 192
to Voltaire), with a second edition in 1773, was presumably that made by Arthur
Murphy (1727–1805), actor, playwright, and miscellaneous writer.

INDEX

Note. This is an index of names of persons occurring in the text and notes. References throughout are to page-numbers, except in the case of Bentham's correspondents, where the figures in italic type after the subheadings 'Letters to' and 'Letters from' refer to the serial numbers of the letters.

In the case of Bentham himself (J.B.), only references to his works are indexed. His father and brother, to whom constant references are made throughout the letters, are indexed only as correspondents.

An analytical index to the correspondence as a whole will be provided in the final volume of this part of the edition.

ABBOT, Charles (later 1st Baron Colchester): 104n., 135, 139, 151, 156, 231, 237, 239n., 260, 273, 287, 327n., 355

ABBOT, Rev. Dr John: 99n., 323n.

ABBOT, John Farr ('Farr'): 104 & n., 134, 148 & n., 151, 154, 156, 163, 231, 237, 239n., 240n., 260, 273, 292, 355

ABBOT, Sarah (née Farr): See BENTHAM, Sarah

ABEL, Karl Friedrich: 295 & n.

ACWORTH, Mrs: 247

ACWORTH, Edward: 247 & n., 256

ADAM, Père: 262, 263, 276

ADAM, William, Snr.: 288n.

ADAMS, Mr: 200

ADDINGTON, Henry, 1st Viscount Sidmouth: 104n.

AINSWORTH, (author): 231

ALBERMARLE, 3rd Earl of: See KEPPEL, George

ALDERSEY, Samuel: 18 & n.

ALEMBERT, Jean le Rond d': 262, 271, 314 & n., 368

ALEXANDER I, Emperor of Russia: 362n.

ALLEN, Miss: 121

ALLEN, Mr: 169, 171

ALLEN, Loder: 121n.

ALLEN, Lydia (née RAY): 121n.

ALMON, John: 87 & n.

ANDERSON, James: 292 & n., 294, 356

ANDERSON, James, niece of: 294

ANDERSON, Mrs (née SETON): 356

ANTIC, Paul Bose d': 372n.

'ARCHANGEL', the (possibly Miss H——): 291 & n., 294, 321, 339 368–9

ARISTOTLE: 59, 60n.

ARNE, Dr Thomas: 14n.

ARNOLD, Samuel: 294, 301n., 362

ARTHUR, Robert: 95n.

ARTHUR, Miss (daughter of Robert ARTHUR): 95n.

ASHBURTON, John, 1st Baron: See DUNNING, John

BACON, Montagu: 121n.

BACON, Nicholas: 121 & n.

BAGOT, Lewis: 33 & n.

BAGOT, Sir Walter, Bart.: 33n.

BANKS, Sir Joseph: 327 & n., 328

BARBEYRAC, Jean: 367

BARBUT, Mrs: 345 & n.

BARKER, Captain: 179, 207, 236

BARKER, Captain, brothers of: 179

BARRET, Mr: 240 & n., 243, 286

BARRINGTON, Hon. Daines: 134n.

BARRY, Mrs: 5

BASKERVILLE, John: 256 & n.

BATHURST, Allen, Baron Bathurst of Battlesden, later 1st Earl: 97 & n.

BECCARIA, Cesare Bonesana, Marchese di: 134n., 367

BECKFORD, William: 272n.

BEDFORD, William, 1st Duke of: See RUSSELL, William

BELIDOR, Bernard Forest de: 262 & n., 270, 271

BENHAM (or Benhall), Mr: 33